HERITAGE

Civilization and the Jews

Source Reader

HERITAGE

Civilization and the Jews

Source Reader

edited by
William W. Hallo
David B. Ruderman
Michael Stanislawski

Editorial Coordinators
Benjamin R. Gampel
Russell H. Herman

Heritage Academic Development Team
Timothy Gunn, Project Director
Robert A. Miller, Project Coordinator

PRAEGER SPECIAL STUDIES • PRAEGER SCIENTIFIC

New York • Philadelphia • Eastbourne, UK
Toronto • Hong Kong • Tokyo • Sydney

Library of Congress Cataloging in Publication Data
Main entry under title:

Heritage : civilization and the Jews : source reader.

Text element for a telecourse assembled by the
Public Broadcasting Service (PBS).
Bibliography: p.
1. Jews—History—Sources. 2. Judaism—History—
Sources, I. Hallo, William W. II. Ruderman, David B.
III. Stanislawski, Michael, 1952–
DS102.H47 1984 909′.04924 84-15012
ISBN 0-03-000479-9 (alk. paper)
ISBN 0-03-000482-9 (pbk. : alk. paper)
ISBN 0-03-001472-7 (faculty manual)

Permission to reprint is gratefully acknowledged in the section "Acknowledgments
and Citations of Source Readings" following Chapter 9.

Published in 1984 by Praeger Publishers
CBS Educational and Professional Publishing
a Division of CBS Inc.
521 Fifth Avenue, New York, NY 10175 USA

456789 052 987654321

Contents

by *Shaye J. D. Cohen*

3   **The Shaping of Traditions (First to Ninth Centuries)**   63
by *David B. Ruderman*

6 Roads from the Ghetto (1789 to 1914)   213
by *Michael Stanislawski*

7 The Golden Land (1654 to 1932)   241
by *Michael Stanislawski*

8 Out of the Ashes (1914 to 1945)   259
by *Michael Stanislawski*

Introduction

The panorama of Jewish history is majestic in its sweep, and unique among national histories. It stretches in time from the beginning of recorded history all the way to the present day, and it reaches in space into nearly every corner of the inhabited world. Yet the bearers of this remarkable history have not been particularly numerous, or powerful, or fortunate. Nor have they been particularly homogeneous. On the contrary, they owe their long survival in part to their adaptability, and their dispersion over the face of the earth to their frequent sufferings at the hands of neighbors more numerous or more powerful than they. Yet the history of this unique people has much to tell about the history of civilization in general. It shows how a small but creative group of people, inspired by a novel religious ideal, emerged in the ancient Near Eastern cradle of civilization and spread with the expansion of civilization, interacting creatively throughout its subsequent history with many other peoples and cultures.

In reconstructing this panorama of Jewish history, the modern scholar utilizes many kinds of sources and resources. In the first place, there are features of the physical and human landscape that survive, more or less unchanged, from the past. A second major source consists of actual objects or pictorial representations preserved or recovered from the various periods and places of the Jewish experience. But the most important evidence is documentary, i.e., the testimony of the countless written records and literary traditions about Jewish life in all lands and all ages. The readings presented below serve to introduce the student to some of the vast array of different documents available to the historian. Although but a tiny fraction of this array, they are carefully selected to illustrate its richness and variety. As explained further in the preface to each chapter, they are also intended to exemplify the interaction of civilization and the Jews.

W.W.H.

xi

1

A People Is Born

William W. Hallo

The origins of the Jewish people are recounted in Genesis, the first book of the Hebrew Bible. This book is a repository of narratives, lists, and poetic passages that collectively enshrine the traditions of Israel's beginnings. These traditions are told in terms of a family history beginning with Adam, the first man, and ending with Joseph. They do not constitute history in the sense of a record or interpretation of events as they actually occurred. Rather they represent protohistory, a mixture of mythological and legendary explanations for some of the questions raised by the conditions of human life in general and of the Israelite experience in particular during later periods. Many of the individual tales of Genesis share significant features with the traditions of other ancient Near Eastern peoples as recovered by modern archaeological excavations. The selections chosen below are intended to illustrate such parallels; they will serve at the same time to silhouette the elements that distinguish the biblical treatments of given themes from their Near Eastern counterparts.* Most often the distinction of the biblical treatment is its conviction that the affairs of men are divinely guided and subject to ethical norms.

The birth of Israel as a nation is recorded in the historical books of the Bible, beginning with Exodus and ending with Judges. A succession of collective experiences gradually transformed a group of individual tribes into a united people. The sense of a collective destiny was forged in the crucible of Egyptian slavery and the dramatic liberation from oppression at the Reed Sea. It was confirmed at Sinai where the whole people entered into a covenant with God, their liberator, under the leadership of Moses. It was tested in the wanderings that ranged from the Sinai peninsula to the lands east of the Jordan River. Finally it was consummated in the conquest and settlement of the Land of Canaan during the time of Joshua and the Judges. For all these constitutive events, the biblical record is our primary source. Only occasionally are there echoes of the events in extra-biblical sources. But there are many documents that confirm the general background against which the events took place. These documents are illustrated in the selections chosen, and again compare and contrast in significant ways with the biblical record. Thus, for example, the covenant with God compares in broad outlines, and

---

*Most of the sections in chapters 1 and 2 of this *Source Reader* consist of parallel readings—one (or more) of them non-biblical and one biblical, or two biblical ones. They are meant to be read in tandem.

1

sometimes even in specific wording, with treaties entered into between Near Eastern vassal kingdoms and the great kings whom they acknowledged as their sovereigns. But the Israelite tradition differed in combining with this covenant a "Book of the Covenant" that spelled out in detail the civil and cultic legislation to which the people subscribed. Again, while Israel shared with its environment the concept of legislation based on wise precedent, it alone preserved the narrative settings that supposedly gave rise to some of these legal innovations.

The rule of God (theocracy) under the temporary stewardship of successive "judges" proved unequal to the challenge of defending the Promised Land against rival claimants. In common with other nations, Israel adopted the institution of kingship. A united monarchy was founded under Saul and consolidated under David, who captured Jerusalem and made it his capital city. It expanded to truly imperial proportions under Solomon who erected the first Temple in Jerusalem. After Solomon, the monarchy was divided, with the kingdom of Israel winning the allegiance of the ten northern tribes, and the kingdom of Judah ruling the two southern ones.

The two kingdoms were sometimes allied against their common enemies, but more often were in opposition to each other. After a little more than two centuries, the northern kingdom fell to the Assyrians (722 B.C.E.). The southern kingdom survived somewhat longer; Jerusalem with its Temple remained the political and religious center of Jewish life until both were destroyed by the Babylonians (586 B.C.E.). The entire period of this "First Commonwealth" is characterized by direct contact with the great powers and city-states of the surrounding Near East. The documents recovered by archaeology become increasingly available to complement and supplement the biblical record. The selections presented below serve to illustrate their role in the reconstruction of Israel's experiment with monarchy.

THE FLOOD

In cuneiform sources the first eight (or ten) kings are followed by a great flood; in Genesis, the first eight generations of men are succeeded by a universal flood, the Deluge. The cuneiform tablet is in Sumerian, probably copied in the eighteenth or seventeenth century B.C.E.

READING 1-1A

All the destructive winds and gales were present together
The flood swept over beyond measure.
After the flood had swept over the nation
For seven days and seven nights,
And the destructive wind had rocked the ark in the high water,
The Sun came out, illuminating heaven and earth.
Ziusudra was able to make an opening in the ark

And the Sun with its rays was brought into the ark.
Ziusudra—though a king—
Prostrated himself before the Sun,
The king slaughters oxen and multiplies sheep on his behalf.

READING 1-1B

This is the line of Noah.—Noah was a righteous man; he was blameless in his age; Noah walked with God.—Noah had three sons: Shem, Ham, and Japheth.

The earth became corrupt before God; the earth was filled with injustice. When God saw how corrupt the earth was, for all flesh had corrupted its ways on earth, God said to Noah, "I have decided to put an end to all flesh, for the earth is filled with lawlessness because of them: I am about to destroy them with the earth. Make yourself an ark of gopher wood; make it an ark with compartments, and cover it inside and out with pitch. This is how you shall make it: the length of the ark shall be three hundred cubits, its width fifty cubits, and its height thirty cubits. Make an opening for daylight in the ark, and terminate it within a cubit of the top. Put the entrance to the ark in its side; make it with bottom, second, and third decks.

"For My part, I am about to bring the Flood—waters upon the earth—to destroy all flesh under the sky in which there is breath of life; everything on earth shall perish. But I will establish My covenant with you, and you shall enter the ark—you, your sons, your wife, and your sons' wives. And of all that lives, of all flesh, you shall take two of each into the ark to keep alive with you; they shall be male and female. From birds of every kind, cattle of every kind, every kind of creeping thing on earth, two of each shall come to you to stay alive. For your part, take of everything that is eaten and store it away, to serve as food for you and for them." Noah did so; just as God commanded him, so he did.

Then the LORD said to Noah, "Go into the ark, you and all your household, for you alone have I found righteous before Me in this generation. Of every clean animal you shall take seven pairs, males and their mates, and of every animal which is not clean, two, a male and its mate; of the birds of the sky also, seven pairs, male and female, to keep seed alive upon all the earth. For in seven days' time I will make it rain upon the earth, forty days and forty nights, and I will blot out from the earth all existence that I created." And Noah did just as the LORD commanded him.

Noah was six hundred years old when the Flood came, waters upon the earth. Noah, with his sons, his wife, and his sons' wives, went into the ark because of the waters of the Flood. Of the clean animals, of the animals that are not clean, of the birds, and of everything that creeps on the ground, two of each, male and female, came to Noah into the ark, as God had commanded Noah. And on the seventh day the waters of the Flood came upon the earth.

In the six hundredth year of Noah's life, in the second month, on the seventeenth day of the month, on that day

All the fountains of the great deep burst apart,
And the flood-gates of the sky broke open.

The rain fell on the earth forty days and forty nights. That same day Noah and Noah's sons, Shem, Ham, and Japheth, went into the ark, with Noah's wife and the three wives of his sons—they and all beasts of every kind, all cattle of every kind, all creatures of every kind that creep on the earth, and all birds of every kind, every bird, every winged thing. They came to Noah into the ark, two each of all flesh in which there was breath of life. Thus they that entered comprised male and female of all flesh, as God had commanded him. And the LORD shut him in.

The Flood continued forty days on the earth, and the waters increased and raised the ark so that it rose above the earth. The waters swelled and increased greatly upon the earth, and the ark drifted upon the waters. When the waters had swelled much more upon the earth, all the highest mountains everywhere under the sky were covered. Fifteen cubits higher did the waters swell, as the mountains were covered. And all flesh that stirred on earth perished—birds, cattle, beasts, and all the things that swarmed upon the earth, and all mankind. All in whose nostrils was the merest breath of life, all that was on dry land, died. All existence on earth was blotted out—man, cattle, creeping things, and birds of the sky; they were blotted from the earth.

[Genesis 6:9–7:23]

JACOB AS HERDSMAN

Both legal theory and practice are revealed in Old Babylonian sources. While the legislative portions of the Bible furnish their closest biblical parallels, the patriarchal narratives provide additional analogies. Thus, for example, when Jacob, the last of the Patriarchs, fled to his kinsman Laban, he undertook to serve as herdsman for the latter's flock. In so doing, he "made good" the natural losses to the flock in the manner and in the very language of an Old Babylonian herding contract (Reading 1-2A) and the Laws of Hammurabi (Reading 1-2B).

READING 1-2A

92 ewes, 20 rams, 22 breeding lambs, 24 [spring(?)]* lambs, 33 she-goats, 4 male goats, 27 kids—total: 158 sheep; total: 64 goats, which Sin-shamuh has entrusted to Dadâ the herdsman. He (i.e., Dadâ) assumes liability (therefore) and will replace any lost (animals). Should Nidnatum, his (i.e., Dadâ's) shepherd boy, absent himself, he (i.e., Nidnatum [?]) will bear responsibility for any (consequent) loss,[1] (and) Dadâ will measure out (i.e., pay) 5 *kōr* of barley. (Three witnesses; date: Samsu-iluna year 1 [?], fourth month, 18th day.)

READING 1-2B

If a herdsman (to whom cattle or sheep were given to pasture) was negligent and lets lameness develop in the fold, the herdsman shall make good in cattle and sheep the loss through the lameness which he let develop in the fold and give (them) to their owner.

---

*The parentheses ( ), square brackets [ ], and spellings used in these readings are as they appeared in the original publications. See "Acknowledgments and Citations" following chapter 9. The editors of the *Source Reader* have added further information that appears either as footnotes or as text notes. The text notes in chapters 1 and 2 have been enclosed in braces { } to distinguish them from previous editors' notations.

[1] *hīṭu*; cognate with Hebrew *ḥeṭ*, or "sin," and with the verb translated "I made good the loss," in Reading 1-2C (Genesis 31:39).

READING 1-2C

Now Jacob became incensed and took up his grievance with Laban. Jacob spoke up and said to Laban, "What is my crime, what is my guilt that you should pursue me? You rummaged through all my things; what have you found of all your household objects? Set it here, before my kinsmen and yours, and let them decide between us two.

"These twenty years I have spent in your service, your ewes and she-goats never miscarried, nor did I feast on rams from your flock. That which was torn by beasts I never brought to you; I myself made good the loss; you exacted it of me, whether snatched by day or snatched by night. Often, scorching heat ravaged me by day and frost by night; and sleep fled from my eyes. Of the twenty years that I spent in your household, I served you fourteen years for your two daughters, and six years for your flocks, since you changed my wages time and again. Had not the God of my father, the God of Abraham and the Fear of Isaac, been with me, you would have sent me away empty-handed. But God took notice of my plight and the toil of my hands, and He gave judgment last night."

[Genesis 31:36–42]

THE COVENANT BETWEEN THE PIECES

The covenant between the pieces of the sacrificial animals which God concluded with Abraham is reminiscent of a comparable ancient Near Eastern practice. At Mari (Reading 1-3A) peace between a tribal group and a vassal kingdom, both subject to the kings of Mari, was concluded by killing a donkey foal. Among the Hittites (Reading 1-3B) the soldiers walked between the pieces of the sacrificial animals to purge themselves from the onus of defeat in battle.

READING 1-3A

To my lord say: Thus Ibal-Il, your servant. The letter (literally: tablet) of Ibal-Adad reached me from Ashlakka and I went to Ashlakka and they brought me a puppy and a she-goat in order to conclude a covenant (literally: to kill a donkey-foal) between the Hanaeans and (the land of) Idamaraz. But, in deference to my lord, I did not permit (the use of) the young dog and the she-goat, but (instead) had a donkey-foal, the young of a she-ass, killed, and thus established a reconciliation between the Hanaeans and (the land of) Idamaraz. In the city of Hurrâ, in all Idamaraz, the Hanaeans will be satisfied, and "a satisfied man has no enmity."

READING 1-3B

When the army is defeated by an enemy, then the following sacrifice is prepared "behind" the river: "behind" the river, a man, a goat, a puppy, and a suckling pig are cut in half. One half is placed on one side, the (other) half on the other. Before it, they make a gate out of white-thorn(?) wood and stretch a cord(?) over it, and in front of the gate they light fires on this side and on that. The troops go through the middle, and when they come to the bank of the river, they sprinkle water over them.

Reading 1-3C

Then He said to him, "I am the LORD who brought you out from Ur of the Chaldeans to give you this land as a possession." And he said, "O Lord GOD, how shall I know that I am to possess it?" He answered, "Bring Me a three-year-old heifer, a three-year-old she-goat, a three-year-old ram, a turtledove, and a young bird." He brought Him all these and cut them in two, placing each half opposite the other; but he did not cut up the birds. Birds of prey came down upon the carcasses, and Abram drove them away. As the sun was about to set, a trance fell upon Abram, and a deep dark dread descended upon him. And He said to Abram, "Know well that your offspring shall be strangers in a land not theirs, and they shall be enslaved and oppressed four hundred years; but I will pass judgment on the nation they shall serve, and in the end they shall go free with great wealth. As for you,

You shall go to your fathers in peace;
You shall be buried at a ripe old age.

And they shall return here in the fourth generation, for the iniquity of the Amorites will not be fulfilled until then."

When the sun set and it was very dark, there appeared a smoking oven, and a flaming torch which passed between those pieces. On that day the LORD made a covenant with Abram, saying, "To your offspring I give this land, from the river of Egypt to the great river, the river Euphrates:[1] the Kenites, the Kenizzites, the Kadmonites, the Hittites, the Perizzites, the Rephaim, the Amorites, the Canaanites, the Girgashites, and the Jebusites."

[Genesis 15:7–21]

JOSEPH IN EGYPT

Joseph, a favorite son of Jacob and the envy of his older brothers, was sold by his brothers into household slavery in Egypt. The adventures that attended his rise to greatness there share many features with late tales in Egyptian and Aramaic. Thus his escapade with and escape from the wife of Potiphar is reminiscent of the Story of the Two Brothers, known from a papyrus dating from approximately the time of the Exodus.

Reading 1-4A

Once upon a time there were two brothers, so the story goes . . . After many [days] following this, while they were in the field, they needed seed. (Anubis) sent his younger brother, saying: You shall go and fetch us seed from town. His younger brother found the wife of his elder brother seated plaiting her (hair). . . . Then she [spoke with] him, saying: There is [great] virility in you, for I have been observing your exertions daily. For it was her desire to know him through sexual intimacy. She got up, seized hold of him, and told him: Come, let's spend for ourselves an hour sleeping (together). Such will be to your advantage, for I will make you fine clothes. Then the youth became like an Upper Egyptian panther in harsh rage over the wicked proposition that she had made to him, and she became exceedingly fearful. He argued with her, saying: Now look, you are (associated) with me after the man-

---

[1]Maximal southern and northern borders of the Promised Land; cf. Readings 1–10B note 1 and 1–16 note 1.

ner of a mother, and your husband is (associated) with me after the manner of a
father, for the one who is older than I it is who has brought me up. What means this
great offence which (you) have said to me? . . . He picked up his load and went off
to the field. . . . The wife of his elder brother was fearful (on account of) the proposition which she had made. She then fetched grease and fat and feigningly became
like one who has been assaulted with the intention of telling her husband: It's your
younger brother who has assaulted (me). . . .

(Dedicated) to the 'soul' of the Scribe of the Treasury Qa-gabu, of
the Treasury of Pharaoh. . . . Done by the Scribe Inena,
the master of this writing.

READING 1-4B

After a time, his master's wife cast her eyes upon Joseph and said, "Lie with
me." But he refused. He said to his master's wife, "Look, with me here, my master
gives no thought to anything in this house, and all that he owns he has placed in my
hands. He wields no more authority in this house than I, and he has withheld nothing from me except yourself, since you are his wife. How then could I do this most
wicked thing, and sin before God?" And much as she coaxed Joseph day after day,
he did not yield to her request to lie beside her, to be with her.

One such day, he came into the house to do his work. None of the household
being there inside, she caught hold of him by his coat and said, "Lie with me!" But
he left his coat in her hand and got away and fled outside." When she saw that he
had left his coat in her hand and had fled outside, she called out to her servants and
said to them, "Look, he had to bring us a Hebrew to dally with us! This one came to
lie with me; but I screamed loud. And when he heard me screaming at the top of my
voice, he left his coat with me and got away and fled outside." She kept his coat
beside her, until his master came home. Then she told him the same story, saying,
"The Hebrew slave, whom you brought into our house, came to me to dally with
me; but when I screamed at the top of my voice, he left his coat with me and fled
outside."

[Genesis 39:7–18]

THE EGYPTIAN OPPRESSION

Egyptian records preserve general descriptions of border crossings
by nomadic tribesmen from the east (Reading 1-5A), their recruitment into
labor gangs for construction projects (Reading 1-5B), and the provisions
of the gangs with carefully allotted rations (Reading 1-5C). These descriptions tally well with the brief delineation of the Egyptian oppression in the
Bible.

READING 1-5A

The scribe Inena communicating to his lord, the Scribe of the Treasury Qa-
g[abu]. . . . We have finished letting the Bedouin tribes of Edom pass the Fortress
of (Pharaoh) Merneptah-Hotephirmaat which is in Tjeku to the pools of Per-Atum[1]

---

[1] I.e., the biblical Pithom (Exodus 1:11)?

of Merneptah-Hotephirmaat which are in Tjeku, to keep them alive and to keep their cattle alive, through the great 'soul' of Pharaoh. . . .

READING 1-5B

Likewise, people are making bricks in their . . . and bring them to work in the house. They are making their quota of bricks daily. I am not slacking over working in the new house. Likewise, I acknowledge the communication which my lord has made. . . .

I am staying at Qenqen-en-to[1], unequipped, and there are neither men to make bricks nor straw in the neighborhood. . . .

READING 1-5C

The scribe Kawiser greets his lord the scribe Bek-en-Ptah. In life, prosperity and health! This letter is for my lord's information. . . . Another message to my lord: I have received the letter which my lord sent to (me) saying: "Give corn-rations to the soldiers and the 'Apiru[2] who are dragging stone to the great pylon of [the house of] Rameses-Miamūn[3]—life, prosperity and health!—'Beloved of Ma'at'[4] which is under the authority of the chief of the Medjay[5] [called] Amon-em-one." I am giving them their corn-rations every month according to the manner which my lord told me. . . .

READING 1-5D

That same day Pharaoh charged the taskmasters and foremen of the people, saying, "You shall no longer provide the people with straw for making bricks as heretofore; let them go and gather straw for themselves. But impose upon them the same quota of bricks as they have been making heretofore; do not reduce it, for they are shirkers; that is why they cry, 'Let us go and sacrifice to our God! Let heavier work be laid upon the men, and let them keep at it and not pay attention to idle chatter."

So the taskmasters and foremen of the people went out and said to the people, "Thus says Pharaoh: I will not give you any straw. You must go and get the straw yourselves wherever you can find it; but there shall be no decrease whatever in your work." Then the people scattered throughout the land of Egypt to gather stubble for straw. And the taskmasters pressed them, saying, "You must complete the same work assignment each day as when you had straw." And the foremen of the Israelites, whom Pharaoh's taskmasters had set over them, were beaten. "Why," they were asked, "did you not complete the prescribed amount of bricks either yesterday or today?"

Then the Israelite foremen came to Pharaoh and cried: "Why do you deal thus with your servants? No straw is issued to your servants, yet they demand of us: Make

---

[1]I.e., "the curse of the land."

[2]A social stratum of "displaced persons" sometimes equated with the biblical Hebrews.

[3]I.e., mer(i)-Amon, beloved of Amon.

[4]An epithet of Rameses II; also the name of a royal palace.

[5]Or Madjoi, mercenaries from south of Egypt.

bricks! Thus your servants are being beaten, when the fault is with your own people." He replied, "You are shirkers, shirkers! That is why you say, 'Let us go and sacrifice to the LORD.' Be off now to your work! No straw shall be issued to you, but you must produce your quota of bricks!"

[Exodus 5:6–18]

THE BIRTH OF MOSES

The birth of Moses is only one (albeit perhaps the oldest) of innumerable versions of the exposed child who is rescued by or returns to the royal court and ends up displacing or defeating the king. A similar tale is told about Sargon of Akkad, the founder of the first great Mesopotamian empire (ca. 2300 B.C.E.), but this version is probably the product of his namesake, Sargon II of Assyria (721–705 B.C.E.).

READING 1-6A

I am Sargon, the great king, king of Akkad. My mother was a high-priestess, my father I did not know [variant: a father I did not have], my paternal kin inhabit the mountain region, my (native) city is Azupirānu {"Saffron-city"}, which is on the banks of the Euphrates. My mother the high-priestess conceived me, in secret she gave birth to me. She placed me in a reed basket, with bitumen she caulked my hatch. She abandoned me to the river from which I could not climb up. The river carried me along; to Aqqi[1] the water drawer it brought me. Aqqi the water drawer when immersing his bucket lifted me up. Aqqi the water drawer raised me as his adopted son. Aqqi the water drawer set me to his garden work. During my garden work the goddess Ishtar fell in love with me and I verily ruled for [fifty]-five years as king.

READING 1-6B

A certain man of the house of Levi went and married a Levite woman. The woman conceived and bore a son; and when she saw how beautiful he was, she hid him for three months. When she could hide him no longer, she got a wicker basket for him and calked it with bitumen and pitch. She put the child into it and placed it among the reeds by the bank of the Nile. And his sister stationed herself at a distance, to learn what would befall him.

The daughter of Pharaoh came down to bathe in the Nile, while her maidens walked along the Nile. She spied the basket among the reeds and sent her slave girl to fetch it. When she opened it, she saw that it was a child, a boy crying. She took pity on it and said, "This must be a Hebrew child." Then his sister said to Pharaoh's daughter, "Shall I go and call you a Hebrew nurse to suckle the child for you?" And Pharaoh's daughter answered, "Yes." So the girl went and called the child's mother. And Pharaoh's daughter said to her, "Take this child and nurse it for me, and I will pay your wages." So the woman took the child and nursed it. When the child grew

---

[1]The name means "I have made a libation (or sacrifice)."

up, she brought him to Pharaoh's daughter, and she made him her son. She named him Moses, saying, "It means: I drew him out of the water."

[Exodus 2:1–10]

THE TEN PLAGUES

A number of Psalms recount the outstanding events of Israel's early history in poetic terms, often with minor variations on the version of the prose narratives of the Pentateuch. The ten plagues (or seven according to Psalm 78) which Moses and Aaron invoke on the pharaoh are reminiscent of traditional Egyptian catalogues of natural disasters such as accompanied the breakdown of pharaonic power in earlier eras. The conditions reflected in the Egyptian text are dated to the "First Intermediate Period" (ca. 2150–2050 B.C.E.) by some scholars, to the "Second Intermediate Period" (ca. 1650–1550 B.C.E.) by others.

READING 1-7A

The Nile overflows, yet none plough for it. Everyone says: "We do not know what will happen throughout the land." Indeed, women are barren and none conceive. Khnum fashions {men} no more because of the condition of the land. . . . Hearts are violent, plague is throughout the land, blood is everywhere . . . , many dead are buried in the river, the stream is a sepulchre and the place of embalming has become a stream. . . . The river is blood, yet men drink of it. Men shrink from [it] as human, and thirst after water. . . . Crocodiles [sink] down because of what they have carried off, for men go to them of their own accord {i.e., they commit suicide}. It is the destruction of the land. . . . Men are few. He that lays his brother in the ground is everywhere. The desert is throughout the land, the nomes {provinces} are laid waste. Barbarians from outside have come to Egypt, there are really no Egyptians anywhere.

READING 1-7B

Then Israel came to Egypt;
 Jacob sojourned in the land of Ham.
He made His people very fruitful,
 more numerous than their foes.
He changed their heart to hate His people,
 to plot against His servants.
He sent His servant Moses,
 and Aaron, whom He had chosen.
They performed His signs among them,
 His wonders, against the land of Ham.
He sent darkness; it was very dark;
 did they not defy His word?
He turned their waters into blood
 and killed their fish.
Their land teemed with frogs,
 even the rooms of their king.

Swarms of insects came at His command,
    lice, throughout their country.
He gave them hail for rain,
    and flaming fire in their land.
He struck their vines and fig trees,
    broke down the trees of their country.
Locusts came at His command,
    grasshoppers without number.
They devoured every green thing in the land;
    they consumed the produce of the soil.
He struck down every firstborn in the land,
    the first fruit of their vigor.
He led Israel out with silver and gold;
    none among their tribes faltered.
Egypt rejoiced when they left,
    for dread of Israel had fallen upon them.

[Psalm 105:23–38]

THE COVENANT AT SINAI

With the growth of empires, sovereigns (suzerains) extended their sway over lesser client-kingdoms and detailed the vassals' obligations in so-called suzerainty-treaties in which the sovereign assumed virtually divine status with respect to the vassal. In subscribing to the Covenant at Sinai, the Israelites similarly entered into a vassal relationship with God as their sovereign.

READING 1-8A[1]

And whoever is evil against the Sun,[2] is considered evil against you. If he is an enemy to the Sun, he shall be an enemy to you.

READING 1-8B[3]

To the enemy of my lord I am hostile, (and) with the friend of my lord (I am) friendly.

READING 1-8C[4]

He who [lives in peace] with the Sun shall live in peace also with you. But he who is an enemy of the Sun, shall also be an enemy [with you].

---

[1]From the Hittite treaty between Shuppiluliuma of the Hittites (ca. 1375–1335 B.C.E.) and Hukkana of Azzi-Hayasha in northeastern Anatolia.

[2]I.e., the king of the Hittites.

[3]From the Akkadian treaty between Shuppiluliuma and Niqma-Addu of Ugarit, a major seaport on the north Syrian coast.

[4]From the Hittite (and Akkadian) treaty between Shuppiluliuma and Aziru of Amurru, the territory around Kadesh.

READING 1-8D[5]

With my friend you shall be friend, and with my enemy you shall be enemy.

READING 1-8E[6]

As he (is) your enemy, so too (is) he the enemy of the Sun. As he (is) the enemy of the Sun, so too he shall be your enemy.

READING 1-8F

I am sending an angel before you to guard you on the way and to bring you to the place which I have made ready. Pay heed to him and obey him; do not defy him, for he will not pardon your offenses, since My Name is in him. But if you obey him and do all that I say, I will be an enemy to your enemies and a foe to your foes.

[Exodus 23:20–22]

THE BOOK OF THE COVENANT

Provisions of civil law are strikingly paralleled in both letter and spirit by the collections of legal precedents issued long before by various Old Babylonian kings. The laws of the goring ox, for example, are already anticipated by the Laws of Hammurabi (Reading 1-9B) and, even more closely, by the earlier Laws of Eshnunna (Reading 1-9A), a city-state on the Diyala River (a tributary of the Tigris River), conquered by Hammurabi.

READING 1-9A

If an ox gores an(other) ox and causes its death, both ox owners shall divide [between themselves] the price of the live ox and the equivalent of the dead ox. If an ox is known to gore habitually and the authorities have brought the fact to the knowledge of its owner, but he does not have his ox dehorned[?], and it gores a man and causes (his) death, then the owner of the ox shall pay two-thirds of a pound of silver {40 shekels}. If it gores a slave and causes [his] death, he shall pay 15 shekels of silver.

READING 1-9B

If an ox, while it is walking along the street, gores a man and causes (his) death, that cause is not subject to claim. If the man's ox is known to gore habitually, and his authorities have brought to his knowledge the fact that it is wont to gore habitually, but he did not plaid its horns (or) tie up his ox, and that ox gores a free man and causes his death, he shall give one-half pound of silver {30 shekels}. If it was the slave of a man, he shall give one-third pound of silver {20 shekels}.

---

[5]From the Hittite and Akkadian versions of the treaty between Murshili of the Hittites (ca. 1334–1306 B.C.E.) and Duppi-Teshub of Amurru.

[6]From the Hittite treaty between Muwatalli of the Hittites (ca. 1306–1282 B.C.E.) and Alakshandu (Alexander) of Wilusha, in southwestern Anatolia.

READING 1-9C

When an ox gores a man or a woman to death, the ox shall be stoned and its flesh shall not be eaten, but the owner of the ox is not to be punished. If, however, that ox has long been a gorer, and its owner, though warned, has failed to guard it, and it kills a man or a woman—the ox shall be stoned and its owner, too, shall be put to death. If ransom is laid upon him, he must pay whatever is laid upon him to redeem his life. So, too, if it gores a minor, male or female, [the owner] shall be dealt with according to the same norm. But if the ox gores a slave, male or female, he shall pay thirty shekels of silver to the master, and the ox shall be stoned. . . .

When a man's ox injures his neighbor's ox and it dies, they shall sell the live ox and divide its price; they shall also divide the dead animal. If, however, the ox has long been known as a gorer, and its owner has failed to guard it, he must restore ox for ox, but shall keep the dead animal.

[Exodus 21:28–32, 35–36]

SPYING OUT THE LAND

Representatives of the twelve tribes were dispatched from Kadesh-barnea to spy out the land, and these reported that the land "does indeed flow with milk and honey" and otherwise painted a glowing picture of its physical attractions in terms long used of Palestine in Egyptian literature, as in the story of Sinuhe.

READING 1-10A

Then (Ammi-enshi, the ruler of Upper Retenu)[1] said to me: "Well, really, Egypt is happy that it knows that (Sesostris I) is flourishing. Now thou art here. Thou shalt stay with me. What I shall do for thee is good." He set me at the head of his children. He married me to his eldest daughter. He let me choose for myself of his country, of the choicest of that which was with him on his frontier with another country. It was a good land, named Yaa. Figs were in it, and grapes. It had more wine than water. Plentiful was its honey, abundant its olives. Every (kind of) fruit was on its trees. Barley was there, and emmer. There was no limit to any (kind of) cattle. Moreover, great was that which accrued to me as a result of the love of me. He made me ruler of a tribe of the choicest of his country. Bread was made for me as daily fare, wine as daily provision, cooked meat and roast fowl, beside the wild beasts of the desert, for they hunted for me and laid before me, beside the catch of my (own) hounds. Many. . . were made for me, and milk in every (kind of) cooking.

READING 1-10B

When Moses sent them to scout the land of Canaan, he said to them, "Go up there into the Negeb {the southernmost portion of the Promised Land} and on into the hill country, and see what kind of country it is. Are the people who dwell in it

---

[1]Northern Canaan and southern and central Syria.

strong or weak, few or many? Is the country in which they dwell good or bad? Are the towns they live in open or fortified? Is the soil rich or poor? Is it wooded or not? And take pains to bring back some of the fruit of the land."—Now it happened to be the season of the first ripe grapes.

They went up and scouted the land, from the wilderness of Zin to Rehob, at Lebo-hamath.[1] They went up into the Negeb and came to Hebron, where lived Ahiman, Sheshai, and Talmai, the Anakites.—Now Hebron was founded seven years before Zoan of Egypt.—They reached the Valley of Eshcol, and there they cut down a branch with a single cluster of grapes—it had to be borne on a carrying frame by two of them—and some pomegranates and figs. That place was named the Valley of Eshcol because of the cluster that the Israelites cut down there.

At the end of forty days they returned from scouting the land.

They went straight to Moses and Aaron and the whole Israelite community at Kadesh in the wilderness of Paran, and they made their report to them and to the whole community, as they showed them the fruit of the land. This is what they told him: "We came to the land you sent us to; it does indeed flow with milk and honey, and this is its fruit. However, the people who inhabit the country are powerful, and the cities are fortified and very large; moreover, we saw the Anakites there. Amalekites dwell in the Negeb region; Hittites, Jebusites, and Amorites inhabit the hill country; and Canaanites dwell by the Sea and along the Jordan."

[Numbers 13:17–29]

BALAAM

The figure of Balaam son of Beor recurs on a seventh-century inscription from Transjordan, again as a master of visions and curses.

READING 1-11A

[This is the inscrip]tion of [Bala]am [son of Be]or. He was a divine seer. And the gods came to him at night, [and they spoke to] him according to the vision of God. And they said to [Bala]am, son of Beor: "This will the [. . .] do in the future. No man has s[een what you have he]ard."

And Balaam arose on the morrow [and fasted for. . .] days, and on the [. . .th] day [he . . .] and he was truly weeping. And his people came to him [and they said] to Balaam son of Beor: "Why do you fast? Why do you weep?" And he said to them: "Be seated and I will inform you what the Shad[day-gods have done], and so, behold the workings of the gods! The gods have joined forces, and the Shadday-gods have established a council. And they have said to Sh[agar-and-Ishtar][2]: 'Sew up, cover up the heavens with a dense cloud, so that darkness, and no brilliance will be there; concealment, and no bristling light (?), that you may instill dread . . . [and mu]ch darkness, and never murmur again!' {There follows Balaam's interpretation of the ominous scene just described, his attempt to free Shagar-and-Ishtar from the destructive power of the divine council, and God's displeasure with Balaam's "in-

---

[1]I.e., from south to north; cf. Reading 1-3C note 1.

[2]A dual fertility deity whose echo may be found, for example, in Deut. 28:18 (see below, Reading 1-24B).

terference." After being taken to the edge of the netherworld (sheol), Balaam is told:} [You are no longer a man fit] to know how to deliver an oracle to his people. You have been condemned for what you have said, and banned from pronouncing words of execration.

READING 1-11B

Balak son of Zippor saw all that Israel had done to the Amorites. Moab was alarmed because that people was so numerous. Moab dreaded the Israelites, and Moab said to the elders of Midian, "Now this horde will lick clean all that is about us as an ox licks up the grass of the field."

Balak son of Zippor, who was king of Moab at that time, sent messengers to Balaam son of Beor in Pethor, which is by the Euphrates, in the land of his kinsfolk, to invite him, saying, "There is a people that came out of Egypt; it hides the earth from view and it is settled next to me. Come then, put a curse upon this people for me, since they are too numerous for me; perhaps I can thus defeat them and drive them out of the land. For I know that he whom you bless is blessed indeed, and he whom you curse falls under the curse."

The elders of Moab and the elders of Midian, versed in divination, set out. They came to Balaam and gave him Balak's message. He said to them, "Spend the night here, and I shall reply to you as the LORD may instruct me." So the Moabite dignitaries stayed with Balaam.

God came to Balaam and said, "What do these people want of you?" Balaam said to God, "Balak son of Zippor, king of Moab, sent me this message: Here is a people that came out from Egypt and hides the earth from view. Come now and damn them for me; perhaps I can engage them in battle and drive them off." But God said to Balaam, "Do not go with them. You must not curse that people, for they are blessed."

[Numbers 22:2–12]

THE "ISRAEL STELA"

Israel's name occurs for the first time outside the Bible in a stela of the Pharaoh Merneptah (ca. 1220–1211 B.C.E.). It is mentioned there in the context of settled cities and peoples on Egypt's Asiatic frontier.

READING 1-12A

> The princes lie prostrate, suing for peace.
> Not one lifts his head among the Nine Bows.[1]
> Destruction for Tehennu![2] Hatti[3] is pacified;
> Canaan is plundered with every evil;
> Ashkelon is taken; Gezer is captured;
> Yanoam is made non-existent;[4]

---

[1]Traditionally the principal enemies of Egypt, though the particular roster that follows here lists only eight.

[2]Libya.

[3]The Hittite empire in Anatolia.

[4]Cities on the southern coast, the central high lands, and the northern Jordan respectively.

Israel lies desolate; its seed is no more;
Hurru[5] has become a widow for Egypt;
All the lands in their entirety are pacified.
Everyone who was a nomad has been curbed by King Mer-ne-Ptah.

READING 1-12B

Who is like You, O LORD, among the celestials;
Who is like You, majestic in holiness,
Awesome in splendor, working wonders!
You put out Your right hand,
The earth swallowed them.
In Your love You lead the people You redeemed;
In Your strength You guide them to Your holy abode.
The peoples hear, they tremble;
Agony grips the dwellers in Philistia.
Now are the clans of Edom dismayed;
The tribes of Moab—trembling grips them;
All the dwellers in Canaan are aghast.
Terror and dread descend upon them;
Through the might of Your arm they are still as stone—
Till Your people pass by, O LORD,
The people pass whom You have ransomed.

[Exodus 15:11–16]

A SYRIAN INTERREGNUM

Twelve judges are known, distributed (more or less) over the twelve tribes. Few if any of them can be connected securely with events recorded in extrabiblical sources. But in the case of the first, Othniel, it can be suggested that King Cushan-rishathaim of Aram (Syria) may be an echo of the Syrian invader, sometimes identified as Irsu, who briefly usurped the Egyptian throne at the very end of the thirteenth century B.C.E.

READING 1-13A

Said King User-maat-Re Meri-Amon[1]—life, prosperity, health!—the great god, to the officials and leaders of the land, the infantry, the chariotry, the Sherden,[2] the many bowmen, and all the souls of Egypt:

Hear ye, that I may make you aware of my benefactions which I accomplished while I was king of the people. The land of Egypt had been cast aside, with every man being his (*own standard of*) *right*. They had no chief spokesman for many years

---

[5]Syria-Palestine as a whole.

---

[1]I.e., Ramses III (ca. 1198–1166 B.C.E.). His throne name is followed by the standard blessing invoked on the pharaoh. For the royal epithet, cf. Reading 1-5D note 3.

[2]The Sherden, one of the Sea Peoples, served as mercenaries in the Egyptian armies at this time or moved westward to colonize the island of Sardinia, named after them.

previously up to other times. The land of Egypt was officials and mayors, one slaying his fellow, both exalted and lowly. Other *times* came afterwards in the empty years, and . . . , a Syrian with them, made himself prince.[3] He set the entire land as tributary before him. One joined his companion that their property might be plundered. They treated the gods like the people, and no offerings were presented in the temples.

But when the gods reversed themselves to show mercy and to set the land right as was its normal state, they established their son, who had come forth from their body, to be Ruler—life, prosperity, health!—of every land, upon their great throne. . . . He brought to order the entire land, which had been rebellious. He slew the disaffected of heart who had been in Egypt. He cleansed the great throne of Egypt.

READING 1-13B

The Israelites settled among the Canaanites, Hittites, Amorites, Perizzites, Hivites, and Jebusites; they took their daughters to wife and gave their own daughters to their sons, and they worshiped their gods. The Israelites did what was offensive to the LORD; they ignored the LORD their God and worshiped the Baalim and the Asheroth {Canaanite divinities}. The LORD became incensed at Israel and surrendered them to King Cushan-rishathaim of Aram-naharaim;[1] and the Israelites were subject to Cushan-rishathaim for eight years. The Israelites cried out to the LORD, and the LORD raised a champion for the Israelites to deliver them: Othniel the Kenizzite, a younger kinsman of Caleb.

The spirit of the LORD descended upon him and he became Israel's chieftain. He went out to war, and the LORD delivered King Cushan-rishathaim of Aram into his hands. He prevailed over Cushan-rishathaim, and the land had peace for forty years.

[Judges 3:5–11]

THE MANNER OF THE KINGSHIP

Faced with the twin threat of Philistines on the west and Ammonites on the east, the twelve tribes demanded, "Appoint a king for us, to govern us like all other nations" (I Samuel 8:5). Samuel countered with a classic defense of theocracy and a warning of the evil consequences of monarchy.

READING 1-14

Samuel reported all the words of the LORD to the people, who were asking him for a king. He said, "This will be the practice of the king who will rule over you: He will take your sons and appoint them as his charioteers and horsemen, and they will serve as outrunners for his chariots. He will appoint them as his chiefs of thousands

---

[3]Alternatively, this line may be translated, "Irsu, a Syrian, was with them as prince."

---

[1]"Aram of the twin rivers," i.e., upper Mesopotamia; the name of its king is artificially modeled on the name of his kingdom; it may mean "Cushan the doubly-wicked one," and thus constitute a deliberate slur.

and of fifties; or they will have to plow his fields, reap his harvest, and make his weapons and the equipment for his chariots. He will take your daughters as perfumers, cooks, and bakers. He will seize your choice fields, vineyards, and olive groves, and give them to his courtiers. He will take a tenth part of your grain and vintage and give it to his eunuchs and courtiers. He will take your male and female slaves, your choice young men, and your asses, and put them to work for him. He will take a tenth part of your flocks, and you shall become his slaves. The day will come when you cry out because of the king whom you yourselves have chosen; and the LORD will not answer you on that day."

[I Samuel 8:10–18]

SAUL AND DAVID

David became the second king of the United Monarchy, having before that served as singer and military leader at the court of Saul. He was the supposed author or subject of numerous poems preserved in the Book of Psalms and elsewhere, some of them celebrating highlights of his life both before and after his accession. Thus, for example, the superscription of Psalm 57 (*al tashhēth*) may be an elliptic allusion to the episode when David restrained his followers from assassinating the sleeping King Saul with the words "Don't do him violence!" (*al tashḥīthēhū*; I Samuel 26:9).

READING 1-15A

The Ziphites came to Saul at Gibeah and said, "David is hiding in the hill of Hachilah facing Jeshimon." Saul went down at once to the wilderness of Ziph, together with three thousand picked men of Israel, to search for David in the wilderness of Ziph, and Saul encamped on the hill of Hachilah which faces Jeshimon, by the road. When David, who was then living in the wilderness, learned that Saul had come after him into the wilderness, David sent out scouts and made sure that Saul had come. David went at once to the place where Saul had encamped, and David saw the spot where Saul and his army commander, Abner son of Ner, lay asleep. Saul lay asleep inside the barricade and the troops were posted around him.

David spoke up and asked Ahimelech the Hittite and Abishai son of Zeruiah, Joab's brother, "Who will go down with me into the camp to Saul?" And Abishai answered, "I will go down with you." So David and Abishai approached the troops by night, and found Saul fast asleep inside the barricade, his spear stuck in the ground at his head, and Abner and the troops sleeping around him. And Abishai said to David, "God has delivered your enemy into your hands today. Let me pin him to the ground with a single thrust of the spear. I will not have to strike him twice." But David said to Abishai, "Don't do him violence! No one can lay hands on the LORD's anointed with impunity." And David went on, "As the LORD lives, the LORD Himself will strike him down, or his time will come and he will die, or he will go down to battle and perish. But the LORD forbid that I should lay a hand on the LORD's anointed! Just take the spear and the water jar at his head and let's be off." So David took away the spear and the water jar at Saul's head, and they left. No one saw or knew or woke up; all remained asleep; a deep sleep from the LORD had fallen upon them.

David crossed over to the other side and stood afar on top of a hill; there was considerable distance between them. And David shouted to the troops and to Abner son of Ner, "Abner, aren't you going to answer?" And Abner shouted back, "Who are you to shout at the king?" And David answered Abner, "You are a man, aren't you? And there is no one like you in Israel! So why didn't you keep watch over your lord the king? For one of [our] troops came to do violence to your lord the king. You have not given a good account of yourself! As the LORD lives, [all of] you deserve to die, because you did not keep watch over your lord, the LORD's anointed. Look around, where are the king's spear and the water jar that were at his head?"

Saul recognized David's voice, and he asked, "Is that your voice, my son David?" And David replied, "It is, my lord king." And he went on, "But why does my lord continue to pursue his servant? What have I done, and what wrong am I guilty of? Now let my lord the king hear his servant out. If the LORD has incited you against me, let Him be appeased by an offering; but if it is men, may they be accursed of the LORD! For they have driven me out today, so that I cannot have a share in the LORD's possession, but am told, 'Go and worship other gods.' Oh, let my blood not fall to the ground, away from the presence of the LORD! For the king of Israel has come out to seek a single flea—as if he were hunting a partridge in the hills."

And Saul answered, "I am in the wrong. Come back, my son David, for I will never harm you again, seeing how you have held my life precious this day. Yes, I have been a fool, and I have erred so very much." David replied, "Here is Your Majesty's spear. Let one of the young men come over and get it. And the LORD will requite every man for his right conduct and loyalty—for this day the LORD delivered you into my hands and I would not raise a hand against the LORD's anointed. And just as I valued your life highly this day, so may the LORD value my life and may He rescue me from all trouble." Saul answered David, "May you be blessed, my son David. You shall achieve, and you shall prevail."

David then went his way, and Saul returned home.

[I Samuel 26]

READING 1-15B

For the leader; *al tashheth*. Of David. A *michtam*,[1] when he fled from Saul into a cave.

> Have mercy on me, O God, have mercy on me,
>> for I seek refuge in You,
>> I seek refuge in the shadow of Your wings,
>> until danger passes.
> I call to God Most High,
>> to God who is good to me.
> He will reach down from heaven and deliver me:
>> God will send down His steadfast love;
>> my persecutor reviles.   *Selah.*
>
> As for me, I lie down among man-eating lions
>> whose teeth are spears and arrows,
>> whose tongue is a sharp sword.

---

[1]A type of prayer, perhaps in the form of a letter or one engraved on a *stela* (= monument).

Exalt Yourself over the heavens, O God,
   let Your glory be over all the earth!
They prepared a net for my feet to ensnare me;
   they dug a pit for me,
   but they fell into it.   *Selah.*

My heart is firm, O God;
   my heart is firm;
   I will sing, I will chant a hymn.
Awake, O my soul!
Awake, O harp and lyre!
I will wake the dawn.
I will praise You among the peoples, O Lord;
   I will sing a hymn to You among the nations;
   for Your faithfulness is as high as heaven;
   Your steadfastness reaches to the sky.
Exalt Yourself over the heavens, O God,
   let Your glory be over all the earth!

[Psalm 57]

THE DEDICATION OF THE TEMPLE

Solomon succeeded his father, David, as king of the United Monarchy. As a man of peace he erected in Jerusalem the first permanent sanctuary to Israel's God. The work began in his fourth year (ca. 960 B.C.E.). It was completed seven years later and was followed by elaborate seven-day dedication ceremonies.

READING 1-16

Then Solomon convoked the elders of Israel—all the heads of the tribes and the ancestral chieftains of the Israelites—before King Solomon in Jerusalem, to bring up the Ark of the Covenant of the Lord from the City of David, that is, Zion.

All the men of Israel gathered before King Solomon at the Feast, in the month of Ethanim—that is, the seventh month. When all the elders of Israel had come, the priests lifted the Ark and carried up the Ark of the Lord. Then the priests and the Levites brought the Tent of Meeting and all the holy vessels that were in the Tent. Meanwhile, King Solomon and the whole community of Israel, who were assembled with him before the Ark, were sacrificing sheep and oxen in such abundance that they could not be numbered or counted.

The priests brought the Ark of the Lord's Covenant to its place underneath the wings of the cherubim, in the Shrine of the House, in the Holy of Holies; for the cherubim had their wings spread out over the place of the Ark, so that the cherubim shielded the Ark and its poles from above. The poles projected so that the ends of the poles were visible in the Sanctuary in front of the Shrine, but they could not be seen outside; and there they remain to this day. There was nothing inside the Ark but the two tablets of stone which Moses placed there at Horeb, when the Lord made [a covenant] with the Israelites after their departure from the land of Egypt.

When the priests came out of the sanctuary—for the cloud had filled the House of the Lord and the priests were not able to remain and perform the service because of the cloud, for the Presence of the Lord filled the House of the Lord—then Solomon declared:

> "The Lord has chosen
> To abide in a thick cloud:
> I have now built for You
> A stately House,
> A place where You
> May dwell forever."

Then, with the whole congregation of Israel standing, the king faced about and blessed the whole congregation of Israel. . . .

When Solomon finished offering to the Lord all this prayer and supplication, he rose from where he had been kneeling, in front of the altar of the Lord, his hands spread out toward heaven. He stood, and in a loud voice blessed the whole congregation of Israel:

"Praised be the Lord who has granted a haven to His people Israel, just as He promised; not a single word has failed of all the gracious promises that He made through His servant Moses. May the Lord our God be with us, as He was with our fathers. May He never abandon or forsake us. May He incline our hearts to Him, that we may walk in all His ways and keep the commandments, the laws, and the rules, which He enjoined upon our fathers. And may these words of mine, which I have offered in supplication before the Lord, be close to the Lord our God day and night, that He may provide for His servant and for His people Israel, according to each day's needs—to the end that all the peoples of the earth may know that the Lord alone is God, there is no other. And may you be wholehearted with the Lord our God, to walk in His ways and keep His commandments, even as now."

The king and all Israel with him offered sacrifices before the Lord. Solomon offered 22,000 oxen and 120,000 sheep as sacrifices of well-being to the Lord. Thus the king and all the Israelites dedicated the House of the Lord. The day the king consecrated the center of the court that was in front of the House of the Lord. For it was there that he presented the burnt offerings, the meal offerings, and the fat parts of the offerings of well-being, because the bronze altar that was before the Lord was too small to hold the burnt offerings, the meal offerings, and the fat parts of the offerings of well-being.

So Solomon and all Israel with him—a great assemblage, [coming] from Lebo-hamath to the Wadi of Egypt[1]—observed the Feast at that time before the Lord our God, seven days and again seven days, fourteen days in all. On the eighth day he let the people go. They bade the king good-bye and went to their homes, joyful and glad of heart over all the goodness that the Lord had shown to His servant David and His people Israel.

[I Kings 8:1–14; 54–66]

---

[1]Cf. Readings 1-3C note 1 and 1-10B note 1.

SOLOMON'S ADMINISTRATIVE SYSTEM

Solomon reorganized the whole governmental structure of the kingdom. Essentially he abolished most of the old tribal boundaries and replaced them, at least in the north, with twelve new provinces. Each of these was responsible for filling the royal coffers during one month of the year. Analogous systems are attested in contemporary Egypt (Reading 1-17A) and in Mesopotamia (Reading 1-17B) more than a thousand years earlier.

READING 1-17A

The king's son, the general Namlot, came into His Majesty's presence and said, 'the House of Arsaphes, the King of the Two Lands,[1] has ceased (making) the daily ox-offering. I found it (the temple) fallen to ruin (from) what (it) had formerly been in the times of the ancestors. It would be well to have it resumed.' Said His Majesty, 'may my *ku* praise thee, my son, who hath come forth from me! Thy heart is like the heart of him who begat thee, my body made young again! It is my father Arsaphes, the King of the Two Lands, the Lord of Herakleopolis {city in Lower Egypt}, that makes sound every utterance of thine in his house, for ever!' A decree was issued in the Palace, L.P.H. {life, prosperity, health}, to supply the House of Arsaphes, the King of the Two, Lands, the Lord of Herakleopolis, and to restore to it this daily ox-offering, as it had been in the times of the ancestors. In proportion to his needs the decree placed a levy for the daily ox-offering on the towns and villages of the Herakleopolite (nome), without exception(?). It shall not be discontinued for him for ever and ever. The King of Upper and Lower Egypt, the Lord of the Two Lands . . . Lord of Diadems, *mry-Imn* Sheshonq,[2] given life like Re {Egyptian sun god} for ever.

There follows the 'quota(?) of the levy which consists of 365 oxen throughout the year, (now) and for ever more.' The remainder of the text is arranged in twelve monthly sections with a final section for the five epagomenal days, and under each are listed the officials and towns responsible for supplying the temple during that month, together with the amount of their levy.

READING 1-17B

Month XII and I:	the governor of Girsu[1]
Month II:	the governor of Umma
Month III:	the governor of Babylon
Month IV:	the governor of Marada
Month V and VI:	the governor of Girsu
Month VII:	the governors of Ishim-Shulgi, etc.

---

[1]Upper and Lower Egypt; equivalent of Hebrew Miṣrayim, the biblical name for Egypt.

[2]Sheshonq I (ca. 940–919 B.C.E.), the biblical Shishak (I Kings 11:4, etc.). For the royal epithet, cf. Reading 1-5D note 3.

---

[1]Girsu and the other places listed are provincial capitals of the Kingdom of Ur in Mesopotamia during the twenty-first century B.C.E.

Month VIII:	the governor of Adab
Month IX:	the prefect of Ur
Month X:	the governor of Shuruppak
Month XI:	the governor of Kazallu

READING 1-17C

Solomon had twelve prefects governing all Israel, who provided food for the king and his household; each had to provide food for one month in the year. And these were their names: Ben-hur, in the hill country of Ephraim; Ben-deker, in Makaz, Shaalbim, Beth-shemesh, and Elon-beth-hanan; Ben-hesed in Arubboth—he governed Socho and all the Hepher area; Ben-abinadab, [in] all of Naphath-dor (Solomon's daughter Taphath was his wife); Baana son of Ahilud [in] Taanach and Megiddo and all Beth-shean, which is beside Zarethan, below Jezreel—from Bethshean to Abel-meholah as far as the other side of Jokmeam; Ben-geber, in Ramothgilead—he governed the villages of Jair son of Manasseh which are in Gilead, and he also governed the district of Argob which is in Bashan, sixty large towns with walls and bronze bars; Ahinadab son of Iddo, in Mahanaim; Ahimaaz, in Naphtali (he too took a daughter of Solomon—Basemath—to wife); Baanah son of Hushi, in Asher and Bealoth; Jehoshaphat son of Paruah, in Issachar; Shimei son of Ela, in Benjamin; Geber son of Uri, in the region of Gilead, the country of Sihon king of the Amorites and Og king of Bashan; and one prefect who was in the land.

Judah and Israel were as numerous as the sands of the sea; they ate and drank and were content.

[I Kings 4:7–20]

THE END OF THE UNITED MONARCHY

The ten northern tribes ("Israel") appealed to Solomon's successor, Rehoboam, to ease their burdens, and he duly consulted with "the elders" and "the young men" in turn (I Kings 12; see also II Chronicles 10). Of these two consultative groups, the former counseled restraint, but the latter advised confrontation and, following ancient literary precedent, as in the story of Gilgamesh and Agga, the latter's counsel prevailed.

READING 1-18A

The envoys of Agga, the son of Enmebaragesi,
Came from Kish to Gilgamesh in Uruk.[1]

Before the elders of his city, Gilgamesh
Set the matter, seeking advice:
"To finish wells, to finish the wells of the land,

---

[1]Gilgamesh of Uruk and Agga of Kish ruled in the Second Early Dynastic Period of Mesopotamian history (ca. 2700–2500 B.C.E.). Their rivalry reflected the long-standing tension between the two halves of lower Mesopotamia later known as Sumer and Akkad.

"To finish the shallow wells of the land,
"To finish the deep wells hung with ropes—
"We must not submit to the house of Kish! Let us fight!"
In the assembly, the elders of his city
Answered Gilgamesh:
"To finish wells, to finish the wells of the land,
"To finish the shallow wells of the land,
"To finish the deep wells hung with ropes—
"Let us submit to the house of Kish! We must not fight!"
Gilgamesh, Lord of Kulaba,[2]
Who trusts in Inanna,
Did not approve the words of the elders of his city.

For a second time, before the able-bodied men of his city,
    Gilgamesh
Set the matter, seeking advice:
"To finish wells, to finish the wells of the land,
"To finish the shallow wells of the land,
"To finish the deep wells hung with ropes—
"We must not submit to the house of Kish! Let us fight!"
In the assembly, the able-bodied men of his city answer Gilgamesh:
"To always be serving and always on duty,
"To be stationed with the king's son,
"To always cleave to the donkey's thigh—
"Who could have enthusiasm for that?
"We must not submit to the house of Kish! Let us fight!
"Uruk, handiwork of the gods,
"Eanna, the temple descended from heaven,
"Whose parts the great gods created,
"Whose great wall hugs the ground like a fog,
"The lofty residence founded by An—
"You watch over it, you are its king and hero!
"O Smasher of heads, prince beloved of An,
"When he (Agga) comes, how they are afraid!
"But that army is small, and disorganized in the rear,
"Its men are incapable of confrontation!"
Then Gilgamesh, lord of Kulaba,
Rejoiced at the words of the able-bodied men of his city, and was
    happy.

He spoke to his servant Enkidu:
"Now then, let the implements and arms of battle be made ready!
"Let the battle mace return to your side!
"Let them create a great and terrifying aura,
"And when he (Agga) comes, my great terror should overwhelm
    him!
"His understanding should become confused, his judgment
    disorganized!"

---

[2]Kulaba (Kullab) was part of Uruk, the biblical Erech (Genesis 10:10).

READING 1-18B

Rehoboam went to Shechem, for all Israel had come to Shechem to acclaim him as king. Jeroboam son of Nebat learned of it while he was still in Egypt; for Jeroboam had fled from King Solomon, and had settled in Egypt. They sent for him; and Jeroboam and all the assembly of Israel came and spoke to Rehoboam as follows: "Your father made our yoke heavy. Now lighten the harsh labor and the heavy yoke which your father laid on us, and we will serve you." He answered them, "Go away for three days and then come back to me." So the people went away.

King Rehoboam took counsel with the elders who had served his father Solomon during his lifetime. He said, "What answer do you advise [me] to give to this people?" They answered him, "If you will be a servant to those people today and serve them, and if you respond to them with kind words, they will be your servants always." But he ignored the advice that the elders gave him, and took counsel with the young men who had grown up with him and were serving him. "What," he asked, "do you advise that we reply to the people who said to me, 'Lighten the yoke that your father placed upon us'?" And the young men who had grown up with him answered, "Speak thus to the people who said to you, 'Your father made our yoke heavy, now you make it lighter for us.' Say to them, 'My little finger is thicker than my father's loins. My father imposed a heavy yoke on you, and I will add to your yoke; my father flogged you with whips, but I will flog you with scorpions.' "

Jeroboam and all the people came to Rehoboam on the third day, since the king had told them: "Come back on the third day." The king answered the people harshly, ignoring the advice that the elders had given him. He spoke to them in accordance with the advice of the young men, and said, "My father made your yoke heavy, but I will add to your yoke; my father flogged you with whips, but I will flog you with scorpions."

[I Kings 12:1–14]

ASSYRIA MOVES WESTWARD

Israel was a prominent member of the alliance that confronted Shalmaneser III of Assyria no less than five times between 853 and 841 B.C.E. In effect, the allies fought him to a standstill. This selection from the annals of Shalmaneser III of Assyria (858–824 B.C.E.) describes the events of his sixth year (853 B.C.E.) including the great battle of Qarqar which pitted the Assyrian king against a western alliance including King Ahab of Israel (874–853 B.C.E.).

READING 1-19

In the year of (the eponym)[1] Daian-Ashur,[2] in the month Aiaru, the 14th day, I departed from Nineveh. I crossed the Tigris and approached the towns of Giammu

---

[1] Assyrian years were named after high officials in predetermined rotations, hence eponym. (cf. below, Reading 2-8.)

[2] Official who gave his name to the 6th year of Shalmaneser III.

on the river Balih.[3] They became afraid of the terror emanating from my position as overlord, as well as of the splendor of my fierce weapons, and killed their master Giammu with their own weapons. I entered the towns Sahlala and Til-sha-Turahi and brought my gods/images into his palaces. I performed the *tašîltu*-festival in his (own) palaces. I opened (his) treasury, inspected what he had hidden; I carried away as booty his possessions, bringing (them) to my town Ashur. From Sahlala I departed and approached Kar-Shalmaneser. I crossed the Euphrates another time at its flood on rafts (made buoyant by means) of (inflated) goatskins. In Ina-Ashur-utir-asbat, which the people of Hattina call Pitru, on the other side of the Euphrates, on the river Sagur, I received tribute from the kings of the other side of the Euphrates—that is, of Sanagara from Carchemish, Kundashpi from Commagene, of Arame, man of Gusi, of Lalli from Melitene . . . , of Haiani, son of Gabari, of Kalparuda from Hattina, (and) of Kalparuda of Gurgum—(consisting of): silver, gold, tin, copper (or bronze), copper containers. I departed from the banks of the Euphrates and approached Aleppo[4]. . . . They (i.e., the inhabitants of A.) were afraid to fight and seized my feet (in submission). I received silver and gold as their tribute and offered sacrifices before the Adad of Aleppo. I departed from Aleppo and approached the two towns of Irhuleni from Hamath[5]. . . . I captured the towns Adennu, Barga (and) Argana his royal residence. I removed from them his booty (as well as) his personal (lit.: of his palaces) possessions. I set his palaces afire. I departed from Argana and approached Karkara. I destroyed, tore down and burned down Karkara, his (text: my) royal residence. He brought along to help him 1,200 chariots, 1,200 cavalrymen, 20,000 foot soldiers of Adad-'idri (i.e. Hadade-zer) of Damascus . . . , 700 chariots, 700 cavalrymen, 10,000 foot soldiers of Irhuleni from Hamath, 2,000 chariots, 10,000 foot soldiers of Ahab, the Israelite . . . , 500 soldiers from Que, 1,000 soldiers from Musri, 10 chariots, 10,000 soldiers from Irqanata, 200 soldiers of Matinu-ba'lu from Arvad, 200 soldiers from Usanata, 30 chariots, I[0?],000 soldiers of Adunu-ba'lu from Shian, 1,000 camel-(rider)s of Gindibu', from Arabia, [. . .],000 soldiers of Ba'sa, son of Ruhubi, from Ammon—(all together) these were twelve kings. They rose against me [for a] decisive battle. I fought with them with (the support of) the mighty forces of Ashur, which Ashur, my lord, has given to me, and the strong weapons which Nergal, my leader, has presented to me, (and) I did inflict a defeat upon them between the towns Karkara and Gilzau. I slew 14,000 of their soldiers with the sword, descending upon them like Adad when he makes a rainstorm pour down. I spread their corpses (everywhere), filling the entire plain with their widely scattered (fleeing) soldiers. During the battle I made their blood flow down the *ḫur-pa-lu* of the district. The plain was too small to let (all) their (text: his) souls descend (into the nether world), the vast field gave out (when it came) to bury them. With their (text: sing.) corpses I spanned the Orontes before there was a bridge. Even during the battle I took from them their chariots, their horses broken to the yoke. . . .

---

[3]Tributary of the Euphrates river.

[4]Major city in Northern Syria.

[5]Another major town in Syria.

TRIBUTE TO ASSYRIA

Having, in effect, fought Shalmaneser to a standstill, Israel for a time enjoyed a respite from the Assyrians, who contented themselves with accepting tribute from the western alliance, as seen in The Black Obelisk of Shalmaneser (Reading 1-20A) and two recently discovered cuneiform inscriptions (1-20B, C).

READING 1-20A

The tribute of Jehu[1] (*Ia-ú-a*), son of Omri (*Hu-um-ri*); I received from him silver, gold, a golden *saplu*-bowl, a golden vase with pointed bottom, golden tumblers, golden buckets, tin, a staff for a king, (and) wooden *puruhtu*.

READING 1-20B

[Tiglath Piles]er,[1] the governor of Enlil, the prince, priest of Ashur
. . . who reme]mbers their places, the vice-regent of
[Assur,] the precious offspring of Baltil
. . . favou]rite of Sarpanitu, the great lady
. . . showed him mercy . . .
[the great king, the mighty king, king of the wo]rld, king of Assur, king of Sumer
[and Akkad, king of the] four [quart]ers, shepherd of mankind,
[decreer of the freed]om of Assur, who pleases . . .
[who broadens] the boundary of Assur
. . .
[At that time As]hur and Enlil
[my fathers] who created [me] sent [me] to strike down the unsubmissive.
. . . In my first regnal year, in the sixth month after [I took my seat majestically on my royal throne],
. . . I mustered] the troops of Assur
[and set off to overthrow the country X.]

The kings of Hatti, the Arameans whom I supplanted,
of the setting sun, Qidri, Aribi.
Kushtashpi of Kummuh
Resin of Damascus
Menahem of Samaria

---

[1]The Black Obelisk of Shalmaneser III is carved with reliefs depicting the submission of various western kings, and thus preserves the only contemporary representation of an Israelite figure known from the Bible. He is identified in an accompanying caption as Jehu who, however, was not a son of Omri nor even a member of the royal house of Omri.

---

[1]Tiglath-pileser III (744–727 B.C.E.) accepted tribute from "Menahem of Samaria" (i.e., Israel) (751–742 B.C.E.).

Tubail of Tyre
Sibatbail of Byblos
Urik of Que
Sulumal of Melid
Uassurme of Tabal
Ushhiti of Atuna
Urballa of Tuhan
Tuhame of Ishtundi
Uirimi of Hushemna
Dadi-il of Kaska
Pisiris of Carchemish
Panammu of Samal
Tarhulara of Gurgum
Zabibe, queen of Arabia
tribute and gifts, silver, gold, tin, iron,
elephant hide, ivory, blue purple and red purple garments,
trimmed linen garments, dromedaries,
she-camels, I imposed upon them.
As for Iranzi of Mannea,
Talta of Ellipi
the chieftains of Namri, of Singibutu,
of all of the mountains of the high country(?)
horses, mules, Bactrian camels
cattle, sheep, I imposed upon them (as tribute).
I received it yearly in Assur.
I made stelae in all(?) the lands.
The great gods, my lords, In engraved thereon.
I depicted a likeness of my majesty on it.

READING 1-20C

To 'Adad,[1] the greatest lord, hero of the gods, mighty one first-born son of Anu, whose fieriness constantly renews itself, the lofty irrigator of heaven and earth, who provides the rain that brings abundance, who dwells in Zamahu, the great lord, his lord: I, Adad-nirari the mighty king, king of the world, king of Assyria, heir of Shamshi-Adad, the king of the world, king of Assyria, heir of Shalmaneser the king of the four regions, mobilized chariots, troops and camps, and ordered a campaign to the Hatti land. In a single year I made the land of Amurru and the Hatti land in its entirety kneel at my feet; I imposed tribute (and) regular tax for future days upon them. He (*sic*) received two thousand talents of silver, one thousand talents of copper, two thousand talents of iron, three thousand multi-coloured garments and (plain) linen garments as tribute from Mari' of the land of Damascus. He received the tribute of Ia'asu the Samaritan,[1] of the Tyrian (ruler) and of the Sidonian (ruler). I marched to the great sea where the sun sets, and erected a stela ("image") of my royal self in the city of Arvad which is in the middle of the sea. I went up the

---

[1]Adad-nirari III (810–783 B.C.E.) accepted tribute from Joash of Israel (797–782 B.C.E.) here called "Ia'asu the Samaritan."

Lebanon mountains and cut down timbers: one hundred mature cedars, material needed for my palace (and) temples. He received tributes from all the kings of the Nairi land.

PROPHET AND PRIEST

Beginning with Amos, the prophets warned of the fragile character of political independence. They coupled these warnings with denunciations of the rich new cosmopolitan life indulged in by the newly emerging royal-urban society. This could lead to confrontations with the established authorities, as in this encounter at Bethel, one of the principal sanctuaries established on the borders of the northern kingdom.

READING 1-21

Amaziah, the priest of Bethel, sent this message to King Jeroboam of Israel: "Amos is conspiring against you within the House of Israel. The country cannot endure the things he is saying. For Amos has said, 'Jeroboam shall die by the sword, and Israel shall be exiled from its soil.' "

Amaziah also said to Amos, "Seer, off with you to the land of Judah! Earn your living there, and do your prophesying there. But don't ever prophesy again at Bethel; for it is a king's sanctuary and a royal palace." Amos answered Amaziah: "I am not a prophet, and I am not a prophet's disciple. I am a cattle breeder and a tender of sycamore figs. But the LORD took me away from following the flock, and the LORD said to me, 'Go, prophesy to My people Israel.' And so, hear the word of the LORD. You say I must not prophesy about the House of Israel or preach about the House of Isaac; but this, I swear, is what the LORD said: Your wife shall play the harlot in the town, your sons and daughters shall fall by the sword, and your land shall be divided up with a measuring line. And you yourself shall die on unclean soil; for Israel shall be exiled from its soil."

This is what my LORD GOD showed me: There was a basket of figs. He said, "What do you see, Amos?" "A basket of figs," I replied. And the LORD said to me: "The hour of doom has come for My people Israel; I will not pardon them again. And the singing women of the palace shall howl on that day—declares my LORD GOD:

> So many corpses
> Left lying everywhere!
> Hush!"

Listen to this, you who devour the needy, annihilating the poor of the land, saying, "If only the new moon were over, so that we could sell grain; the sabbath, so that we could offer wheat for sale, using an ephah that is too small, and a shekel that is too big, tilting a dishonest scale, and selling grain refuse as grain! We will buy the poor for silver, the needy for a pair of sandals. the LORD swears by the Pride of Jacob: "I will never forget any of their doings."

[Amos 7:10–8:7]

THE FALL OF SAMARIA

In 722 B.C.E. Samaria, the capital of Israel, fell to the Assyrian armies, and the entire northern kingdom was incorporated into the Assyrian provincial system. The event is recorded both in the Bible and in the "Babylonian Chronicle," a detailed and objective record of events compiled continuously by the priesthood of Babylon beginning in 747 B.C.E.

READING 1-22A

The second year: Tiglath-pileser (III) died in the month Tebet. For [*eighteen*] years Tiglath-pileser (III) ruled Akkad and Assyria. For two of these years he ruled in Akkad. On the twenty-fifth day of the month Tebet Shalmaneser (V) ascended the throne in Assyria [and Akkad]. He ravaged Samaria. The fifth year: Shalmaneser (V) died in the month Tebet. For five years Shalmaneser (V) ruled Akkad and Assyria. On the twelfth day of the month Tebet Sargon (II) ascended the throne in Assyria. In the month Nisan Merodach-baladan (II) ascended the throne in Babylon.

READING 1-22B

In the twelfth year of King Ahaz of Judah, Hoshea son of Elah became king over Israel in Samaria—for nine years. He did what was displeasing to the LORD, though not as much as the kings of Israel who preceded him. King Shalmaneser marched against him, and Hoshea became his vassal and paid him tribute. But the king of Assyria caught Hoshea in an act of treachery: he had sent envoys to King So of Egypt, and he had not paid the tribute to the king of Assyria, as in previous years. And the king of Assyria arrested him and put him in prison. Then the king of Assyria marched against the whole land; he came to Samaria and besieged it for three years. In the ninth year of Hoshea, the king of Assyria captured Samaria. He deported the Israelites to Assyria and settled them in Halah, at the [River] Habor, at the River Gozan, and in the towns of Media.

This happened because the Israelites sinned against the LORD their God, who had freed them from the land of Egypt, from the hand of Pharaoh king of Egypt. They worshipped other gods and followed the customs of the nations which the LORD had dispossessed before the Israelites and the customs which the kings of Israel had practiced. The Israelites committed against the LORD their God acts which were not right: They built for themselves shrines in all their settlements, from watchtowers to fortified cities; they set up pillars and sacred posts for themselves on every lofty hill and under every leafy tree; and they offered sacrifices there, at all the shrines, like the nations whom the LORD had driven into exile before them. They committed wicked acts to vex the LORD, and they worshiped fetishes concerning which the LORD had said to them, "You must not do this thing."

The LORD warned Israel and Judah by every prophet [and] every seer, saying: "Turn back from your wicked ways, and observe My commandments and My laws, according to all the Teaching that I commanded your fathers and that I transmitted to you through My servants the prophets." But they did not obey; they stiffened their necks, like their fathers who did not have faith in the LORD their God; they spurned His laws and the covenant which He had made with their fathers, and the warnings He had given them. They went after delusion and were deluded; [they imitated] the nations that were about them, which the LORD had forbidden them to emulate. They rejected all the commandments of the LORD their God; they made molten idols for themselves—two calves—and they made a sacred post and they bowed down to all the host of heaven, and they worshiped Baal. They consigned their sons and daughters to the fire; they practiced augury and divination, and gave themselves over to what was displeasing to the LORD and vexed Him. The LORD was incensed at Israel and He banished them from His presence; none was left but the tribe of Judah alone.

[II Kings 17:1–18]

THE SIEGE OF JERUSALEM (701 B.C.E.)

After weathering Sennacherib's siege of Jerusalem in 701 B.C.E., King Hezekiah (716–687 B.C.E.) fell ill and addressed God by means of a letter-prayer (Reading 1-23C). The Assyrian king used a similar format to report on the campaign (Reading 1-23A) and, long before, a Babylonian king had similarly prayed for relief from illness in a letter to his goddess (1-23B).

READING 1-23A[1]

[. . . Anshar, my lord, encourag]ed me, and against the land of Ju[dah I marched. In] the course of my campaign, the tribute of the Ki[ngs (?) of Philistia (?)] I received . . [. with the mig]ht of Anshar, my lord, the province of [Hezek]iah of Judah like [. . .] the city of Azekah, his stronghold, which is between my [bo]rder and the land of Judah [. . . like the nest of the eagle (?)] located on a mountain ridge; like pointed iron (?) daggers without number reaching high to heaven [. . . its walls] were strong and rivaled the highest mountains; to the (mere) sight, as if from the sky [appears its head (?) . . . by means of beaten (earth) ra]mps, mighty (?) battering rams brought near, with the attack by foot soldiers (using) mi[nes, breaches . . .] they had seen [the approach of my cav]alry and they had heard the roar of the mighty troops of the god Anshar and their hearts became afraid [. . . The city Azekah I besieged,] I captured, I carried off its spoil, I destroyed, I devastated, [I burned with fire . . .]

[The city of Gath (?)], a royal [city] of the Philistines, which H[ezek]iah had captured and strengthened for himself [. . .] like a tree [standing out on a ridge (?) . . .] surrounded with great towers and exceedingly difficult [its ascent (?) . . .], palace like a mountain was barred in front of them and high is [its top (?) . . .]. It was dark and the sun never shone on it; its waters were situated in darkness and [its] overflow [. . .], its [mou]th (?) was cut with axes and a moat was dug around it [. . . warriors] skillful in battle he caused to enter into it, their weapons he bound (on them) to [offer battle . . .] I caused the warriors of Amurru, all of them, to carry earth [. . .] against them. In the seventh time his [. . .] the great like a pot [of clay (?) I smashed (?) . . . cattle and she]ep I carried out from its midst [and counted as] spo[il . . .].

---

[1]Sennacherib's almost lyrical account of the unsuccessful Assyrian siege of Jerusalem in 701 B.C.E. It may constitute a letter-prayer to Anshar (Ashur), the national deity of Assyria.

READING 1-23B[1]

To Nin-isina, beloved daughter of lofty An, mistress of Egalmah, speak!
To the chair-bearer of the Orient, the counselor of the netherworld,
The beloved (chief-)wife of the warrior Pabilsag, the senior daughter-in-law
    of Ki'ur,
The senior record-keeper of An and Enlil, proudest of goddesses,
Who perfects the attributes of Duranki in Nippur,
Who makes their exaltation appear in Egalmah, the house of her queenship,
Who has founded (in) Larak the Eniggar (as) a throne, the Esabad, the house of
    . . . , (as) their lofty dais,
Like the mother who bore me, who verily took me from the womb(?), have mercy
    man,
    Mother of the nation, merciful one, who loves prayer and supplication,
    My lady, say furthermore to her —
    (This is) what Sin-iddinam, the king of Larsa, says:

Since the day of my birth, after you spoke to Utu (and) he gave me the shepherdship
    over his nation,
I do not neglect my duties, I do not sleep sweetly, I seek life (or: I work all my life).
To the gods greatly in my worship
I perform prayers and sacrifices, I have withheld nothing from them.
Asalluhi the king of Babylon, son of Ilurugu (the divine Ordeal-river), persisting [in
    wrath?],
Their city against my city daily overruns the land,
Their king seeks out the king of Larsa as an evildoer.
    (Though) I, not being the shepherd over their nation, have not coveted(?) their
    sacrifices,
    A young man to me at night in the guise of a dream passed by me on his feet,
    He stood at my head, I myself saw this terrible glance,
    Carrying a river-oar(?), having cast a spell most evilly.

Since that day my manhood is not in order, his hand has seized me.
I cannot escape from my fears by myself, an evil sickness has seized me.
My sickness is an unlit darkness, not visible to man.
The physician cannot look upon it, cannot [soothe?] it with a bandage,
The exorcists cannot recite the spell(?), since suddenly(?) my sickness has no diag-
    nosis.
My sickness: its (healing) herb has not sprouted forth on plain (or) mountain, no one
    gets it for me.
Healing my sickness is with you (alone), let me declare your supremacy:
    "As my [mother] has abandoned me since my childhood
    I am one who has no [mother], no one recites my lament to you, you are my
    mother!
    Except [for you], I do not have another personal goddess, no one pleads for
    mercy to you on my behalf,
    No one seeks [for mercy?] from you for me, you are my personal goddess!"

---

[1]The letter-prayers of King Sin-iddinam of Larsa in Babylonia (ca. 1849–1843 B.C.E.)
were still being copied as models of their kind in seventh-century Assyria. One of them was
addressed by the ailing king to the healing goddess Nin-isina.

I am verily your constable (and) dog, I do not cease from being tied to you.
Damu, your beloved son: I am verily his private soldier (and) weapon holder,
May you plead for mercy for me before him!
My sickness has been changed into (worse) sickness, one does not know how to rec-
tify it.
At midday I am not given any sustenance, by night I cannot sleep.
My very own mother(?), holy Nin-isina, verily you are the merciful lady,
With my not sleeping, let me bring my wailing to you at night:

"Let me behold your favorable glance, give me sweet life!

As for me, like a bird fleeing from a falcon, I am seeking to save my life.

As for me, let me enter your lap in the face of Death (Fate), save me from (its)
hand.

I am a young man, I set up lamentation in the face of Death, my life ebbs away
from me."

Like a mother-cow, have mercy on me!
Like a [. . .], have mercy on me!
Like the mother who bore me, who verily took me from the womb(?), have mercy
on me!
(Like) the father who . . . , hear the . . . , the disobedient . . .

Damu, your beloved son, the great healer of Enlil,

He knows the plant of life, knows the water of life,

. . . , the god who cre[ated (?) me], who can [. . .] to you?

Asalluhi, son of Ilurugu, has verily spoken: "Let him live!"

READING 1-23C

In those days Hezekiah fell dangerously ill. The prophet Isaiah son of Amoz
came and said to him, "Thus said the LORD: Set your affairs in order, for you are
going to die; you will not get well." Thereupon Hezekiah turned his face to the wall
and prayed to the LORD. "Please, O LORD," he said, "remember how I have walked
before You sincerely and wholeheartedly, and have done what is pleasing to You."
And Hezekiah wept profusely.

Then the word of the LORD came to Isaiah: "Go and tell Hezekiah: Thus said
the LORD, the God of your father David: I have heard your prayer, I have seen your
tears. I hereby add fifteen years to your life. I will also rescue you and this city from
the hands of the king of Assyria. I will protect this city. And this is the sign for you
from the LORD that the LORD will do the thing which He has promised: I am going to
make the shadow on the steps, which has descended on the dial of Ahaz because of
the sun, recede ten steps." And the sun['s shadow] receded ten steps, the same steps
it had descended.

A poem[1] by Hezekiah king of Judah when he recovered from the illness he had
suffered:

I had thought:
I must depart in the middle of my days;
I have been consigned to the gates of Sheol
For the rest of my years.

---

[1]Other translations have: "a writing" or "a psalm." The later meaning of the Hebrew term
is "a letter."

I thought, I shall never see Yah,
Yah in the land of the living,
Or ever behold men again
Among those who inhabit the earth.
My dwelling is pulled up and removed from me
Like a tent of shepherds;
My life is rolled up like a web
And cut from the thrum.

Only from daybreak to nightfall
Was I kept whole,
Then it was as though a lion
Were breaking all my bones;
I cried out until morning.
(Only from daybreak to nightfall
Was I kept whole.)
I piped like a swift or a crane,
I moaned like a dove,
As my eyes, all worn, looked to heaven:
"My Lord, I am in straits;
Be my surety!"

What can I say? He promised me,
And He it is who has wrought it.
All my sleep had fled
Because of the bitterness of my soul.
My Lord, for all that and despite it
My life-breath is revived;
You have restored me to health and revived me.
Truly, it was for my own good
That I had such great bitterness:
You saved my life
From the pit of destruction,
For You have cast behind Your back
All my offenses.
For it is not Sheol that praises You,
Not [the Land of] Death that extols You;
Nor do they who descend into the Pit
Hope for Your grace.
The living, only the living
Can give thanks to You
As I do this day;
Fathers relate to children
Your acts of grace:
[It has pleased] the Lord to deliver us,
That is why we offer up music
All the days of our lives
At the House of the Lord."

[Isaiah 38:1–20]

TREATY-CURSES

God became Israel's sovereign overlord, and Deuteronomy the vassal-treaty that confirmed the relationship. Some of its provisions clearly paralleled the treaties between the Assyrian kings and their vassals. This is particularly true of the curses foreseen for violations of the treaty.

READING 1-24A

(If you sin against this treaty of Esarhaddon)[1]

(37) May Ashur, king of the gods, who determines the fates, decree for you an evil, unpropitious fate, and not grant you fatherhood, old age, . . . ripe old age.

(49) May Nergal, the warrior among the gods, extinguish your life with his merciless dagger, may he plant carnage and pestilence among you.

(63) May all the gods who are named in this treaty tablet reduce your soil in size to be as narrow as a brick, turn your soil into iron, so that no one may cut a furrow in it.

(64) Just as rain does not fall from a copper sky, so may there come neither rain nor dew upon your fields and meadows, but let it rain burning coals in your land instead of dew.

(48) May Ishtar, lady of battle, break your bow in a heavy battle, tie your arms, and have you crouch at the feet of your enemy.

(41) May Ninurta, leader of the gods, fell you with his fierce arrow, and fill the plain with your corpses, give your flesh to eagles and vultures to feed upon.

(39) May Sin, the luminary of heaven and earth, clothe you in leprosy and (thus) not permit you to enter the presence of god and king; roam the open country as a wild ass or gazelle!

(40) May Shamash, the light of heaven and earth, not give you a fair and equitable judgment, may he take away your eyesight; walk about in darkness!

(42) May Venus, the brightest among the stars, let your wives lie in the embrace of your enemy before your very eyes, may your sons not have authority over your house, may a foreign enemy divide your possessions.

READING 1-24B

But if you do not heed the word of the LORD your God to observe faithfully all His commandments and laws which I enjoin upon you this day, all these curses shall come upon you and take effect:

Cursed shall you be in the city and cursed shall you be in the country.

Cursed shall be your basket and your kneading bowl.

---

[1]In 672 B.C.E. King Esarhaddon (680–669 B.C.E.) forced his Iranian vassals to swear to support the accession of his sons in Assyria and Babylonia after his death, on pain of dreadful curses such as those enumerated above. They have been rearranged to correspond to the sequence of curses in Deuteronomy 28. Cf., for example, no. 37 with Deut. 28:20; no. 49 with 28:21; nos. 63–64 with 28:23–24; no. 48 with 28:25; no. 41 with 28:26; no. 39 with 28:27; no. 40 with 28:28–29; no. 42 with 28:30–34.

Cursed shall be the issue of your womb and the produce of your soil, the calving of your herd and the lambing of your flock.[1]

Cursed shall you be in your comings and cursed shall you be in your goings.

The LORD will let loose against you calamity, panic, and frustration in all the enterprises you undertake, so that you shall soon be utterly wiped out because of your evildoing in forsaking Me. The LORD will make pestilence cling to you, until He has put an end to you in the land which you are invading to occupy. The LORD will strike you with consumption, fever, and inflammation, with scorching heat and drought, with blight and mildew; they shall hound you until you perish. The skies above you shall be copper and the earth under you iron. The LORD will make the rain of your land dust, and sand shall drop on you from the sky, until you are wiped out.

The LORD will put you to rout before your enemies; you shall march out against them by a single road, but flee from them by many roads; and you shall become a horror to all the kingdoms of the earth. Your carcasses shall become food for all the birds of the sky and all the beasts of the earth, with none to frighten them off.

The LORD will strike you with the Egyptian inflammation, with hemorrhoids, boil-scars, and itch, from which you shall never recover.

The LORD will strike you with madness, blindness, and dismay. You shall grope at noon as a blind man gropes in the dark; you shall not prosper in your ventures, but shall be constantly abused and robbed, with none to give help.

If you pay the bride-price for a wife, another man shall enjoy her. If you build a house, you shall not live in it. If you plant a vineyard, you shall not harvest it. Your ox shall be slaughtered before your eyes, but you shall not eat of it; your ass shall be seized in front of you, and it shall not be returned to you; your flock shall be delivered to your enemies, with none to help you. Your sons and daughters shall be delivered to another people, while you look on; and your eyes shall strain for them constantly, but you shall be helpless. A people you do not know shall eat up the produce of your soil and all your gains; you shall be abused and downtrodden continually, until you are driven mad by what your eyes behold. The LORD will afflict you at the knees and thighs with a severe inflammation, from which you shall never recover—from the sole of your foot to the crown of your head.

[Deuteronomy 28:15–35]

THE SIEGE OF JERUSALEM (597 B.C.E.)

Two of Nebuchadnezzar's major campaigns were directed against Jerusalem. The first, in 597 B.C.E., was duly chronicled by the Babylonians in words supplementing the biblical account but similar to it.

READING 1-25A

In the seventh years of his reign, in the month of Kislev [December 598], the king of Akkad [Nebukadnezar] mobilized his army and marched against the Hittite

---

[1]Cf. Reading 1-11A note 1.

land [Syria-Palestine] and pitched his camp in front of the city of Judaea [Jerusalem], and in the month of Addar, on the second day of the month [March 16, 597 B.C.E.], he seized the city, he captured the king, he appointed a king of his own choosing in the midst [of Jerusalem], he accepted heavy tribute from it and brought it to Babylon.

READING 1-25B

Jehoiachin was eighteen years old when he became king, and he reigned three months in Jerusalem; his mother's name was Nehushta daughter of Elnathan of Jerusalem. He did what was displeasing to the Lord, just as his father had done. At that time, the troops of King Nebuchadnezzar of Babylon marched against Jerusalem, and the city came under siege. King Nebuchadnezzar of Babylon advanced against the city while his troops were besieging it. Thereupon King Jehoiachin of Judah, along with his mother, and his courtiers, commanders, and officers, surrendered to the king of Babylon. The king of Babylon took him captive in the eighth year of his reign. He carried off from Jerusalem all the treasures of the House of the Lord and the treasures of the royal palace; he stripped off all the golden decorations in the Temple of the Lord—which King Solomon of Israel had made—as the Lord had warned. He exiled all of Jerusalem: all the commanders and all the warriors—ten thousand exiles—as well as all the craftsmen and smiths; only the poorest people in the land were left. He deported Jehoiachin to Babylon; and the king's wives and officers and the notables of the land were brought as exiles from Jerusalem to Babylon. All the able men, to the number of seven thousand—all of them warriors, trained for battle—and a thousand craftsmen and smiths were brought to Babylon as exiles by the king of Babylon.

And the king of Babylon appointed Mattaniah, Jehoiachin's uncle, king in his place, changing his name to Zedekiah.

[II Kings 24:8–17]

2

The Power of the Word

William W. Hallo

After a period of exile in Babylonia, the Judaean leadership returned to Jerusalem to establish the Second Commonwealth. The Temple was rebuilt and the theocracy restored in place of the fallen monarchy. Prophecy, which had guided kings and people in the ways of God both before and during the exile, was gradually replaced by other forms of communication with the deity. Diaspora communities grew up in the lands of dispersion—Babylonia, Persia, Egypt, and others—and the conception of God changed to a universal power to be worshipped wherever the Jews settled, and ruling the affairs of all peoples. Israel was thus spiritually conditioned for the encounter with new cultures on its own soil and abroad.

Under the Persian (Achemenid) Empire, Judaea was a small and relatively insignificant subdivision of the great *satrapy* (province) called "Across the River" (i.e., west of the Euphrates). Contact was maintained with exiles in Egypt, notably at the colony of Elephantine on the upper Nile, and with those who had chosen to stay behind in the hospitable environment of Babylonia. The Book of Esther tells of the fate of the exiles at the Persian capital city of Shushan. In Judaea itself the Jews were permitted to reconstruct their religious life, subject only to their continued political loyalty to their Persian overlords.

When Alexander the Great toppled the Persian Empire (ca. 333 B.C.E.) and Greek rule replaced Persian rule throughout the Near East, the Jews welcomed the change. They continued as active partners in the economic life of the various successor states that divided Alexander's heritage among themselves. Judaea became a part, first of the Ptolemaic kingdom centered in Egypt, then of the Seleucid kingdom centered in Syria and Babylonia. But religious toleration gradually gave way to pressures—internal and external—to adopt the newer Hellenistic patterns of culture and belief. The Maccabean (Hasmonean) revolt restored not only traditional Jewish values but also political independence, yet as the Roman Empire expanded into the Near East that independence became ever more difficult to maintain. A number of client states arose, and the priestly leadership formed a party that generally favored accommodation to Roman rule. But other groupings competed for the loyalty of the people. Amid the increasing unrest, all of Jewish Palestine was gradually incorporated into the provincial system of the growing Roman Empire. A desperate attempt to throw off the Roman yoke ended in failure with the destruction of the Second Temple in 70 C.E.

The social and political unrest of the second temple period went hand in hand with religious diversity. Many "sects" and schools of thought arose, among them the Pharisees, the Sadducees, the Essenes, and the early Christians. Each of these groups advocated a different approach to the Bible, Jewish law, and theology.

The selections chosen for this period reflect the growing degree of direct contact between Israel and her neighbors.

TWO VIEWS OF THE EXILE

While the psalmist stressed the more melancholy aspect of exile, the prophet encouraged a realistic effort to make the best of the new situation.

READING 2-1A

> By the rivers of Babylon,
>   there we sat,
>   sat and wept,
>   as we thought of Zion.
> There on the poplars
>   we hung up our lyres,
>   for our captors asked us there for
>   songs,
>   our tormentors, for amusement,
>   "Sing us one of the songs of Zion."
> How can we sing a song of the LORD
>   on alien soil?
> If I forget you, O Jerusalem,
>   let my right hand wither;
>   let my tongue stick to my palate
>   if I cease to think of you,
>   if I do not keep Jerusalem in memory
>   even at my happiest hour.

[Psalm 137:1–6]

READING 2-1B

This is the text of the letter which the prophet Jeremiah sent from Jerusalem to the priests, the prophets, the rest of the elders of the exile community, and to all the people whom Nebuchadnezzar had exiled from Jerusalem to Babylon—after King Jeconiah, {i.e., Jehoiachin} the queen mother, the eunuchs, the officials of Judah and Jerusalem, and the craftsmen and smiths had left Jerusalem. [The letter was sent] through Elasah son of Shaphan and Gemariah son of Kilkiah, whom King

Zedekiah of Judah had dispatched to Babylon, to King Nebuchadnezzar of Babylon.

Thus said the LORD of Hosts, the God of Israel, to the whole community which I exiled from Jerusalem to Babylon: Build houses and live in them, plant gardens and eat their fruit. Take wives and beget sons and daughters; and take wives for your sons, and give you daughters to husbands, that they may bear sons and daughters. Multiply there, do not decrease. And seek the welfare of the city to which I have exiled you and pray to the LORD in its behalf; for in its prosperity you shall prosper.

For thus said the LORD of Hosts, the God of Israel: Let not the prophets and diviners in your midst deceive you, and pay no heed to the dreams they dream. For they prophesy to you in My name falsely; I did not send them—declares the LORD.

For thus said the LORD: When seventy years of Babylon are over, I will take note of you, and I will fulfill to you My promise of favor—to bring you back to this place. For I am mindful of the plans I have made concerning you—declares the LORD—plans for your welfare, not for disaster, to give you a hopeful future. When you call Me, and come and pray to Me, I will give heed to you. You will search for Me and you will find Me, if only you seek Me wholeheartedly. I will be at hand for you—declares the LORD—and I will restore your fortunes. And I will gather you from all the nations and from all the places to which I have banished you—declares the LORD—and I will bring you back to the place from which I have exiled you.

[Jeremiah 29:1–14]

JEHOIACHIN IN EXILE

Jehoiachin, the exiled king of Judah, was provisioned from the royal coffers. This is reported both in the Bible (II Kings 25:27–30; compare Jeremiah 52:34) and on fragmentary administrative documents found in Babylon in which the king's name is written Ia-'-kin, Ia-'-ú-kin, or Ia-ku-ú-ki-nu.

READING 2-2A

   . . . t[o?] *Ia-'-ú-kin*, king . . .
to the *qîpūtu*-house of . . .
   . . . for Shalamiamu, the . . .
   . . . for 126 men from Tyre . . .
   . . . for Zabiria, the Ly[dian] . . .

   10 (*sila*[1] of oil) to . . . [*Ia*]-'-*kin*, king of *Ia*[. . .]
   2½ *sila* (oil) to [. . . so]ns of the king of Judah
(*Ia-a-ḫu-du*)
    4 *sila* to 8 men from Judah (*[amel]Ia-a-ḫu-da-a-a*) . . .

---

[1]A *sila* is a measure of volume comparable to a quart.

1½ *sila* (oil) for 3 carpenters from Arvad, ½ *sila* each
11½ *sila* for 8 ditto from Byblos, 1 sila each . . .
3½ *sila* for 7 ditto, Greeks, ½ sila each
½ *sila* to *Nabû-êṭir* the carpenter
10 (*sila*) to *Ia-ku-ú-ki-nu*, the son of the king of *Ia-ku-du* (i.e. Judah)
2½ *sila* for the 5 sons of the king of Judah (*Ia-ku-du*)
through Qana'a [. . .]

READING 2-2B

In the thirty-seventh year of the exile of King Jehoiachin of Judah, on the twenty-seventh day of the twelfth month, King Evil-merodach of Babylon, in the year he became king, took note of King Jehoiachin of Judah and released him from prison. He spoke kindly to him, and gave him a throne above those of other kings who were with him in Babylon. His prison garments were removed, and [Jehoiachin] received regular rations by his favor for the rest of his life. A regular allotment of food was given him at the instance of the king—an allotment for each day—all the days of his life.

[II Kings 25:27–30]

THE CHALDEAN DYNASTY

The Chaldeans constituted the "tenth" and last independent dynasty of Babylon (625–558 B.C.E.). Called "Kasdim" in the Bible, their name became synonymous with Arameans on the one hand and astrologers on the other.

The end of the Chaldean empire was hastened by its last king, Nabonidus, whose strange policies were remembered in the Book of Daniel (though there attributed to Nebuchadnezzar), and in the Aramaic prayer of Nabonidus found in the library of Qumran (Reading 2-3B). The policies were equally puzzling to and unpopular among his Babylonian contemporaries, as seen in the "Verse Account" of Nabonidus, an Akkadian text of the early Persian period (Reading 2-3A).

READING 2-3A

[As to Nabonidus] (his) protective deity became hostile to him,
[And he, the former favorite of the g]ods (is now) seized by misfortunes;
[. . . against the will of the g]ods he performed an unholy action,
[. . .] he thought out something worthless: . . .

After he had obtained what he desired, a work of utter deceit,
Had built (this) abomination, a work of unholiness
  —when the third year was about to begin—
He entrusted the "Camp" to his oldest (son), the firstborn,
The troops everywhere in the country he ordered under his (command).

He let (everything) go, entrusted the kingship to him
And, himself, he started out for a long journey,
The (military) forces of Akkad marching with him;
He turned towards Tema (deep) in the west.

He started out the expedition on a path (leading) to a distant (region). When he
  arrived there,
He killed in battle the prince of Tema,
Slaughtered the flocks of those who dwell in the city (as well as) in the countryside,
And he, himself, took his residence in [Te]ma, the forces of Akkad [were also sta-
  tioned] there.

READING 2-3B

The words of the prayer which Nabonidus king of Ass[yria and Baby]lonia, the
[great] king, prayed [when he was afflicted] with a severe inflammation at the command of the [high]est God in [the city of] Teima. ["With a severe inflammation] I
was afflicted for seven years, and I was dist[ant from my throne. But when I had
confessed my transgression] and my sin, he forgave it. A diviner, being a Judaean of
[the exiles in Babylon] interpreted and wrote: (it means one is) to ascribe glory and
gran[deur of majesty] to the name of the [highest] God and [thus he wrote: When]
you were afflicted with a severe inflammation . . . in Teima at the command of the
highest God for seven years, you [prayed to] the gods of silver and gold, [bronze and
iron], wood, stone, clay, because [you believed] that they were gods. . . .

READING 2-3C

All this befell King Nebuchadnezzar.[1] Twelve months later, as he was walking
on the roof of the royal palace at Babylon, the king exclaimed, "There is great Babylon, which I have built by my vast power to be a royal residence for the glory of my
majesty!" The words were still on the king's lips, when a voice fell from heaven, "It
has been decreed for you, O King Nebuchadnezzar: The kingdom has passed out of
your hands. You are being driven away from men, and your habitation is to be with
the beasts of the field. You are to be fed grass like cattle, and seven seasons will pass
over you until you come to know that the Most High is sovereign over the realm of
man and He gives it to whom He wishes." There and then the sentence was carried
out upon Nebuchadnezzar. He was driven away from men, he ate grass like cattle,
and his body was drenched with the dew of heaven until his hair grew like eagle's
[feathers] and his nails like [the talons of] birds.

"When the time had passed, I, Nebuchadnezzar, lifted my eyes to heaven, and
my reason was restored to me. I blessed the Most High, and praised and glorified the
Ever-Living One,

Whose dominion is an everlasting dominion
And whose kingdom endures throughout the generations.

---

[1]Although these events are associated here with Nebuchadnezzar, they clearly befell Nabonidus. The removal of the Chaldean court from Babylon to the oasis city of Teima, deep in
the Arabian Desert, is here linked to the greatest member of the dynasty instead of its last king.

All the inhabitants of the earth are of no account.
He does as He wishes with the host of heaven,
And with the inhabitants of the earth.
There is none to stay His hand
Or say to Him, 'What have You done?'

There and then my reason was restored to me, and my majesty and splendor were restored to me for the glory of my kingdom. My companions and nobles sought me out, and I was reestablished over my kingdom, and added greatness was given me.

[Daniel 4:25–33]
[English Bible: 4:28–36]

THE CALL OF CYRUS

The Medes and Persians had united under a powerful new leader, Cyrus, the descendant of Achemenes, and were forging a new Persian (or Achemenid) empire under his auspices. Jews and Babylonians alike welcomed him as a relief from the apparent madness of Nabonidus and even employed curiously similar language to express themselves.

READING 2-4

Cyrus' Proclamation

Daily (Nabonidus) used to do evil against (Marduk's) city. He (tormented) its (inhabitants) with a yoke without relief, he ruined them all. Upon their complaints the lord of the gods became terribly angry and (he departed from) their region,

(also) the (other) gods living among them left their mansions, wroth that he had brought (them) into Babylon.[2]

(But) Marduk . . . on account of (the fact that) the sanctuaries of all their settlements were in ruins and the inhabitants of Sumer and Akkad had become like (living) dead, turned back (his countenance, his anger abated) and he had mercy (upon them).

He scanned and looked (through) all the countries, searching for a righ-

Isaiah[1]

47.5f. O daughter of the Chaldeans, you showed them (the Judeans) no mercy; on the aged you made your yoke exceeding heavy. 47.6 I (Yahweh) was angry with my people, I profaned my heritage, I gave them into your (the Babylonians') hand.

40.1f. Comfort, comfort my people, says your God. Speak tenderly to Jerusalem and cry to her that her warfare is ended, that her iniquity is pardoned, that she has received from Yahweh's hand double for all her sins.

42.6 I am Yahweh, I have called you (Cyrus) in righteousness, I have taken you by the hand and kept you.

---

[1]The translation of the biblical text is taken from Morton Smith, "II Isaiah and the Persians," *Journal of the American Oriental Society,* 83 (1963), p. 416.

[2]Not paralleled in Isaiah. Compare Ezekiel 8–11.

teous ruler willing to lead him (Marduk) (in the annual procession).

(Then) he pronounced the name of Cyrus, King of Anshan, pronounced (his) name to (become) the ruler of the world.

He made the Guti country and all the Manda hordes bow in submission to his (Cyrus) feet.

And he (Cyrus) did always endeavour to treat according to justice the black-headed (people) whom he (Marduk) had made him conquer.

Marduk, the great lord, a protector of his people, beheld with pleasure his (Cyrus') good deeds and his upright mind (and therefore) ordered him to march against his city Babylon. He made him set out on the road to Babylon, going at his side like a real friend.

His widespread troops—their number, like that of the water of a river, could not be established—strolled along, their weapons packed away. Without any battle he made him enter his town Babylon, sparing Babylon any calamity. He delivered into his hands Nabonidus, the king who did not worship him (Marduk). All the inhabitants of Babylon as well as of the entire country of Sumer and Akkad, princes and governors (included), bowed to him (Cyrus) and kissed his feet, jubilant that he (had received) the kingship and with shining faces.[3]

Happily they greeted him as a master through whose help they had come (again) to life from death (and) had all been spared damage and disaster, and they worshiped his name.

45.1ff. Thus saith Yahweh to his anointed, to Cyrus, whose right hand I have grasped to subdue nations before him . . . I call you by your name.

45.14 The wealth of Egypt and the merchandise of Ethiopia and the Sabaeans . . . shall come over to you . . . and bow down to you.

42.1 (Cyrus) will bring forth justice to the nations . . . He will not fail . . . till he has established justice in the earth.

42.1 Behold my servant whom I upheld, my chosen, in whom my soul delights; . . . he will bring forth justice.

48.14 Yahweh loves him; he shall perform Yahweh's purpose on Babylon.

43.14 I (Yahweh) will send (Cyrus) to Babylon.

45.1f. Thus saith Yahweh to Cyrus, whose right hand I have grasped, . . . I will go before you.

44.28a. (Yahweh) says of Cyrus, My friend.

41.2 (Yahweh) will make his swordsmen (numerous) as the dust, (the arrows of) his bowman like driven stubble; he will pursue and pass by in peace.

45.2 I will break in pieces the doors of brass and cut asunder the bars of iron.

47.3–10 I will take vengeance (because) . . . you (Babylon) said in your heart, I am, and there is none besides me.

42.6 I (Yahweh) have given you (Cyrus) as a covenant to the people, a light to the nations, to open the eyes that are blind, to bring out the prisoners from the dungeon, from prison those who sit in darkness.

---

[3]Compare Isaiah 45:14 above.

THE EDICT OF CYRUS

Cyrus secured the loyalty of his innumerable subject-peoples, not by terror and deportation like his predecessors, but by returning them to their ancestral lands, allowing them to restore their native cults, and extending a measure of autonomy to them. These enlightened policies, proclaimed in a lengthy inscription, applied to numerous exiled populations and the cult statues of their deities. The great "Cyrus Cylinder" from which this passage is taken became the centerpiece of the celebrations that marked the 2500th year of the Persian Empire in 1971 C.E.

READING 2-5

I am Cyrus, king of the world, great king, legitimate king, king of Babylon, king of Sumer and Akkad, king of the four rims (of the earth), son of Cambyses, great king, king of Anshan, grandson of Cyrus, great king, king of Anshan, descendant of Teispes, great king, king of Anshan, of a family (which) always (exercised) kingship; whose rule Bel and Nebo love, whom they want as king to please their hearts.

When I entered Babylon as a friend and (when) I established the seat of the government in the palace of the ruler under jubilation and rejoicing, Marduk, the great lord, [induced] the magnanimous inhabitants of Babylon [to love me], and I was daily endeavouring to worship him. My numerous troops walked around in Babylon in peace, I did not allow anybody to terrorize (any place) of the [country of Sumer] and Akkad. I strove for peace in Babylon and in all his (other) sacred cities. As to the inhabitants of Babylon, [who] against the will of the gods [had/were . . . , I abolished] the corvée (lit.: yoke) which was against their (social) standing. I brought relief to their dilapidated housing, putting (thus) an end to their (main) complaints. Marduk, the great lord, was well pleased with my deeds and sent friendly blessings to myself, Cyrus, the king who worships him, to Cambyses, my son, the offspring of [my] loins, as well as to all my troops, and we all [praised] his great [godhead] joyously, standing before him in peace.

All the kings of the entire world from the Upper to the Lower Sea, those who are seated in throne rooms, (those who) lie in other [types of buildings as well as] all the kings of the West land living in tents, brought their heavy tributes and kissed my feet in Babylon. (As to the region) from . . . as far as Ashur and Susa, Agade, Eshnunna, the towns Zamban, Me-Turnu, Der as well as the region of the Gutians, I returned to (these) sacred cities on the other side of the Tigris, the sanctuaries of which have been ruins for a long time, the images which (used) to live therein and established for them permanent sanctuaries. I (also) gathered all their (former) inhabitants and returned (to them) their habitations. Furthermore, I resettled upon the command of Marduk, the great lord, all the gods of Sumer and Akkad whom Nabonidus has brought into Babylon to the anger of the lord of the gods, unharmed, in their (former) chapels, the places which make them happy.

May all the gods whom I have resettled in their sacred cities ask daily Bel and Nebo for a long life for me and may they recommend me (to him); to Marduk, my lord, they may say this: "Cyrus, the king who worships you, and Cambyses, his son, . . ." . . . all of them I settled in a peaceful place . . . ducks and doves, . . . I endeavoured to fortify/repair their dwelling places. . . .

THE EGYPTIAN DIASPORA:
THE LETTER TO BAGOAS

When the Persians conquered Egypt, they engaged Jews as mercenary soldiers, first to guard the frontier between Egypt and Nubia, and
soon enough, no doubt, to help control the local population as well. The
natives responded by pillaging the temple, and the Jews appealed to their
brethren in Judaea and Samaria for help. The appeal is preserved in a
letter found on the island of Elephantine, located in the Nile just below the
present Aswan Dam. At the time it was the site of the Jewish mercenary
colony.

READING 2-6

To our lord Bagoas, governor of Judah, your servants Yedoniah and his colleagues, the priests who are in the fortress of Elephantine. May the God of Heaven
seek after the welfare of our lord exceedingly at all times and give you favor before
King Darius {Darius (II), Persian emperor (423–405 B.C.E.)} and the nobles a
thousand times more than now. May you be happy and healthy at all times. Now,
your servant Yedoniah and his colleagues depose as follows: In the month of Tammuz in the 14th year of King Darius, when Arsames departed and went to the king,
the priests of the god Khnub, who is in the fortress of Elephantine, conspired with
Vidaranag, who was commander-in-chief here, to wipe out the temple of the god
Yaho {an Aramaic form of the Hebrew name of God} from the fortress of Elephantine. So that wretch Vidaranag sent to his son Nefayan, who was in command of the
garrison of the fortress of Syene, this order, "The temple of the god Yaho in the
fortress of Yeb is to be destroyed." Nefayan thereupon led the Egyptians with the
other troops. Coming with their weapons to the fortress of Elephantine, they entered that temple and razed it to the ground. The stone pillars that were there they
smashed. Five "great" gateways built with hewn blocks of stone which were in that
temple they demolished, but their doors *are standing*, and the hinges of those doors
are of bronze; and *their* roof of cedarwood, all of it, with the . . . and whatever else
was there, everything they burnt with fire. As for the basins of gold and silver and
other articles that were in that temple, they carried all of them off and made them
their own.—Now, our forefathers built this temple in the fortress of Elephantine
back in the days of the kingdom of Egypt, and when Cambyses {Persian emperor
(529–522 B.C.E.)} came to Egypt he found it built. They knocked down all the
temples of the gods of Egypt, but no one did any damage to this temple. But when
this happened, we and our wives and our children wore sackcloth, and fasted, and
prayed to Yaho the Lord of Heaven, who has let us see our desire upon that Vidaranag. The dogs took the fetter out of his feet, and any property he had gained
was lost; and any men who have sought to do evil to this temple have all been killed
and we have seen our desire upon them.—We have also sent a letter before now,
when this evil was done to us, [to] our lord and to the high priest Johanan and his
colleagues the priests in Jerusalem and to Ostanes the brother of Anani and the nobles of the Jews. Never a letter have they sent to us. Also, from the month of Tammuz, year 14 of King Darius, to this day, we have been wearing sackcloth and fasting, making our wives as widows, not anointing ourselves with oil or drinking wine.
Also, from then to now, in the year 17 of King Darius, no meal-offering, in[cen]se,

nor burnt offering have been offered in this temple. Now your servants Yedoniah, and his colleagues, and the Jews, the citizens of Elephantine, all say thus: If it please our lord, take thought of this temple to rebuild it, since they do not let us rebuild it. Look to your well-wishers and friends here in Egypt. Let a letter be sent from you to them concerning the temple of the god Yaho to build it in the fortress of Elephantine as it was built before; and the meal-offering, incense, and burnt offering will be offered in your name, and we shall pray for you at all times, we, and our wives, and our children, and the Jews who are here, all of them, if you do thus, so that that temple is rebuilt. And you shall have a merit before Yaho the God of Heaven more than a man who offers to him burnt offering and sacrifices worth a thousand talents of silver and (because of) gold. Because of this we have written to inform you. We have also set the whole matter forth in a letter in our name to Delaiah and Shelemiah, the sons of Sanballat the governor of Samaria. Also, Arsames knew nothing of all that was done to us. On the 20th of Marheshwan, year 17 of King Darius.

THE BABYLONIAN DIASPORA: THE HOUSE OF MURASHU

The exiles who chose to remain in Babylonia were quickly and fully integrated into the thriving commercial life of the country. A great banking house like that of "Murashu & Sons" at Nippur, though not itself Jewish, dealt on many occasions with persons with distinctly Jewish names. The transactions are recorded in numerous documents of the fifth century B.C.E.

READING 2-7

Contents: Agreement to abandon legal proceedings. An inhabitant of Nippur complains to *Bêl-nâdin-shumu*, that the latter's servants, in collusion with his own brother and nephew, have robbed his house. On the property being restored, he agrees for himself and his children to take no legal proceedings against the servants or their master.

Udarna'[1] (= *Hydarnes*), son of *Raḥîm-ili*, of Nippur, spoke to *Bêl-nâdin-shumu*, son of *Murashû*, thus: Thy bondslaves, thy messenger and thy servants, in collusion with *Zabdiia*, my brother, and *Bêl-ittannu*, his son, have entered my house and carried off my property and my household goods. Whereupon *Bêl-nâdin-shumu* examined his bondslaves, his messenger, his servants, *Zabdiia* and *Bêl-ittannu*, took that property away from them and returned it to *Udarna'*. That property *Udarna'* has received from *Bêl-nâdin-shumu*, his bondslaves and his messenger and his servants. There shall be no legal proceedings of *Udarna'* and his children on account of that property against *Bêl-nâdin-shumu*, his bondslaves, his messenger and his servants *in perpetuo*; *Udarna'* and his children shall not bring suit again on account of that property against *Bêl-nâdin-shumu*, his bondslaves and his messenger and his servants *in perpetuo*.

---

[1]Udarna', his father Raḥîm-ili, his brother Zabdiia, his nephew(?) Bel-îttannu, and his son Ḥananiiâma were all members of a Jewish family. The other names in this text belong to native Babylonians.

Names of twenty-two witnesses and the scribe—Seals of *Udarna'* and his son, Ḥananiiâma, who acts as a witness, and of five other witnesses.

THE PERSIAN DIASPORA: THE *PURU* OF JAHALI

In the absence of significant contemporary documentation from Susa, the biblical Book of Esther must serve as the principal source for life in the Iranian Diaspora. And in fact it preserves authentic touches as in the use of lots or dice, *purim*, to determine high affairs of state.

One such lot, a *puru*, has survived from antiquity. It was inscribed with a prayer by Jahali (Iahali), a high Assyrian official, and was used to determine the year that was to be known by his name.

READING 2-8

Oh Assur the great lord, oh Adad the great lord, the lot of Iahali the grand vizier of Salmaneser king of Assyria, governor-of-the-land (for) the city of Kibshuni (in) the land of Qumeni, the land of Mehrani, Uqu and the Cedar Mountain, and minister of trade—in his year assigned to him by lot may the harvest of the land of Assyria prosper and thrive; in front of the gods Assur and Adad may his lot fall.

POSTEXILIC PROPHECY: HAGGAI

Imperial permission and even financial support were secured to rebuild the temple on its ancient sacred site. The Jewish governor of Judaea, the high priest, and prophets like Haggai and Zechariah all encouraged the work.

READING 2-9

In the second year of King Darius, on the first day of the sixth month, this word of the LORD came through the prophet Haggai to Zerubbabel son of Shealtiel, the governor of Judah, and to Joshua son of Jehozadak, the high priest:

Thus said the LORD of Hosts: These people say, "The time has not yet come, for rebuilding the House of the LORD."

And the word of the LORD through the prophet Haggai continued:

It is a time for you to dwell in your paneled houses, while this House is lying in ruins? Now thus said the LORD of Hosts: Consider how you have been faring! You have sowed much and brought in little; you eat without being satisfied; you drink without getting your fill; you clothe yourselves, but no one gets warm; and he who earns anything earns it for a leaky purse. . . .

Thus said the LORD of Hosts: Consider how you have fared: Go up to the hills and get timber, and rebuild the House; then I will look on it with favor and I will be glorified—said the LORD.

[Haggai 1:1–8]

THE PROBLEM OF INTERMARRIAGE

Under the leadership of Nehemiah and Ezra in the fifth century, special precautions were taken in Jerusalem to prevent (and even to undo) intermarriages between Jews and Samaritans. Nehemiah also opposed intermarriage between Jews and other neighboring peoples including the Moabites (Reading 2-10A). But his sentiments were not universally shared. The Book of Ruth derives no less a hero than King David himself from the marriage between Boaz of Judah and Ruth the Moabitess (2-10B). It may have been written at this time to counter Nehemiah's exclusivism.

READING 2-10A

Also at that time, I saw that Jews had married Ashdodite, Ammonite, and Moabite women; a good number of their children spoke the language of Ashdod and the language of those various peoples, and did not know how to speak Judean. I censured them, cursed them, flogged them, tore out their hair, and adjured them by God, saying, "You shall not give your daughters in marriage to their sons, or take any of their daughters for your sons or yourselves. It was just in such things that King Solomon of Israel sinned! Among the many nations there was not a king like him, and so well loved was he by his God that God made him king of Israel, yet foreign wives caused even him to sin. How, then, can we acquiesce in your doing this great wrong, breaking faith with our God by marrying foreign women?" One of the sons of Joiada son of the high priest Eliashib was a son-in-law of Sanballat the Horonite; I drove him away from me.

Remember to their discredit, O my God, how they polluted the priesthood, the covenant of the priests and Levites. I purged them of every foreign element, and arranged for the priests and the Levites to work each at his task by shifts, and for the wood offering [to be brought] at fixed times and for the firstfruits.

O my God, remember it to my credit!

[Nehemiah 13:23–31]

READING 2-10B

In the days when the chieftains {literally, "judges"} ruled, there was a famine in the land; and a man of Bethlehem in Judah, with his wife and two sons, went to reside in the country of Moab. The man's name was Elimelech, his wife's name was Naomi, and his two sons were named Mahlon and Chilion—Ephrathites of Bethlehem in Judah. They came to the country of Moab and remained there.

Elimelech, Naomi's husband, died; and she was left with her two sons. They married Moabite women, one named Orpah and the other Ruth, and they lived there about ten years. Then those two—Mahlon and Chilion—also died; so the woman was left without her two sons and without her husband.

She started out with her daughters-in-law to return from the country of Moab; for in the country of Moab she had heard that the LORD had taken note of His people and given them food. Accompanied by her two daughters-in-law, she left the place where she had been living; and they set out on the road back to the land of Judah.

But Naomi said to her two daughters-in-law, "Turn back, each of you to her mother's house. May the LORD deal kindly with you, as you have dealt with the dead and with me! May the Lord grant that each of you find security in the house of a husband!" And she kissed them farewell. They broke into weeping and said to her, "No, we will return with you to your people."

But Naomi replied, "Turn back, my daughters! Why should you go with me? Have I any more sons in my body who might be husbands for you? Turn back, my daughters, for I am too old to be married. Even if I thought there was hope for me, even if I were married tonight and I also bore sons, should you wait for them to grow up? Should you on their account debar yourselves from marriage? Oh no, my daughters! My lot is far more bitter than yours, for the hand of the Lord has struck out against me."

They broke into weeping again, and Orpah kissed her mother-in-law farewell. But Ruth clung to her. So she said, "See, your sister-in-law has returned to her people and her gods. Go follow your sister-in-law." But Ruth replied, "Do not urge me to leave you, to turn back and not follow you. For wherever you go, I will go; wherever you lodge, I will lodge; your people shall be my people, and your God my God. Where you die, I will die, and there I will be buried. Thus and more may the Lord do to me if anything but death parts me from you." When [Naomi] saw how determined she was to go with her, she ceased to argue with her; and the two went on until they reached Bethlehem.

When they arrived in Bethlehem, the whole city buzzed with excitement over them. The women said, "Can this be Naomi?" "Do not call me Naomi," she replied. "Call me Mara, for Shaddai has made my lot very bitter. I went away full, and the Lord has brought me back empty. How can you call me Naomi, when the Lord has dealt harshly with me, when Shaddai has brought misfortune upon me!"

Thus Naomi returned from the country of Moab; she returned with her daughter-in-law Ruth the Moabite. They arrived in Bethlehem at the beginning of the barley harvest. . . .

Now Naomi had a kinsman on her husband's side, a man of substance, of the family of Elimelech, whose name was Boaz. . . .

So Boaz married Ruth; she became his wife, and he cohabited with her. The Lord let her conceive, and she bore a son. And the women said to Naomi, "Blessed be the Lord, who has not withheld a redeemer from you today! May his name be perpetuated in Israel! He will renew your life and sustain your old age; for he is born of your daughter-in-law, who loves you and is better to you than seven sons."

Naomi took the child and held it to her bosom. She became its foster mother, and the women neighbors gave him a name, saying, "A son is born to Naomi!" They named him Obed; he was the father of Jesse, father of David.

This is the line of Perez: Perez begot Hezron, Hezron begot Ram, Ram begot Amminadab, Amminadab begot Nahshon, Nahshon begot Salmon, Salmon begot Boaz, Boaz begot Obed, Obed begot Jesse, and Jesse begot David.

[Ruth 1; 2:1; 4:13–22]

THE SAMARITAN SCHISM: THE DALIYEH PAPYRI

The Samaritans opposed Alexander, and many of them perished for their pains in the caves around Samaria where they had fled for safety. The papyrus documents that they took with them for safekeeping provide a precious glimpse into their last years. The first fragment is from a sealing affixed to the remnants of a papyrus. The other fragments are preserved on another papyrus.

READING 2-11

. . . yahū, son of [San]ballat, governor of Samaria.

[Before Yeš]ūaʻ son of Sanballaṭ (and) Ḥanan the prefect.
This document was written in Samaria.

JUDAEA UNDER THE PTOLEMIES: THE ZENON PAPYRI

Ptolemaic rule in Judaea lasted until 200 B.C.E., illuminated in part by records of Zenon, an Egyptian official. Among the papyri of Zenon was found a letter from the Jew Tobias (Toubias) to Apollonios, Zenon's master in Egypt, with a copy of Tobias's letter to King Ptolemy II himself.

READING 2-12

Toubias to Apollonios, greeting. Just as you wrote me to send presents for the king in the month of Xandikos, I sent on the tenth of Xandikos my man Aineas with two horses, six dogs, one wild mule (born) out of a donkey, two white Arabian donkeys, two foals (born) out of wild mules and one foal (born) out of a wild ass, but they are tame. I have sent to you also the letter written by me about the presents to the king, and likewise also a copy of it (for you) so that you may be informed.
      Goodbye.

Year 29, Xandikos 10
[12 May, 257 B.C.E.]

(The copy)
      To King Ptolemy greeting from Toubias. I have sent you two horses, six dogs, one wild mule out of a donkey, two white Arabian donkeys, two foals out of wild mules, one foal out of a wild ass.
      Farewell.

(On the back of the papyrus)
(The address) To Apollonios
(A docket, or memo) Toubias (re) the things sent the king, and the copy of his letter to the king. Year 29, Artemision 16 [17 June, 257 B.C.E.], in Alexandria.

JUDAEA UNDER THE SELEUCIDS: APOCALYPTIC

The Seleucid rulers were determined to impose Greek patterns of culture and conduct. But only the "Hellenizers" among the Jews were prepared to abandon their own traditions. In terms not unlike their Babylonian contemporaries, they depicted the Seleucids as merely the latest in a succession of rulers who, too, were bound to pass from the scene.

The Book of Daniel typifies the replacement of prophecy by apocalypse, in which past history is presented as prediction of the future and veiled allusions replace explicit identifications. Thus, four kingdoms here are probably meant to stand for the Babylonians, Medes, Persians, and Macedonian Greeks.

A late cuneiform text of a prophetic or apocalyptic character, the Akkadian "Dynastic Prophecy" describes the history of successive dynasties ruling Mesopotamia in the guise of a forecast of events made long before the events occurred. The dynasties are identified by thinly veiled allusions: the "dynasty of Harran" refers to the Chaldeans, "Elam" to Persia, and the "Hanaeans" to the Greeks.

READING 2-13A

Iacuna

. . . [. . . . . .]
. . . [. . . . . .]
. . . [. . . . . .]
will go up from [. . . . . .]
will overthrow[. . . . . .]
For three years [he will exercise sovereignty].
Borders and . . . [. . . . . .]
For his people he will [. . . . . .]
After his (death) his son will [ascend] the throne ([. . .])
(But) he will not [*be master of the land*].

A re[bel] prince will arise ([. . .])
The dynasty of Harran [*he will establish*].
For seventeen years [he will exercise sovereignty].
He will oppress (lit. 'be stronger than') the land and the *festival* of Esa[*gil* he will *cancel*].
A fortress in Babylon [he will build].
He will plot evil against Akkad.

A king of Elam will arise, the sceptre . . . [. . .]
He will remove him from his throne and ([. . .])
He will take the throne and the king who arose [from] the throne ([. . .])
The king of Elam will change his place ([. . .])
He will settle him in another land ([. . .])
That king will oppress (lit. 'be stronger than') the land an[d (. . .)]
All the lands [*will bring to him*] tribute.
During his reign Akkad [will not enjoy] a peaceful abode.

[. . .] . . . [. . . . . .]
. . . kings . . . [. . . . . .]
Which/of his father . . . [. . . . . .]
For two years [he will exercise sovereignty].
a eunuch [*will murder*] that king.

Any prince [*will arise*],
will attack and [seize] the thr[one].
For five years [he will exercise] sovereignty.
The army of the Hanaeans [. . .]
will attack . . . . . . [. . .]
[*The Hanaeans will bring about the defeat of*] his army.
They will plunder and rob him. Afterwards he (the king) will
refit [his] army and ra[ise] his weapons.

Enhi, Shamash, and [*Marduk*]
will go at the side of his army [and]
the overthrow of the army of the Hanaean he will [bring about].
He will carry off his extensive booty and
[*bring (it)*] into his palace.
The people who *had* [*experienced*] misfortune
[*will enjoy*] well-being.
The mood of the land [will be a happy one].
Tax exemption [. . . . . .]

READING 2-13B

As for me, Daniel, my spirit was disturbed within me and the vision of my mind alarmed me. I approached one of the attendants and asked him the true meaning of all this. He gave me this interpretation of the matter: 'These great beasts, four in number [mean] four kingdoms will arise out of the earth; then holy ones of the Most High will receive the kingdom, and will possess the kingdom forever—forever and ever.' Then I wanted to ascertain the true meaning of the fourth beast, which was different from them all, very fearsome, with teeth of iron, claws of bronze, that devoured and crushed, and stamped the remains; and of the ten horns on its head; and of the new one that sprouted, to make room for which three fell—the horn that had eyes, and a mouth that spoke arrogantly, and which was more conspicuous than its fellows. (I looked on as that horn made war with the holy ones and overcame them, until the Ancient of Days came and judgment was rendered in favor of the holy ones of the Most High, for the time had come, and the holy ones took possession of the kingdom.) This is what he said: 'The fourth beast [means]—there will be a fourth kingdom upon the earth which will be different from all the kingdoms; it will devour the whole earth, tread it down, and crush it. And the ten horns [mean]—from that kingdom, ten kings will arise, and after them another will arise. He will be different from the former ones, and will bring low three kings. He will speak words against the Most High, and will harass the holy ones of the Most High. He will think of changing times and laws, and they will be delivered into his power for a time, times, and half a time. Then the court will sit and his dominion will be taken away, to be destroyed and abolished for all time. The kingship and dominion and grandeur belonging to all the kingdoms under heaven will be given to the people of the holy ones of the Most High. Their kingdom shall be an everlasting kingdom, and all dominions shall serve and obey them.' "
Here the account ends.

[Daniel 7:15–28]

THE FESTIVAL OF HANUKKAH[1]
by Shaye J. D. Cohen

The festival of Hanukkah (literally, dedication) was instituted by the Maccabees to commemorate their victory over the Seleucids, the Macedonian kings of Syria and Asia, and their purification of the temple in 164 B.C.E. The first reading is from the First Book of Maccabees, which was written in Hebrew in the latter part of the second century B.C.E. It is a court history and reflects the views of the Maccabees, the Jewish leaders of the revolt. In it the Maccabees purify the temple precincts, make new utensils, reinstitute the sacrificial cult, and establish the new holiday.

The second reading is from the Babylonian *Talmud* and gives the rabbinic view of the origins of Hanukkah. Instead of emphasizing the Maccabean victory and purification of the temple, the rabbis ascribe the origins of Hanukkah to a miraculous event: a cruse of oil that should have been exhausted after only one day provided oil for eight days until a new supply could be readied. This story is not mentioned in the First Book of Maccabees, which states simply that the Jews "lit the lamps," and gives no reason for the eight-day duration of the festival. This rabbinic story thus "demilitarizes" Hanukkah, commemorating a deed of God, not a deed of man. The rabbis followed a quietistic political policy and did not admire revolutionaries who fought against the state (see Reading 2-16).

Both First Maccabees and the rabbinic account agree that the festival was instituted by the Maccabees themselves. This is important, because the Bible nowhere allows the Jews to institute a new festival through a vote or an acclamation by the people. The institution of an annual festival to commemorate a victory was a Greek custom that was imported into Judaism by Judah and his followers. Judah was prepared to follow the ways of the Greeks as long as they did not conflict with the ways of Judaism.

READING 2-14A

Then said Judas and his brothers, "Behold, our enemies are crushed; let us go up to cleanse the sanctuary and dedicate it." So all the army assembled and they went up to Mount Zion. And they saw the sanctuary desolate, the altar profaned, and the gates burned. In the courts they saw bushes sprung up as in a thicket, or as on one of the mountains. They saw also the chambers of the priests in ruins. Then they rent their clothes, and mourned with great lamentation, and sprinkled themselves with ashes. They fell face down on the ground, and sounded the signal on the trumpets, and cried out to Heaven. Then Judas detailed men to fight against those in the citadel until he had cleansed the sanctuary.

He chose blameless priests devoted to the law, and they cleansed the sanctuary and removed the defiled stones to an unclean place. They deliberated what to do about the altar of burnt offering, which had been profaned. And they thought it

---

[1]Selections 2-14 to 2-19 edited by Shaye J. D. Cohen.

best to tear it down, lest it bring reproach upon them, for the Gentiles had defiled it. So they tore down the altar, and stored the stones in a convenient place on the temple hill until there should come a prophet to tell what to do with them. Then they took unhewn stones, as the law directs, and built a new altar like the former one. They also rebuilt the sanctuary and the interior of the temple, and consecrated the courts. They made new holy vessels, and brought the lampstand, the altar of incense, and the table into the temple. Then they burned incense on the altar and lighted the lamps on the lampstand, and these gave light in the temple. They placed the bread on the table and hung up the curtains. Thus they finished all the work they had undertaken.

Early in the morning on the twenty-fifth day of the ninth month, which is the month of Chislev {also "Kislew"}, in the one hundred and forty-eighth year {164 B.C.E.}, they rose and offered sacrifice, as the law directs, on the new altar of burnt offering which they had built. At the very season and on the very day that the Gentiles had profaned it, it was dedicated with songs and harps and lutes and cymbals. All the people fell on their faces and worshiped and blessed Heaven, who had prospered them. So they celebrated the dedication of the altar for eight days, and offered burnt offerings with gladness; they offered a sacrifice of deliverance and praise. They decorated the front of the temple with golden crowns and small shields; they restored the gates and the chambers for the priests, and furnished them with doors. There was very great gladness among the people, and the reproach of the Gentiles was removed.

ery year at that season the days of the dedication of the altar should be observed with gladness and joy for eight days, beginning with the twenty-fifth day of the month of Chislev.

READING 2-14B

What is [the reason of] *Hanukkah?* For our Rabbis taught: On the twenty-fifth of Kislew [commence] the days of *Hanukkah*, which are eight on which a lamentation for the dead and fasting are forbidden. For when the Greeks entered the Temple, they defiled all the oils therein, and when the Hasmonean dynasty prevailed against and defeated them, they made search and found only one cruse of oil which lay with the seal of the High Priest, but which contained sufficient for one day's lighting only; yet a miracle was wrought therein and they lit [the lamp] therewith for eight days. The following year these [days] were appointed a Festival with [the recital of] Hallel[1] and thanksgiving.

THE MACCABEES' CONQUESTS

As soon as they gained control of Judaea the Maccabees launched a series of attacks on their neighbors to expand the amount of territory under Jewish control. In this excerpt from the First Book of Maccabees, Simon (who ruled Judaea 142–135 B.C.E.) explains to Antiochus VII (who ruled the Seleucid empire 139–129 B.C.E.) that the Maccabean conquests were motivated by the desire to reclaim the ancestral inheritance

[1]A collection of psalms recited at festive occasions.

of the Jews. Such was Maccabean ideology; a similar ideology probably motivated those rebelling against Rome in 66–74 C.E. This excerpt also illustrates the instability in the Seleucid empire that gave the Maccabees the freedom to pursue their aggressive policy. When the Seleucid throne was contested by various claimants, the Maccabees played one pretender against another and thereby strengthened their own hand. In the excerpt, Simon is prepared to support Antiochus VII in his war against Trypho (who had killed Simon's brother).

READING 2-15

And Simon sent to Antiochus two thousand picked men, to fight for him, and silver and gold and much military equipment. But he refused to receive them, and he broke all the agreements he formerly had made with Simon, and became estranged from him. He sent to him Athenobius, one of his friends, to confer with him, saying, "You hold control of Joppa and Gazara and the citadel in Jerusalem; they are cities of my kingdom. You have devastated their territory, you have done great damage in the land, and you have taken possession of many places in my kingdom. Now then, hand over the cities which you have seized and the tribute money of the places which you have conquered outside the borders of Judea; or else give me for them five hundred talents of silver, and for the destruction that you have caused and the tribute money of the cities, five hundred talents more. Otherwise we will come and conquer you."

So Athenobius the friend of the king came to Jerusalem, and when he saw the splendor of Simon, and the sideboard with its gold and silver plate, and his great magnificence, he was amazed. He reported to him the words of the king, but Simon gave him this reply: "We have neither taken foreign land nor seized foreign property, but only the inheritance of our fathers, which at one time had been unjustly taken by our enemies. Now that we have the opportunity, we are firmly holding the inheritance of our fathers. As for Joppa and Gazara, which you demand, they were causing great damage among the people and to our land; for them we will give a hundred talents." Athenobius did not answer him a word, but returned in wrath to the king and reported to him these words and the splendor of Simon and all that he had seen. And the king was greatly angered.

RABBAN YOḤANAN BEN ZAKKAI AND THE DESTRUCTION OF JERUSALEM

Neither Josephus, the Jewish historian and general in the first century C.E., nor the rabbis admired the rebels who fought against Rome in 66–74 C.E. Their major failing was failure. The war they began ended not with victory but with defeat and the destruction of the Temple. In this excerpt the rabbinic attitude is evident. Vespasian, the Roman general, offers the Jews quarter but is rebuffed; Rabban Yoḥanan ben Zakkai (also "Joḥanan") pleads with the rebels to surrender, but he too is rebuffed. The rabbi flees from the city with his two disciples, is granted the right to establish an academy at Jamnia (the Greek form of *Yavneh*, a city west-north-west of Jerusalem), and hails Vespasian as a future emperor (*Lebanon* was used by the rabbis as an allegorical name for the Temple). Both of the rabbi's prophecies are soon realized: Vespasian becomes emperor and destroys the Temple.

The historicity of this narrative is very suspect. Vespasian's ascent to the rulership of the Empire is described incorrectly, and the idea that Rabban Yoḥanan prophesied Vespasian's future greatness was probably derived from Josephus, who told a similar story about himself. The story's importance lies in the fact that it shows that the rabbis regarded Rabban Yoḥanan, and not the revolutionaries, as the real hero of the war.

By his action Rabban Yoḥanan ensured the survival of Judaism. His emergence from the coffin is symbolic: he escapes from the Jerusalem of the revolutionaries, a city of death, and emerges to a new life at Yavneh, whose academy of sages laid the foundations of rabbinic Judaism. The rabbis, like Jeremiah, believed that they should support the state in return for religious toleration; messianic deliverance could not be hastened by the actions of men.

READING 2-16

Now, when Vespasian came to destroy Jerusalem he said to the inhabitants: "Fools, why do you seek to destroy this city and why do you seek to burn the Temple? For what do I ask of you but that you send me one bow or one arrow, and I shall go off from you?"

They said to him: "Even as we went forth against the first two who were here before thee and slew them, so shall we go forth against thee and slay thee."

When Rabban Joḥanan ben Zakkai heard this, he sent for the men of Jerusalem and said to them: "My children, why do you destroy this city and why do you seek to burn the Temple? For what is it that he asks of you? Verily he asks naught of you save one bow or one arrow, and he will go off from you."

They said to him: "Even as we went forth against the two before him and slew them, so shall we go forth against him and slay him."

Vespasian had men stationed inside the walls of Jerusalem. Every word which they overheard they would write down, attach (the message) to an arrow, and shoot it over the wall, saying that Rabban Joḥanan ben Zakkai was one of the Emperor's friends.

Now, after Rabban Joḥanan ben Zakkai had spoken to them one day, two and three days, and they still would not attend to him, he sent for his disciples, for Rabbi Eliezer and Rabbi Joshua.

"My sons," he said to them, "arise and take me out of here. Make a coffin for me that I might lie in it."

Rabbi Eliezer took hold of the head end of it, Rabbi Joshua took hold of the foot; and they began carrying him as the sun set, until they reached the gates of Jerusalem.

"Who is this?" the gatekeepers demanded.

"It's a dead man," they replied. "Do you not know that the dead may not be held overnight in Jerusalem?"

"If it's a dead man," the gatekeepers said to them, "take him out."

So they took him out and continued carrying him until they reached Vespasian. They opened the coffin and Rabban Joḥanan stood up before him.

"Art thou Rabban Joḥanan ben Zakkai?" Vespasian inquired; "tell me, what may I give thee?"

"I ask naught of thee," Rabban Joḥanan replied, "save Jamnia, where I might go and teach my disciples and there establish a prayer [house] and perform all the commandments."

"Go," Vespasian said to him, "and whatever thou wishest to do, do."

Said Rabban Joḥanan to him: "By thy leave, may I say something to thee?"

"Speak," Vespasian said to him.

Said Rabban Joḥanan to him: "Lo, thou art about to be appointed king."

"How dost thou know this?" Vespasian asked.

Rabban Joḥanan replied: "This has been handed down to us, that the Temple will not be surrendered to a commoner, but to a king; as it is said, *And he shall cut down the thickets of the forest with iron, and Lebanon shall fall by a mighty one*" (Isa. 10:34).

It was said: No more than a day, or two or three days, passed before messengers reached him from his city (announcing) that the emperor was dead and that he had been elected to succeed as king.

A catapult was brought to him, drawn up against the wall of Jerusalem. Boards of cedar were brought to him which he set into the catapult, and with these he struck against the wall until he made a breach in it. A swine's head was brought and set into the catapult, and this he hurled toward the (sacrificial) limbs which were on the altar.

It was then that Jerusalem was captured.

Meanwhile Rabban Joḥanan ben Zakkai sat and waited trembling, the way Eli had sat and waited; as it is said, *Lo, Eli sat upon his seat by the wayside watching; for his heart trembled for the ark of God* (I Sam. 4:13). When Rabban Joḥanan ben Zakkai heard that Jerusalem was destroyed and the Temple was up in flames, he tore his clothing, and his disciples tore their clothing, and they wept, crying aloud and mourning.

THE JEWISH SECTS

In several passages of his *Jewish War* and *Jewish Antiquities* Josephus describes the three *haireseis* ("schools of thought,") which existed among the Jews. The Greek word *hairesis* gives us the English *heresy*, but it is clear that Josephus does not intend to describe "heretical" groups. He is describing various "sects," "parties," and "movements," three of which he considers "legitimate" (the Pharisees, Sadducees, and Essenes), one of which he considers "intrusive" and illegitimate (the revolutionaries), and the remainder of which he ignores.

In this passage Josephus distinguishes one school from another by three different criteria: their social standing, their philosophy, and their way of life. The Pharisees have the support of the masses, believe in immortality of the soul and in a combination of fate and free will, and lead a simple way of life. The Sadducees have the support only of the well-to-do, deny the immortality of the soul, affirm absolute free will, and are very disputatious. The Essenes are a small group, believe in the absolute power of God, and lead a life of virtue. The fourth group agrees with the Pharisees in all respects except that it follows the anarchistic ideology "No king but God!" and thereby disqualifies itself, according to Josephus. Numerous aspects of these descriptions are obscure and are debated by scholars. The passage clearly shows, however, the plurality of ancient Judaism.

READING 2-17

The Jews, from the most ancient times, had three philosophies pertaining to their traditions, that of the Essenes, that of the Sadducees, and, thirdly, that of the group called the Pharisees. To be sure, I have spoken about them in the second book of the *Jewish War*, but nevertheless I shall here too dwell on them for a moment.

The Pharisees simplify their standard of living, making no concession to luxury. They follow the guidance of that which their doctrine has selected and transmitted as good, attaching the chief importance to the observance of those commandments which it has seen fit to dictate to them. They show respect and deference to their elders, nor do they rashly presume to contradict their proposals. Though they postulate that everything is brought about by fate, still they do not deprive the human will of the pursuit of what is in man's power, since it was God's good pleasure that there should be a fusion and that the will of man with his virtue and vice should be admitted to the council-chamber of fate. They believe that souls have power to survive death and that there are rewards and punishments under the earth for those who have led lives of virtue or vice: eternal imprisonment is the lot of evil souls, while the good souls receive an easy passage to a new life. Because of these views they are, as a matter of fact, extremely influential among the townsfolk; and all prayers and sacred rites of divine worship are performed according to their exposition. This is the great tribute that the inhabitants of the cities, by practising the highest ideals both in their way of living and in their discourse, have paid to the excellence of the Pharisees.

The Sadducees hold that the soul perishes along with the body. They own no observance of any sort apart from the laws; in fact, they reckon it a virtue to dispute with the teachers of the path of wisdom that they pursue. There are but few men to whom this doctrine has been made known, but these are men of the highest standing. They accomplish practically nothing, however. For whenever they assume some office, though they submit unwillingly and perforce, yet submit they do to the formulas of the Pharisees, since otherwise the masses would not tolerate them.

The doctrine of the Essenes is wont to leave everything in the hands of God. They regard the soul as immortal and believe that they ought to strive especially to draw near to righteousness. They send votive offerings to the temple, but perform their sacrifices employing a different ritual of purification. For this reason they are barred from those precincts of the temple that are frequented by all the people and perform their rites by themselves. Otherwise they are of the highest character, devoting themselves solely to agricultural labour. They deserve admiration in contrast to all others who claim their share of virtue because such qualities as theirs were never found before among any Greek or barbarian people, nay, not even briefly, but have been among them in constant practice and never interrupted since they adopted them from of old. Moreover, they hold their possessions in common, and the wealthy man receives no more enjoyment from his property than the man who possesses nothing. The men who practise this way of life number more than four thousand. They neither bring wives into the community nor do they own slaves, since they believe that the latter practice contributes to injustice and that the former opens the way to a source of dissension. Instead they live by themselves and perform menial tasks for one another. They elect by show of hands good men to receive their revenues and the produce of the earth and priests to prepare bread and other food. Their manner of life does not differ at all from that of the so-called Ctistae among the Dacians, but is as close to it as could be.

As for the fourth of the philosophies, Judas the Galilaean set himself up as leader of it. This school agrees in all other respects with the opinions of the Pharisees, except that they have a passion for liberty that is almost unconquerable, since they are convinced that God alone is their leader and master. They think little of submitting to death in unusual forms and permitting vengeance to fall on kinsmen and friends if only they may avoid calling any man master. Inasmuch as most people have seen the steadfastness of their resolution amid such circumstances, I may forgo any further account. For I have no fear that anything reported of them will be considered incredible. The danger is, rather, that report may minimize the indifference with which they accept the grinding misery of pain. The folly that ensued began to afflict the nation after Gessius Florus, who was governor, had by his overbearing and lawless actions provoked a desperate rebellion against the Romans. Such is the number of the schools of philosophy among the Jews.

JOSEPHUS ON JESUS

The following excerpt is probably the single most famous paragraph of the *Jewish Antiquities* of Josephus. Known as the *Testimonium Flavianum*, or the testimony of Flavius Josephus to Jesus Christ, it is found in all the manuscripts of the *Jewish Antiquities*, although its authenticity is suspect. The context of the passage is a series of troubles that befell the Jews in the 30's C.E. during the tenure of Pontius Pilate, the Roman governor of Palestine. Most scholars agree that in its original form this paragraph narrated briefly the career of Jesus, the troubles which he caused, his execution by Pilate, and the fact that his followers continued to be active even after his death because they believed that he had been resurrected. Later Christian copyists "improved" the original by adding references to Jesus' divinity and messiahship and by rephrasing the passage to indicate that Josephus too acknowledged the miracle of the resurrection. This passage is important because it provides an outsider's view of Jesus and because it demonstrates how easy it was to tamper with the literature of antiquity.

READING 2-18

About this time there lived Jesus, a wise man, if indeed one ought to call him a man. For he was one who wrought surprising feats and was a teacher of such people as accept the truth gladly. He won over many Jews and many of the Greeks. He was the Messiah. When Pilate, upon hearing him accused by men of the highest standing amongst us, had condemned him to be crucified, those who had in the first place come to love him did not give up their affection for him. On the third day he appeared to them restored to life, for the prophets of God had prophesied these and countless other marvellous things about him. And the tribe of the Christians, so called after him, has still to this day not disappeared.

THE JEWISH DIASPORA IN THE FIRST CENTURY C.E.

The festival of Pentecost (literally, fifty) was celebrated fifty days after Passover. In this passage, the disciples of Jesus receive the Holy Spirit and begin to speak in many different languages, thereby symbolizing the universality of the Christian mission. The numerous Jews in Jerusalem who hailed from foreign countries recognized their own native languages. This passage shows the extent of the Jewish Diaspora in the first century, the adoption of Judaism by proselytes, and the centrality of Jerusalem for all Jews. *Asia* refers to the Roman province of Asia, the western part of Turkey.

READING 2-19

Now there were dwelling in Jerusalem Jews, devout men from every nation under heaven. And at this sound the multitude came together, and they were bewildered, because each one heard them speaking in his own language. And they were amazed and wondered, saying, "Are not all these who are speaking Galileans? And how is it that we hear, each of us in his own native language? Parthians and Medes and Elamites and residents of Mesopotamia, Judea and Cappadocia, Pontus and Asia, Phrygia and Pamphylia, Egypt and the parts of Libya belonging to Cyrene, and visitors from Rome, both Jews and proselytes, Cretans and Arabians, we hear them telling in our own tongues the mighty works of God."

3

The Shaping of Traditions
(First to Ninth Centuries)

David B. Ruderman

The destruction of the Jerusalem Temple at the hands of the Romans in 70 C.E. marks a major turning point in Jewish history. In the aftermath of the Temple's destruction, the program of the revolutionaries was discredited. In its place, a rabbi named Yoḥanan ben Zakkai and his followers established a new seat of Jewish learning in the town of Yavneh, and with it created a new lease on life in which to restructure the foundations of Judaism.

From the last decades of the first century C.E. until the end of the fifth century the values and the laws and institutions designed by the rabbis of Yavneh and their successors in Palestine and later in Babylonia shaped Jewish communities. Throughout this period, rabbinic institutions of learning and legal formulation rose to prominence; Jewish law, as interpreted by the rabbis, was adapted to the exigencies of life both in Israel and in the Diaspora; the central corpus of rabbinic legal and homiletic writing—the *Mishnah*, *Midrash*, and *Talmud*—was composed and redacted.

The rabbinic age in Jewish history left a decisive imprint on the development of Christianity as well. Even while the rabbis sought universal acceptance of their path of religious salvation within the Jewish community, the followers of Jesus, and later Paul, were offering their hope of salvation through a redeeming Christ to a swelling constituency of Jewish Christians and, later, gentiles living beyond the confines of the Jewish community. The diverging paths of the two faiths led to their ultimate separation. The Jewish rejection of the messiahship and divinity of Jesus elicited the hostility of anti-Judaism among the leadership of the early Church. In order to legitimate their own claims to being the true faith of Israel, the Church fathers felt the intrinsic need to deprecate the Jewish faith and practice. With the ascendancy of Christianity as the official religion of the Roman Empire and later of medieval Europe, Christian theological attitudes toward the Jews often were reflected in social policy as well. The Jews were to be allowed to exist, albeit in a pariah status, doomed to wander the earth as witnesses of the ultimate truth of Christianity.

The seventh century marked a further permutation in Jewish history with the rise of the new religion of Islam. Islam, like Christianity, was indebted to Judaism for its singular passion for monotheism, its concept of divine revelation, and its preoccupation with ethical obligation as a fundamental dimension of fulfilling God's will. During that time, the Jews too, despite occasional disabilities, flourished socially, culturally, and economically throughout the first centuries of Muslim rule, especially at the height of the Abbasid dynasty (end of eighth to tenth centuries).

JOSEPHUS' ACCOUNT OF THE FALL OF MASADA

By 73 C.E. only one rebel fortress stubbornly resisted the formidable Roman forces, which already had conquered Judaea and left Jerusalem and its Temple in ruins. Masada, overlooking the southwest shore of the Dead Sea, was a high, steep mountain that had previously been fortified by earlier rulers, most recently by Herod the Great. The rebels withstood the Roman legions until they realized their imminent defeat. Eleazar ben Yair, the leader of the Masada band, finally acknowledged in a speech before his soldiers, (as reported by Flavius Josephus, the first-century Jewish historian) the futility of further resistance and the inevitable conclusion to be drawn from Jerusalem's destruction: that mass suicide—dying as free men—was preferable to surrendering to the Romans as slaves. When the Romans reached the top of the mountain, they discovered that almost the entire Masada community had heeded Eleazar's advice and died as martyrs.

The following selection is taken from Eleazar's last speech to the rebels as related by Josephus in the seventh book of his *The Jewish War*.

READING 3-1

And where now is that great city, the mother-city of the whole Jewish race, intrenched behind all those lines of ramparts, screened by all those forts and massive towers, that could scarce contain her munitions of war, and held all those myriads of defenders? What has become of her that was believed to have God for her founder? Uprooted from her base she has been swept away, and the sole memorial of her remaining is that of the slain still quartered in her ruins! Hapless old men sit beside the ashes of the shrine and a few women, reserved by the enemy for basest outrage.

Which of us, taking these things to heart, could bear to behold the sun, even could he live secure from peril? Who such a foe to his country, so unmanly, so fond of life, as not to regret that he is still alive to-day? Nay, I would that we had all been dead ere ever we saw that holy city razed by an enemy's hands, that sacred sanctuary so profanely uprooted! But seeing that we have been beguiled by a not ignoble hope, that we might perchance find means of avenging her of her foes, and now that hope has vanished and left us alone in our distress, let us hasten to die honourably; let us have pity on ourselves, our children and our wives, while it is still in our power to find pity from ourselves. For we were born for death, we and those whom we have begotten; and this even the fortunate cannot escape. But outrage and servitude and the sight of our wives being led to shame with their children—these are no necessary evils imposed by nature on mankind, but befall, through their own cowardice, those who, having the chance of forestalling them by death, refuse to take it. But we, priding ourselves on our courage, revolted from the Romans, and now at the last, when they offered us our lives, we refused the offer. Who then can fail to foresee their wrath if they take us alive? Wretched will be the young whose vigorous frames can sustain many tortures, wretched the more advanced in years whose age is incapable of bearing such calamities. Is a man to see his wife led off to violation, to hear the voice of his child crying 'Father!' when his own hands are bound? No, while those hands are free and grasp the sword, let them render an honourable service. Unenslaved by the foe let us die, as free men with our children and wives let us quit this life together! This our laws enjoin, this our wives and children implore of us. The need for this is of God's sending, the reverse of this is the Romans' desire, and their fear is lest a single one of us should die before capture. Haste we then to leave them, instead of their hoped-for enjoyment at securing us, amazement at our death and admiration for our fortitude.

YOHANAN BEN ZAKKAI'S PRESCRIPTION FOR JEWISH SURVIVAL

Rabban Yohanan ben Zakkai, the leader of the Pharisees at the time of the destruction of Jerusalem in 70 C.E., reacted differently to the national disaster than did his countryman Eleazar ben Yair. He chose instead to save his own life and those of his followers by submitting to Roman rule. He thus succeeded in securing from the Romans the town of Yavneh, where he was able to restructure the foundations of the Jewish community and its religious faith. Yohanan elected a strategy of collective survival rather than collective suicide; he offered the Jewish survivors of Jerusalem's tragedy the reassuring comfort that they could overcome their present devastation by obeying "the will of God" and by "acts of loving kindness." The following selection attributed to Yohanan is preserved in rabbinic literature.

READING 3-2

Once as Rabban Yohanan ben Zakkai was coming forth from Jerusalem, Rabbi Joshua followed after him and beheld the Temple in ruins.

"Woe unto us!" Rabbi Joshua cried, "that this, the place where the iniquities of Israel were atoned for, is laid waste!"

"My son," Rabban Yohanan said to him, "be not grieved; we have another atonement as effective as this. And what is it? It is acts of loving-kindness, as it is said, *For I desire mercy and not sacrifice.*" [Hosea 6:6]

AN EARLY DEFENSE OF JUDAISM

By the end of the first century C.E., large numbers of Jews were living outside the land of Israel, dispersed throughout the Roman Empire in what had come to be known as the Diaspora. Flavius Josephus, the Jewish historian, who already had written two major works, *The Jewish War* and *The Jewish Antiquities*, was then living in Rome. About 96 C.E., he composed another short treatise, which he called *Against Apion*, in order to defend the integrity of Judaism against the misrepresentations of pagan writers, especially Apion, a first-century anti-Jewish author from Alexandria, Egypt. Josephus constructed his apologia of the Jewish religion and especially Jewish law in the context of a society that valued Greek cultural ideals highly. In arguing passionately for the superior moral and spiritual life of the Jewish community, Josephus assumed a function to be shared by many future spokesmen of Diaspora Judaism: to justify and legitimate the existence of this singular minority and its culture in the eyes of an unsympathetic and often hostile majority.

READING 3-3

Seeing, however, that Apollonius Molon,[1] Lysimachus,[2] and others, partly from ignorance, mainly from ill will, have made reflections, which are neither just nor true, upon our lawgiver Moses and his code, maligning the one as a charlatan and impostor, and asserting that from the other we receive lessons in vice and none in virtue, I desire to give, to the best of my ability, a brief account of our constitution as a whole and of its details. From this, I think, it will be apparent that we possess a code excellently designed to promote piety, friendly relations with each other, and humanity towards the world at large, besides justice, hardihood, and contempt of death. . . .

For us, with our conviction that the original institution of the Law was in accordance with the will of God, it would be rank impiety not to observe it. What could one alter in it? What more beautiful one could have been discovered? What improvement imported from elsewhere? Would you change the entire character of the constitution? Could there be a finer or more equitable polity than one which sets God at the head of the universe, which assigns the administration of its highest affairs to the whole body of priests, and entrusts to the supreme high-priest the direction of the other priests? These men, moreover, owed their original promotion by the legislator to their high office, not to any superiority in wealth or other accidental advantages. No; of all his companions, the men to whom he entrusted the ordering of divine worship as their first charge were those who were pre-eminently gifted with persuasive eloquence and discretion. But this charge further embraced a strict superintendence of the Law and of the pursuits of everyday life; for the appointed

---

[1] Rhetorician in Rhodes and in Rome; teacher of Cicero and Julius Caesar.
[2] Alexandrian author.

duties of the priests included general supervision, the trial of cases of litigation, and the punishment of condemned persons.

Could there be a more saintly government than that? Could God be more worthily honoured than by such a scheme, under which religion is the end and aim of the training of the entire community, the priests are entrusted with the special charge of it, and the whole administration of the state resembles some sacred ceremony? Practices which, under the name of mysteries and rites of initiation, other nations are unable to observe for but a few days, we maintain with delight and unflinching determination all our lives.

An infinity of time has passed since Moses, if one compares the age in which he lived with those of other legislators; yet it will be found that throughout the whole of that period not merely have our laws stood the test of our own use, but they have to an ever increasing extent excited the emulation of the world at large.

Our earliest imitators were the Greek philosophers, who, though ostensibly observing the laws of their own countries, yet in their conduct and philosophy were Moses' disciples, holding similar views about God, and advocating the simple life and friendly communion between man and man. But that is not all. The masses have long since shown a keen desire to adopt our religious observances; and there is not one city, Greek or barbarian, nor a single nation, to which our custom of abstaining from work on the seventh day has not spread, and where the fasts and the lighting of lamps and many of our prohibitions in the matter of food are not observed. Moreover, they attempt to imitate our unanimity, our liberal charities, our devoted labour in the crafts, our endurance under persecution on behalf of our laws. The greatest miracle of all is that our Law holds out no seductive bait of sensual pleasure, but has exercised this influence through its own inherent merits; and, as God permeates the universe, so the Law has found its way among all mankind.

Upon the laws it was unnecessary to expatiate. A glance at them showed that they teach not impiety, but the most genuine piety; that they invite men not to hate their fellows, but to share their possessions; that they are the foes of injustice and scrupulous for justice, banish sloth and extravagance, and teach men to be self-dependent and to work with a will; that they deter them from war for the sake of conquest, but render them valiant defenders of the laws themselves; inexorable in punishment, not to be duped by studied words, always supported by actions. For actions are our invariable testimonials, plainer than any documents. I would therefore boldly maintain that we have introduced to the rest of the world a very large number of very beautiful ideas. What greater beauty than inviolable piety? What higher justice than obedience to the laws? What more beneficial than to be in harmony with one another, to be a prey neither to disunion in adversity, nor to arrogance and faction in prosperity; in war to despise death, in peace to devote oneself to crafts or agriculture; and to be convinced that everything in the whole universe is under the eye and direction of God? Had these precepts been either committed to writing or more consistently observed by others before us, we should have owed them a debt of gratitude as their disciples. If, however, it is seen that no one observes them better than ourselves, and if we have shown that we were the first to discover them, then the Apions and Molons and all who delight in lies and abuse may be left to their own confusion.

FROM THE LITERATURE OF THE RABBIS

The rabbinic age in Jewish history (roughly the first five centuries of the Common Era), like the patristic age in Christian history to which it corresponds, played a decisive role in the shaping of a new religious civilization. The rabbis, like the Church fathers, produced an overwhelming body of theological speculation, a voluminous legal code, a richly diversified homiletical and ethical literature, liturgy, and scriptural exegesis, all of which established the classical foundations of their historic faith.

Among the major components of this extraordinary literary output, the *Mishnah*, the *Midrash*, and the *Talmud* especially should be noted. The *Mishnah*, redacted by Judah ha-nasi around 200 C.E. in Palestine, constitutes a law code, textbook, and condensation of the vast body of orally transmitted rulings of centuries of rabbinic literature in Palestine. The *Midrash* consists of collections of rabbinic commentaries on the Hebrew Bible, either of legal rulings (called *Midreshei Halakhah*) or of narrative portions (called *Midreshei Aggadah*). The latter kind of *Midrash* includes rabbinic homily, theological speculation, and ethical teaching; it, especially, gave full expression to the rabbis' attempt to communicate the values of Judaism. The *Talmud*, of which two versions exist, one compiled in Palestine and one in Babylonia, was completed roughly by the fifth century. It consists of the *Mishnah*, followed by an elaborate amplification called the *Gemara*. It constitutes a code of law but it also includes vigorous discussion, debate, and homiletic and ethical teaching. Above all it represents an invitation to uninterrupted learning, an "oral law" never closed or canonized, but open to continuous elaboration, refutation, and counter-refutation. The *Talmud* was thus both a work of law and an educational program.

It is virtually impossible to capture the flavor of the rabbinic corpus in a few short selections. The four examples following provide only a faint expression of some of the modes of rabbinic writing. The first selection (Reading 3-4A) is taken from the first chapter of *Pirke Avot* (Ethics of the Fathers), a unique anthology of rabbinic ethical teachings found in the *Mishnah*. Its opening paragraph provides an interesting "chain of tradition," linking the authority of the rabbis back to the prophets and to the divine revelation at Sinai. The second selection (Reading 3-4B) is from the tractate *Pesaḥim* of the *Mishnah*, describing the rabbinic ritual of the Passover meal. The third selection (Reading 3-4C) is from the Palestinian *Midrash* called *Mekhilta de Rabbi Ishmael*. The third of nine treatises of this *Midrash* on the Book of Exodus is called *Shirta* (the Song, a commentary on the biblical Song of the Sea, preserved in Exodus 15). The section given provides a rich example of rabbinic homily, treating one verse on the wondrous nature of God (Exodus 15:11). The final selection (Reading 3-4D) is from the Babylonian *Talmud*, tractate *Yoma* 82a–b (concerning the ritual of Yom Kippur, the day of atonement). It considers the extreme case of a pregnant woman who holds a morbid desire to eat pork on the fast of Yom Kippur. The rabbis utilize this example to underscore the importance of human life and to limit severely the occasions where taking one's life is religiously justifiable.

READING 3-4A

Avot ('The Fathers')

Moses received the Law from Sinai and committed it to Joshua, and Joshua to the elders, and the elders to the Prophets, and the Prophets committed it to the men of the Great Synagogue. They said three things: Be deliberate in judgement, raise up many disciples, and make a fence around the Law.

Simeon the Just was of the remnants of the Great Synagogue. He used to say: By three things is the world sustained: by the Law, by the [Temple-]service, and by deeds of loving-kindness.

Antigonus of Soko received [the Law] from Simeon the Just. He used to say: Be not like slaves that minister to the master for the sake of receiving a bounty, but be like slaves that minister to the master not for the sake of receiving a bounty; and let the fear of Heaven be upon you.

Jose b. Joezer of Zeredah and Jose b. Johanan of Jerusalem received [the Law] from them. Jose b. Joezer of Zeredah said: Let thy house be a meeting-house for the Sages and sit amid the dust of their feet and drink in their words with thirst.

Jose b. Johanan of Jerusalem said: Let thy house be opened wide and let the needy be members of thy household; and talk not much with womankind. They said this of a man's own wife: how much more of his fellow's wife! Hence the Sages have said: He that talks much with womankind brings evil upon himself and neglects the study of the Law and at the last will inherit Gehenna.

Joshua b. Perahyah and Nittai the Arbelite received [the Law] from them. Joshua b. Perahyah said: Provide thyself with a teacher and get thee a fellow[-disciple] and when thou judgest any man incline the balance in his favour.

Nittai the Arbelite said: Keep thee far from an evil neighbour and consort not with the wicked and lose not belief in retribution.

Judah b. Tabbai and Simeon b. Shetah received [the Law] from them. Judah b. Tabbai said: Make not thyself like them that would influence the judges; and when the suitors stand before thee let them be in thine eyes as wicked men, and when they have departed from before thee let them be in thine eyes as innocent, so soon as they have accepted the judgement.

Simeon b. Shetah said: Examine the witnesses diligently and be cautious in thy words lest from them they learn to swear falsely.

Shemaiah and Abtalion received [the Law] from them. Shemaiah said: Love labour and hate mastery and seek not acquaintance with the ruling power.

Abtalion said: Ye Sages, give heed to your words lest ye incur the penalty of exile and ye be exiled to a place of evil waters, and the disciples that come after you drink [of them] and die, and the name of Heaven be profaned.

Hillel and Shammai received [the Law] from them. Hillel said: Be of the disciples of Aaron, loving peace and pursuing peace, loving mankind and bringing them nigh to the Law.

He used to say: A name made great is a name destroyed, and he that increases not decreases, and he that learns not is worthy of death, and he that makes worldly use of the crown shall perish.

He used to say: If I am not for myself who is for me? and being for mine own self what am I? and if not now, when?

Shammai said: Make thy [study of the] Law a fixed habit; say little and do much, and receive all men with a cheerful countenance.

Rabban Gamaliel said: Provide thyself with a teacher and remove thyself from doubt, and tithe not overmuch by guesswork.

Simeon his son said: All my days have I grown up among the Sages and I have found naught better for a man than silence; and not the expounding [of the Law] is the chief thing but the doing [of it]; and he that multiplies words occasions sin.

Rabban Simeon b. Gamaliel said: By three things is the world sustained: by truth, by judgement, and by peace, as it is written, *Execute the judgement of truth and peace*.

READING 3-4B

Pesaḥim

On the eve of Passover, from about the time of the Evening Offering, a man must eat naught until nightfall. Even the poorest in Israel must not eat unless he sits down to table, and they must not give them less than four cups of wine to drink, even if it is from the [Paupers'] Dish.[1]

After they have mixed him his first cup, the School of Shammai say: He says the Benediction first over the day and then the Benediction over the wine. And the School of Hillel say: He says the Benediction first over the wine and then the Benediction over the day.

When [food] is brought before him he eats it seasoned with lettuce, until he is come to the breaking of bread; they bring before him unleavened bread and lettuce and the *haroseth*,[2] although *haroseth* is not a religious obligation. R. Eliezer b. R. Zadok says: It is a religious obligation. And in the Holy City they used to bring before him the body of the Passover-offering.

They then mix him the second cup. And here the son asks his father (and if the son has not enough understanding his father instructs him [how to ask]), 'Why is this night different from other nights? For on other nights we eat seasoned food once, but this night twice; on other nights we eat leavened or unleavened bread, but

---

[1] A communal institution for support of the poor.

[2] A mixture of nuts, fruit, and wine reminiscent of the mortar used by the Hebrew slaves to make bricks in Egypt.

this night all is unleavened,[3] on other nights we eat flesh roast, stewed, or cooked, but this night all is roast.[4] And according to the understanding of the son his father instructs him. He begins with the disgrace[5] and ends with the glory; and he expounds from *A wandering Aramean was my father . . .* until he finishes the whole section.[6]

Rabban Gamaliel used to say: Whosoever has not said [the verses concerning][7] these three things at Passover has not fulfilled his obligation. And these are they: Passover, unleavened bread, and bitter herbs: 'Passover'—because God passed over the houses of our fathers in Egypt; 'unleavened bread'—because our fathers were redeemed from Egypt; 'bitter herbs'—because the Egyptians embittered the lives of our fathers in Egypt. In every generation a man must so regard himself as if he came forth himself out of Egypt, for it is written, *And thou shalt tell thy son in that day saying, It is because of that which the Lord did for me when I came forth out of Egypt.* Therefore are we bound to give thanks, to praise, to glorify, to honour, to exalt, to extol, and to bless him who wrought all these wonders for our fathers and for us. He brought us out from bondage to freedom, from sorrow to gladness, and from mourning to a Festival-day, and from darkness to great light, and from servitude to redemption; so let us say before him the *Hallelujah.*[8]

READING 3-4C

Shirta

WHO IS LIKE UNTO THEE, O LORD, AMONG THE 'LYM (GODS): When Israel saw that Pharaoh and his troops perished in the Reed Sea, that the empire of the Egyptians was over and done with, and that disasters were inflicted on their idols, they all burst forth with the exclamation, "Who is like unto Thee, O Lord, among the gods!"

And it was not Israel alone that recited the Song, but the Nations of the World too recited the Song. When the Nations of the World heard that Pharaoh and his troops had perished in the Sea, that the empire of the Egyptians was over and done with, and that disasters had been inflicted on their idols, all of them renounced their own idol worship and acknowledging God they all burst forth with the exclamation, "Who is like unto Thee, O Lord, among the gods!"

You will find the same true of the Nations, that in the Future they will renounce their idol worship, as it is said, "O Lord, my strength and my stronghold, and my refuge, in the day of affliction; unto Thee shall the Nations come . . . Shall a man make unto himself gods" etc.; (Jer. 16:19–20); and it says, "In that day a man shall cast away his idols of silver" etc., (Isa. 2:20), and it goes on, "To go into the cleft of the rocks" etc. (Isa. 2:21); and in the latter connection what else is written? "And the idols shall utterly pass away." (Isa. 2:18).

---

[3]Some texts add: "On other nights we eat all other manner of vegetables, but this night bitter herb."

[4]Some texts add: "On other nights we dip only once, but this night twice."

[5]Slavery and Idolatry.

[6]Deuteronomy 26:5.

[7]Exodus 12:27, 39; 1:14.

[8]Referring to Psalms 113–118.

Another interpretation of WHO IS LIKE UNTO THEE, O LORD, AMONG THE 'LYM: Note the spelling 'lm: (That is to say,) Who among those capable of mighty deeds ('lmym) is like unto Thee, who can be the likes of Thee in the miracles and mighty deeds Thou didst perform at the Sea, as it is said, ". . . Awesome things by the Reed Sea" etc. (Ps. 106:22)—"And He rebuked the Reed Sea, and it was dried up." (Ps. 106:9).

WHO IS LIKE UNTO THEE, O LORD, AMONG THE 'LYM: Who is like unto Thee, O Lord, among the mute ones ('ylmym), who can be the likes of Thee beholding Thy children disgraced and yet Thou keepest still, as it is said, "I have a long time held My peace, I have been still, and restrained Myself; now will I cry like a travailing woman, gasping and panting at once." (Isa. 42:14)—In the past "I have been still and restrained Myself"; henceforth, however, "I will cry like a travailing woman, gasping and panting at once I shall lay waste" etc. (Isa. 41:14 f.).

Another interpretation of WHO IS LIKE UNTO THEE, O LORD, AMONG THE 'LYM: Who is like unto Thee among those who minister before Thee on high, as it is said, "For who in the skies can be compared . . . A God dreaded in the great council of the holy ones . . . O Lord God of hosts, who is a mighty one, like unto Thee, O Lord." (Ps. 89:7–9).

WHO IS LIKE UNTO THEE, O LORD, AMONG THE 'LYM: Who is like unto Thee among those who call themselves divine? Pharaoh called himself divine, as it is said, "Because he hath said: Mine is my river and I, I made it for myself." (Ezek. 29:3, 9). Sennacherib called himself divine, as it is said, "Who are they among all the gods of these countries" etc. (Isa. 36:20). Nebuchadnezzar called himself divine, as it is said, "I will ascend above the heights of the clouds" etc. (Isa. 14:14). The Prince of Tyre called himself divine, as it is said, "Son of man, say unto the Prince of Tyre: Thus saith the Lord God: Because thy heart is lifted up" etc. (Ezek. 28:2).

WHO IS LIKE UNTO THEE, O LORD, AMONG THE 'LYM: Who is like unto Thee among those whom others call divine and there is absolutely nothing to them? It is of them that it is said, "They have mouths, but they speak not" etc. (Ps. 115:5 ff.)—these "have mouths but cannot speak." But that is not the case with Him Who Spake and the World Came to Be! On the contrary, in one utterance He says two things, something impossible for flesh and blood to do, as it is said, "God hath spoken one word, but in this we have heard two" etc., (Ps. 62:12), "Is not My word like as fire" etc. (Jer. 23:29); it is also written, ". . . And speech goeth out of His mouth" (etc.). (Job 37:2 ff.).

READING 3-4D

Babylonian Talmud, Yoma 82a–82b

MISHNAH. If a woman with child smelt[1] she must be given to eat until she feels restored. A sick person is fed at the word of experts.[2] And if no experts are there, one feeds him at his own wish until he says: enough.

GEMARA. Our Rabbis taught: if a woman with child smelt the flesh of holy flesh, or of pork, we put for her a reed into the juice and place it upon her mouth. If

---

[1] A pregnant woman smelt a dish of holy flesh or pork (prohibited to eat on any day, and especially on the Day of Atonement) on the Day of Atonement and strongly desires it.

[2] Physicians.

thereupon she feels that her craving has been satisfied, it is well. If not, one feeds her with the juice itself. If thereupon her craving is satisfied it is well, if not one feeds her with the fat meat itself, for there is nothing that can stand before [the duty of] saving life, with the exception of idolatry, incest,[3] and bloodshed [which are prohibited in all situations]. Whence do we know that about idolatry? For it was taught: R. Eliezer said: Since it is said, *With all thy soul*, why is it said: *With all thy might.*[4] And since it is said: '*With all thy might*', why is it said: '*With all thy soul*'? [It but comes to tell you that] if there be a man whose life is more cherished by him than his money, for him it is said: '*With all thy soul*'; and if there be a person to whom his money is dearer than his life, for him it is said: '*With all thy might*'.[5] Whence do we know it about incest and bloodshed?—Because it was taught: Rabbi said, *For as when a man rises against his neighbour, and slayeth him, even so is this matter.*[6] What matter do we infer for [the rape of] a betrothed maiden from a murderer?—Rather: What was meant to teach, learns itself,[7] just as in the case of a betrothed maiden it is lawful to save her at the expense of his [the would-be raper's] life, thus also in the case of a murderer. And just as in the case of [an order to] shed blood one should rather be killed oneself than transgress [the prohibition of murder], thus also in the case of a [command to rape a] betrothed maiden, one should rather be killed than transgress [the prohibition of violating her]. [82*b*] But whence do we know that this principle applies in the case of a murder?—This is reasonable. For there was a man who came before Raba and said to him: The lord of my village told me: Kill so-and-so, and if you will not, I shall kill you!—He [Raba] answered: Let him kill you, but do not kill! What makes you see that your blood is redder than his?[8] Perhaps the blood of that man is redder than yours?

FROM THE NEW TESTAMENT

The Parable of the Vineyard

The disciples of Jesus were faced with a formidable crisis for Christian faith with the crucifixion. Seen in the context of Jewish messianic teaching, Jesus' death constituted an obvious paradox. If Jesus was, in fact, the messiah, how was it possible for him to expire on a cross? The explanation that arose in the aftermath of the crucifixion was that the religious leadership of Israel was responsible for his death and that the crucifixion represented only the culmination of a series of crimes perpetrated by an unbelieving Jewish people. This explanation finds its best expres-

---

[3]Including adultery.

[4]Referring here to economic might, money.

[5]It would appear superfluous to mention loving God with all one's money, since most people value their life more than their wealth.

[6]Referring to the rape of a betrothed maiden.

[7]Literally, Behold this one comes to teach and turns out a learner.

[8]Do not assume your neighbor's life is any dearer to God than your own.

sion in the parable of the vineyard (Mark 12:1–12; Matthew 21:33–46; Luke 20:9–19). Here the vineyard owner (God) leaves his vineyard (Israel) in the hands of tenants (the Jews). He occasionally sends his servants (the prophets) to obtain his share of the fruit. The unfaithful servants, however, kill the servants until the owner decides to send his own son (Jesus) to represent his interests. But "they took him and killed him and cast him out of the vineyard." Rather than a statement of historic reality, the deicide theme, exemplified by the parable, arose out of a critical need to polemicize with Judaism in order to authenticate Christian belief in the years following Jesus' death.

READING 3-5A

And he began to speak to them in parables. "A man planted a vineyard, and set a hedge around it, and dug a pit for the wine press, and built a tower, and let it out to tenants, and went into another country. When the time came, he sent a servant to the tenants, to get from them some of the fruit of the vineyard. And they took him and beat him, and sent him away empty-handed. Again he sent to them another servant, and they wounded him in the head, and treated him shamefully. And he sent another, and him they killed; and so with many others, some they beat and some they killed. He had still one other, a beloved son; finally he sent him to them, saying, 'They will respect my son.' But those tenants said to one another, 'This is the heir; come, let us kill him, and the inheritance will be ours.' And they took him and killed him, and cast him out of the vineyard. What will the owner of the vineyard do? He will come and destroy the tenants, and give the vineyard to others. Have you not read this scripture:

'The very stone which the builders rejected
has become the head of the corner;
this was the Lord's doing,
and it is marvelous in our eyes'?"

And they tried to arrest him, but feared the multitude, for they perceived that he had told the parable against them; so they left him and went away.

[Mark 12:1–12]

From the Gospel of John

More than any other work of the Christian canon, the fourth Gospel, according to John, served to encourage and buttress anti-Judaic sentiments in future generations. Written after the other three "synoptic" Gospels—Matthew, Mark, and Luke—it effectively expressed some of the central theological convictions of early Christianity. At the same time, its vilification of the Jews, its labeling of the entire Jewish nation as Christ-killers, and its explicit designation of the Jews as the children of the devil, gave ultimate theological expression to the roots of anti-Jewish attitudes in the continuing Church tradition. The eighth chapter of John records a lengthy dispute between the Jews and Jesus where the level of religious hostility is especially pronounced.

READING 3-5B

Again he said to them, "I go away, and you will seek me and die in your sin; where I am going, you cannot come." Then said the Jews, "Will he kill himself, since he says, 'Where I am going, you cannot come'?" He said to them, "You are from below, I am from above; you are of this world, I am not of this world. I told you that you would die in your sins, for you will die in your sins unless you believe that I am he." They said to him, "Who are you?" Jesus said to them, "Even what I have told you from the beginning. I have much to say about you and much to judge; but he who sent me is true, and I declare to the world what I have heard from him." They did not understand that he spoke to them of the Father. So Jesus said, "When you have lifted up the Son of man, then you will know that I am he, and that I do nothing on my own authority but speak thus as the Father taught me. And he who sent me is with me; he has not left me alone, for I always do what is pleasing to him." As he spoke thus, many believed in him.

Jesus then said to the Jews who had believed in him, "If you continue in my word, you are truly my disciples, and you will know the truth, and the truth will make you free." They answered him, "We are descendants of Abraham, and have never been in bondage to any one. How is it that you say, 'You will be made free'?"

Jesus answered them, "Truly, truly, I say to you, every one who commits sin is a slave to sin. The slave does not continue in the house for ever; the son continues for ever. So if the Son makes you free, you will be free indeed. I know that you are descendants of Abraham; yet you seek to kill me, because my word finds no place in you. I speak of what I have seen with my Father, and you do what you have heard from your father."

They answered him, "Abraham is our father." Jesus said to them, "If you were Abraham's children, you would do what Abraham did, but now you seek to kill me, a man who has told you the truth which I heard from God; this is not what Abraham did. You do what your father did." They said to him, "We were not born of fornication; we have one Father, even God." Jesus said to them, "If God were your Father, you would love me, for I proceeded and came forth from God; I came not of my own accord, but he sent me. Why do you not understand what I say? It is because you cannot bear to hear my word. You are of your father the devil, and your will is to do your father's desires. He was a murderer from the beginning, and has nothing to do with the truth, because there is no truth in him. When he lies, he speaks according to his own nature, for he is a liar and the father of lies. But, because I tell the truth, you do not believe me. Which of you convicts me of sin? If I tell the truth, why do you not believe me? He who is of God hears the words of God; the reason why you do not hear them is that you are not of God."

[John 8:21–47]

FROM THE HOMILIES OF JOHN CHRYSOSTOM AGAINST THE JEWS

From about the second to the sixth centuries the Church fathers continued to employ and embellish themes found in the New Testament to demonstrate the veracity of the Christian faith by underscoring the perversities and blindness of Judaism. Their *adversos Judaeos* tracts emerged as an essential part of the literature of the early Church. John Chrysostom, the presbyter of Antioch at the end of the fourth century, was a particularly vituperative spokesman of this tradition. Drawing from Old and New Testament passages, he sought to emphasize the diabolical character of the Jews and the inferior status of their law and practice. He was especially agitated by the habit of some Christians in Antioch of celebrating Jewish holidays in the synagogue with the Jews. In the heat of his anger, he dramatically identified the Jews of his day with those whom he considered to be murderers of Christ.

READING 3-6

Do not be surprised if I have called the Jews wretched. They are truly wretched and miserable for they have received many good things from God yet they have spurned them and violently cast them away. The sun of righteousness rose on them first, but they turned their back on its beams and sat in darkness. But we, who were nurtured in darkness, welcomed the light and we were freed from the yoke of error. The Jews were branches of the holy root, but they were lopped off. We were not part of the root, yet we have produced the fruits of piety. They read the prophets from ancient times, yet they crucified the one spoken of by the prophets. We had not heard the Holy Scriptures, yet now we worship the one about whom the prophets speak. This is why they are wretched, because when others embraced and welcomed the good things given to them, the Jews refused them.

They were called to sonship, but they degenerated to the level of dogs. But we who were dogs were by the grace of God able to cast off our former irrationality to be elevated to the dignity of sons. How do I know this? "It is not right to take the children's bread and throw it to the dogs" (Matt 15:26). Jesus was speaking there to the Canaanite woman and he called the Jews "beloved children" and the Gentiles "dogs." But note how the order is reversed later; they have become "dogs" and we are "beloved children." Paul said this about them, "Beware of those dogs and their malpractices. Beware of those who insist on mutilation—'circumcision' I will not call it; we are the circumcised" (Phil 3:2–3). Don't you see how those who were formerly beloved children have become dogs? . . .

Consider with me how the prophet intimates that they [the Jews] are unmanageable. For he did not say, "You threw off my yoke," but "you broke my yoke." This is the shortcoming of wild animals, unused to the reins, who refuse to be tamed. Where does this stiffness come from? From gluttony and drunkenness. Moses himself said, "Israel ate, and he was well fed and grew fat, and the beloved became recalcitrant" (Deut 32:15). Just as animals, when they are allowed to eat as much as they want, grow fat and become stubborn and hard to hold, and neither the yoke, nor the bridle, nor the hand of the driver can restrain them, so also the Jewish people, by drunkenness and overeating have been driven to the ultimate evil. They have kicked up their hooves refusing to bear the yoke of Christ and to draw the plow of his teaching. One prophet intimated this when he said, "Israel has run wild, wild as a heifer." (Hos 4:16). Another called Israel an "unbroken calf" (Jer 31:18). Such animals, unfit for any useful work, are fit only for slaughter. This is what has happened since they made themselves unsuitable for any task. They are suited only for slaughter. This is why Christ said, "Those enemies of mine who did not want me for their king, bring them here and slaughter them" (Luke 19:27). . . .

I know that many have high regard for the Jews and they think that their present way of life is holy. That is why I am so anxious to uproot this deadly opinion. I said that the synagogue is no better than the theater and I submitted proof from the prophet. The Jews are not more trustworthy than the prophets. What did the prophet say? "Yours was a harlot's brow, and you were resolved to show no shame." (Jer 3:3). A place where a prostitute offers her wares is a house of prostitution. But the synagogue is not only a house of prostitution and a theater, it is also a hideout for thieves and a den of wild animals. "Your house has become for me a hyena's den." (Jer 7:11). But it is not simply the den of a wild animal but of an unclean one at that. Further, "I have forsaken my house, I have cast off my inheritance" (Jer 12:7). When God leaves, what hope of salvation remains? When God forsakes a place it becomes a dwelling place for demons.

Surely they say that they worship God. Away with such talk! No Jew worships God. Who says these things? The son of God. "If you knew me you would know my father as well. You know neither me nor my father." (John 8:19). What testimony can I offer that is more trustworthy than this one?

If they are ignorant of the Father, if they crucified the son, and spurned the aid of the Spirit, can one not declare with confidence that the synagogue is a dwelling place of demons? God is not worshipped there. Far from it! Rather the synagogue is a temple of idolatry. Nevertheless some go to these places as though they were sacred shrines. I am not imagining such things. I know them from my own experience.

ST. AUGUSTINE ON THE JEWS

The view of St. Augustine (345–430), bishop of Hippo in North Africa, is representative of the emerging position of the Jews in Christian society in late antiquity and the early Middle Ages. Augustine's attitude, eventually became the dominant theological view of the Church toward the Jews living in its domain, rather than that of Chrysostom and others like him whose verbal assaults could easily have been translated by extremists into physical abuse. Rather than charging that Jews should be killed, Augustine argued for a place among the living for them, albeit a life of misery and debasement. Since the Jews killed Christ, they deserved death but, like Cain who murdered his brother Abel, they were not to die but rather were doomed to wander the earth as witnesses to the ultimate truth of Christianity. The Jews were to exist in a pariah status, always present to testify to the final triumph of the Church. When Christ returns, the Jews finally would acknowledge their error, convert to Christianity, or be condemned to final damnation.

READING 3-7

Then God says to Cain: "Thou art cursed from the earth, which hath opened its mouth to receive thy brother's blood at thy hand. For thou shalt till the earth, and it shall no longer yield unto thee its strength. A mourner and an abject shalt thou be on earth." It is not, Cursed is the earth, but, Cursed art thou from the earth, which hath opened its mouth to receive thy brother's blood at thy hand. So the unbelieving people of the Jews is cursed from the earth, that is, from the Church, which in the confession of sins has opened its mouth to receive the blood shed for the remission of sins by the hand of the people that would not be under grace, but under the law. And this murderer is cursed by the Church; that is, the Church admits and avows the curse pronounced by the apostle: "Whoever are the works of the law are under the curse of the law." Then, after saying, Cursed art thou from the earth, which has opened its mouth to receive thy brother's blood at thy hand, what follows is not, For thou shalt till it, but, Thou shalt till the earth, and it shall not yield to thee its strength. The earth he is to till is not necessarily the same as that which opened its mouth to receive his brother's blood at his hand. From this earth he is cursed, and so he tills an earth which shall no longer yield to him its strength. That is, the Church admits and avows the Jewish people to be cursed, because after killing Christ they continue to till the ground of an earthly circumcision, an earthly Sabbath, an earthly passover, while the hidden strength or virtue of making known Christ, which this tilling contains, is not yielded to the Jews while they continue in impiety and unbelief, for it is revealed in the New Testament. While they will not turn to God, the veil which is on their minds in reading the Old Testament is not taken away. This veil is taken away only by Christ, who does not do away with the reading of the Old Testament, but with the covering which hides its virtues. So, at the crucifixion of Christ, the veil was rent in twain, that by the passion of Christ hidden mysteries might be revealed to believers who turn to Him with a mouth opened in confession to drink His blood. In this way the Jewish people, like Cain, continue tilling the ground, in the carnal observance of the law, which does not yield to them its strength, because they do not perceive in it the grace of Christ. So, too, the flesh of Christ was the ground from which by crucifying Him the Jews produced our salvation, for He died for our offences. But this ground did not yield to them its strength, for they were not justified by the virtue of His resurrection, for He arose again for our justification. As the apostle says: "He was crucified in weakness, but He liveth by the power of God." This is the power of that ground which is unknown to the ungodly and unbelieving. When Christ rose, He did not appear to those who had crucified Him. So Cain was not allowed to see the strength of the ground which he tilled to sow his seed in it; as God said, "Thou shalt till the ground, and it shall no longer yield unto thee its strength."

"Groaning and trembling shalt thou be on the earth." Here no one can fail to see that in every land where the Jews are scattered they mourn for the loss of their kingdom, and are in terrified subjection to the immensely superior number of Christians. So Cain answered, and said: "My case is worse, if Thou drivest me out this day from the face of the earth, and from Thy face shall I be hid, and I shall be a mourner and an outcast on the earth; and it shall be that every one that findeth me shall slay me." Here he groans indeed in terror, lest after losing his earthly possession he should suffer the death of the body. This he calls a worse case than that of the ground not yielding to him its strength, or than that of spiritual death. For his mind is carnal; for he thinks little of being hid from the face of God, that is, of being under the anger of God, were it not that he may be found and slain. This is the carnal mind that tills the ground, but does not obtain its strength. To be carnally minded is death; but he, in ignorance of this, mourns for the loss of his earthly possession, and is in terror of bodily death. But what does God reply? "Not so," He says;

"but whosoever shall kill Cain, vengeance shall be taken on him sevenfold." That is, It is not as thou sayest; not by bodily death shall the ungodly race of carnal Jews perish. For whoever destroys them in this way shall suffer sevenfold vengeance, that is, shall bring upon himself the sevenfold penalty under which the Jews lie for the crucifixion of Christ. So to the end of the seven days of time, the continued preservation of the Jews will be a proof to believing Christians of the subjection merited by those who, in the pride of their kingdom, put the Lord to death.

ROMAN LAW CONCERNING THE JEWS

When the Emperor Constantine (306–37) converted to Christianity, Christianity gradually was transformed from a persecuted faith into the official religion of the Roman Empire. With the ascendancy of Christianity, the political and social status of the Jews gradually deteriorated, especially under the statutes of Theodosius II of the the fifth century and, later, under the revisions of Justinian in the sixth century. Shorter revisions of the Code of Justinian were incorporated into canon law and eventually served as the basis for medieval Christian legislation.

The following excerpts of specific laws pertaining to the Jews illustrate the increasing disabilities they faced within a political state under the direct influence of Christian theology: the Jews were prohibited from proselytizing Christians, from owning Christian slaves, and from marrying Christians; they were excluded from holding all civil and military offices, from building new synagogues or repairing old ones, and from bearing witness in court against orthodox Christians. Thus Christian theology deleteriously affected the political and economic status of the Jews living within the Roman Empire—both in the East and the West—and directly influenced their subsequent status in medieval Christian and Muslim societies.

READING 3-8

Laws of Constantine the Great, October 18, 315

We wish to make it known to the Jews and their elders and their patriarchs that if, after the enactment of this law, any one of them dares to attack with stones or some other manifestation of anger another who has fled their dangerous sect and attached himself to the worship of God [Christianity], he must speedily be given to the flames and burnt together with all his accomplices.

Moreover, if any one of the population should join their abominable sect and attend their meetings, he will bear with them the deserved penalties.

Laws of Constantius, August 13, 339

This pertains to women, who live in our weaving factories and whom Jews, in their foulness, take in marriage. It is decreed that these women are to be restored to the weaving factories. [Marriages between Jews and Christian women of the imperial weaving factory are to be dissolved.]

This prohibition [of intermarriage] is to be preserved for the future lest the Jews induce Christian women to share their shameful lives. If they do this they will subject themselves to a sentence of death. . . .

If any one among the Jews has purchased a slave of another sect or nation, that slave shall at once be appropriated for the imperial treasury.

If, indeed, he shall have circumcised the slave whom he has purchased, he will not only be fined for the damage done to that slave but he will also receive capital punishment.

If, indeed, a Jew does not hesitate to purchase slaves—those who are members of the faith that is worthy of respect [Christianity]—then all these slaves who are found in his possession shall at once be removed. No delay shall be occasioned, but he is to be deprived of the possession of those men who are Christians.

A Law of Theodosius II, January 31, 439

Wherefore, although according to an old saying [of the Greek Hippocrates, the "father" of medicine] "no cure is to be applied in desperate sicknesses," nevertheless, in order that these dangerous sects which are unmindful of our times may not spread into life the more freely, in indiscriminate disorder as it were, we ordain by this law to be valid for all time:

No Jew—or no Samaritan who subscribes to neither [the Jewish nor the Christian] religion—shall obtain offices and dignities; to none shall the administration of city service be permitted; nor shall any one exercise the office of a defender [that is, overseer] of the city. Indeed, we believe it sinful that the enemies of the heavenly majesty and of the Roman laws should become the executors of our laws—the administration of which they have slyly obtained—and that they, fortified by the authority of the acquired rank, should have the power to judge or decide as they wish against Christians, yes, frequently even over bishops of our holy religion themselves, and thus, as it were, insult our faith.

Moreover, for the same reason, we forbid that any synagogue shall rise as a new building. However, the propping up of old synagogues which are now threatened with imminent ruin is permitted. To these things we add that he who misleads a slave or a freeman against his will or by punishable advice, from the service of the Christian religion to that of an abominable sect and ritual, is to be punished by loss of property and life.

POPE GREGORY I ON THE JEWS

Gregory the Great (590–604) was one of the first of the popes to formulate a coherent policy toward the Jews, laying the foundation for later medieval canon law intended to regulate Jewish life in Christian Europe. His position closely followed the previous regulations of Roman legislation; it also approximated the Augustinian theology of tolerating the Jews while allowing them to suffer punishment for their infidelity. When Christians sought to go beyond this policy by injuring Jewish life or property, however, he vigorously protested. In the two letters below, he objects to forced baptism and to the seizure of a synagogue by Church officials.

When a synagogue was consecrated as a church, making its return to the Jewish community impossible, he attempted to secure restitution for the Jews in monetary payment and to relocate lost religious articles.

READING 3-9

June 591—Gregory to Virgilius, Bishop of Arles, and Theodorus, Bishop of Marseilles, in Gaul

Though the opportunity of a suitable time and suitable persons for writing to your Fraternity and duly returning your salutation has failed me so far, the result has been that I can now at one and the same time acquit myself of what is due to love and fraternal relationship, and also touch on the complaint of certain persons which has reached us, with respect to the way in which the souls of the erring should be saved.

Very many, though indeed of the Jewish religion, resident in this province [Rome], and from time to time traveling for various matters of business to the regions of Marseilles, have apprized us that many of the Jews settled in those parts have been brought to the font of baptism more by force than by preaching. Now I consider the intention in such cases to be worthy of praise, and allow that it proceeds from the love of our Lord. But I fear lest this same intention, unless adequate justification from [a verse of] Holy Scripture accompany it, should either have no profitable effect; or there will ensue further (God forbid) the loss of the very souls which we wish to save.

For, when any one is brought to the font of baptism, not by the sweetness of preaching but by compulsion, he returns to his former superstition, and dies the worse from having been born again.

Let, therefore, your Fraternity stir up such men by frequent preaching, to the end that through the sweetness of their teacher they may desire the more to change their old life. For so our purpose is rightly accomplished, and the mind of the convert returns not again to his former vomit. Wherefore discourse must be addressed to them, such as may burn up the thorns of error in them, and illuminate what is dark in them by preaching, so that your Fraternity may through your frequent admonition receive a reward for them, and lead them, so far as God may grant it, to the regeneration of a new life.

October 598—Gregory to Fantinus, Defensor [papal administrator] of Palermo

A little time ago we wrote to Victor, our brother and fellow-bishop, that—inasmuch as certain of the Jews have complained in a petition presented to us that synagogues with their guest-chambers [for the poor and ailing], situated in the city of Palermo, had been unreasonably taken possession of by him—he should keep aloof from the consecration of them [as churches] until it could be ascertained whether this thing had actually been done, lest perchance injury should appear to have been alleged by the Jews of their own [ill] will. And, indeed, having regard to his priestly office, we could not easily believe that our aforesaid brother [Victor] had done anything unsuitably.

But, we found from the report of Salarius, our notary, who was afterwards there, that there had been no reasonable cause for taking possession of those synagogues, and that they had been unadvisedly and rashly consecrated. We therefore enjoin thy Experience (since what has been once consecrated cannot any more be restored to the Jews) that it be thy care to see that our aforesaid brother and fellow-bishop pay the price at which our sons, the glorious Venantius the Patrician and Urbicus the Abbot, may value the synagogues themselves with the guest-chambers that are under them or annexed to their walls, and the gardens thereto adjoining. Thus what he has caused to be taken possession of may belong to the Church, and they [the Jews] may in no wise be oppressed or suffer any injustice.

Moreover, let books or ornaments that have been carried off be in like manner sought for. And, if any have been openly taken away, we desire them also to be restored without any question. For, as there ought to be no license for them to do anything in their synagogues beyond what is decreed by law, so neither damage nor any cost ought to be brought upon them contrary to justice and equity, as we have ourselves already written. [Gregory here refers to his letter of June, 598, to Victor, Bishop of Palermo: "Just as one ought not to grant any freedom to the Jews in their synagogues beyond that permitted by law, so should the Jews in no way suffer in those things already conceded to them."]

THE *KORAN* ON THE "CHILDREN OF ISRAEL"

The rise of Islam in the seventh century C.E. had far-reaching consequences for Jewish life. Jewish civilization, in turn, left a noticeable impact on Islamic faith and practice. As early as Muhammad's initial years in Mecca and Medina, he undoubtedly established intimate contacts with members of the Jewish community long settled in the Arabian peninsula. The *Koran*, the written record of Muhammad's revelation, amply testifies to his debt to Jewish traditions. Not only did he appropriate Abraham and Moses (as well as Jesus) as prophets of the new faith who preceded the seal of Muhammad's prophecy; he also freely utilized Jewish concepts and literary motifs throughout Muslim scripture. Rabbinic Judaism thus left a fundamental imprint on Islam from its inception, as it had similarly done with respect to Christianity.

Sura Two, entitled "The Cow" (*al-Baquarah*), is a summary of the essential aspects of Muhammad's revelation and also relates the prophet's experiences with Jews, his discussions with them, and his efforts to persuade them of the veracity of his new faith. The selections below illustrate Muhammad's use of biblical themes; his contention that he had not come to abrogate the truths of Judaism and Christianity but to fulfill them; his view that Abraham was neither a Jew nor a Christian but the true expounder of ethical monotheism; and that the *Koran*, as revealed to Muhammad by Allah, embodied the true revelation which both the Jews and Christians fail to follow.

READING 3-10

To Moses We gave the Scriptures and after him We sent other apostles. We gave Jesus the son of Mary veritable signs and strengthened him with the Holy Spirit. Will you then scorn each apostle whose message does not suit your fancies, charging some with imposture and slaying others?

They say: 'Our hearts are sealed.' But Allah has cursed them for their unbelief. They have but little faith.

And now that a Book confirming their Scriptures has been revealed to them by Allah, they deny it, although they know it to be the truth and have long prayed for help against the unbelievers. May Allah's curse be upon the infidels! Evil is that for which they have bartered away their souls. To deny Allah's own revelation, grudging that He should reveal His bounty to whom He chooses from His servants! They have incurred Allah's most inexorable wrath. An ignominious punishment awaits the unbelievers.

When it is said to them: 'Believe in what Allah has revealed,' they reply: 'We believe in what was revealed to *us*.' But they deny what has since been revealed, although it is the truth, corroborating their own scriptures.

Say: 'Why did you kill the prophets of Allah, if you are true believers? Moses came to you with veritable signs, but in his absence you worshipped the calf and committed evil.'

When We made a covenant with you and raised the Mount above you, saying: 'Take what We have given you with willing hearts and hear Our commandments,' you replied: 'We hear but disobey.' . . .

Children of Israel, remember that I have bestowed favours upon you and exalted you above the nations. Fear the day when every soul shall stand alone: when neither intercession nor ransom shall be accepted from it, nor any help be given it.

When his Lord put Abraham to the proof by enjoining on him certain commandments and Abraham fulfilled them, He said: 'I have appointed you a leader of mankind.'

'And what of my descendants?' asked Abraham.

'My covenant,' said He, 'does not apply to the evil-doers.'

We made the House a resort and a sanctuary for mankind, saying: 'Make the place where Abraham stood a house of worship.' We enjoined Abraham and Ishmael to cleanse Our House for those who walk round it, who meditate in it, and who kneel and prostrate themselves.

'Lord,' said Abraham, 'make this a land of peace and bestow plenty upon its people, those of them that believe in Allah and the Last Day.'

'As for those that do not,' He answered, 'I shall let them live awhile and then drag them to the scourge of Hell. Evil shall be their fate.'

Abraham and Ishmael built the House and dedicated it, saying: 'Accept this from us, Lord. You hear all and You know all. Make us submissive to You; make of our descendants a nation that will submit to You. Teach us our rites of worship and turn to us mercifully; You are forgiving and merciful. Send forth to them an apostle of their own who shall declare to them Your revelations and instruct them in the Scriptures and in wisdom and purify them of sin. You are the Mighty, the Wise One.'

Who but a foolish man would renounce the faith of Abraham? We chose him in this world, and in the world to come he shall dwell among the righteous. When his

Lord said to him: 'Submit,' he answered: 'I have submitted to the Lord of the Creation.'

Abraham enjoined the faith on his children, and so did Jacob, saying: 'My children, Allah has chosen for you the true faith. Do not depart this life except as men who have submitted to Him.'

Were you present when death came to Jacob? He said to his children: 'What will you worship when I am gone?' They replied: 'We will worship your God and the God of your forefathers Abraham and Ishmael and Isaac: the One God. To Him we will surrender ourselves.'

That nation have passed away. Theirs is what they did, and yours what you have done. You shall not be questioned about their actions.

They say: 'Accept the Jewish or the Christian faith and you shall be rightly guided.'

Say: 'By no means! We believe in the faith of Abraham, the upright one. He was no idolater.'

Say: 'We believe in Allah and that which is revealed to us; we believe in what was revealed to Abraham, Ishmael, Isaac, Jacob, and the tribes; to Moses and Jesus and the other prophets. We make no distinction between any of them, and to Allah we have surrendered ourselves.' . . .

THE PACT OF UMAR

By the middle of the seventh century the legal treatment of the Jews in Muslim society already was established. The Jews were part of a protected minority called *dhimmis*, which included Christians, Zoroastrians, and a few other communities. In return for payment of a poll tax (*jizya*) and a land tax (*kharāj*) and for tolerating other discriminatory practices, many of which had been present in Roman, Byzantine, and Persian law, the *dhimmis* received assurances of religious tolerance and security for their lives and property. Most importantly, their religious communities were allowed to live under their own jurisdiction without excessive governmental interference. In contrast to their more problematic status in Christian lands, the Jews enjoyed considerable protection and privileges within Muslim societies and usually were not subject to physical abuse.

The pact of Umar, a document of surrender extended by the second caliph Umar b. al-Khattāb (ruled 634–44) to the patriarch of Jerusalem, became the model for the treatment of *dhimmis* in the new Muslim empire. Whether or not the actual text is genuine, it embodies the basic provisions and restrictions underlying the policy of the Muslim state towards "the people of the Book."

READING 3-11

Abd al-Raḥmān b. Ghanam [died 697 C.E.] related the following: When Umar b. al-Khaṭṭāb—may Allah be pleased with him—made peace with the Christian inhabitants of Syria, we wrote him the following.

In the name of Allah, the Merciful, the Beneficent.

This letter is addressed to Allah's servant Umar, the Commander of the Faithful, by the Christians of such-and-such city. When you advanced against us, we asked you for a guarantee of protection for our persons, our offspring, our property, and the people of our sect, and we have taken upon ourselves the following obligations toward you, namely:

We shall not build in our cities or in their vicinity any new monasteries, churches, hermitages, or monks' cells. We shall not restore, by night or by day, any of them that have fallen into ruin or which are located in the Muslims' quarters.

We shall keep our gates wide open for passersby and travelers. We shall provide three days' food and lodging to any Muslims who pass our way.

We shall not shelter any spy in our churches or in our homes, nor shall we hide him from the Muslims.

We shall not teach our children the Koran.

We shall not hold public religious ceremonies. We shall not seek to proselytize anyone. We shall not prevent any of our kin from embracing Islam if they so desire.

We shall show deference to the Muslims and shall rise from our seats when they wish to sit down.

We shall not attempt to resemble the Muslims in any way with regard to their dress, as for example, with the *qalansuwa* [a conical cap], the turban, sandals, or parting the hair (in the Arab fashion). We shall not speak as they do, nor shall we adopt their *kunyas* [the Arabic byname, formed with *abū* (father of, or possessor of)].

We shall not ride on saddles.

We shall not wear swords or bear weapons of any kind, or ever carry them with us.

We shall not engrave our signets in Arabic.

We shall not sell wines.

We shall clip the forelocks of our head.

We shall always adorn ourselves in our traditional fashion. We shall bind the *zunnar* [a kind of belt] around our waists.

We shall not display our crosses or our books anywhere in the Muslims' thoroughfares or in their marketplaces. We shall only beat our clappers in our churches very quietly. We shall not raise our voices when reciting the service in our churches, nor when in the presence of Muslims. Neither shall we raise our voices in our funeral processions.

We shall not display lights in any of the Muslim thoroughfares or in their marketplaces.

We shall not come near them with our funeral processions.

We shall not take any of the slaves that have been allotted to the Muslims.

We shall not build our homes higher than theirs.

(When I brought the letter to Umar—may Allah be pleased with him—he added the clause "We shall not strike any Muslim.")

We accept these conditions for ourselves and for the members of our sect, in return for which we are to be given a guarantee of security. Should we violate in any way these conditions which we have accepted and for which we stand security, then there shall be no covenant of protection for us, and we shall be liable to the penalties for rebelliousness and sedition.

Then Umar—may Allah be pleased with him—wrote: "Sign what they have requested, but add two clauses that will also be binding upon them; namely, they shall not buy anyone who has been taken prisoner by the Muslims, and that anyone who deliberately strikes a Muslim will forfeit the protection of this pact."

THE ITINERARY OF THE RADHANITE JEWISH MERCHANTS

Writing at the end of the ninth century, a Muslim geographer named ibn Khurradadhbih described the existence of a group of long-distance traders who lived in the eighth century, called the Radhanites, apparently from a region near Baghdad. These merchants, trading in slaves and luxury goods, traveled from the Middle East to the Slavic regions of the North, across Europe to Spain, and finally returned home via North Africa. They also traveled to the Far East, to India, and to China. In a period with relatively few links between the East and the West, this notable group functioned as intermediaries between the two continents and foreshadowed the vigorous mercantile activities of Jewish merchants from the ninth through twelfth centuries recorded in the Cairo *genizah* (storehouse of discarded Jewish writings).

READING 3-12

They speak Arabic, Persian, Greek, Frankish, Andalusian, and Slavonic. They travel from East to West and from West to East by both land and sea. From the West, they bring adult slaves, girls and boys, brocade, beaver pelts, assorted furs, sables, and swords. They sail from the Land of the Franks [possibly the Frankish-ruled part of Italy] on the Western Sea (the Mediterranean) and set out for al-Faramā (Pelusium—a port on the easternmost branch of the Nile). There they transport their merchandise by pack animal to al-Qulzum [a port on the Red Sea], which is twenty-five parasangs away [a parasang is six kilometers]. At al-Qulzum they set sail for al-Jār [on the Red Sea coast of Arabia, the port of Medina] and Jidda [the port of Mecca] after which they proceed to Sind [the lower Indus River valley and delta], India, and China. From China they bring musk, aloeswood, camphor, cinnamon, and other products obtained from those regions, as they make their way back to al-Qulzum. Then they transport it overland to al-Faramā, there setting sail on the Western Sea once again. Some go straight to Constantinople to sell their merchandise to the Byzantines, while others go to the capital of the king of the Franks and sell their goods there.

Sometimes they choose to take their merchandise from the Land of the Franks across the Western Sea to Antioch, and thence overland on a three-day journey to al-Jābiya [a town south of Damascas], from which they sail down the Euphrates to Baghdad, then down the Tigris to Ubulla [a port in southern Iraq]. From Ubulla they sail to Oman, Sind, India, and China—in that order.

As for their overland itinerary—those of them that set out from Spain or the Land of the Franks can cross over to the Further Sūs [probably the Berber region of Southwest Morocco], go from there to Tangier, and then across to Ifrīqiya (Tunisia), Egypt, Ramle, Damascus, Kufa, Baghdad, Basra, Ahwaz, Fars, Kirman, Sind, India, and finally, China. Sometimes they take the route behind the Byzantine Empire through the Land of the Slavs to Khamlīj, the capital of the Khazars. Then they cross the Sea of Jurjān (the Caspian) toward Balkh and Transoxania. From there they continue to Yurt and Tughuzghuzz [in Central Asia], and finally to China.

NATHAN THE BABYLONIAN ON THE INSTALLATION OF THE EXILARCH

With the rise of the Abbasid capital of Baghdad in the eighth century, the Jewish community of the region (which formerly had been called Babylonia) gradually rose to a position of renewed prominence. The academies of Sura and Pumbedita were revived and functioned as centers of rabbinic learning and codification as they had done in previous centuries. The head of the academy was called a *Gaon* (*Geonim*, plural), and his authority both in Baghdad and throughout the Abbasid realm was even greater at times than that of the exilarch, the other leader of the community, who claimed to be a descendant of the house of David.

A precious Hebrew chronicle of the early tenth century, written by one Nathan the Babylonian, provides a revealing portrait of the academies of Baghdad, the power of the *geonim*, and especially that of a few families of court bankers known as the Bnai Aaron and Netira families. By virtue of their considerable economic standing at the caliphate court, these bankers were able to exercise substantial influence in the political affairs of the Jewish community. The selection below provides a vivid account of the installation of the exilarch, the pomp and circumstance surrounding the ceremony, the role of the *geonim* in the ceremony, and generally the political and social life of the community's leadership.

READING 3-13

R. Nathan ha-Kohen [ha-Bavlī] went on to describe the appointment of the Exilarch and how the people paid their allegiance to him at that time. It was as follows:

When there was a communal consensus on the appointment, the two Heads of the Yeshivot, together with their students, all the leaders of the congregation, and the elders, would gather in some prominent individual's house in Baghdad. He would be one of the greatest of that generation, such as Netira or the like. The man in whose home they gather is singled out for honor by this and receives much praise. His standing is enhanced by this meeting of the leaders and elders in his home.

The community would gather in the main synagogue on Thursday. The Exilarch would be installed by the laying of hands. The shofar was sounded to let all the people know from the youngest to the eldest. And when everyone heard it, each of them would send him a gift—each according to his means. All the leaders of the congregation and the wealthy would send him fine clothes, jewelry, and gold and silver vessels—each as he saw fit. The Exilarch, for his part, would take great pains in preparing a feast for Thursday and Friday which included all kinds of food and drink, and all sorts of confections, such as various sweets.

When he arose on Saturday to go to the synagogue, many of the prominent members of the community would join him in order to accompany him there. At the synagogue a wooden dais has already been specially prepared for him. It was seven cubits in length and three in width. It was entirely covered with fine fabrics of blue, purple, and crimson silk. Under the dais stood young men who had been chosen from amongst the leading families of the community. These young men were distinguished for their sweet, pleasant voices. They had to be well versed in all aspects of prayer.

Meanwhile, the Exilarch himself was hidden from sight together with the Heads of the Yeshivot [academies]. So at this time, while the youths were standing beneath the dais, there was no one at all sitting on it. . . .

When everyone was seated, the Exilarch would emerge from the place where he was hidden, and when the people saw him, they would all rise to their feet and remain standing until he was seated alone on the dais that had been set up for him. Next, the Head of the Sura Yeshiva would come out and take a seat on the dais after bowing to the Exilarch, who would return the bow. After him, the Head of the Pumbeditha Yeshiva emerges, bows, and sits to the Exilarch's left. Throughout all this, the people remain standing until all three have taken their seats—the Exilarch in the center, the Sura Gaon on his right, and the Pumbeditha Gaon on his left. An empty space remained between each of the Geonim and the Exilarch. Over his head was spread a canopy of precious fabric which was suspended by a cord of fine linen and purple.

At this point, the Cantor would lean his head under the canopy and bless the Exilarch with benedictions which had been specially composed for the occasion one or two days before. He would do this in a low voice which could only be heard by those seated on the dais and by the choir under it. As he is blessing him, the young men would respond in loud chorus "Amen!" But the entire congregation remains silent throughout his blessing.

The Exilarch now begins the sermon, expounding on the Torah portion for that Sabbath. Or, he might give permission to the Sura Gaon to open with the sermon, and the Sura Gaon, in turn, would grant permission to the Pumbeditha Gaon. In this way, they show their deference to one another, until finally, the Head of the Sura Yeshiva begins. An interpreter who is standing near him passes his words on to the people. He would deliver the sermon in an awe-inspiring manner with his eyes closed. He would envelop himself in his prayershawl which he pulled over his head and down to the brow. No one in the congregation would open his mouth, twitter, or say a word while he was speaking. Should he feel, however, that someone was talking, he would open his eyes, and fear and trembling would descend over the congregation. At the conclusion of the sermon, he would present a problem with the formula: "Indeed, you should study." A wise and learned elder would stand, give an answer, and then sit down again.

The Cantor now recited the Kaddish [the Aramaic doxology recited at the conclusion of various parts of the service]. When he reached the words "in your lifetime and in your days," he would add "and during the lifetime of our Prince, the Exilarch" before continuing with "and during the lifetime of all the House of Israel." Upon finishing the Kaddish, he again blessed the Exilarch, and after him the Heads of the Yeshivot. With the blessings completed, he now declares: "Such-and-such a city and its villages have contributed such-and-such a sum to the Yeshiva. He mentions all the cities that have sent contributions, and he blesses them. Next, he blesses those individuals who are responsible for collecting the contributions and who look after them until they reach the Yeshivot. . . .

As the Exilarch departs, all the people accompany him to his house in a procession, going before and after him, singing his praises. The Heads of the Yeshivot, however, do not go with him. The Exilarch does not permit any of the scholars who have accompanied him to his house to leave until they have enjoyed at least seven days' hospitality. From that time on, he does not leave his house. People gather and pray with him there, be it on secular days, sabbaths, or holidays. If he does have to go out on some business, he rides in the litter of an official similar to that of the Caliph's ministers. He would be beautifully attired. Behind him would walk a train of as many as fifteen men. His servant would run after him. Should he happen to pass any Israelites, they would run up to him, touch his hands, and greet him. As many as fifty or sixty people might do this both on his way to his destination and upon his return home. This is the custom. He would never go out without his entourage, just like any of the Caliph's ministers.

Whenever the Exilarch wishes to appear before the Caliph either to request something or simply to wait upon him, he asks the Caliph's viziers and servants who have regular entry to his court to speak to the Caliph, so that he may grant him the permission to come into his presence. The Caliph then grants the permission and orders the guards at the palace gate to admit him. When the Exilarch enters, the Caliph's slaves would run before him. He comes prepared with dinars and dirhams in his pocket to distribute to all those slaves who usher him in. He would continually be putting his hand into his bosom pocket and giving each and every one whatever God had ordained for him. They in turn treat him with honor and touch his hand until he comes into the presence of the Caliph and bows to him. The Caliph signals to one of his retainers who takes the Exilarch by the hand and seats him in the spot which the Caliph has indicated. The Exilarch then converses with the Caliph. The latter would ask after his health and his affairs, and the purpose of the visit. The Exilarch then requests permission to address him which is immediately granted. He then begins with praises and blessings formally prepared beforehand in which he eulogizes the Caliph's ancestors. He conciliates him with kind words until his request is granted and he is given what he has asked. The Caliph then commands that a decree be written to that effect, and the Exilarch retires, happily taking his leave.

FROM *THE BOOK OF BELIEFS AND OPINIONS* OF SAADIA GAON

Political and economic interaction between Jews and Muslims in Baghdad also was translated into cultural dialogue. Of particular importance in this regard was the revival of Greek philosophical and scientific learning at the Abbasid court and its impact on Islamic and Jewish theology. Muslim philosophers, especially those associated with the school of the *Kalam*, strove to harmonize their own faith with rational thought as conceived by Greek philosophy. In a similar manner, Jewish thinkers struggled with the same problem of reconciling the truths of their divine revelation with those of Aristotle and Plato. The most important Jewish philosopher in Baghdad was Saadia Gaon (882–942). Born in Egypt, he eventually settled in Baghdad where he pursued a stormy community and literary career. Saadia saw himself as the foremost representative of rabbinic Judaism in his era and expended all his energy in defending it against its detractors: Karaites, who challenged the authority of the rabbis to interpret the *Torah*, Palestinian rabbis who challenged rabbinic hegemony in Baghdad, and philosophic skeptics. Saadia's philosophical treatise, *The Book of Beliefs and Opinions*, from which the excerpt below is taken, attempts to demonstrate the authenticity and rationality of divine revelation as understood by the rabbis. For Saadia, Judaism's validity rested on its demonstrability. Subjective certitude was no longer enough; a Jewish religious thinker now was required to substantiate philosophically what already was revealed. Still, a Jewish philosopher needed the immediate certitude and emotional assurance that belief in divine revelation could offer him. Reprinted from *Three Jewish Philosophers* by permission of Hebrew Publishing Company.

READING 3-14

The reader of this book should know that we inquire and speculate in matters of our religion for two reasons: (1) in order that we may find out for ourselves what we know in the way of imparted knowledge from the Prophets of God; (2) in order that we may be able to refute those who attack us on matters connected with our religion. For our Lord (be He blessed and exalted) instructed us in everything which we require in the way of religion, through the intermediacy of the Prophets after having established for us the truth of prophecy by signs and miracles. He commanded us to believe these matters and to keep them. He also informed us that by speculation and inquiry we shall attain to certainty on every point in accordance with the Truth revealed through the words of His Messenger.

In this way we speculate and search in order that we may make our own what our Lord has taught us by way of instruction. There is, however, another objection which we have to consider. It may be asked: If the doctrines of religion can be discovered by rational inquiry and speculation, as God has told us, how can it be reconciled with His wisdom that He announced them to us by way of prophetic Revelation and verified them by proofs and signs of a visible character, and not by rational arguments? To this we will give a complete answer with the help of God. We say: God knew in His wisdom that the final propositions which result from the labour of speculation can only be attained in a certain measure of time. Had he, therefore, made us depend on speculation for religious knowledge, we should have existed without religion for some time until the work of speculation was completed and our labour had come to an end. Perhaps many of us would never have completed the work because of their inability and never have finished their labour because of their lack of patience; or doubts may have come upon them, and confused and bewildered their minds. From all these troubles God (be He exalted and glorified) saved us quickly by sending us His Messenger, announcing through him the Tradition, and allowing us to see with our own eyes signs in support of it and proofs which cannot be assailed by doubts, and which we can find no ground for rejecting, as is said, 'Ye yourselves have seen that I have talked with you from heaven.' He spoke to His Messenger in our presence, and He based on this fact our obligation to believe him for ever, as He said, 'That the people may hear when I speak with thee, and may also believe thee for ever.' So we were immediately obliged to accept the teaching of religion with all that it implies since it was verified by the testimony of sense perception, and its acceptance is obligatory on the strength of the reliable Tradition which has been handed down to us as we shall explain. He commanded us to inquire patiently until the truth of Tradition was brought out by speculation, and not to depart from our religious position before its truth was verified, since we are obliged to believe in it on account of what we saw with our eyes and heard with our ears. In the case of some of us it may take a very long time until our speculation is completed, but we shall be none the worse for that, and if another one is held up in his studies on account of some hindrance, he will nevertheless not remain without religion. Even women and children and people incapable of speculation will possess a complete religion and be aware of its truths, for all human beings are equal so far as the knowledge of the senses is concerned. Praise unto Him Whose wisdom guideth man! This is why we find that the Torah mentions in many passages children and women in addition to the men when speaking of signs and miracles.

A KARAITE REFUTATION OF SAADIA'S DEFENSE OF RABBINIC JUDAISM

Widespread sectarian conflict was present in Islamic society during the early Middle Ages and was mirrored in Jewish society as well. The most significant sectarian challenge to rabbinic Judaism was offered by a sect called the Karaites (from the Hebrew *mikra*, "scriptures"). Founded by Anan ben David around 760, the Karaites emerged as a powerful movement in the tenth and eleventh centuries. The later Karaites emphatically rejected rabbinic legal authority, encouraged individualistic biblical interpretation, and demonstrated great interest in theological speculation. They produced a rich literature in Arabic and Hebrew in such areas as law, biblical exegesis, Hebrew philology, and philosophy.

Saadia's polemic against the Karaites, which helped launch his own literary career, ironically generated a virtual outpouring of theological response on the part of Karaite thinkers. One of the most outspoken of the Karaite critics of Saadia and rabbinic Judaism was Solomon ben Yeruḥam (ca. 910 to after 960). Solomon's principal work was a polemical epistle, written in rhymed quatrains in Hebrew, and possibly in Arabic as well, entitled *Book of the Wars of the Lord* (*Sefer Milḥamot ha-Shem*). His arguments against the Fayyumite (Saadia) concern the validity of the oral law of the rabbis, especially the lack of unanimity among the rabbis of the *Mishnah* and the *Talmud*.

READING 3-15

I have discovered in my heart another argument,
  A handsome one, and majestic enough
To be placed as a crown for the Karaites,
  To be their ornament, pride, and glory.
I have looked again into the six divisions of the Mishnah,
  And behold, they represent the words of modern men.
There are no majestic signs and miracles in them,
  And they lack the formula: "And the Lord spoke unto Moses
    and unto Aaron."
I therefore put them aside, and I said, There is no true Law in
    them,
  For the Law is set forth in a different manner,
In a majestic display of prophets, of signs, and of miracles;
  Yet all this majestic beauty we do not see in the whole
    Mishnah. . . .
I have set the six divisions of the Mishnah before me,
  And I looked at them carefully with mine eyes.
And I saw that they are very contradictory in content,
  This one Mishnaic scholar declares a thing to be forbidden to the
    people of Israel, while that one declares it to be permitted.
My thoughts therefore answer me,
  And most of my reflections declare unto me,
That there is in it no Law of logic,
  Nor the Law of Moses the Wise.
I said, Perhaps one of the two did not know the right way,
  Wherefore he did not know how to reason it out with his
    companion;
Perhaps the truth lies with his companion;
  Let me look into his words; perchance I will find relief from
    my perplexity.
But instead I found there other men—
  Sometimes they say, "Others say,"
While anon the scholars issue a decision,
  Agreeing neither with the one nor with the other, but
    contradicting both.

Had I been among them—I say, had I been among them—
   I would not have accepted the words of these "others" and
     "scholars."
Rather would I have weighed the word of the Lord with them,
   And I would have judged accordingly every word which they
     had contrived. . . .
Hearken unto me and I will speak further:
   If thou shouldst say, "This took place in the days of the
     Prophets and in the days of Ezra";
Why is there no mention in it of these Prophets
   In the same manner as the names of the Prophets are recorded
     throughout Scripture?
Be silent, and I will teach thee wisdom,
   If it be thy desire to learn wisdom.
It is written: *The Law of the Lord is perfect*
   What profit be there for us, then, in the written Mishnah?
Moreover, if the Talmud originated with our master Moses,
   What profit is there for us in "another view,"
And what can a third and a fourth view teach us,
   When they tell us first that the interpretation of this problem
     in law is thus-and-so, and then proceed to explain it with
     "another view?"
The truth stands upon one view only,
   For this is so in the wisdom of all mankind,
And right counsel cannot be based upon two contradictory
     things.
   Now in this one thing he has fallen down and cannot stand up:
If the Talmud is composed of the words of prophets,
   Why are contradictory views found in it?
Now it is evident that this view of Sa'adiah's is foolishness, and
     the words of fools.
   So testify all mankind.

AGOBARD OF LYONS' COMPLAINTS ABOUT JEWISH INFLUENCE ON CHRISTIAN SOCIETY

By the ninth century firm evidence exists for Jewish settlement in western Europe. In the Carolingian period Charlemagne and his son, Louis the Pious, made a special effort to attract Jewish merchants to their northern French and German lands. Jews were offered a stipulated legal status within Christian society and the benefit of physical protection in return for the fiscal and administrative benefits they provided feudal lords and, later, the kings.

Church officials soon realized that, solely on the basis of mutual economic self-interest, the Jews were fashioning a favorable relationship with ruling Christian authorities, who appeared oblivious to existing theological concepts regarding these relations. Between 822–828, Agobard, the archbishop of Lyons, voiced alarm at what he considered to be an emerging feudal "anarchy" within the Carolingian order. He objected to the preferential treatment afforded Jews at court, the promotion of their trade at public fairs, their ownership of Christian slaves, and their growing influence over Christians. From his canonical and theological perspective, the new charters were undermining the idealized position of Jewish social inferiority and separation from the Christian body politic.

READING 3-16

Letter to Nibridus, Archbishop of Narbonne

True Christians . . . should separate themselves from the company of infidels . . . especially Jews, who are quite well settled in this city. . . . For it seems to be most unworthy and improper for our faith that the sons of light be led into obscurity by associating themselves with the sons of darkness, and that the Church of Christ, which must be fittingly prepared without stain or blotch for the embraces of her celestial spouse, should be discolored through contact with the repudiated and reddled synagogue.

Yet, we see this evil (of comradeship, dining in common and even sexual debauchery through which the faith is endangered) growing and increasing daily. . . . Particularly, as once the law of God ordered that Jews neither join themselves in marriage with the nations nor celebrate feasts with them in common, lest through the bond of marriage and the conviviality of the repast they fall away from the divine service and thus direct their spiritual liberty into the yoke of idolatry, so now our people too should be equally restrained . . . lest they be caught up in the inextricable bonds of error. So then, blessed father . . . stay firm and intrepid . . . against the winds of adverse tempest; for these winds may have the power to shake the fundament of the house of God, but they are unable to destroy it, for even the gates of hell could not prevail against Him. . . .

4

The Crucible of Europe
(Ninth to Fifteenth Centuries)

David B. Ruderman

By the second half of the tenth century the Spanish Jewish community began to assert its independence from the hegemony of Baghdadian Jewry. Spanish Jewry's rise to prominence was spurred in part by the Jewish physician and courtier, Hasdai ibn Shaprut (905–75), who functioned as the leading figure within the Jewish community and helped to establish the unique literary ambiance that marked the efflorescence of Jewish culture in medieval Spain. Despite the political decline and dismemberment of the Spanish Muslim state, Jewish cultural creativity in poetry, in philosophy, and in traditional modes of rabbinic learning continued unabated for the next two centuries, even reaching new heights through the literary achievements of Judah ha-Levi (ca. 1035–1145) and Moses Maimonides (1135–1204).

Jews had settled in northern Europe as early as the ninth century, receiving privileges of domicile from feudal lords in return for their administrative and fiscal services. They lived relatively unmolested until the first crusade in 1096 where several thousand Jews, especially those living in the Rhineland, were brutalized by fanatical crusaders on their way to "liberate" the Holy Land. From the twelfth century on, Jewish life in Christian Europe steadily eroded, facilitated in part by the crusader violence. Jewish legal and economic status declined, the Church became more aggressive in its anti-Judaic policies, and the negative popular image of Jews became more visible and pervasive throughout European society and culture.

Despite Christian hostility toward its Jewish minority, Jewish culture in northern Europe flourished. Biblical and Talmudic scholarship was noteworthy, of which the most important contributions were made by Rashi (1040–1105) and his students known as the *ba'alei ha-tosafot* or glossators. Talmudic scholarship, combined with Jewish philosophy and Jewish mysticism, also constituted a central component of Spanish and Provencel Jewish culture. In the thirteenth century Jewish mystical activity became especially prominent, particularly in areas of shrinking opportunities for cultural interchange and religious dialogue with Christians. Still, these activities, like rabbinic learning, offered Jewish intellectuals spiritual replenishment. They also served to focus Jewish creative energies in a world increasingly unsympathetic, and often antagonistic, towards Jews and their cultural legacy.

Of all the medieval Jewish communities living within the Christian orbit, Spanish Jewry was the oldest and numerically the largest. Until the end of the fourteenth century, despite the conquest of most of Spain by the Christians, Jewish community life generally remained intact. Beginning in 1391, however, the situation changed for the worse. Spanish Jewry was physically assaulted by hostile Christians and spiritually demoralized by an aggressive clerical leadership. At this time large numbers of Jews converted to Christianity, creating an unprecedented number of "New Christians" living within Spanish society. The Spanish Inquisition, established by the end of the fifteenth century, directed much of its energies to uprooting what it considered to be a major problem of heresy—that of new converts secretly practicing Judaism. When the Jews of Spain finally were expelled in 1492, their removal was viewed by the authorities as the most effective strategy for dealing with Marrano (Crypto-Jewish) heresy. The expulsion constituted a painful blow to Jewish life throughout Europe, signaling the retreat of the Jewish presence from most of the European continent.

THE ASSERTION OF SPANISH JEWRY'S INDEPENDENCE UNDER ḤASDAI IBN SHAPRUT

Under the leadership of the powerful court physician, Ḥasdai ibn Shaprut (905–75), who served the caliphs Abd al-Raḥman III and al-Ḥakam in Cordova, the Spanish Jewish community began to assert its independence of the hegemony of Baghdadian Jewry. An astute Muslim writer named Said al-Andalusi, in describing his native Spain of the tenth century, noticed this development especially. By declaring Spanish Jewry's prerogative to determine its own mathematical calculation of the Jewish calendar, Ḥasdai virtually assumed the right of this community to establish its own autonomous political, economic, and religious status. Al-Andalusi's comments, confirmed independently by other Jewish sources, point to a development within Spanish Jewry directly related to the gradual erosion of political power and cultural vitality of Baghdadian Jewry's major institution, the *gaonate*, by the second half of the tenth century. This cultural and political shift within the Jewish world corresponded as well to a similar transfer of power from east to west within the entire Muslim empire.

READING 4-1

There were a number of Jewish men of science in Spain. Among those who took an interest in medicine was Ḥasday b. Isaac (Ibn Shaprut), who was in the service of al-Ḥakam b. Abd al-Raḥmān al-Nāṣir li-Dīn Allāh. He specialized in the art of medicine and had an exemplary knowledge of the science of Jewish law. He was the first to open for Andalusian Jewry the gates of their science of jurisprudence, chronology, and other subjects. Previously, they had recourse to the Jews of Baghdad in order to learn the law of their faith and in order to adjust the calendar and determine the dates of their holidays. They used to bring from them (the Jews of Baghdad) a calculation for a span of a number of years, and from it, they were able to know when their seasons began and when their year commenced.

When Ḥasday became attached to al-Ḥakam II, gaining his highest regard for his professional ability, his great talent, and his culture, he was able to procure through him the works of the Jews in the East which he desired. Then he taught the Jews of Spain that of which they had previously been ignorant. They were able as a result of this to dispense with the inconvenience which had burdened them.

ḤASDAI IBN SHAPRUT'S EPISTLE TO THE KING OF THE KHAZARS

Ḥasdai ibn Shaprut's political power allowed him to function as the chief patron of the Spanish Jewish community and its principal spokesman for other Jewish communities. In his first role, Ḥasdai promoted the composition and recitation of secular poetry by accomplished Hebrew poets. In his later role, he corresponded with various Jewish communities in Europe and tried especially to establish liaisons with the King of the Khazars, an empire between the Black and Caspian Seas, whose royal household had converted to Judaism by Ḥasdai's time.

In his Hebrew letter to the Khazar king Ḥasdai portrays himself as the Jewish monarch of the West, striving to communicate with his Jewish counterpart in the East. His letter portrays Jewish political power, comparable in his estimation to that of the Christians and Muslims. Yet despite the security of his position in Cordova, he also reveals an impulse characteristic of later generations of Spanish Jews, the yearning for messianic redemption. This Spanish courtier's outward success in erecting a wide-ranging program of Jewish cultural and political autonomy in Spain appears somewhat tempered by his anxious hope for Israel's ultimate salvation, so poignantly expressed in this epistle.

READING 4-2

I, Ḥasdai, son of Isaac, son of Ezra, belonging to the exiled Jews of Jerusalem, in Spain, a servant of my Lord the King, bow to the earth before him and prostrate myself towards the abode of your Majesty, from a distant land. I rejoice in your tranquillity and magnificence, and stretch forth my hands to God in heaven, that

He may prolong your reign in Israel. But who am I? and what is my life that I should dare to indite a letter to my Lord the King, and to address your Majesty? I rely, however, on the integrity and uprightness of my object. How, indeed, can an idea be expressed in fair words by those who have wandered into captivity, who have forgotten their homes, and from whom the honour of the kingdom has departed; who have long suffered afflictions and calamities, and see their signs in the land no more? We, indeed, who are of the remnant of the captive Israelites, servants of my Lord the King, are dwelling peacefully in the land of our sojourning (for our God has not forsaken us, nor has His shadow departed from us). When we had transgressed He brought us into judgment, cast affliction upon our loins, and stirred up the minds of those who had been set over the Israelites to appoint collectors of tribute over them, who aggravated the yoke of the Israelites, oppressed them cruelly, humbled them grievously, and inflicted great calamities upon them. But when God saw their misery and labour, and that they were helpless, He led me to present myself before the King, and has graciously turned his heart to me, not because of mine own righteousness, but for his mercy and His covenant's sake. And by this covenant the poor of the flock were exalted to safety, the hands of the oppressors themselves were relaxed, they refrained from further oppression, and through the mercy of our God the yoke was lightened. . . .

Wherefore I have written this epistle to your Majesty, in which I submissively entreat you not to refuse my request, but to command your servant to write to me about all these things: viz., what is your State, what is the nature of your land, what tribes inhabit it, what is the manner of the government, how kings succeed one another, whether they are chosen from a certain tribe or family, or whether sons succeed their fathers, as was customary among our ancestors when they dwelt in their own land. Would my Lord the King also inform me as to the extent of his country, its length, and breadth; what walled cities, and what open towns it has; whether it be watered by artificial or natural means; and how far his dominion extends; also the number of his armies, and their leaders. Let not my Lord take it ill, I pray, that I enquire about the number of his forces ("may the Lord add unto them," etc.). My Lord sees that I enquire about this with no other object than that I may rejoice when I hear of the increase of the holy people. I wish, too, that he would tell me of the number of the provinces which he rules over, the amount of tribute paid to him, if they give him tithes, whether he dwells continually in the royal city or goes about through the whole extent of his dominions, if there are any islands in the neighbourhood, and if any of their inhabitants conform to Judaism; if he judges his own people himself, or appoints judges over them; how he goes up to the house of God; with what peoples he wages war; whether he allows war to set aside the observance of the Sabbath; what kingdoms or nations are on his borders, what are their names, and those of territories; what are the cities near to his kingdom called Chorasan, Berdaa, and Bab Al Abuab; in what way their caravans proceed to his territory; how many kings ruled before him, what were their names, how many years each of them ruled, and what is the current language of the land. In the time of our fathers there was among us a certain Israelite, an intelligent man, who belonged to the tribe of Dan, who traced his descent back to Dan, the son of Jacob. He spoke elegantly, and gave everything its name in the holy language. Nor was he at a loss for any expression. When he expounded the Law he was accustomed to say, "Thus has Othniel, son of Kenaz, handed down by tradition from the mouth of Joshua, and he from the mouth of Moses who was inspired by the Almighty." One thing more I ask of my Lord, that he would tell me whether there is among you any computation concerning the final redemption which we have been awaiting so many years, whilst we went from one captivity to another, from one exile to another. How strong is the hope of him who awaits the realisation of these events! And oh, that I might shed my life's blood on account of the desolation of the house of our glory, and for the sake of those who, escaping the sword, have passed through fire and water, so that the remnant is but small! We have been cast down from our glory, so that we have nothing to reply when they say daily unto us, "Every other people has its kingdom, but of yours there is no memorial on the earth." Hearing, therefore, the fame of my Lord the King, as well as the power of his dominions, and the multitude of his forces, we were amazed, we lifted up our head, our spirit revived, and our hands were strengthened, and the kingdom of my Lord furnished us with an argument in answer to this taunt. May this report be substantiated; for that would add to our greatness. Blessed be the Lord God of Israel who has not left us without a kinsman as defender, nor suffered the tribes of Israel to be without an independent kingdom. May my Lord the King prosper for ever!

SAMUEL HA-NAGID'S VICTORY OVER IBN ABBAD

The most powerful Spanish Jewish courtier of the eleventh century was Samuel ibn Naghrela (933–1055 or 1056, who referred to himself by the title *nagid,* or Jewish prince) of the Berber kingdom of Granada. Samuel meteorically rose from rags to riches to assume the viziership of the state and the leadership of an army of Muslims. Never lacking in self-confidence, Samuel was well aware of his multiple administrative, martial, and literary talents. He lavishly documented his dramatic accomplishments on the battlefield in his Hebrew poems, which demonstrated as well his brilliant mastery of the Hebrew language.

The poem below celebrates Samuel's impressive victory over the forces of Isma'il ibn Abbad, the commander of the forces of the kingdom of Seville in 1040. Having recently defeated the army of the state of Almeria and having captured its vizier, ibn Abbad, Samuel was particularly jubilant in achieving an even more impressive military prize. What characterizes Samuel's military poems especially is his constant invocation of divine protection. In this case, the victory over Seville constituted a particular favor for Samuel from God for his unwavering religious loyalty.

READING 4-3

Will You do wonders for me each year
As You have done for the patriarchs and saints?
Will You slay lions for me like he-goats
Sacrifice them in my behalf like ewes?
Will the depths of the sea that I cross each year
Be turned into paved highways?

Each year into fire I enter,—
Will its flames be transformed into dew?
To You O Rock praise is fitting,
For You are God and might is from your hand.
You entice those who run away,—for their end has come,
And on the day of vengeance You remove the impure.
I will speak of your glory in the gates
And give thanks to You among the multitudes.
I will tell of your wondrous deeds in the assembly of the saints
And of your miracles among those clothed with fringes.

About a year ago, on a fearful day
You redeemed me, making the foe my ransom.
Now after the death of Ben 'Abbas,
I am filled with fear as Ben 'Abbad approaches.
They both pursued me, though upon the latter's head
Sits the crown of royalty, while the former was a commoner.

By his decree nobles are raised up to rule over their
Dominions and by his command they are removed.
By his leave the mighty are given lands
To control and at his wish they are put to death.
The Berber captains heed his words
And he is acclaimed by the princes of the Arabs.
They wait for his command as for the early showers
And anticipate his murmurings like the rain.

Now there were quarrels and jealousy between him and my king.
And they remained apart in their own lands.
Both were like cedars among royalty
And all the earth's monarchs were like saplings.
Both learned how to ravage kings
While the mighty were consumed by their swords.
For a long time they slew kings like paupers
And slaughtered the powerful like rams.
There was no one in Spain to stand up to them
To defy them or rise in revolt. . . .

In the month of the Mighty Ones.
After the passage of ninety-nine years
Salvation blossomed for me like a plant.
For You were a sanctuary to me and from the foe
You preserved me even from the hosts of the uncircumcised.
You extended your right hand to me in help
And against my enemies with hurting blows.
The angels of harm and destruction who make
The heaven and earth to shudder, were given orders.
For they hurled upon them vessels of wrath
Like the rains and anger like the issue of a storm-cloud.
You gave your servant to drink of the cup of salvation

And to his adversaries, the poisonous cup.
There was light for me on the eve of the festival of the Harvest
    Gathering
And it brightened all my darkened paths,
As it did on the night of Abram and the night of Moses,
As on Joshua's afternoon, as on the night when the burden of siege
    was removed!

I observed properly the Lord's festivals
As was the practice among the Dwellers in Tents,
Even the Sabbath days and the day of the Shofar and Atonement
The days of the Booth until the exit of the pilgrims.
The dread of profaning them was like a fire
In my heart, though there were some less scrupulous.
God granted that the armies were freed from their labors
On the days that work was forbidden!

I will multiply my songs to God
For the wonders which He did increase.
He makes a laughing stock out of the scoffers
And fulfills the desires of the humble workers.
I will relate his praises abroad and tell them
To the generations to come, the children of wanderers and exiles.
Though the dwellers of heaven and earth
Be unable to laud his name for this cause.

At the time that the people brought into their booths
Myrtle from the rock and branches of the palm tree,
The Rock exalted me with the palm of his hand and his booth
Was my shelter like a sealed up fortress.
When they brought their willow, He made the steppes
Into a city of walls and ramparts for his servant's son.
He plucked out the glory of my enemies as they harvested
The yield from the splendid trees they planted.
And the leaves of the myrtle made atonement for
Me like the burnt offerings or the half-shekel.
He magnified himself by the waters while the people were occupied
With the four kinds that grow upon the waters.

As my enemies drew near to eat my flesh
I rose up while they fell down enfeebled.
They brought pain to my heart but God
Sent healing balm at the time of suffering and anguish.
He commanded the ministering angels and they were
My help from the heavens, descending and ascending;
Even to the nation which thought to divide
The booty of his people, He allotted ruin in his wrath.
We will build the *succot* with joy
While they lament in their shame.

We will recite the *Hallel* with gladness
While they chant the dirge and bewail.

Is this done for me? For I am a worm and not a man
Despised among people, lowliest among the low.
Who am I and what is my life, my Lord?
I am great with sin, evil in deeds;
I am puny and unworthy of these triumphs,
And all your gracious gifts.
If You reward me for my merits in this world
And requite me according to my righteousness
How shall I fare on the day of judgment,
And how shall my guilt and sins be forgiven?
To the God of strength who appears in the storm
And in the whirlwind against the idol-worshippers,
Who has not given his glory to another
Nor bequeathed his praise to statues,
To him I have heretofore composed a *Shira*
And now a *Tehilla* which is bright as the stars.
Its form is similar to that of its sister.
In number of lines it is like the Psalmist's praises.
Its subject matter is more precious than pearls
With stanzas balanced in measures of verse.
The creators of verse are barren unable to bear its like.
Even the fathers of poetry are bereaved.
Both of them all the days of my life shall be
Bracelets upon my arm and rings in my ears.
On the judgment day they shall speak in my behalf
With words dripping myrrh and aloes.

Children of my people, join me in this praise.
Put it at the head of all laudations.
Set its words in proper order
In the mouths of old and young.
For when in future times your sons will ask:
"What is this?" You will then to the questioner reply:
"A song of praise it is to God who redeemed his beloved,
Who composed it for the redeemed to recite.
It is a song of praise, great and glorious
To the glory of God and his mighty works."

A POETICAL ATTACK ON THE JEWS OF GRANADA

Samuel ha-Nagid's well-publicized career, his inflated ego, and his own national chauvinism, so obvious in his writings, vividly exemplify the aristocratic delusions of grandeur that characterized the attitudes of some of the elite Jewish class. Certainly so ostentatious an expression of Jewish pride did not go unnoticed by traditional-minded Muslim contemporaries. A number of contemporary Muslim writers openly attacked what they considered to be Jewish pretentiousness. The poem of Abūj Ishār of Elvira called for the death of Joseph ha-Nagid, Samuel's son and successor, along with his fellow Granadan Jews. Such literary vituperation was translated into physical assault. Joseph was assassinated by a hostile mob that also ransacked the Jewish quarter of Granada in 1066.

READING 4-4

Go, tell all the Ṣanhāja [the great confederation of Berbers]
    the full moons of our time, the lions in their lair
The words of one who bears them love, and is concerned
    and counts it a religious duty to give advice.
Your chief has made a mistake
    which delights malicious gloaters
He has chosen an infidel as his secretary
    when he could, had he wished, have chosen a believer.
Through him, the Jews have become great and proud
    and arrogant—they, who were among the most abject
And have gained their desires and attained the utmost
    and this happened suddenly, before they even realised it.
And how many a worthy Muslim humbly obeys
    the vilest ape among these miscreants.
And this did not happen through their own efforts
    but through one of our own people who rose as their accomplice.
Oh why did he not deal with them, following
    the example set by worthy and pious leaders?
Put them back where they belong
    and reduce them to the lowest of the low,
Roaming among us, with their little bags,
    with contempt, degradation and scorn as their lot,
Scrabbling in the dunghills for colored rags
    to shroud their dead for burial.
They did not make light of our great ones
    or presume against the righteous,
Those low-born people would not be seated in society
    or paraded along with the intimates [of the ruler].
Bādīs! [king of Granada] You are a clever man
    and your judgment is sure and accurate.
How can their misdeeds be hidden from you
    when they are trumpeted all over the land?
How can you love this bastard brood
    when they have made you hateful to all the world?
How can you complete your ascent to greatness
    when they destroy as you build?
How have you been lulled to trust a villain
    and made him your companion—though he is evil company?
God has vouchsafed in His revelations
    a warning against the society of the wicked.

Do not choose a servant from among them
  but leave them to the curse of the accurst!
For the earth cries out against their wickedness
  and is about to heave and swallow us all.
Turn your eyes to other countries
  and you will find the Jews there are outcast dogs.
Why should you alone be different and bring them near
  when in all the land they are kept afar?
—You, who are a well-beloved king,
  scion of glorious kings,
And are the first among men
  as your forbears were first in their time.
I came to live in Granada
  and I saw them frolicking there.
They divided up the city and the provinces
  with one of their accursed men everywhere.
They collect all the revenues
  they munch and they crunch
They dress in the finest clothes
  while you wear the meanest.
They are the trustees of your secrets
  —yet how can traitors be trusted?
Others eat a dirham's worth, afar,
  while they are near, and dine well.
They challenge you to your God
  and they are not stopped or reproved.
They envelop you with their prayers
  and you neither see nor hear.
They slaughter beasts in our markets
  and you eat their *trefa* [ritually unfit meat].
Their chief ape has marbled his house
  and led the finest spring water to it.
Our affairs are now in his hands
  and we stand at his door.
He laughs at us and at our religion
  and we return to our God.
If I said that his wealth is as great
  as yours, I would speak truth.
Hasten to slaughter him as an offering,
  sacrifice him, for he is a fat ram
And do not spare his people
  for they have amassed every precious thing.
Break loose their grip and take their money
  for you have a better right to what they collect.
Do not consider it a breach of faith to kill them
  —the breach of faith would be to let them carry on.
They have violated our covenant with them
  so how can you be held guilty against the violaters?
How can they have any pact
  when we are obscure and they are prominent?

Now we are the humble, beside them,
    as if we had done wrong, and they right!
Do not tolerate their misdeeds against us
    for you are surety for what they do.
God watches His own people
    and the people of God will prevail.

A SPANISH JEWISH CURRICULUM OF JEWISH AND SECULAR STUDIES

In the image of Ḥasdai ibn Shaprut and Samuel ha-Nagid, a Jewish courtier class emerged in Spain that dominated Spanish Jewry for generations to come. For this group of Jewish literati study of the *Torah* alone did not make the complete Jewish gentleman; their dignity and high social status were the result of systematic training in literature, science, and philosophy. They attempted to harmonize Jewish learning and "Greek wisdom" as Saadia had done in Baghdad but their curriculum of Jewish and "Greek" studies strove for a social as well as an intellectual ideal. Scholarly attainment in both traditional and secular fields of learning led ultimately, in their minds, to a nobility of character, to the forging of a complete human being who embodied the best of Jewish and Muslim cultures. The curriculum of Joseph ben Judah ibn Aqnin of the late twelfth century illustrates the cultural ideal of Spanish Jewry's courtier class.

READING 4-5

READING AND WRITING: The method of instruction must be so arranged that the teacher will begin first with the script, in order that the children may learn their letters, and this is to be kept up until there is no longer any uncertainty among them. This script is, of course, the "Assyrian," [the Aramaic square script] the use of which has been agreed upon by our ancestors. Then he is to teach them to write until their script is clear and can be read easily. He should not however keep them too long at work striving for beauty, decorativeness, and special elegance of penmanship. On the contrary, that which we have already mentioned will be sufficient.

TORAH, MISHNAH, AND HEBREW GRAMMAR: Then he is to teach them the Pentateuch, Prophets, and Hagiographa, that is the Bible, with an eye to the vocalization and the modulation in order that they may be able to pronounce the accents correctly. . . . Then he is to have them learn the Mishnah until they have acquired a fluency in it. The teacher is to continue this until they are ten years of age, for the sages said "At five years the age is reached for the study of the Scriptures, at ten for the study of the Mishnah." The children are then to be taught the inflections, declensions, and conjugations, the regular verbs . . . and other rules of grammar. . . .

POETRY: Then the teacher is to instruct his pupils in poetry. He should, for the most part, have them recite religious poems and whatever else of beauty is found in the different types of poetry, and is fit to develop in them all good qualities. . . .

TALMUD: Then say the wise "At fifteen the age is reached for the study of the Talmud." Accordingly when the pupils are fifteen years of age the teacher should give them much practice in Talmud-reading until they have acquired fluency in it.

Later, when they are eighteen years of age, he should give them that type of instruction in it which lays emphasis on deeper understanding, independent thinking, and investigation. . . .

PHILOSOPHIC OBSERVATIONS ON RELIGION: When the students have spent considerable time in study which is directed toward deeper comprehension and thoroughness, so that their mental powers have been strengthened; when the Talmud has become so much a part of them that there is hardly any chance of its being lost, and they are firmly entrenched in the Torah and the practice of its commands; then the teacher is to impart to them the third necessary subject. This is the refutation of the errors of apostates and heretics and the justification of those views and practices which the religion prescribes. . . .

PHILOSOPHIC STUDIES: . . . These studies are divided into three groups. The first group is normally dependent on matter, but can, however, be separated from matter through concept and imagination. This class comprises the mathematical sciences. In the second group speculation cannot be conceived of apart from the material, either through imagination or conception. To this section belong the natural sciences. The third group has nothing to do with matter and has no material attributes; this group includes in itself metaphysics as such.

LOGIC: But these sciences are preceded by logic which serves as a help and instrument. It is through logic that the speculative activities, which the three groups above mentioned include, are made clear. Logic presents the rules which keep the mental powers in order, and lead man on the path of clarity and truth in all things wherein he may err. . . .

MATHEMATICS, ARITHMETIC: The teacher will then lecture to his students on mathematics, beginning with arithmetic or geometry, or instruct them in both sciences at the same time. . . .

GEOMETRY: With respect to geometry two things are included in this term, practical and theoretical geometry. . . .

OPTICS: Then the students are introduced into the third of the mathematical sciences, namely optics. . . .

ASTRONOMY: Then they pass on to astronomy. This includes two sciences. First, astrology, that is, the science wherein the stars point to future events as well as to many things that once were or now are existent. Astrology is no longer numbered among the real sciences. It belongs only to the forces and secret arts by means of which man can prophesy what will come to pass, like the interpretation of dreams, fortune-telling, auguries, and similar arts. This science, however, is forbidden by God. . . . The second field of astronomy is mathematical. This field is to be included among mathematics and the real sciences. This science concerns itself with the heavenly bodies and the earth. . . .

MUSIC: After studying the science of astronomy the teacher will lecture on music to his students. Music embraces instruction in the elements of the melodies and that which is connected with them, how melodies are linked together, and what condition is required to make the influence of music most pervasive and effective. . . .

MECHANICS: . . . This includes two different things. For one thing it aims at the consideration of heavy bodies insofar as they are used for measurements. . . . The second part includes the consideration of heavy bodies insofar as they may be moved or insofar as they are used for moving. It treats, therefore, of the principles concerning instruments whereby heavy objects are raised and whereby they are moved from one place to another. . . .

NATURAL SCIENCES, MEDICINE: Let us now speak of the second section of the philosophic disciplines, that is, the natural sciences. After the students have assimilated the sciences already mentioned the teachers should instruct them in the natural sciences. The first of this group that one ought to learn is medicine, that is, the art which keeps the human constitution in its normal condition, and which brings back to its proper condition the constitution which has departed from the normal. This latter type of activity is called the healing and cure of sickness, while the former is called the care of the healthy. This art falls into two parts, science and practice. . . .

After the students have learned this art the teacher should lecture to them on the natural sciences as such. This discipline investigates natural bodies and all things whose existence is incidentally dependent on these bodies. This science also makes known those things out of which, by which, and because of which these bodies and their attendant phenomena come into being. . . .

METAPHYSICS: After this one should concern himself with the study of metaphysics, that which Aristotle has laid down in his work, *Metaphysics*. This science is divided into three parts. The first part investigates "being" and whatever happens to it insofar as it is "being." The second part investigates the principles with respect to proofs which are applied to the special speculative sciences. These are those sciences, each one of which elucidates, along speculative lines, a definite discipline, as for instance, logic, geometry, arithmetic, and the other special sciences which are similar to those just mentioned.

Furthermore, this part investigates the principles of logic, of the mathematical sciences, and of natural science, and seeks to make them clear, to state their peculiarities, and to enumerate the false views which have existed with respect to the principles of these sciences. In the third part there is an investigation of those entities which are not bodies nor a force in bodies. . . .

This is the first among sciences. All the other sciences, which are but the groundwork of philosophy, have this discipline in mind. . . .

FROM THE HEBREW POETS OF MEDIEVAL SPAIN

Ḥasdai ibn Shaprut's patronage of Hebrew poets at the court of Cordova served to establish a new Jewish attitude toward poetry. For centuries, beginning in Palestine, Hebrew poets had written poems solely for the purpose of prayer. Inspired by the Arabic example, Spanish Jews now wrote poems in Hebrew, writing no longer just for liturgical use but even simply to flatter their patrons. The professional Hebrew poet asserted his own religious and cultural distinctiveness by writing poems using the Hebrew rather than Arabic scriptures as his model. But by composing poems on love, wine, women, and the glorification of nature, he celebrated a lifestyle of an elite society indistinguishable from its Arab counterparts. More than any writing, the numerous poems of the Spanish Hebrew poets came to extol and propagate the values of the new Jewish patriciate.

The following poems of Moses ibn Ezra (1070–1139) and Judah ha-Levi (1085–1142) provide a modest illustration of the literary virtuosity of Spanish Jewish poets. Strikingly, both men lived during the twilight of Jewish community life in Muslim Spain, a period of instability, dislocation, and decline. Their poems reflect an environment increasingly ridden with anxiety and uncertainty. Ha-Levi's poems, especially his odes to Zion, suggest a sense of growing impatience and disillusionment in the already shaky edifice of Spanish Jewry's political power and cultural élan, which was crumbling dramatically in the early twelfth century.

READING 4-6A

Moses ibn Ezra

Trembling We Seek the House of Prayer

Trembling, we seek the house of prayer
To confess our iniquities,
And to recite the vicissitudes of our lives
With all that has befallen us.
Oh, that the Rock of our salvation
Would come forth to meet us,
To deliver our souls from death
And to grant us life!

What shall we say—
For we are smitten by our own illdoing;
And our sins are like veils upon our faces,
Hiding from us our Maker!
Yea, we are like cattle
That would make the world their manger;
Like jackals, panting for the scent of their delights.

But this day, bowed low,
We hasten to the house of God, our Refuge—
For our feet are swift to run after Him
In the time of their distress.

They that have forgotten God,
Where is their gold?
Where are the jewels of their adornment?
Is there any among them that shall live,
Seeing that their origin is of the dust?
When the hand of Death is raised against them,
Shall their treasures aught avail?

Foolishly they imagined that from the lion's corse
Honey would drip upon their hands;

And they bore not in mind their latter end—
Now, therefore, do they bear their shame.

Bethink Thee, O God! Bethink Thee, and shine forth!
Oh, cease from Thine anger
Against them that fear the day of Thy judgment,
And grant them peace.
For unto Thee they yearn,
But there is none to intercede for them.
And though they have done wickedly before Thee,
Yet justify the mortals that lament their trespasses.
Oh, make known that Thou hast accepted them
And hast forgiven their sins!

Winter Hath Vanished

Winter with its rains hath vanished,
Vanished with its trampling horses,
With the tumult of its riders;
Now the sun—his law fulfilling
In his circling of the heavens—
Comes again unto the ram's head,
As a king comes to his table.

On their heads the hills are binding
Turbans of bright flowers; the valley,
Gay in mantle of green grasses,
Sends forth to regale our senses
Spicy odors, as of incense
She had treasured in her bosom
Through the days of chill and gloom.

Fetch the cup—for joy it throneth
In the heart, and drives out sorrow—
With my tears assuage its burning,
For the wine is wroth, and flameth.

Guard thee against Fate; like venom
With a little honey mingled,
Are his gifts. Yet should he bring thee
Good at morn, accept, enjoy it;
Knowing surely, that ere nightfall
Into evil will he turn it.

Drink with day till he departeth,
Till the sun o'erlay his silver
With the hues of ruddy gold;
Drink with night until she leave thee—
Flying fast—a shape of blackness,
And the roseate hand of morning
Stretcheth out to seize her heel.

The World Is Like a Woman of Folly

The world is like a woman of folly,
Vain are her pomp and glory;
She speaks sweet words, but verily
Under her tongue is a snare.
O brother of wisdom, frustrate her cunning;
Turn thou her glory into shame.
Hasten, and send her from thee forever—
Her bill of divorcement in her hand!

READING 4-6B

Judah ha-Levi

Wedding Song

REJOICE, O young man, in thy youth,
And gather the fruit thy joy shall bear;
Thou and the wife of thy youth,
Turning now to thy dwelling to enter there.

Glorious blessings of God, who is One,
Shall come united upon thine head;
Thine house shall be at peace from dread,
Thy foes' uprising be undone.
Thou shalt lay thee down in a safe retreat;
Thou shalt rest, and thy sleep be sweet.

In thine honour, my bridegroom, prosper and live;
Let thy beauty arise and shine forth fierce;
And the heart of thine enemies God shall pierce,
And the sins of thy youth will he forgive,
And bless thee in increase and all thou shalt do,
When thou settest thine hand threto.

And remember thy Rock, Creator of thee,
When the goodness cometh which he shall bring;
For sons out of many days shall spring,
And ev'n as thy days thy strength shall be.
Blessed be thou when thou enterest
And thy going out shall be blest.

'Mid the perfect and wise shall thy portion lie,
So thou be discreet where thou turnest thee;
And thine house shall be builded immovably,
And "Peace" thou shalt call; and God shall reply;
And peace shall be thine abode; and sealed
Thy bond with the stones of the field.

Thy glory shall rise, nor make delay;
And thee shall he call and choose; and thy light,
In the gloom, in the darkness of the night,

Then shall break forth like the dawn of day;
   And out from the shining light of the morn
   Shall the dew of thy youth be born.

Where Shall I Find Thee?

O LORD, where shall I find thee?
All-hidden and exalted is thy place;
   And where shall I not find thee?
Full of thy glory is the infinite space.

   Found near-abiding ever,
He made the earth's ends, set their utmost bar;
   Unto the nigh a refuge,
Yea, and a trust to them who wait afar.
     Thou sittest throned between the cherubim,
     Thou dwellest high above the cloud-rack dim.
Praised by thine hosts and yet beyond their praises
   For ever far exalt;
The endless whirl of worlds cannot contain thee,
   How then one heaven's vault?

   And thou, withal uplifted
O'er man, upon a mighty throne apart,
   Art yet for ever near him,
Breath of his spirit, life-blood of his heart.
     His own mouth speaketh testimony true
     That thou his Maker art alone; for who
Shall say he hath not seen thee? Lo! the heavens
   And all their host aflame
With glory, show thy fear in speech unuttered,
   With silent voice proclaim.

   Longing I sought thy presence,
Lord, with my whole heart did I call and pray,
   And going out toward thee,
I found thee coming to me on the way;
     Yea, in thy wonders' might as clear to see
     As when within the shrine I looked for thee.
Who shall not fear thee? Lo! upon their shoulders
   Thy yoke divinely dread!
Who shall forbear to cry to thee, that givest
   To all their daily bread?

   And can the Lord God truly—
God, the Most High—dwell here within man's breast?
   What shall he answer, pondering—
Man, whose foundations in the dust do rest?
     For thou art holy, dwelling 'mid the praise
     Of them who waft thee worship all their days.

Angels adoring, singing of thy wonder,
   Stand upon heaven's height;
And thou, enthroned o'erhead, all things upholdest
   With everlasting might.

My Heart Is in the East

My heart is in the east, and I in the uttermost west—
How can I find savour in food? How shall it be sweet to me?
How shall I render my vows and my bonds, while yet
Zion lieth beneath the fetter of Edom, and I in Arab chains?
A light thing would it seem to me to leave all the good things of Spain—
Seeing how precious in mine eyes to behold the dust of the desolate sanctuary.

On the Sea

My God, break not the breakers of the sea,
   Nor say Thou to the deep, 'Be dry',
Until I thank Thy mercies, and I thank
   The waves of the sea and the wind of the west;
Let them waft me to the place of the yoke of Thy love,
   And bear far from me the Arab yoke.
And how shall my desires not find fulfilment,
   Seeing I trust in Thee, and Thou art pledged to me?

JUDAH HA-LEVI'S *SEFER HA-KUZARI*

Judah ha-Levi's major philosophical work was the *Sefer ha-Kuzari*. In it ha-Levi constructed an imaginary discussion among the Khazar king (the subject of Ḥasdai ibn Shaprut's earlier correspondence), representatives of the three major faiths, and a philosopher; all had been summoned by the ruler to present his opinion about Judaism. Within the framework of this philosophical dialogue ha-Levi offered a "defense of the despised faith," a defense against the intellectual assaults of Christianity and Islam from without and against the spiritual erosion caused by philosophy from within Judaism.

Ha-Levi ringingly denounced the integration of Spanish society's values and thought into Judaism in the ideals of the Jewish courtier class. He decried the fusion of Judaism and philosophy; Judaism, he argued, was comprehensible in historical, not philosophical terms. The Land of Israel, not Spain, was the only geographical location where Jews totally could fulfill their spiritual ideals and religious obligations, where prophecy could be realized, and from which the messiah would appear.

The following selection illustrates ha-Levi's view of the Jewish people's unique vocation among the nations of the world.*

---

*Reprinted from *Three Jewish Philosophers* by permission of Hebrew Publishing Company.

READING 4-7

THE KHAZARI: So you are today a body without either head or heart?

THE RABBI: So it is. Or rather: we are not even a body, only scattered limbs, like the dry bones Ezekiel saw. However, O King of the Khazars, these bones, which have retained a trace of vital power and have once been the seat of a heart, head, spirit, soul, and intellect, are better than bodies formed of marble and plaster, endowed with heads, eyes, ears, and all limbs, in which there never dwelt the spirit of life, nor can it dwell therein, since they are but imitations of men, not men in reality.

THE KHAZARI: It is as thou sayest.

THE RABBI: The dead religious communities, which desired to be equal to the living one, achieved nothing more than an external resemblance. They built houses to God, but no trace of His (presence) was visible therein. They lived as hermits and ascetics in order to derive inspiration, but they did not derive it. They deteriorated, became disobedient, and wicked; yet no fire fell down from heaven upon them, nor swift pestilence, to be distinguished as God's punishment for their disobedience. If their heart—I mean their temple—was destroyed, their status has not changed; it changed only in proportion to their greatness or smallness, strength or weakness, disunion or unity, according to natural or accidental causes. We, however, since our heart, the Holy House, was destroyed, were also lost; if it be restored, we, too, will be restored, be we few or many, and whatever be our status. For our leader is the living God; He is our King, who keeps us in our present status of dispersion and exile.

THE KHAZARI: Certainly. Such a dispersion of a people is inconceivable without the same people being absorbed by another, especially after so long a period. How many nations which lived after your (ruin) have perished without leaving a trace, as Edom, Moab, Ammon, Aram, the Philistines, Chaldeans, Medians, Persians, Greeks, Brahmans, Sabaeans and many others!

THE RABBI: Do not believe that I, though agreeing with thy (former) words, admit that we are like the dead. We still hold connection with that Divine power through the laws He has placed as a link between us and Him, e.g. circumcision, of which is said 'My covenant shall be in your flesh for an everlasting covenant', and the Sabbath, which is called 'a sign between Me and you throughout your generations'. Besides this there is the covenant with the fathers and the covenant of the Torah, first granted on Horeb and then in the plains of Moab, in connection with promises and warnings and His words: 'If any of thine be driven out into the utmost parts of heaven, thence will God gather and fetch thy people'; and 'thou shalt return unto the Lord thy God' and the song 'Give ear, O heavens', and other places. We resemble, therefore, not the dead, but rather a person sick unto death, who has been given up by the physicians, and yet hopes for recovery through miracles or extraordinary events, as it is said: 'With these bones live'; and in the parable: 'He is ugly and homely, like one from whom men hide their faces'; which means that, on account of his deformity and repulsive visage, he resembles an unclean thing, which man only beholds with disgust, and rejects; 'despised and rejected of men, a man of pain, acquainted with disease'.

THE KHAZARI: How can this serve as a comparison for Israel, as it is said: 'Surely he has borne our diseases'? That which has befallen Israel, befell it on account of its sins only!

THE RABBI: Israel amidst the nations is like the heart amidst the organs: it is the most sick and the most healthy of them all.

THE KHAZARI: Make this clearer.

THE RABBI: The heart is visited without interruption by all sorts of diseases, as sadness, anxiety, envy, wrath, enmity, love, hate, and fear. Its constitution changes continually according to the vigour and weakness of respiration, inappropriate meat and drink, movement, exertion, sleep or wakefulness. These all affect the heart, whilst the limbs rest uninjured.

THE KHAZARI: I understand how far it is the sickest of all organs. But in which sense is it the healthiest of them all?

THE RABBI: Is it possible that in the heart there should settle a humour producing an inflammation, a cancer, a wart, etc., as is possible in other organs?

THE KHAZARI: Impossible. For the smallest trace of these would bring on death. On account of its extreme sensibility, caused by the purity of its blood and its abundance of animal spirit, it feels the slightest symptom and expels it as long as it is able to do so. The other organs lack this fine sensibility, and it is, therefore, possible for humours to settle in them which produce diseases.

THE RABBI: Thus its sensibility and feeling expose it to many diseases, but they are also the cause of the expulsion of the same at the very beginning, before they have taken root.

THE KHAZARI: Quite so.

THE RABBI: The relation of the Divine power to us is the same as that of the soul to the heart. For this reason it is said: 'You only have I known among all the families of the earth, therefore I will punish you for all your iniquities'. He does not allow our sins to accumulate—and to destroy us completely by their multitude, as He did in the case of the Amorites, of whom it is said: 'The iniquity of the Amorites is not yet full'; God left them alone, till the ailment of their sins became rooted and deadly. And just as the heart is pure in substance and matter, and of even temperament, in order to be accessible to the intellectual soul, so is Israel in its substance and matter; but in the same way as the heart may be affected by diseases from the other organs, viz. the lusts of the liver, stomach and genitals, by reason of their bad temperament, thus also diseases befell Israel in consequence of its assimilation to the Gentiles, as it is said: 'They were mingled among the heathens and learned their works'. It cannot seem strange, therefore, that it is said: 'Surely, he has borne our disease and carried our griefs'. Now we are oppressed, whilst the whole world enjoys rest and prosperity. But the trials which meet us serve to purify our piety, to cleanse us and to remove all taint from us.

LAW AND PHILOSOPHY IN THE WRITING OF MOSES MAIMONIDES

Moses Maimonides (1135–1204) was the dominant cultural figure within the Jewish world of his day and for centuries following his death. Forced to leave Spain as a youth, he wandered through North Africa and Palestine and eventually settled in Cairo where he was appointed house physician to the vizier of Egypt. Maimonides' writings reflect a three-pronged intellectual commitment that was reflected in his daily life. As a physician, he devoted himself to patient care and authored scientific treatises on various medical problems. As a Jewish legal scholar, he composed a number of major *halakhic* (legal) works, of which his comprehensive code of Jewish law, called the *Mishneh Torah* (The Repetition of the Law), was the most important. As a philosopher, his masterpiece, *The Guide of the Perplexed*, originally written in Arabic, soon achieved a revered status within the Jewish, Muslim, and Christian intellectual worlds.

In contrast to ha-Levi Maimonides strove to realize the overall unity of all learning, a unity of the practical and theoretical, of divine law and Aristotelian philosophy. Attacking the simplistic and naive rationalism of earlier philosophers, Maimonides strove for a more honest and sophisticated confrontation between revelation and reason than that of Saadia before him. Judaism could not insulate itself from the larger intellectual community; it needed to project a profile of "a wise and understanding people" (Deut. 4:7). For Maimonides Jewish law was grounded in reason. Striving to comprehend that rationality with the aid of philosophy became for him the supreme religious ideal. Judaism's spiritual maturation as a religious civilization was dependent, so he argued, on its mutual dialogue and interaction with the outside world.

The brief sampling below from Maimonides' work includes (1) the introductory sections of Maimonides' law code in which he summarizes some of the essential beliefs of Judaism, underscoring the unity of philosophy and law; (2) a chapter from the *Guide* (3:31) in which he insists upon the need for a rationalistic interpretation of the commandments in order to preserve Judaism's credibility; (3) the beginning of his famous chapter in the *Guide* (3:51) on the parable of the castle, an explicit formulation of the exalted place of the intellect and of philosophic speculation in realizing the religious ideal in Judaism.

READING 4-8A

Mishneh Torah, Book of Knowledge, Basic Principles of the *Torah*, Chapter One

1. The basic principle of all basic principles and the pillar of all sciences is to realize that there is a First Being who brought every existing thing into being. All existing things, whether celestial, terrestrial, or belonging to an intermediate class, exist only through His true Existence.

2. If it could be supposed that He did not exist, it would follow that nothing else could possibly exist.

3. If, however, it were supposed that all other beings were non-existent, He alone would still exist. Their non-existence would not involve His non-existence. For all beings are in need of Him; but He, blessed be He, is not in need of them nor of any of them.

4. This is what the prophet means when he says "But the Eternal is the true God"; that is, He alone is real, and nothing else has reality like His reality. The same

thought the Torah expresses in the text: "There is none else besides Him"; that is: There is no being besides Him, that is really like Him. . . .

6. To acknowledge this truth is an affirmative precept, as it is said "I am the Lord, thy God". And whoever permits the thought to enter his mind that there is another deity besides this God, violates a prohibition; as it is said "Thou shalt have no other gods before me", and denies the essence of Religion—this doctrine being the great principle on which everything depends. . . .

8. That the Holy One, blessed be He, is not a physical body, is explicitly set forth in the Pentateuch and in the Prophets, as it is said "(Know therefore) that the Lord, He is God in Heaven above, and upon the Earth beneath"; and a physical body is not in two places at one time. Furthermore, it is said, "For Ye saw no manner of similitude"; and again it is said, "To whom then will Ye liken me, or shall I be equal?". If He were a body, He would be like other bodies.

9. Since this is so, what is the meaning of the following expressions found in the Torah: "Beneath his feet"; "Written with the finger of God"; "The hand of God"; "The eyes of God"; "The ears of God"; and similar phrases? All these expressions are adapted to the mental capacity of the majority of mankind who have a clear perception of physical bodies only. The Torah speaks in the language of men. All these phrases are metaphorical like the sentence "If I whet my glittering sword". Has God then a sword and does he slay with a sword? The term is used allegorically and all these phrases are to be understood in a similar sense. That this view is correct is proved by the fact that one prophet says that he had a vision of the Holy One, blessed be He, "Whose garment was white as snow", while another says that he saw Him "with dyed garments from Bozrah". Moses, our teacher, himself saw Him at the Red Sea as a mighty man waging war and on Sinai, as a Congregational Reader wrapped (in his Talith)—all indicating that in reality He has no form or figure. These only appeared in a prophetic vision. But God's essence as it really is, the human mind does not understand and is incapable of grasping or investigating. And this is expressed in the scriptural text "Canst thou, by searching, find out God? Canst thou find out the Almighty unto perfection? . . ."

12. This being so, the expressions in the Pentateuch and books of the Prophets already mentioned, and others similar to these, are all of them metaphorical and rhetorical, as for example, "He that sitteth in the heavens shall laugh", "They have provoked me to anger with their vanities", "As the Lord rejoiced", etc. To all these phrases, applies the saying "The Torah speaks in the language of men." So too, it is said "Do they provoke Me to anger?"; and yet it is said "I am the Lord, I change not." If God was sometimes angry and sometimes rejoiced, He would be changing. All these states exist in physical beings that are of obscure and mean condition, dwelling in houses of clay, whose foundation is in the dust. Infinitely blessed and exalted above all this, is God, blessed be He.

READING 4-8B

The Guide of the Perplexed, Part III, Chapter 31

There is a group of human beings who consider it a grievous thing that causes should be given for any law; what would please them most is that the intellect would not find a meaning for the commandments and prohibitions. What compels them to feel thus is a sickness that they find in their souls, a sickness to which they are unable to give utterance and of which they cannot furnish a satisfactory account. For they think that if those laws were useful in this existence and had been given to us for this or that reason, it would be as if they derived from the reflection and the understanding of some intelligent being. If, however, there is a thing for which the intellect could not find any meaning at all and that does not lead to something useful, it indubitably derives from God; for the reflection of man would not lead to such a thing. It is as if, according to these people of weak intellects, man were more perfect than his Maker; for man speaks and acts in a manner that leads to some intended end, whereas the deity does not act thus, but commands us to do things that are not useful to us and forbids us to do things that are not harmful to us. But He is far exalted above this; the contrary is the case—the whole purpose consisting in what is useful for us, as we have explained on the basis of its dictum: *For our good always, that He might preserve us alive, as it is at this day.* And it says: *Which shall hear all these statutes and say: Surely this great community is a wise and understanding people.* Thus it states explicitly that even all the *statutes* will show to all the nations that they have been given with *wisdom and understanding.* Now if there is a thing for which no reason is known and that does not either procure something useful or ward off something harmful, why should one say of one who believes in it or practices it that he is *wise and understanding* and of great worth? And why should the religious communities think it a wonder? Rather things are indubitably as we have mentioned: every *commandment* from among these *six hundred and thirteen commandments* exists either with a view to communicating a correct opinion, or to putting an end to an unhealthy opinion, or to communicating a rule of justice, or to warding off an injustice, or to endowing men with a noble moral quality, or to warning them against an evil moral quality. Thus all [the commandments] are bound up with three things: opinions, moral qualities, and political civic actions. We do not count speeches as one of these things since the speeches that the Law enjoins or forbids belong in part to the class of civic actions, and in part are meant to cause opinions, and in part are meant to cause moral qualities. Therefore we have limited ourselves here, in giving reasons for every law, to these three classes.

READING 4-8C

The Guide of the Perplexed, Part III, Chapter 51

This chapter that we bring now does not include additional matter over and above what is comprised in the other chapters of this Treatise. It is only a kind of a conclusion, at the same time explaining the worship as practiced by one who has apprehended the true realities peculiar only to Him after he has obtained an apprehension of what He is; and it also guides him toward achieving this worship, which is the end of man, and makes known to him how providence watches over him in this habitation until he is brought over to the *bundle of life.*

I shall begin the discourse in this chapter with a parable that I shall compose for you. I say then: The ruler is in his palace, and all his subjects are partly within the city and partly outside the city. Of those who are within the city, some have turned their backs upon the ruler's habitation, their faces being turned another way. Others seek to reach the ruler's habitation, turn toward it, and desire to enter it and to stand before him, but up to now they have not yet seen the wall of the habitation. Some of those who seek to reach it have come up to the habitation and walk around it searching for its gate. Some of them have entered the gate and walk about in the antechambers. Some of them have entered the inner court of the habitation and have come to be with the king, in one and the same place with him, namely, in the ruler's habitation. But their having come into the inner part of the habitation does not mean that they see the ruler or speak to him. For after their coming into the inner part of the habitation, it is indispensable that they should make another effort; then they will be in the presence of the ruler, see him from afar or from nearby, or hear the ruler's speech or speak to him.

Now I shall interpret to you this parable that I have invented. I say then: Those who are outside the city are all human individuals who have no doctrinal belief, neither one based on speculation nor one that accepts the authority of tradition: such individuals as the furthermost Turks found in the remote North, the Negroes found in the remote South, and those who resemble them from among them that are with us in these climes. The status of those is like that of irrational animals. To my mind they do not have the rank of men, but have among the beings a rank lower than the rank of man but higher than the rank of the apes. For they have the external shape and lineaments of a man and a faculty of discernment that is superior to that of the apes.

Those who are within the city, but have turned their backs upon the ruler's habitation, are people who have opinions and are engaged in speculation, but who have adopted incorrect opinions either because of some great error that befell them in the course of their speculation or because of their following the traditional authority of one who had fallen into error. Accordingly because of these opinions, the more these people walk, the greater is their distance from the ruler's habitation. And they are far worse than the first. They are those concerning whom necessity at certain times impels killing them and blotting out the traces of their opinions lest they should lead astray the ways of others.

Those who seek to reach the ruler's habitation and to enter it, but never see the ruler's habitation, are the multitude of the adherents of the Law, I refer to *the ignoramuses who observe the commandments*.

Those who have come up to the habitation and walk around it are the jurists who believe true opinions on the basis of traditional authority and study the law concerning the practices of divine service, but do not engage in speculation concerning the fundamental principles of religion and make no inquiry whatever regarding the rectification of belief.

Those who have plunged into speculation concerning the fundamental principles of religion, have entered the antechambers. People there indubitably have different ranks. He, however, who has achieved demonstration, to the extent that that is possible, of everything that may be demonstrated; and who has ascertained in divine matters, to the extent that that is possible, everything that may be ascertained; and who has come close to certainty in those matters in which one can only come close to it—has come to be with the ruler in the inner part of the habitation.

Know, my son, that as long as you are engaged in studying the mathematical sciences and the art of logic, you are one of those who walk around the house searching for its gate, as [the Sages], *may their memory be blessed*, have said resorting to a parable: *Ben Zoma is still outside.* If, however, you have understood the natural things, you have entered the habitation and are walking in the antechambers. If, however, you have achieved perfection in the natural things and have understood divine science, you have entered in the ruler's place *into the inner court* and are with him in one habitation. This is the rank of the men of science; they, however, are of different grades of perfection.

There are those who set their thought to work after having attained perfection in the divine science, turn wholly toward God, may He be cherished and held sublime, renounce what is other than He, and direct all the acts of their intellect toward an examination of the beings with a view to drawing from them proof with regard to Him, so as to know His governance of them in whatever way it is possible. These people are those who are present in the ruler's council. This is the rank of the prophets. Among them there is he who because of the greatness of his apprehension and his renouncing everything that is other than God, may He be exalted, has attained such a degree that it is said of him, *And he was there with the Lord*, putting questions and receiving answers, speaking and being spoken to, in that holy place. And because of his great joy in that which he apprehended, *he did neither eat bread nor drink water.* For his intellect attained such strength that all the gross faculties in the body ceased to function. I refer to the various kinds of the sense of touch. Some prophets could only see, some of them from close by and some from afar, as [a prophet] says: *From afar the Lord appeared unto me.* The various degrees of prophecy have already been discussed by us. Let us now return to the subject of this chapter, which is to confirm men in the intention to set their thought to work on God alone after they have achieved knowledge of Him, as we have explained. This is the worship peculiar to those who have apprehended the true realities; the more they think of Him and of being with Him, the more their worship increases. . . .

SELECTIONS FROM MAIMONIDES' LETTERS

Maimonides' extensive correspondence provides another perspective on his personality, concerns, and convictions. The following selections* offer rare glimpses of Maimonides the person: (1) a letter to Samuel ibn Tibbon describing his exhausting professional and community responsibilities in Egypt; (2) a letter of sincere encouragement to a convert to Judaism; and (3) a letter to Ḥasdai ha-Levi, expressing a universal love for all humanity.

READING 4-9A

Maimonides to Samuel ibn Tibbon

God knows that, in order to write this to you, I have escaped to a secluded spot, where people would not think to find me, sometimes leaning for support against the wall, sometimes lying down on account of my excessive weakness, for I have grown old and feeble.

---

*Reprinted from Franz Kobler, *Letters of Jews through the Ages*, by permission of Hebrew Publishing Company.

But with respect to your wish to come here to me, I cannot but say how greatly your visit would delight me, for I truly long to commune with you, and would anticipate our meeting with even greater joy than you. Yet I must advise you not to expose yourself to the perils of the voyage, for, beyond seeing me, and my doing all I could to honour you, you would not derive any advantage from your visit. Do not expect to be able to confer with me on any scientific subject for even one hour, either by day or by night. For the following is my daily occupation:

I dwell at Mizr [Fostat] and the Sultan resides at Kahira [Cairo]; these two places are two Sabbath days' journey distant from each other. My duties to the Sultan are very heavy. I am obliged to visit him every day, early in the morning; and when he or any of his children, or any of the inmates of his harem, are indisposed, I dare not quit Kahira, but must stay during the greater part of the day in the palace. It also frequently happens that one or two royal officers fall sick, and I must attend to their healing. Hence, as a rule, I repair to Kahira very early in the day, and even if nothing unusual happens, I do not return to Mizr until the afternoon. Then I am almost dying with hunger. . . . I find the antechambers filled with people, both Jews and Gentiles, nobles and common people, judges and bailiffs, friends and foes—a mixed multitude who await the time of my return.

I dismount from my animal, wash my hands, go forth to my patients, and entreat them to bear with me while I partake of some slight refreshment, the only meal I take in the twenty-four hours. Then I go forth to attend to my patients, and write prescriptions and directions for their various ailments. Patients go in and out until nightfall, and sometimes even, I solemnly assure you, until two hours or more in the night. I converse with and prescribe for them while lying down from sheer fatigue; and when night falls, I am so exhausted that I can scarcely speak.

In consequence of this, no Israelite can have any private interview with me, except on the Sabbath. On that day the whole congregation, or at least the majority of the members, come to me after the morning service, when I instruct them as to their proceedings during the whole week; we study together a little until noon, when they depart. Some of them return, and read with me after the afternoon service until evening prayers. In this manner I spend that day. I have here related to you only a part of what you would see if you were to visit me.

Now, when you have completed for our brethren the translation you have commenced, I beg that you will come to me, but not with the hope of deriving any advantage from your visit as regards your studies; for my time is, as I have shown you, excessively occupied.

READING 4-9B

Maimonides to Obadiah the Proselyte

Thus says Moses the son of Rabbi Maimon, one of the exiles from Jerusalem, who lived in Spain:

I received the question of the master Obadiah, the wise and learned proselyte, may the Lord reward him for his work, may a perfect recompense be bestowed upon him by the Lord of Israel, under whose wings he has sought cover.

You ask me if you, too, are allowed to say in the blessings and prayers you offer alone or in the congregation: '*Our* God' and 'God of *our* Fathers,' 'Thou who hast sanctified *us* through Thy commandments,' 'Thou who hast separated *us*,' 'Thou who hast chosen *us*,' 'Thou who hast inherited *us*,' 'Thou who hast brought *us* out of the land of Egypt,' 'Thou who hast worked miracles to *our* fathers,' and more of this kind.

Yes, you may say all this in the prescribed order and not change it in the least. In the same way as every Jew by birth says his blessing and prayer, you, too, shall bless and pray alike, whether you are alone or pray in the congregation. The reason for this is, that Abraham, our father, taught the people, opened their minds, and revealed to them the true faith and the unity of God; he rejected the idols and abolished their adoration; he brought many children under the wings of the Divine Presence; he gave them counsel and advice, and ordered his sons and the members of his household after him to keep the ways of the Lord forever, as it is written, 'For I have known him to the end that he may command his children and his household after him, that they may keep the way of the Lord, to do righteousness and justice.' Ever since then whoever adopts Judaism and confesses the unity of the Divine Name, as it is prescribed in the Torah, is counted among the disciples of Abraham, our father, peace be with him. These men are Abraham's household, and he it is who converted them to righteousness.

In the same way as he converted his contemporaries through his words and teaching, he converts future generations through the testament he left to his children and household after him. Thus Abraham, our father, peace be with him, is the father of his pious posterity who keep his ways, and the father of his disciples and of all proselytes who adopt Judaism.

Therefore you shall pray, 'Our God' and 'God of our fathers,' because Abraham, peace be with him, is *your* father. And you shall pray, 'Thou who hast taken for his own our fathers,' for the land has been given to Abraham, as it is said, 'Arise, walk through the land in the length of it and in the breadth of it; for I will give it unto thee.' As to the words, 'Thou who hast brought us out of the land of Egypt' or 'Thou who hast done miracles to our fathers'—these you may change, if you will, and say, 'Thou who hast brought Israel out of the land of Egypt' and 'Thou who hast done miracles to Israel.' If, however, you do not change them, it is no transgression, because since you have come under the wings of the Divine Presence and confessed the Lord, no difference exists between you and us, and all miracles done to us have been done as it were to us and to you. Thus it is said in the book of Isaiah, 'Neither let the son of the stranger, that hath joined himself to the Lord, speak, saying "The Lord hath utterly separated me from His people." ' There is no difference whatever between you and us. You shall certainly say the blessing, 'Who has chosen us,' 'Who has given us,' 'Who hast taken us for Thine own' and 'Who has separated us': for the Creator, may He be extolled, has indeed chosen you and separated you from the nations and given you the Torah. For the Torah has been given to us *and* to the proselytes, as it is said, 'One ordinance shall be both for you of the congregation, and also for the stranger that sojourneth with you, an ordinance for ever in your generations; as you are, so shall the stranger be before the Lord,' Know that our fathers, when they came out of Egypt, were mostly idolators; they had mingled with the pagans in Egypt and imitated their way of life, until the Holy One, may He be blessed, sent Moses, our teacher, the master of all prophets, who separated us from the nations and brought us under the wings of the Divine Presence, us and all proselytes, and gave to all of us one Law.

Do not consider your origin as inferior. While we are the descendants of Abraham, Isaac and Jacob, you derive from Him through whose word the world was created. As is said by Isaiah: 'One shall say, I am the Lord's, and another shall call himself by the name of Jacob.' . . .

READING 4-9C

Maimonides to Hasdai ha-Levi

. . . As to your question about the nations, know that the Lord desires the heart, and that the intention of the heart is the measure of all things. That is why our sages say, 'The pious men among the Gentiles have a share in the World-to-Come,' namely, if they have acquired what can be acquired of the knowledge of God, and if they ennoble their souls with worthy qualities. There is no doubt that every man who ennobles his soul with excellent morals and wisdom based on the faith in God, certainly belongs to the men of the World-to-Come. That is why our sages said, 'Even a non-Jew who studies the Torah of our master Moses resembles a High Priest.' What is essential is nothing else than that one tries to elevate his soul towards God through the Torah. Thus said David, 'I put the Lord always before me; because He is on my right hand I do not waver.' And Moses is praised for this reason: 'This man was very humble' because this is the height of perfection. Our sages said also, 'Be exceedingly humble.' . . . And the philosophers declared that it is very difficult to find a man who is completely perfect in morality and wisdom. He in whom this perfection is found is called a Saint, and surely such a man is on the steps which lead to the higher world. . . . Besides, there is no doubt that the Patriarchs as well as Noah and Adam, who obviously did not observe the Torah, by no means became denizens of Gehinnom. On the contrary: as they achieved what pertains to the ennoblement of man they are raised aloft. All this cannot be secured by fasting, praying and lamentation if knowledge and true faith are absent, because in such behaviour God can be near to the mouth but far from the heart. The basis of all things is [knowledge] that nothing is eternal save God alone. . . .

THE CHARTER OF BISHOP RUDIGER OF SPEYER

In 1084 Rudiger, the Biship of Speyer, invited the Jews from the neighboring town of Mainz, whose homes had been destroyed by fire, to settle in his village. Hopeful of improving Speyer's economy through the presence of the Jews, he offered them physical protection, trading rights, and freedom to live under their own religious laws. The resulting charter, like the earlier ones of the Carolingian era which had been contracted with individual Jews, provided this small Jewish community with a legal status and a modicum of security in return for the services they rendered. Rudiger's agreement to build a wall around the Jewish quarter suggests the potential violence the Jews may have come to expect by then, twelve years before the first crusade. A brief notice in Hebrew written by a twelfth-century Speyer Jew provides additional information about the circumstances surrounding Rudiger's grant.

READING 4-10

The Latin Document

In the name of the holy and undivided Trinity. When I wished to make a city out of the village of Speyer, I Rudiger, surnamed Huozmann, bishop of Speyer, thought that the glory of our town would be augmented a thousandfold if I were to bring Jews.

1. Those Jews whom I have gathered I placed outside the neighborhood and residential area of the other burghers. In order that they not be easily disrupted by the insolence of the mob, I have encircled them with a wall.
2. The site of their residential area I have acquired properly—first the hill partially by purchase and partially by exchange; then the valley I received by gift of the heirs. I have given them that area on the condition that they pay annually three and one-half pounds in Speyer currency for the shared use of the monks.
3. I have accorded them the free right of exchanging gold and silver and of buying and selling everything they use—both within their residential area and, outside, beyond the gate down to the wharf and on the wharf itself. I have given them the same right throughout the entire city.
4. I have, moreover, given them out of the land of the Church burial ground to be held in perpetuity.
5. I have also added that, if a Jew from elsewhere has quartered with them, he shall pay no toll.
6. Just as the mayor of the city serves among the burghers, so too shall the Jewish leader adjudicate any quarrel which might arise among them or against them. If he be unable to determine the issue, then the case shall come before the bishop of the city or his chamberlain.
7. They must discharge the responsibility of watch, guard, and fortification only in their own area. The responsibility of guarding they may discharge along with their servants.
8. They may legally have nurses and servants from among our people.
9. They may legally sell to Christians slaughtered meats which they consider unfit for themselves according to the sanctity of their law. Christians may legally buy such meats.

In short, in order to achieve the height of kindness, I have granted them a legal status more generous than any which the Jewish people have in any city of the German kingdom.

Lest one of my successors dare to deny this grant and concession and force them to a greater tax, claiming that the Jews themselves usurped this status and did not receive it from the bishop, I have given them this charter of the aforesaid grant as proper testimony. In order that the meaning of this matter remains throughout the generations, I have strengthened it by signing it and by the imposition of my seal; as may be seen below, I have caused it to be sealed.

This charter has been given on September 13, 1084 A.D.

The Hebrew Report

At the outset, when we came to establish our residence in Speyer—may its foundations never falter!—it was as a result of the fire that broke out in the city of Mainz.

The city of Mainz was the city of our origin and the residence of our ancestors, the ancient and revered community, praised above all communities in the empire. All the Jews' quarter and their street was burned, and we stood in great fear of the burghers. At the same time, Meir Cohen came from Worms, bearing a copy of *Torat Cohanim* [either Leviticus itself or the midrash on Leviticus]. The burghers thought that it was silver or gold and slew him . . .

R. Meshullam said to them: "Fear not, for all this was ordained." We then decided to set forth from there and to settle wherever we might find a fortified city. Perhaps the compassionate Lord might show compassion and the merciful One might exhibit mercy and the All-Helpful might help to sustain us, as in fact He does this very day.

The bishop of Speyer greeted us warmly, sending his ministers and soldiers after us. He gave us a place in the city and expressed his intention to build about us a strong wall to protect us from our enemies, to afford us fortification. He pitied us as a man pities his son. We then set forth our prayers before our Creator, morning and evening, for a number of years.

THE CRUSADERS AT MAINZ

In 1096 the Pope called for a massive army of crusaders to liberate the Holy Land from the polluted hands of the Muslim "infidels." Undisciplined and theologically unsophisticated, thousands of Europeans gathered to "atone" for their sins and to do battle for Christ. The crusading hordes swarmed dangerously across the European continent, constituting a major threat to the welfare and security of the communities in their path. To European Jews, especially those living in the Rhineland, the crusader presence proved to be particularly alarming. For many crusaders it seemed preposterous, so they thought, to set out on a long journey to kill God's enemies while his worst enemies, those who had murdered him, the Jews, were dwelling in the midst of the Christian world. Accordingly, some five thousand Jews lost their lives during the first crusade, either massacred by Christians or having taken their own lives as martyrs.

The memory of the massacres is preserved in three major Hebrew chronicles, in Hebrew liturgical poems, and in some shorter Christian accounts. One of the chronicles, written by Solomon bar Samson around 1140 excerpted below, provides not only a relatively accurate picture of the Christian atrocities but also a lucid account of the Jewish responses to the new Christian aggressiveness. This reading documents the singular response of the Jewish victims dying as religious martyrs. During their confrontation with the crusaders these Jews openly revealed their willingness to testify to the truth of their faith and to repudiate Christianity by

taking their own lives. The willing acceptance of martyrdom by Ashkenazic (German) Jewry as delineated below stands in sharp contrast to the
emphatic warnings of Maimonides and other Spanish rabbis who counseled the Jews in similar circumstances either to escape or to accept a
forced conversion.

READING 4-11

It was on the third of Siwan . . . at noon [Tuesday, May 27], that Emico [one of
the crusader leaders] the wicked, the enemy of the Jews, came with his whole army
against the city gate, and the citizens opened it up for him. Then the enemies of the
Lord said to each other: "Look! They have opened up the gate for us. Now let us
avenge the blood of 'the hanged one' [Jesus]."

The children of the holy covenant who were there, martyrs who feared the
Most High, although they saw the great multitude, an army numerous as the sand
on the shore of the sea, still clung to their Creator. Then young and old donned their
armor and girded on their weapons, and at their head was Rabbi Kalonymus ben
Meshullam, the chief of the community. Yet because of the many troubles and the
fasts which they had observed they had no strength to stand up against the enemy.
Then came gangs and bands, sweeping through like a flood, until Mayence was
filled from end to end.

The foe Emico proclaimed in the hearing of the community that the enemy be
driven from the city and be put to flight. Panic was great in the town. Each Jew in
the inner court of the bishop girded on his weapons, and all moved towards the
palace gate to fight the crusaders and the citizens. They fought each other up to the
very gate, but the sins of the Jews brought it about that the enemy overcame them
and took the gate.

The hand of the Lord was heavy against His people. All the Gentiles were gathered together against the Jews in the courtyard to blot out their name, and the
strength of our people weakened when they saw the wicked Edomites [Christians]
overpowering them. The bishop's men, who had promised to help them, were the
very first to flee, thus delivering the Jews into the hands of the enemy. They were
indeed a poor support; even the bishop himself fled from his church for it was
thought to kill him also because he had spoken good things of the Jews. . . .

When the children of the holy covenant saw that the heavenly decree of death
had been issued and that the enemy had conquered them and had entered the courtyard, then all of them—old men and young, virgins and children, servants and
maids—cried out together to their Father in heaven and, weeping for themselves
and for their lives, accepted as just the sentence of God. One to another they said:
"Let us be strong and let us bear the yoke of the holy religion, for only in this world
can the enemy kill us—and the easiest of the four deaths is by the sword. But we,
our souls in paradise, shall continue to live eternally, in the great shining reflection
[of the divine glory]."

With a whole heart and with a willing soul they then spoke: "After all it is not
right to criticize the acts of God—blessed be He and blessed be His name—who has
given to us His Torah and a command to put ourselves to death, to kill ourselves for
the unity of His holy name. Happy are we if we do His will. Happy is anyone who is
killed and slaughtered, who dies for the unity of His name, so that he is ready to

enter the World to Come, to dwell in the heavenly camp with the righteous—with Rabbi Akiba and his companions, the pillars of the universe, who were killed for His name's sake. Not only this; but he exchanges the world of darkness for the world of light, the world of trouble for the world of joy, and the world that passes away for the world that lasts for all eternity." Then all of them, to a man, cried out with a loud voice: "Now we must delay no longer, for the enemy are already upon us. Let us hasten and offer ourselves as a sacrifice to the Lord. Let him who has a knife examine it that it not be nicked, and let him come and slaughter us for the sanctification of the Only One, the Everlasting, and then let him cut his own throat or plunge the knife into his own body."

As soon as the enemy came into the courtyard they found some of the very pious there with our brilliant master, Isaac ben Moses. He stretched out his neck, and his head they cut off first. The others, wrapped in their fringed praying-shawls, sat by themselves in the courtyard, eager to do the will of their Creator. They did not care to flee into the chamber to save themselves for this temporal life, but out of love they received upon themselves the sentence of God. The enemy showered stones and arrows upon them, but they did not care to flee; and "with the stroke of the sword, and with slaughter, and destruction" the foe killed all of those whom they found there. When those in the chambers saw the deed of these righteous ones, how the enemy had already come upon them, they then cried out, all of them: "There is nothing better than for us to offer our lives as a sacrifice."

The women there girded their loins with strength and slew their sons and their daughters and then themselves. Many men, too, plucked up courage and killed their wives, their sons, their infants. The tender and delicate mother slaughtered the babe she had played with; all of them, men and women arose and slaughtered one another. The maidens and the young brides and grooms looked out of the windows and in a loud voice cried: "Look and see, O our God, what we do for the sanctification of Thy great name in order not to exchange you for a hanged and crucified one. . . ."

Thus were the precious children of Zion, the Jews of Mayence, tried with ten trials like Abraham, our father, and like Hananiah, Mishael, and Azariah. They tied their sons as Abraham tied Isaac his son, and they received upon themselves with a willing soul the yoke of the fear of God, the King of the Kings of Kings, the Holy One, blessed be He, rather than deny and exchange the religion of our King for "an abhorred offshoot [Jesus]. . . ." They stretched out their necks to the slaughter and they delivered their pure souls to their Father in heaven. Righteous and pious women bared their throats to each other, offering to be sacrificed for the unity of the Name. A father turning to his son or brother, a brother to his sister, a woman to her son or daughter, a neighbor to a neighbor or a friend, a groom to a bride, a fiancé to a fiancée, would kill and would be killed, and blood touched blood. The blood of the men mingled with their wives', the blood of the fathers with their children's, the blood of the brothers with their sisters', the blood of the teachers with their disciples', the blood of the grooms with their brides', the blood of the leaders with their cantors', the blood of the judges with their scribes', and the blood of infants and sucklings with their mothers'. For the unity of the honored and awe-inspiring Name were they killed and slaughtered.

The ears of him who hears these things will tingle, for who has ever heard anything like this? Inquire now and look about, was there ever such an abundant sacrifice as this since the days of the primeval Adam? Were there ever eleven hundred offerings on one day, each one of them like the sacrifice of Isaac, the son of Abraham?

For the sake of Isaac who was ready to be sacrificed on Mount Moriah, the world shook, as it is said: "Behold their valiant ones cry without; the angels of peace weep bitterly and the heavens grow dark." Yet see what these martyrs did! Why did the heavens not grow dark and the stars not withdraw their brightness? Why did not the moon and the sun grow dark in their heavens when on one day, on the third of Siwan, on a Tuesday, eleven hundred souls were killed and slaughtered, among them so many infants and sucklings who had not transgressed nor sinned, so many poor, innocent souls?

Wilt Thou, despite this, still restrain Thyself, O Lord? For Thy sake it was that these numberless souls were killed. Avenge quickly the blood of Thy servants which was spilt in our days and in our sight. Amen.

BERNARD OF CLAIRVAUX ON PROTECTING THE JEWS FROM CRUSADER VIOLENCE

Neither the Church nor the secular princes empowered to protect the Jews were prepared to offer formidable resistance to the crusaders. Both were caught by surprise; both proved incapable of controlling the unruly crowds that burst upon defenseless Jewish communities to act out a hatred nurtured by years of Church teaching, goaded by infectious crowd hysteria.

When Bernard, the abbot of Clairvaux, organized a second crusade in the middle of the twelfth century, he was determined to avert a repetition of the tragedies. In 1146, in a widely distributed missive to the leaders of his newly assembled army, he demanded that Jewish life and property not be harmed. He reminded them of the Augustinian doctrine which said that although the Jews were damnable, they ought to be preserved until the end of time. Fully aware that the Church's position regarding the Jews had been violated by crusader violence, he attempted to walk the fine line of Christian teaching, insisting that the Jews be protected, even while portraying them as enemies of Christ.

READING 4-12

I address myself to you, the people of England, in the cause of Christ, in whom lies your salvation. I say this so that the warrant of the Lord and my zeal in his interests may excuse my hardihood in addressing you. I am a person of small account, but my desire for you in Christ is not small. This is my reason and motive for writing, this is why I make bold to address you all by letter. I would have preferred to do so by word of mouth had I but the strength to come to you as I desire. . . .

Now is the acceptable time, now is the day of abundant salvation. The earth is shaken because the Lord of heaven is losing his land, the land in which he appeared to men, in which he lived amongst men for more than thirty years; the land made glorious by his miracles, holy by his blood; the land in which the flowers of his resurrection first blossomed. And now, for our sins, the enemy of the Cross has begun to lift his sacrilegious head there, and to devastate with the sword that blessed land, that land of promise. Alas, if there should be none to withstand him, he will soon invade the very city of the living God, overturn the arsenal of our redemption, and defile the holy places which have been adorned by the blood of the immaculate lamb. They have cast their greedy eyes especially on the holy sanctuaries of our Christian Religion, and they long particularly to violate that couch on which, for our sakes, the Lord of our life fell asleep in death.

What are you doing, you mighty men of valour? What are you doing, you servants of the Cross? Will you thus cast holy things to dogs, pearls before swine? How great a number of sinners have here confessed with tears and obtained pardon for their sins since the time when these holy precincts were cleansed of pagan filth by the swords of our fathers! The evil one sees this and is enraged, he gnashes his teeth and withers away in fury. He stirs up his vessels of wrath so that if they do but once lay hands upon these holy places there shall be no sign or trace of piety left. Such a catastrophe would be a source of appalling grief for all time, but it would also be a source of confusion and endless shame for our generation. What think you, my brethren? Is the hand of the Lord shortened and is he now powerless to work salvation, so that he must call upon us, petty worms of the earth, to save and restore to him his heritage? Could he not send more than twelve legions of angels, or even just say the word and save his land? Most certainly he has the power to do this whenever he wishes, but I tell you that God is trying you. 'He looks down from heaven at the race of men to find one soul that reflects and makes God its aim', one soul that sorrows for him. For God has pity on his people and on those who have grievously fallen away and has prepared for them a means of salvation. Consider with what care he plans our salvation, and be amazed. Look, sinners, at the depths of his pity, and take courage. He does not want your death but rather that you should turn to him and live. So he seeks not to overthrow you but to help you. When Almighty God so treats murderers, thieves, adulterers, perjurers, and such like, as persons able to find righteousness in his service, what is it but an act of exquisite courtesy all God's own? Do not hesitate. God is good, and were he intent on your punishment he would not have asked of you this present service or indeed have accepted it even had you offered it. Again I say consider the Almighty's goodness and pay heed to his plans of mercy. He puts himself under obligation to you, or rather feigns to do so, so that he can help you to satisfy your obligations towards himself. He puts himself in your debt so that, in return for your taking up arms in his cause, he can reward you with pardon for your sins and everlasting glory. I call blessed the generation that can seize an opportunity of such rich indulgence as this, blessed to be alive in this year of jubilee, this year of God's choice. The blessing is spread throughout the whole world, and all the world is flocking to receive this badge of immortality.

Your land is well known to be rich in young and vigorous men. The world is full of their praises, and the renown of their courage is on the lips of all. Gird yourselves therefore like men and take up arms with joy and with zeal for your Christian name, in order to 'take vengeance on the heathen, and curb the nations.' For how long will your men continue to shed Christian blood; for how long will they continue to fight amongst themselves? You attack each other, you slay each other and by each other you are slain. What is this savage craving of yours? Put a stop to it now, for it is not fighting but foolery. Thus to risk both soul and body is not brave but shocking, is not strength but folly. But now, O mighty soldiers, O men of war, you have a cause for which you can fight without danger to your souls; a cause in which to conquer is glorious and for which to die is gain.

But to those of you who are merchants, men quick to seek a bargain, let me point out the advantages of this great opportunity. Do not miss them. Take up the sign of the Cross and you will find indulgence for all the sins which you humbly confess. The cost is small, the reward is great. Venture with devotion and the gain will be God's kingdom. They do well therefore who have taken up this heavenly sign, and they also will do well, and profit themselves, who hasten to take up what will prove to be for them a sign of salvation.

For the rest, not I but the Apostle warns you, brethren, not to believe every spirit. I have heard with great joy of the zeal for God's glory which burns in your midst, but your zeal needs the timely restraint of knowledge. The Jews are not to be persecuted, killed or even put to flight. Ask anyone who knows the Sacred Scriptures what he finds foretold of the Jews in the psalm. 'Not for their destruction do I pray', it says. The Jews are for us the living words of Scripture, for they remind us always of what our Lord suffered. They are dispersed all over the world so that by expiating their crime they may be everywhere the living witnesses of our redemption. Hence the same psalm adds, 'only let thy power disperse them'. And so it is: dispersed they are. Under Christian princes they endure a hard captivity, but 'they only wait for the time of their deliverance'. Finally we are told by the Apostle that when the time is ripe all Israel shall be saved. But those who die before will remain in death. I will not mention those Christian money lenders, if they can be called Christian, who, where there are no Jews, act, I grieve to say, in a manner worse than any Jew. If the Jews are utterly wiped out, what will become of our hope for their promised salvation, their eventual conversion? If the pagans were similarly subjugated to us then, in my opinion, we should wait for them rather than seek them out with swords. But as they have now begun to attack us, it is necessary for those of us who do not carry a sword in vain to repel them with force. It is an act of Christian piety both to vanquish the proud and also 'to spare the subjected', especially those for whom we have a law and a promise, and whose flesh was shared by Christ whose name be for ever blessed.

THE POPULAR IMAGE OF THE JEW IN MEDIEVAL CHRISTIAN SOCIETY

From the twelfth century onward Jewish life throughout Christian Europe steadily deteriorated. The events of 1096 and their aftermath contributed to an atmosphere of growing intolerance and antagonism toward Jews, but constituted only one of many factors—economic, political, and psychological—in the growing tide of Christian hostility toward the Jewish minority.

Most alarming of all was the popular image of the Jew emerging in Christian civilization. A characterization of Jewish civilization appeared in ballads, poetry, songs, plays, and especially in art work that was far worse than the official view held by either the Church or the secular governments of Europe. The popular charges against the Jews focused on their image as a diabolical people; the Jew was considered an enemy of mankind, an anti-Christ, a sorcerer, an economic exploiter and pitiless usurer, and a murderer of innocent Christian children. All of these themes, some depicted below in a typical ballad originating in England representing an early version of Shakespeare's Shylock, served to conjure up quite a horrific portrait. They allow us to understand the popular support that the Church and state possessed in carrying out their anti-Jewish policies.

READING 4-13

Gernutus the Jew of Venice

The First Part

In Venice towne not long agoe
    A cruel Jew did dwell,
Which lived all on usurie,
    As Italian writers tell.

Gernutus called was the Jew,
    Which never thought to dye,
Nor ever yet did any good
    To them in streets that lie.

His life was like a barrow hogge,
    That liveth many a day,
Yet never once doth any good,
    Until men will him slay,

Or like a filthy heap of dung,
    That lyeth in a whoard;
Which never can do any good,
    Till it be spread abroad.

So fares it with the usurer,
    He cannot sleep in rest
For feare the thiefe will him pursue,
    To plucke him from his nest.

His heart doth thinke on many a wile
    How to deceive the poore;
His mouth is almost ful of mucke,
    Yet still he gapes for more.

His wife must lend a shilling,
    For every weeke a penny;

Yet bring a pledge that is double worth,
    If that you will have any.

And see, likewise, you keepe your day,
    Or else you loose it all:
This was the living of the wife,
    Her cow she did it call.

Within that city dwelt that time
    A marchant of great fame,
Which being distressed in his need,
    Unto Gernutus came:

Desiring him to stand his friend
    For twelvemonth and a day;
To lend to him an hundred crowns;
    And he for it would pay.

Whatsoever he would demand of him,
    And pledges he should have:
"No," quoth the Jew, with flearing lookes
    "Sir, aske what you will have.

"No penny for the loane of it
    For one year you shall pay;
You may doe me as good a turne,
    Before my dying day.

"But we will have a merry jeast,
    For to be talked long:
You shall make me a bond," quoth he,
    "That shall be large and strong.

"And this shall be the forfeyture,—
    Of your owne fleshe a pound:
If you agree, make you the bond,
    And here is a hundred crownes."

"With right good will," the marchant he says,
    And so the bond was made,
When twelve month and a day drew on,
    That backe it should be payd,

The marchant's ships were all at sea,
    And money came not in;
Which way to take, or what to doe,
    To thinke he doth begin.

And to Gernutus strait he comes,
    With cap and bended knee;
And sayde to him, "Of curtesie,
    I pray you beare with mee.

"My day is come, and I have not
    The money for to pay;
And little good the forfeyture
    Will doe you, I dare say."

"With all my heart," Gernutus sayd,
    "Commaund it to your minde:
In thinges of bigger weight than this
    You shall me ready finde."

He goes his way; the day once past,
    Gernutus doth not slacke
To get a sergiant presently,
    And clapt him on the backe.

And layd him into prison strong,
    And sued his bond withall;
And when the judgement day was come,
    For judgement he did call.

The marchant's friends came thither fast,
    With many a weeping eye,
For other means they could not find,
    But he that day must dye.

The Second Part

Some offered for his hundred crownes
    Five hundred for to pay;
And some a thousand, two or three,
    Yet still he did denay.

And at the last ten thousand crownes
    They offered, him to save:
Gernutus sayd, "I will no gold,
    My forfeite I will have.

"A pound of fleshe is my demand,
    And that shall be my hire."
Then sayd the judge, "Yet, good my friend,
    Let me of you desire

"To take the fleshe from such a place,
    As yet you let him live:
Do so, and lo! an hundred crownes
    To thee here will I give."

"No, no," quoth he, "no judgement here;
    For this it shall be tride;
For I will have my pound of fleshe
    From under his right side."

It grieved all the companie
    His crueltie to see,

For neither friend nor foe could helpe
    But he must spoyled bee.

The bloudie Jew now ready is
    With whetted blade in hand,
To spoyle the bloud of innocent,
    By forfeit of his bond.

And as he was about to strike
    In him the deadly blow,
"Stay," quoth the judge, "thy crueltie;
    I charge thee to do so.

"Sith needs thou wilt thy forfeit have,
    Which is of flesh a pound,
See that thou shed no drop of bloud,
    Nor yet the man confound.

"For if thou doe, like murderer
    Thou here shalt hanged be:
Likewise of flesh see that thou cut
    No more than longes to thee.

"For if thou take either more or lesse,
    To the value of a mite,
Thou shalt be hanged presently,
    As is both law and right."

Gernutus now waxt franticke mad,
    And wotes not what to say;
Quoth he at last, "Ten thousand crownes
    I will that he shall pay;

"And so I graunt to set him free."
    The judge doth answere make;
"You shall not have a penny given;
    Your forfeyture now take."

At the last he doth demaund
    But for to have his owne:
"No," quoth the judge, "doe as you list,
    Thy judgement shall be showne.

"Either take you pound of flesh," quoth he,
    "Or cancell me your bond:"
"O cruell judge," then quoth the Jew,
    "That doth against me stand!"

And so with griping grieved mind
    He biddeth them fare-well:
Then all the people prays'd the Lord,
    That ever this heard tell.

> Good people, that doe heare this song,
>   For trueth I dare well say,
> That many a wretch as ill as hee
>   Doth live now at this day;
>
> That seeketh nothing but the spoyle
>   Of many a wealthy man,
> And for to trap the innocent
>   Deviseth what they can.
>
> From whome the Lord deliver me,
>   And every Christian too,
> And send to them like sentence eke
>   That meaneth so to do.

THE ACCUSATION OF RITUAL MURDER AT BLOIS

A dramatic demonstration of the increased level of Christian hostility toward the Jews was the infamous blood libel. Appearing first in the town of Norwich, England, in 1144, the accusation rapidly spread to the Continent, becoming a permanent feature of Jewish-Christian relations through the twentieth century. Jews were falsely accused of capturing an innocent Christian child and ritually murdering him in order to utilize his blood for the production of *matzot*, the unleavened Passover bread. One of the most publicized of such accusations was the alleged ritual murder in Blois, northern France, in 1171. Here a Jew was accused of killing a child whose corpse had never been found. Theobald V, the count of Blois, officially accepted the accusation as true and thirty-one Jews were killed for it. The following account is taken from a Hebrew chronicle of the twelfth century written by Ephraim ben Jacob, a German Jew.

READING 4-14

What shall we say before God? What shall we speak? How can we justify ourselves? God must have found out our iniquity.

In the year 4931 [1171], evil appeared in France, too, and great destruction in the city of Blois, in which at that time there lived about forty Jews. It happened on that evil day, Thursday, toward evening, that the terror came upon us. A Jew [Isaac bar Eleazar] rode up to water his horse; a common soldier—may he be blotted out of the book of life—was also there watering the horse of his master. The Jew bore on his chest an untanned hide, but one of the corners had become loose and was sticking out of his coat. When, in the gloom, the soldier's horse saw the white side of the hide, it was frightened and sprang back, and it could not be brought to water.

The Christian servant hastened back to his master and said: "Hear, my lord, what a certain Jew did. As I rode behind him toward the river in order to give your horses a drink, I saw him throw a little Christian child, whom the Jews have killed, into the water. When I saw this, I was horrified and hastened back quickly for fear he might kill me too. Even the horse under me was so frightened by the splash of the water when he threw the child in that it would not drink." The soldier knew that his master would rejoice at the fall of the Jews, because he hated a certain Jewess, influential in the city. He as much as put the following words into his master's mouth: "Now I can wreak my vengeance on that person, on that woman Pulcelina."

The next morning the master rode to the ruler of the city, to the cruel Theobald, son of Theobald—may his unrighteousness and bitter, evil curses fall upon his head. He was a ruler that listened to falsehood, for his servants were wicked.

When he heard this he became enraged and had all the Jews of Blois seized and thrown into prison. But Dame Pulcelina encouraged them all, for she trusted in the affection of the ruler who up to now had been very attached to her. However, his cruel wife, a Jezebel, swayed him, for she also hated Dame Pulcelina. All the Jews had been put into iron chains except Pulcelina, but the servants of the ruler who watched her would not allow her to speak to him at all, for fear she might get him to change his mind.

The ruler was revolving in his mind all sorts of plans to condemn the Jews, but he did not know how. He had no evidence against them until a priest appeared— may he be destroyed and may his memory be uprooted from the land of the living— who said to the ruler: "Come, I'll advise you how you can condemn them. Command that the servant who saw the Jew throw the child into the river be brought here, and let him be tested by the ordeal in a tank of water to discover if he has told the truth."

The ruler commanded and they brought him, took off his clothes, and put him into a tank filled with holy water to see what would happen. If he floated, his words were true; if he sank, he had lied. Such are the laws of the Christians who judge by ordeals—bad laws and customs by which one cannot live! The Christians arranged it in accordance with their wish so that the servant floated, and they took him out and thus they declared the wicked innocent and the righteous guilty. [In this ordeal the normal procedure appears to have been reversed. Generally the innocent sank and the guilty floated.]

The ruler had started negotiations for a money settlement before the coming of the priest who incited the ruler not to accept any ransom for the dead child. He had sent a Jew to the Jews [of the other communities] and had asked how much they would give him. The Jews consulted with their Christian friends and also with the Jews in the dungeon, and these latter advised offering only one hundred pounds and in addition their uncollected debts amounting to the sum to one hundred eighty pounds.

In the meantime the priest arrived on the scene, and from this time on the ruler paid no attention to the Jews and did not listen to them, but only to the instruction of the priest. In the day of wrath money could not help them. At the wicked ruler's command they were taken and put into a wooden house around which were placed thornbushes and faggots. As they were led forth they were told: "Save your lives. Leave your religion and turn to us." They mistreated them, beat them, and tortured them, hoping that they would exchange their glorious religion for something worthless, but they refused. Rather did they encourage each other and say to one another: "Persist in the religion of the Almighty!"

At the command of the oppressor they then took the two [Jewish] priests, the pious Rabbi Jehiel, the son of Rabbi David Ha-Kohen, and the just Rabbi Jekutiel Ha-Kohen, the son of Rabbi Judah, and tied them to a single stake in the house where they were to be burned. They were both men of valor, disciples of Rabbi Samuel and Rabbi Jacob [the grandsons of Rashi]. They also tied the hands of Rabbi

Judah, the son of Aaron, and then set fire to the faggots. The fire spread to the cords on their hands so that they snapped, and all three came out and spoke to the servants of the oppressor:"The fire has no power over us. Why should we not go free?" The enemy answered: "By our lives! You shall not get out." They kept on struggling to get out but they were pushed back into the house. They came out again and seized hold of a Christian to drag him along with them back onto the pyre. When they were right at the fire the Christians pulled themselves together, rescued the Christian from their hands, killed them with their swords, and then threw them into the fire. Nevertheless they were not burnt, neither they nor all those thirty-one persons. Only their souls were released by the fire; their bodies remained intact. When the Christians saw it they were amazed and said to one another: "Truly these are saints."

A certain Jew by the name of Rabbi Baruch, the son of David, a priest, was there and saw all this at that time with his own eyes. He lived in the territory of that ruler and had come there to arrange terms for the Jews of Blois, but, because of our sins, he had no success. However, a settlement was made by him for one thousand pounds to save the other Jews of that accursed ruler. He also saved the scrolls of the Torah and the rest of their books. This happened in the year 4931 on Wednesday, the 20th of the month of Siwan [May 26, 1171]. This day ought to be established as a fast day like the Fast of Gedaliah. All these facts were written down by the Jews of Orleans—a city close by that of the martyrs—and made known to the teacher, our master Rabbi Jacob [ben Rabbi Meir, Rashi's grandson].

It was also reported in that letter that as the flames mounted high the martyrs began to sing in unison a melody that began softly but ended with a full voice. The Christian people came and asked us: "What kind of a song is this for we have never heard such a sweet melody?" We knew it well for it was the song: "It is incumbent upon us to praise the Lord of all."

O daughters of Israel, weep for the thirty-one souls that were burnt for the sanctification of the Name, and let your brothers, the entire house of Israel, bewail the burning.

Because of our sins these men were not even given a Jewish burial but were left at the bottom of the hill on the very spot where they had been burnt. It was only later the Jews came and buried their bones. There were about thirty-two holy souls who offered themselves as a sacrifice to their Creator; and God smelled the sweet savor, for him whom He has chosen does He cause to come nigh unto Him.

Of their own free will all the communities of France, England, and the Rhineland observed Wednesday, the 20th of Siwan, 4931, as a day of mourning and fasting. This was also the command of our great teacher Jacob, the son of Rabbi Meir, who wrote letters to them informing them that it was proper to fix this day as a fast for all our people, and that it must be greater even than the Fast of Gedaliah ben Ahikam; it was to be like the Day of Atonement.

FORCED DISPUTATION AT BARCELONA

A critical feature of the new Christian aggressiveness against Judaism in the twelfth and thirteenth centuries was the forced public disputation. The disputation was not an open debate between two equal partners;

it was, rather, an artificial demonstration of Christian intellectual superiority. In a forced "disputation" held in Paris in 1239, Nicholas Donin, a recent convert, argued that the *Talmud* was the primary cause of Jewish perfidiousness and antipathy toward Christianity and it should therefore be burned. Indeed, Talmudic tomes were burned throughout France.

In the city of Barcelona in 1263 Pablo Christiani, another former Jew, employed other tactics to defeat his Jewish opponent, the distinguished rabbi Moses b. Nahman (Nahmanides). Pablo argued that rabbinic literature could be used to demonstrate Christian truth. By combing Jewish homiletical literature with which he was familiar, he sought to demonstrate that the messiah already had come. That Donin's and Christiani's strategy of denigrating rabbinic literature while using it as evidence for Christian dogma was self-contradictory did not prove to be an obstacle for these clerics. Both debating tactics were employed for missionizing Jews; consistency did not represent a special virtue.

Two accounts of the Barcelona disputation are extant: a Christian one and another Jewish, the latter penned by Nahmanides himself. The two differ in the name of the ultimate victor in the debate. Despite Nahmanides' defiant narrative, however, he was not permitted to emerge triumphant. Indeed, his subsequent departure for the Land of Israel offers the most telling evidence of the hopelessness of any Jewish victory within such Christian forums. The Latin report is presented below.

READING 4-15

On July 20, 1263, in the presence of the lord king of Aragon and many other barons, prelates, clerics, and knights, in the palace of the lord king at Barcelona, Moses the Jew, called "rabbi" was summoned from Gerona by the lord king, at the request of the Dominicans, and was present there, along with many other Jews who seemed and were reputed among other Jews more learned. Deliberation was undertaken with the lord king and with certain Dominicans and Franciscans who were present, not that the faith of the Lord Jesus Christ—which because of its certitude cannot be placed in dispute—be put in the center of attention with the Jews as uncertain, but that the truth of that faith be made manifest in order to destroy the Jews' errors and to shake the confidence of many Jews. Since they could not defend their errors, these Jews indicated that the said rabbi could sufficiently reply to each and every question which would be placed before them.

Friar Paul proposed to the said rabbi that, with the aid of God, he would prove from writings shared and accepted by the Jews the following contentions, in order: that the messiah, who is called Christ, whom the Jews anticipate, has surely come already; also that the messiah, as prophesied, should be divine and human; also that he suffered and was killed for the salvation of mankind; also that the laws and ceremonials ceased and should have ceased after the advent of the said messiah. When the said Moses was asked whether he wished to respond to these contentions which have been indicated, he said and affirmed that he would and that, if necessary, he would remain at Barcelona for that purpose not only for a day or a week or a month, but even for a year. When it was proved to him that he should not be called "rabbi," because no Jew should be designated by that title from the time of the Passion of Christ, he conceded at least that this was true for the previous eight hundred years.

Then it was indicated to him that when Friar Paul had come to Gerona for the purpose of conferring with him on these matters, which pertain to salvation, and had expostulated carefully concerning the Holy Trinity, both about the unity of the divine essence and about the trinity of beings, the beliefs which Christians hold, he had conceded that, if Christians believed in the manner explained to him, he would believe indeed that so it should be held. When this was repeated before the king, he did not contradict. Rather he was silent, and thus by remaining silent he conceded.

Then in the palace of the lord king, the said Jew was asked whether the messiah, who is called Christ, has come. He responded with the assertion that he has not come. He added that the messiah and Christ are the same and that, if it could be proved to him that the messiah had come, it could be believed to refer to none other than him, namely Jesus Christ, in whom the Christians believe, since no one else has come who has dared to usurp for himself this title nor has there been anyone else who had been believed to be Christ. It was then proved to him clearly, both through authoritative texts of the law and the prophets as well as through the Talmud, that Christ has truly come, as Christians believe and preach. Since he was unable to respond, vanquished by proper proofs and authoritative texts, he conceded that Christ or the messiah had been born in Bethlehem a thousand years ago and had subsequently appeared in Rome to some. When he was asked where that messiah who he said was born and appeared at Rome might be, he replied that he did not know. Subsequently he said that the messiah lives in a terrestrial paradise with Elijah. He also said that, although the messiah has been born, he has still not come, since the messiah may be said to have come when he achieves dominion over the Jews and liberates them and when the Jews follow him. Against this response was adduced the authority of the Talmud, which clearly says that the messiah would come to them daily, if they would hear his voice and not harden their heart, as is said in Psalms: "Today if you will listen to his voice."

It was added that the messiah was born among men, that he came among men, and that he could not otherwise be or be understood. To this he was unable to respond. Also among the proofs presented concerning the advent of the messiah was that from Genesis: "The sceptre shall not pass from Judah, nor the staff from his descendants." Since therefore he must acknowledge that there is neither sceptre nor staff, he acknowledges that the messiah who was to be sent has come. To this he responded that the sceptre has not been removed. It is merely temporarily absent, as happened during the time of the Babylonian captivity. It was proved to him that in Babylonia the Jews had exilarchs with jurisdiction, while after the death of Christ they had neither a staff nor a prince nor exilarchs according to the prophecy of Daniel nor a prophet nor any jurisdiction, as is manifestly obvious every day. It is thus certain that the messiah has come. He then said that he would prove that the Jews had the aforesaid exilarchs after Jesus, but he was able to show nothing in these matters. On the contrary he confessed that they have not had the aforesaid exilarchs for the past 850 years. Therefore it is clear that the messiah has come, since an authoritative text cannot lie.

The said Moses claimed that Jesus Christ should not be called the messiah, since the messiah, he said, should not die, as is said in Psalms: "He asked of thee life and thou didst give it him, length of days for ever and ever." Rather he should live eternally, both he and those whom he would liberate. It was therefore asked of him whether chapter 53 of Isaiah—"Who could have believed what we have heard"— which according to the Jews begins at the end of chapter 52, where it is said: "Behold my servant shall prosper," speaks of the messiah. Although he consistently claimed that this passage in no way speaks of the messiah, it was proved to him through many authoritative texts in the Talmud which speak of the passion and death of Christ, which they prove through the said chapter, that the aforesaid chapter of Isaiah must be understood as related to Christ, in which the death, passion, burial, and resurrection of Christ is obviously contained. Indeed forced by authoritative texts, he confessed that this section must be understood and explained as relating to Christ. From this it is clear that the messiah was to suffer.

Since he did not wish to confess the truth unless forced by authoritative texts, when he was unable to explain these authoritative texts, he said publicly that he did not believe these authoritative texts which were adduced against him—although found in ancient and authentic books of the Jews—because they were, he claimed, sermons in which their teachers often lied for the purpose of exhorting the people. As a result he reproved both the teachers and the scriptures of the Jews. Moreover, all these issues, or almost all, which he confessed or which were proved to him, he first negated; then confuted by authoritative texts and confused, he was forced to assent. Moreover, since he was unable to respond and was often publicly confused and since both Jews and Christians insulted him, he persistently claimed before all that he would in no way respond, since the Jews prohibited him and Christians, namely Friar P. de Janua and certain upstanding men of the city, had sent him messages advising that he in no way respond. Concerning this lie he was publicly refuted by the said Friar P. and by these upstanding men. Whence it is clear that he tried to escape the disputation by lies. Moreover, although he promised before the king and many others that before a few he would answer concerning his faith and his law, when the said lord was outside the city, he secretly fled and departed. Whence it is clear that he did not dare nor was he able to defend his erroneous belief.

We James, by the grace of God king of Aragon, Majorca and Valencia, count of Barcelona and Urgel, and lord of Montpellier, confirm and acknowledge that each and every statement and action took place in our presence and in the presence of many others, as contained above in the present letter. In testimony of this we have caused our seal to be appended as a perpetual memorial.

THE ETHICAL WILLS OF JUDAH IBN TIBBON AND ELEAZAR OF MAINZ

Jewish life in medieval Europe represented more than a series of Christian atrocities and Jewish responses. Despite the incessant pressure exerted by Christian society on its Jewish minority, Jewish culture continued to flourish and respond to the challenges of its surroundings. The dominant mode of Jewish culture in Ashkenazic Europe was rabbinic scholarship: biblical exegesis, rabbinic commentaries; and *responsa*. In northern Spain and Provence, rabbinic learning was accompanied by philosophic and mystical speculation. In Germany a small community of pietists introduced a unique social philosophy and set of religious practices.

The many-sided nature of medieval Jewish cultural expression can hardly be distilled in a few brief selections. The ethical wills presented below illustrate one genre of medieval Jewish literature, common to all regions of European Jewry. These moral testaments, composed by Jewish fathers for their progeny, generally presented idealized goals. As one would expect in such sources, language is often mundane and stereotypical; yet, one occasionally finds the rewarding touch of a real individual with concrete demands and expectations.

Such is the case of the two ethical wills presented below. The first, written by the erudite physician and translator Judah ibn Tibbon (1120–ca. 1190), reflects the broad cultural horizons of Jewish intellectuals living in Spain and Provence in the twelfth century. The second, written by one Eleazar of Mainz (d. 1357), portrays the simple moral and spiritual concerns of a surviving member of a Jewish community that only recently had experienced the disquieting spectacle of the Black Death and the destruction of its Jewish quarter.

READING 4-16A

Judah ibn Tibbon

My son, listen to my precepts, neglect none of my injunctions. Set my Admonition before thine eyes, thus shalt thou prosper and prolong thy days in pleasantness! . . .

Thou knowest, my son, how I swaddled thee and brought thee up, how I led thee in the paths of wisdom and virtue. I fed and clothed thee; I spent myself in educating and protecting thee. I sacrificed my sleep to make thee wise beyond thy fellows, and to raise thee to the highest degree of science and morals. These twelve years I have denied myself the usual pleasures and relaxations of men for thy sake, and I still toil for thine inheritance.

I have honored thee by providing an extensive library for thy use, and have thus relieved thee of the necessity to borrow books. Most students must bustle about to seek books, often without finding them. But thou, thanks be to God, lendest and borrowest not. Of many books, indeed, thou ownest two or three copies. I have besides made for thee books on all sciences, hoping that thy hand might "find them all as a nest." Seeing that thy Creator had graced thee with a wise and understanding heart, I journeyed to the ends of the earth, and fetched for thee a teacher in secular sciences. I minded neither the expense nor the danger of the ways. Untold evil might have befallen me and thee on those travels, had not the Lord been with us!

But thou, my son! didst deceive my hopes. Thou didst not choose to employ thine abilities, hiding thyself from all thy books, not caring to know them or even their titles. Hadst thou seen thine own books in the hand of others, thou wouldst not have recognized them; hadst thou needed one of them, thou wouldst not have known whether it was with thee or not, without asking me; thou didst not even consult the Catalogue of thy library. . . .

All this thou hast done. Thus far thou hast relied on me to rouse thee from the sleep of indolence, thinking that I would live with thee for ever! Thou didst not bear in mind that death must divide us, and that there are daily vicissitudes in life. But who will be as tender to thee as I have been, who will take my place—to teach thee out of love and good-will? Even if thou couldst find such a one, lo! thou seest how the greatest scholars, coming from the corners of the earth, seek to profit by my society and instruction, how eager they are to see me and my books. But thou, though all this was thine without silver and price, thou wert unwilling; and the Lord hath not given thee a heart to know, eyes to see, or ears to hearken unto this day. May thy God endow thee with a new heart and spirit, and instil into thee a desire to retrieve the past, and to follow the true path henceforward! . . .

Therefore, my son! Exert thyself whilst still young, the more so as thou even now complainest of weak memory. What, then, wilt thou do in old age, the mother of forgetfulness? Awake, my son! from thy sleep; devote thyself to science and religion; habituate thyself to moral living, for "habit is master over all things." As the Arabian philosopher holds, there are two sciences, ethics and physics; strive to excel in both!

See to it that thy penmanship and handwriting is as beautiful as thy style. Keep thy pen in fine working order, use ink of good color. Make thy script as perfect as possible, unless forced to write without proper materials, or in a pressing emergency. The beauty of a composition depends on the writing, and the beauty of the writing on pen, paper, and ink; and all these excellencies are an index to the author's worth. . . .

Examine thy Hebrew books at every new moon, the Arabic volumes once in two months, and the bound codices once every quarter. Arrange thy library in fair order, so as to avoid wearying thyself in searching for the book thou needest. Always know the case and chest where the book should be. A good plan would be to set in each compartment a written list of the books therein contained. If, then, thou art looking for a book, thou canst see from the list the exact shelf it occupies without disarranging all the books in the search for one. Examine the loose leaves in the volumes and bundles, and preserve them. These fragments contain very important matters which I collected and copied out. Do not destroy any writing or letter of all that I have left. And cast thine eye frequently over the Catalogue so as to remember what books are in thy library.

Never intermit thy regular readings with thy teacher, study in the college of thy master on certain evenings before sitting down to read with the young. Whatever thou hast learned from me or from thy teachers, impart it again regularly to worthy pupils, so that thou mayest retain it, for by teaching it to others thou wilt know it by heart, and their questions will compel thee to precision, and remove any doubts from thine own mind.

READING 4-16B

The Testament of Eleazar of Mainz

[My grandfather's Testament to his children; and as it is a rule good for every God-fearer, I write it here, that all men may follow it.]

[A worthy Testament, whose ways are ways of pleasantness; proven and seemly for publishing to all the people.]

These are the things which my sons and daughters shall do at my request.

My daughters must obey scrupulously the rules applying to women; modesty, sanctity, reverence, should mark their married lives. They should carefully watch for the signs of the beginning of their periods and keep separate from their husbands at such times. Marital intercourse must be modest and holy, with a spirit of restraint and delicacy, in reverence and silence. They shall be very punctilious and careful with their ritual bathing, taking with them women friends of worthy character. They shall cover their eyes until they reach their home, on returning from the bath, in order not to behold anything of an unclean nature. They must respect their husbands, and must be invariably amiable to them. Husbands, on their part, must honor their wives more than themselves, and treat them with tender consideration.

If they can by any means contrive it, my sons and daughters should live in communities, and not isolated from other Jews, so that their sons and daughters may learn the ways of Judaism. Even if compelled to solicit from others the money to pay a teacher, they must not let the young, of both sexes, go without instruction in the Torah. Marry your children, O my sons and daughters, as soon as their age is ripe, to members of respectable families. Let no child of mine hunt after money by making a low match for that object; but if the family is undistinguished only on the mother's side, it does not matter, for all Israel counts descent from the father's side.

Every Friday morning, they shall put themselves in careful trim for honoring the Sabbath, kindling the lamps while the day is still great, and in winter lighting the furnace before dark, to avoid desecrating the Sabbath (by kindling fire thereon). For due welcome to the Sabbath, the women must prepare beautiful candles. As to games of chance, I entreat my children never to engage in such pastimes. During the leisure of the festival weeks they may play for trifling stakes in kind, and the women may amuse themselves similarly on New Moons, but never for money. In their relation to women, my sons must behave continently, avoiding mixed bathing and mixed dancing and all frivolous conversation, while my daughters ought not to speak much with strangers, nor jest nor dance with them. They ought to be always at home, and not be gadding about. They should not stand at the door, watching whatever passes. I ask, I command, that the daughters of my house be never without work to do, for idleness leads first to boredom, then to sin. But let them spin, or cook, or sew. . . .

Be very particular to keep your houses clean and tidy. I was always scrupulous on this point, for every injurious condition, and sickness and poverty, are to be found in foul dwellings. Be careful over the benedictions; accept no divine gift without paying back the Giver's part; and His part is man's grateful acknowledgment.

Every one of these good qualities becomes habitual with him who studies the Torah; for that study indeed leads to the formation of a noble character. Therefore, happy is he who toils in the Law! For this gracious toil fix daily times, of long or short duration, for 'tis the best of all works that a man can do. Week by week read at least the set portion with the commentary of Rashi. And when your prayer is ended day by day, turn ever to the word of God, in fulfilment of the Psalmist's injunction, "passing from strength to strength."

And O, my sons and daughters, keep yourselves far from the snare of frivolous conversation, which begins in tribulation and ends in destruction. Nor be ye found in the company of these light talkers. Judge ye rather every man charitably and use your best efforts to detect an honorable explanation of conduct however suspicious. Try to persuade yourselves that it was your neighbor's zeal for some good end that led him to the conduct you deplore. This is the meaning of the exhortation: "In righteousness shalt thou judge thy neighbour." To sum up, the fewer one's idle words the less one's risk of slander, lying, flattery,—all of them, things held in utter detestation by God.

On holidays and festivals and Sabbaths seek to make happy the poor, the unfortunate, widows and orphans, who should always be guests at your tables; their joyous entertainment is a religious duty. Let me repeat my warning against gossip and scandal. And as ye speak no scandal, so listen to none, for if there were no receivers there would be no bearers of slanderous tales; therefore the reception and credit of slander is as serious an offence as the originating of it. The less you say, the less cause you give for animosity, while "in the multitude of words there wanteth not transgression."

Always be of those who see and are not seen, who hear and are not heard. Accept no invitations to banquets, except to such as are held for religious reasons: at weddings and at meals prepared for mourners, at gatherings to celebrate entry into the covenant of Abraham, or at assemblies in honor of the wise. Games of chance for money stakes, such as dicing, must be avoided. And as I have again warned you on that head, again let me urge you to show forbearance and humility to all men, to ignore abuses levelled at you, but the indignant refutation of charges against your moral character is fully justifiable. . . .

I beg of you, my sons and daughters, my wife, and all the congregation, that no funeral oration be spoken in my honor. Do not carry my body on a bier but in a coach. Wash me clean, comb my hair, trim my nails, as I was wont to do in my life-time, so that I may go clean to my eternal rest, as I went clean to Synagogue every Sabbath day. If the ordinary officials dislike the duty, let adequate payment be made to some poor man who shall render this service carefully and not perfunctorily. At a distance of thirty cubits from the grave, they shall set my coffin on the ground, and drag me to the grave by a rope attached to the coffin. Every four cubits they shall stand and wait awhile, doing this in all seven times, so that I may find atonement for my sins. Put me in the ground at the right hand of my father, and if the space be a little narrow, I am sure that he loves me well enough to make room for me by his side. If this be altogether impossible, put me on his left, or near my grandmother, Yuta. Should this also be impractical, let me be buried by the side of my daughter.

FROM THE *RESPONSA* OF RABBI MEIR OF ROTHENBURG

Rabbinical *responsa*—legal queries addressed to rabbinical authorities and their answers—constitute an invaluable source of information on the many-sided life of medieval Jewry. The voluminous *responsa* of Rabbi Meir of Rothenburg, the principal Talmudic scholar of Franco-German Jewry in the second half of the thirteenth century, provide eloquent testimony to the activities of the Jewish community in the Middle Ages, especially the dynamic interplay of social, cultural, and economic forces that fashioned its group life. They also indicate the growing complexities of Jewish life in a Christian environment increasingly hostile and intolerant toward its Jewish minority. The selections from Rabbi Meir's *responsa* illustrate some of the problems faced by this community: the issue of drinking ritually "forbidden wine;" the problem of Jews swearing by Christian oaths; the question of the authority of the community over its constituents; and the relationship between the Jewish community and unjust royal authority.

READING 4-17A

Q. Thieves entered a place where many casks of wine were stored. Some of the casks were provided with faucets, while others were entirely sealed. The thieves inserted a faucet in one of the sealed casks and drew part of its wine. I believe that the wine in the casks which have faucets should be considered "forbidden wine" since we suspect that the thieves drew wine from these casks also.

A. We must not be too strict in our ruling when it is uncertain whether wine has been dedicated to an idol. Since there is no indication that the casks which had faucets were tampered with by the thieves, we do not assume that the thieves drew wine from them. Faucets are usually inserted in casks which contain ordinary wine, while sealed casks are used for wine of superior quality. The thieves preferred to insert a faucet in a sealed cask probably in order to draw the superior wine rather than obtain inferior wine from the open casks. Moreover, they did not draw out all the wine even from the sealed cask. There is no reason to suspect, therefore, that they also drew wine from the open casks.

READING 4-17B

"They that swear by the sin of Samaria" and mainly rely on Christian oaths in the conduct of their business are guilty of a misconduct. I have often protested most vigorously against it, but they would not heed me. I have often repeated that on account of such practices family fortunes have been ruined and investments lost, but I have been unable to abate these practices; for those who indulge in them state that they rely on great authority, on R. Tam [a French rabbinical authority of the twelfth century], who permitted such practices on the ground that the Gentiles of today were not idolators. Nowadays the Gentiles swear by their sacred objects but do not consider the objects themselves to be deities. Though they appeal to Heaven and mean Jesus, they do not expressly mention his name. [Regarding the prohibition involved, see Sanh. 43b]. Moreover, since these Jews do not heed outright prohibitions, how can one expect them to abstain from practices that some authorities permit? However, the person who reported to you that I sanction such practices, did not speak the truth; for whenever a difference of opinion exists between our great authorities I follow the strict opinion, except when the lenient ruling has been widely accepted as an ancient custom.

READING 4-17C

Q. Ten Jewish adult males were inhabitants of the town of T. One of them wanted to leave [temporarily for the holidays]. His leaving would disrupt congregational prayers. Could the other members compel him to remain?

A. It is an accepted custom throughout the Diaspora for small communities to hire one or two adult males whenever it is necessary to complete a *minyan* (quorum) for the high holidays. Therefore, if there are exactly ten adult males in the community, the other remaining members can compel the member seeking to leave either to remain in town or to hire somebody else in his stead. But, if there are eleven adult males in the community, no single member can be restrained from leaving; for he does not have to provide for the possibility of another member becoming sick or indisposed. However, if two out of the eleven want to leave, both have to share the expenses of hiring a person to complete the *minyan*.

Q. When nine Jews have to hire a tenth in order to complete the *minyan* (quorum), or when they have to hire a cantor for the holidays, do the members share equally in expenses, or do they pay in proportion to their wealth?

A. Since the members do not join a large community for the high-holyday prayers because they do not want to leave their homes, their possessions, and their investments, the forming of the local *minyan* is dependent upon monetary considerations, and the expenses thereof should be shared by the members in proportion to their wealth.

READING 4-17D

Q. The king's deputy made unjust demands on the community of T in the name of the king. The Jews answered him brazenly and thus aroused his ire to the extent that he sought means of coercing them and of punishing them, and he even attempted to kill them. Thereupon the members of the community incarcerated the deputy, thus preventing him from carrying out his evil design. One member of the community even struck the Gentile. The king became enraged, arrested the Jews of T, brought false accusations against them, and forced them to pay ransom. Now A, a resident of T, charges that the community, by its rash acts, caused him a loss of money. He demands that the community make good this loss.

A. The community was not at fault. The king had no right to make unjust demands upon it, for his deputy was in the wrong, not the community. The king, most certainly, had no right to punish the Jews of T for the sin of a single Jew who struck the Gentile. The acts of the community leaders, and the misdemeanor of the Jew were mere excuses for the extortion but not the cause thereof. Therefore, A is not entitled to collect any damages from the community.

SOLOMON IBN ADRET ON THE PLACE OF PHILOSOPHY AND MYSTICISM IN JUDAISM

The colorful career of Solomon ibn Adret (ca. 1235–ca. 1310), Spanish rabbi and one of the foremost Jewish scholars of his day, vividly reveals the sharp cultural tensions of European Jewish life in the late Middle Ages. Although he considered himself a student of both rationalism and mysticism, he was disquieted by the corrosive effect of both these trends. He concluded that, for many, philosophy led to religious scepticism. The allegorical methods of interpreting scripture, prevalent among rationalists in Provence and in France, were undermining traditional authority. The mystics also were capable of endangering Jewish life, especially extreme visionaries with delusions of grandeur like Adret's contemporary Abraham Abulafia (1240–92). In response to the first group, Adret issued a ban (the first selection below) in 1305 prohibiting the study of philosophy to students under the age of twenty-five. He did not categorically reject all study of philosophy; he only was concerned with the danger philosophy might have on undisciplined and unsophisticated students who had not yet undertaken thorough rabbinic training. In another *responsum* (from which one passage appears below, second selection, he objected to the unrestrained pursuit of mystical speculation, especially that of Abulafia.

READING 4-18A

Epistle Prohibiting Anyone Under Twenty-Five Years of Age to Study Philosophy

It is now some time since our attention has been drawn by people from the land of Provence, the chosen remnant, who were jealous for the faith of Moses and the Jews, to the fact that there are men there who falsify the Law, and that he is regarded wise who sits down to demolish the walls and who destroys the words of the Law. They hew out for themselves cisterns, broken cisterns, and they impute unto the words of the Law and the words of the sages things which are not right. Concerning the two Laws they expound in the synagogues and in the houses of study words by which none can live. To provoke the eyes of the Glory of all Israel they break down all the fences of the Law; and even against our holy fathers they put forth their tongue, a thing which the worshippers of idols have not done. For they say that Abraham and Sarah represent matter and form, and that the twelve tribes of Israel are the twelve constellations. Has a nation ever heard such an evil thing since the world was divided into territories? Or has such a thing ever been heard, that men should reduce everything to chaos? The blasphemers of God further say that the holy vessels which were sanctified, the Urim and the Thummim, are the instrument known as astrolabe, which men make for themselves. Have such false children ever been found before? They in truth bite the people more dangerously than do the fiery serpents. Without any benefit and without any cause they commit the sin of slander, and say that the four who fought against the five are the four elements and the five senses. May the souls of these men be wholly consumed as offerings! A man who does such things reduces the entire Bible to useless allegories; indeed they trifle with, and pervert all the commandments in order to make the yoke of their burden lighter unto themselves. Their reports terrify us, and all who arrive here tell us new things. Truth has stumbled in the street, for some of them say that all that is written from the section of *Bereshit* as far as the giving of the Law is nothing more than an allegory. May such men become a proverb and a by-word, and may they have no stay and no staff. Indeed they show that they have no faith in the plain meaning of the commandments; they inscribe on their hearts and on the walls of their altars that they have no portion in the God of Israel, nor in the Torah which their fathers had received on Sinai. They are more estranged than the Gentiles; for the latter fulfil some of the commandments in the proper form, while they (may they have no remnant in the land!) strongly desire to uproot all. The chief reason of all this is because they are infatuated with alien sciences, Zidonian and Moabitish [ancient peoples], and pay homage to the Greek books. They mingle with strangers, and bear them children. The children that are consecrated unto heaven from their birth and from their mothers' womb are drawn away from the breasts, and are taught the books and the language of the Chaldeans instead of rising early to study the Jewish faith in the house of their teachers. . . .

We have therefore interdicted in a perfect manner of interdiction, as ye see recorded with writing of truth in the book of the covenant which we made with our God, any one to teach or to learn these sciences, until the student and the teacher are twenty-five years old, and until they have become full of the delicacies of the Law, so that they will not remove it from being queen; for he who espouses it in his youth will not turn away from it even when he grows old. And indeed we shall not have done our duty, until we have pursued them, and brought them low, and removed the abominations from between their teeth; the books which they composed should be burned in the public place in their presence. It is about three years now since we have endeavored to carry out our wish in accordance with our aim; we have made many supplications, asking, requesting, and praying, to restore the crown of the Torah to its pristine glory, in its place. All this did we, so that the sword should not be against the dove which is foolish and without understanding, and that we should not afterwards be reviled by the mouth of the reviler. Our words, however, did not enter into their ears; they made their words, which are directed against us, harsher still, because of their ability to write and to speak. Nevertheless we did not cease to write to them. But many strict communities of those provinces inscribed their name to God, and decided to ban and excommunicate them, and they acted wisely after us, as ye see from the copies of their letters. . . .

READING 4-18B

To Israel, the heir of the religion of truth, the children of Jacob, the man of truth. [. . .] it is easier to bear the burden of exile than to believe in anything before it is thoroughly and repeatedly examined and all its dross has been purged away, even though it appears to be a sign or a miracle. The undeniable evidence for Israel's love of truth and rejection of anything which is doubtful can be seen in the relation of the people of Israel to Moses. In spite of the fact they they were crushed by slavery, yet when Moses was told to bring them tidings of their redemption, he said to the Lord: "Behold, they will not believe me, nor hearken to my voice, for they will say: 'The Lord hath not appeared unto me'." Moses had to bring evidence. Thus it is characteristic of our people not to be satisfied unless exhaustive examination has proven a matter to be true.

SOLOMON ALAMI'S EXPLANATION OF THE POGROMS OF 1391

Until the end of the fourteenth century, Jewish community life in Spain generally remained unviolated despite Christian hostility against Jews elsewhere in Europe. All of this changed in 1391. Aggravated by economic instability, class hatred, and religious fanaticism, anti-Jewish violence erupted throughout all the major cities of Castille and Aragon. While similar patterns of anti-Jewish aggression previously had occurred throughout western Europe, the massacres of 1391 were unique in one aspect: the reaction of the victims. For the first time in Jewish history thousands of Jews converted en masse to Christianity in order to save their lives and property.

Solomon Alami (ca. 1370–1420) was an eyewitness to the events of 1391. In 1415 he composed a Hebrew work entitled *Iggeret Musar* (*Epistle of Ethical Admonition*) in an effort to explain the causes of the tragedy. His answer was simply the traditional recognition that "we ourselves have dug the pit in which we have fallen." He singled out the moral shortcomings of wealthy Jews, philosophers, and rabbis as the reasons why the catastrophe had befallen the community. His critique was cast in the mold of biblical prophecy, providing him a theological rubric within which to explain contemporary Jewish suffering.

READING 4-19

"Rejoice not, O Israel! Exult not like the peoples." Forget not the evil decrees hurled against us since the year 4908 [1148], when the Almohades made themselves masters in Spain and persecuted our communities and seats of learning. A few years later destruction came to the eastern countries. Moses Maimonides lived at that time; both in his youth and in his old age he witnessed the hardships of his people. Because of our many sins the community of Lucena was reduced to ruins. Lucena, "a city and a mother in Israel," a center of learning for many generations.

The next period brought the expulsion from England [1290], from France [1306], and from other realms. From that time on we sank deeper and deeper, and our Torah was delivered unto flames. Our wives and daughters were defiled; the others were deprived of their honor. Deep calls to deep, calls for sword, famine, and captivity. Death seems preferable to such a life. Very recently, in the year 5151 [1391], we suffered much destruction in all the provinces of Castile and in the kingdom of Catalonia. Our communities in Aragon, too, were gravely tried and had to endure famine and thirst, homelessness and the death of many children.

This we cannot forget. But if we ask ourselves why all this happened to us, then we have to accept the truth: we ourselves are at fault. God is just and righteous and it was in His power to help us. We and our own iniquities caused this evil to happen.

Our sages were jealous of each other and disrespectful. Their main attention was given to minor details, to novel explanations, clever elucidations. They did not pay much attention to the Book before them, and its counsel of justice and sanctity. There was much quarreling among the wise men. What the one proved, the other disproved; what the one forbade, the other permitted. Thus the Torah, which was one, fell apart. People did not feel obliged to follow such blind leadership, and no wonder.

Then there were those scholars who attempted to interpret the Scriptures in the Greek manner and clothe it in a Greek dress. They believed that Plato and Aristotle had brought us more light than Moses our master.

Now, if a man should not be able to "live by his faith," why should he suffer death for it and endure the yoke and the shame of dispersion among the nations? It serves no good purpose to quote Scriptures as support for philosophical opinions; the way of reason and the way of faith are too far apart and will never meet. No prophets are found among the followers of Aristotle while many prophets, young and old, arose in Israel's ancient land. Those who read a few columns in a book of Greek philosophy will soon tear to shreds the scroll of the Torah, scoff at the laws, and dispute the validity of tradition. They will never know the thought of the Lord, never understand His counsel.

The next in line of decadence were the leaders of the communities and those favored and trusted by the kings. Their riches and high position made them forsake humility and forget the general misery. "Israel hath forgotten his Maker and builded palaces." They acquired costly wagons and horses, dressed in precious garments; the wives and daughters of these leaders carried themselves like princesses, and proudly displayed their jewelry.

They gave up study and industry, and cultivated idleness, vainglory, and inordinate ambition. Law and wisdom, our ancient heirloom, no longer counted for them. Everyone chased after coveted positions; envy estranged a man from his fellow and they didn't mind denouncing one another before the Court. Little did they realize that their souls were the price they paid and that they faced a bitter end. They oppressed the wretched, and the poor became the victims of their tyranny. The burden of taxation they shifted to the poorer class. In the end, the Court itself found them despicable and removed them from their power. No Jew was left who could represent the cause of the people before the king and say a good word in behalf of a fellow Jew in need. Down to the ground fell the glory of the "mighty." It is time to wake up from the slumber of foolishness.

There are still other reasons for our miseries and hardships. Our heart lacks faith and modesty; we refuse to admit our failings; our good deeds lack sincerity; our prayers are light-hearted. If you take from your face the mask of hypocrisy and if you have eyes to see you will recognize that the majority of our nation have abandoned truth.

The Sabbath is being profaned and those who try to voice admonition are quickly silenced; no one likes the moralist. The seer shall not see. "Speak to us smooth things, prophesy illusions."

There are many among us who repudiate the belief in divine providence, and only few who retain the idea of reward and punishment.

There is no communal spirit among us. People quarrel over trifles. Strict honesty is no longer observed; there is overreaching, and deceit is practiced even in dealing with the people at large: thus do we desecrate in their midst the Holy Name of our God.

Who among us is ready to give up the love of the world and to consider his end? Who will repent his treason and return to his God with a perfect heart? Who will again dedicate himself to the Covenant of Israel, and in his youth or, later, in his maturity enter the service of his God? Not one man will you find among us who will seriously reflect on the fall of our own kingdom, the decline of wisdom, the cessation of prophecy, the destruction of our Temple, and the desecration of the Name of God who is our glory. Not one will divest himself of his ornaments in mourning over the disgrace of the Torah, the martyrdom of our sages—events which our eyes have seen and our ears have heard—the loss of our congregation and our homes.

Surrounded by people suffering persecution, expulsion, forced conversion, some there are who manage to hold banquets, listen to music, and imitate the Gentiles in their clothes and hairdress. . . .

Among the scholars, teachers of the laws, authors of books, you find vanity and contentiousness competing with scholarship and piety. Many study in order to get a position, they teach for the fee; pretense rates higher than quiet work; the handsome speaker displaces the solid one, the flatterer pushes aside the honest man. Simple teachings are made complicated by unproductive sophistry, just in order to parade something "novel." Little men, poor of mind, write books of no use to anybody; they carry copies to their sponsors, who give them some money; they should be ashamed to disgrace our ancient writings.

Worse, of course, is the half-educated crowd, philosophers in their bedrooms who, blind to true knowledge, believe that the world stands and falls on their doings. What they read but don't understand, they reject as of no value; what they do grasp, they have known all along. In Portugal, I found a whole class of semischolars who had put their noses into various books; yet before they had time to learn anything they already felt qualified to judge others. They appeared as the protagonists of whatever was being much talked about; they memorized pertinent quotations from fashionable philosophers and from writers in vogue; they were the heralds of every newest craze. Recently, in Elvas, a man was ready to found a society for the support of some latest rage, sure of the acclaim of the young ladies.

The right way is to listen to the teachings of the prophets and of the sages of old; to advance humility, loving-kindness, and virtue; to love Israel and its Torah, and to be forbearing with the faults of our brethren. May they learn to act out of true fear of God and not out of worldly vanity. If people could be taught to restrain their desires, to be content, and to trust in divine providence, then much of what saddens my heart would be overcome and our good would increase with the good of man. May what happened to our philosophers in Catalonia not happen to us: their strength of faith was surpassed by simple people, by women and children.

The promise of our Scriptures upholds me; so great is the power of this promise, so deep the fountain of our hope, that I do not despair of the future of Israel, which one day will recognize its failings and receive forgiveness.

PROFIAT DURAN'S POLEMICAL LETTER ON THE CONVERSION OF HIS FRIEND

Among the large number of converts to Christianity in the aftermath of 1391 was the Jewish grammarian and philosopher, Profiat Duran (Efodi; d. ca. 1414). Duran may have lived as a Christian in the town of Perpignan for some years after his conversion. On the basis of his writings, however, he appears to have continued to believe and act as a Jew. In 1394 or 1395 he composed a biting satire entitled *Al Tehi ka-Avotekha* (Don't be like your fathers) to his friend David Bonet Bonjorn who had converted with him and had remained a sincere Christian. Written with purposeful ambiguity the author hoped to disguise his work as a panegyric on Christianity while in fact ridiculing the Church, its irrational dogma, and its emphasis on faith at the expense of reason. As earlier Jewish polemicists had done before him, he underscored the superiority of Jewish faith which did not contradict reason. Some years later he developed these themes in his masterful *Kelimat ha-Goyim*, one of the most informed and penetrating polemical works against Christianity written by a Jew in the Middle Ages. Duran's first work is excerpted below.*

READING 4-20

Now, my brother, I became aware of thy good intentions, and that all thou dost is for the sake of the Lord. Faith is for thee a girdle round the loins, and Reason with all her lies is unable to entice thee and divert thy paths. Therefore I made up my mind to show thee clearly the ways of the faith which thou hast chosen as thy compass in the light of the Messiah.

Be not like unto thy fathers, who believed in one God from whose unity they removed any plurality. They have erred indeed, when they said, 'Hear Israel, the Lord is One!', when they understood this unity in the purest sense without inclusion of species, kind or number. *Not so thou!* Thou shalt believe that one can become three, and that three united make one. Lips will never tell it, ears can never take it in. . . .

Be not like unto thy fathers, who by close scrutiny tried to find a deep philosophical meaning in the account of creation, and who had much to disclose about the first human couple, about the four rivers, the tree of knowledge, the serpent, and the coats of skin which the Lord made them for clothing. *Not so thou!* Conceive al this literally! Add, however, yet an inner punishment to Adam's misfortune, increase through it the burden of his bitter fate that he has to carry on his back. He will never get rid of it, and is entirely in the grip of Satan, until the Redeemer comes and purifies him by his death. Now that sin is abolished, although it is not mentioned in our holy Scripture, while the other curses, the punishments of hell, remain for ever. . . .

---

*Reprinted from Franz Kobler, *Letters of Jews Through the Ages*, by permission of Hebrew Publishing Company.

Be not like unto thy fathers, who were continuously engaged in sciences of all kinds, in mathematics, metaphysics and logic, and tried to penetrate to the foundations of truth. *Not so thou!* Far be it from thee to recognize the first fundamental rule of reasoning in logic. For this would entice thee to deny thy faith by saying: God is Father; the Son, too, is God truly: the Son is therefore the Father. Brother, stick to this belief! It will lead thee to eternal life, and God will be with thee. . . . Alas, thy fathers ate the bread of affliction, suffered thirst and hunger; thou, however, hast saved thy soul, thou eatest and becomest satisfied, thou rejoicest in the Lord and praisest the Holy One of Israel. . . .

Be not like unto thy fathers, upon whom the holy Torah of Moses was bestowed as heritage and possession, when they strove after spiritual perfection in thought and deed, when they called that godly doctrine the crown of their head, and kept faithfully the commandments and prohibitions, according to the saying, 'The secret things belong unto the Lord our God; but those things which are revealed belong unto us and to our children for ever.' Every prophet points to this, even the last one declares it through his last word. *Not so thou!* For this would be shameful. If thou beget sons, do not introduce them into the covenant of the fathers! Take no heed of the multitude of those ancient laws of marriage. Neither change thy garb to sanctify the Sabbaths and Festivals. When the great, the only day of the long fast approaches, tell thyself: 'Now, eat and drink, for thou art without any guilt!' Eat leavened bread on the Passover; eat also meat and milk together! Where penalties threaten, believe that it is always better to permit. Eat of pork, of all animals in the water, on the earth and in the air, which have been interdicted thee once. . . .

Behold! I should like to come to thee, my brother, and to thy new teacher, with all these and many other scruples, because I know that the holy spirit speaks through you, elected men! No secret exists for you, thanks to the Lord, who has chosen you. . . . There is one thing, however, which I want to tell thee. . . . Do not care for the shame in thy soul, or the mark on thy forehead, when the enemies will perhaps offend thee in future, for some of them will say 'Apostate' and others 'circumcised Jew': as a reward thy soul will share the eternal pleasures, and thou wilt see the faces of the king and of the queen beside him.

I wonder that thou—methinks, just as it is the way of fools—warnest me writing that my friends try to perplex me. For ever and anon I strove seriously after truth, in thought and deed. Thou knowest this very well. I live entirely for my Lord, with all my heart, and with all my soul, today and always. It is my hope and my profound trust that *that* Messiah will come who carries His name. Behold, this is my song and praise, my pleasure, strength and power. To this faith I have clung for many years, without change, without apostasy, and I shall cling for ever.

I should like, however, to ask thee one thing, this thing only, please, do it for my sake: do not call thyself any longer after the honoured name of thy wise father, may his memory be blessed! For his advice does not suit thee any more, and his merit does not shine upon thee. For if he were alive he would say to-day: 'Better no son than such a son!' And his soul in its resting place laments now, too, over thee and thy way. May the Messiah, he to whom thou adherest, he alone and nobody else, give thee light and peace for ever!

He who is writing this loves thee with all his heart. And if thou wilt choose the right way and listen to the voice of the Lord, He will always be with thee. As it is

said, 'In all places where I record my name, I will bless thee.' And then thou wilt
again be to me a brother and darling son.

He who wrote this is thy brother.

Profiat Duran, Efodi

THE EXPULSION FROM SPAIN:
A CONTEMPORARY ACCOUNT

In early 1492 Ferdinand and Isabella conquered Granada, the last
Muslim stronghold of the Iberian peninsula. Soon after, the king and
queen signed an edict expelling all Jews living in united Spain. Motivated
primarily by the desire to see recent converts to Christianity relinquish
their ties with their former coreligionists, and perhaps spurred in part by
the promise of economic profits to be gained through confiscation of Jewish property, the monarchs were responsible for the exodus of some
200,000 Jews from Spanish soil.

The expulsion of Spanish Jewry represented more than an isolated
national tragedy. It was not only more massive than any previous expulsion; it was also the only instance, with the exception of the relatively
small English Jewish community, where all the Jews of one nation simultaneously had been banished. Beyond the physical suffering and displace-
ment it engendered, its symbolism did not go unnoticed by those of the
exiled generation. Spain was not just another nation of the Jewish Diaspora; it held the largest, the most dynamic, and the proudest of Jewish
communities. The Spanish eviction thus represented the culmination of
all previous Jewish expulsions from Christian lands.

One of the contemporary Jewish accounts of the expulsion is presented below, taken from the writing of the last of Spanish Jewry's great
courtiers, Don Isaac Abravanel (1437–1508).

READING 4-21

In 1492 the King of Spain seized the great city of Granada, together with the
whole kingdom. His haughtiness brought a change of character; his power led him
to sin against his God. He thought to himself: "How can I better show my gratitude
to my God, Who gave victory to my army and put this city into my power, than by
bringing under His wing the scattered flock of Israel that walks in darkness? How
shall I better serve Him than to bring back to His faith the apostate daughter? Or, if
they remain stiffnecked, to drive them to another land so that they will not dwell
here nor be seen in my presence?" Consequently the King enacted a decree as fixed
as the law of the Medes and the Persians. He commanded that the children of Israel
could remain in the country only if they submitted to baptism; but if they were
unwilling to embrace Christian faith, they must leave the territories of Spain, Sicily,

Majorca, and Sardinia. "Within three months," he decreed, "there must not remain in my kingdoms a single Jew."

I was at court when the decree was proclaimed. I was disconsolate with grief. Thrice I addressed the King, imploring his mercy: "O King, save your loyal subjects. Why do you act so cruelly toward us? We have prospered in this land and we would gladly give all we possess for our country." I begged my noble friends at court to intercede for my people. The King's most trusted counsellors pleaded desperately that he revoke the decree and turn from his design to destroy the Jews. But his ears were closed as though he were stone deaf. The Queen, seated at his right, opposed revoking the decree; she pressed him to complete the task he had begun. Our exertions were therefore without effect. Despite the fact that I neither rested nor relaxed, the thunderbolt struck.

When the dreadful news reached the people, they mourned their fate; and wherever the report of the decree spread, Jews wept bitterly. The terror and lamentation were greater than at any time since the expulsion of our forefathers from their own soil in Judah to foreign strands. However, they bravely encouraged each other: "Let us cling unflinchingly to our faith, holding our heads with pride before the voice of the enemy that taunts and blasphemes. If they let us live, we will live; if they kill us, we will perish. But we will not break our Divine Covenant nor shall we turn back. We will go forth in the name of the Lord our God."

In this spirit the people, old and young, women and children, a multitude of 300,000 from every province, went forth on one day, unarmed and afoot. I was among them. They went whithersoever the wind carried them. Some fled to the kingdom of Portugal, others to the kingdom of Navarre. Many chose the way of the sea and were lost, drowned, burnt to death, and sold into slavery. They suffered the curses written in our Scriptures: "The Lord will cause thee to be smitten before thine enemies; thou shalt flee seven ways before them; thou shalt be a horror to all the kingdoms of the earth." Of this vast host, only a small number survived. Blessed be the name of the Lord!

I, too, chose the path of my people, departing on a seagoing vessel. I went into exile with my whole family and came to this glorious city of Naples, whose kings are merciful. Thereupon I decided to pay my vow to God by setting upon the task of writing a commentary on the books of Kings. It was a time to recall the destruction of our Holy Temple and the Exile of our people, which are recorded in these books. It was a time to remember our glories and our misfortunes.

5

The Search for Deliverance
(1492 to 1789)

David B. Ruderman

The period from the Spanish expulsion of 1492 until the French Revolution in 1789 was characterized by a series of momentous demographic,
political, and cultural changes in Jewish society. Demographically, the
Jews dramatically migrated from west to east. The Spanish emigrés,
forced out of the Iberian peninsula, relocated in the eastern half of the
Mediterranean basin, in the Ottoman Empire, Italy, and, later, in Amsterdam. The Jews of Germanic origin settled in the lands of Eastern Europe.
Politically, Jews were denied the opportunity to settle in most of Western
Europe, but received more favorable political privileges in the Ottoman
Empire and in Eastern Europe. Culturally the Jewish community experienced a virtual explosion of literary and spiritual creativity: rabbinic scholarship in Eastern Europe and in the Ottoman Empire; a kabbalistic and
messianic effervescence in the Land of Israel and a pietistic revival in
Eastern Europe; and stimulating cultural interaction in Italy, Amsterdam,
and elsewhere, producing a virtual outpouring of historical, theological,
homiletical, and scientific writing.

These Jewish transformations coincided with major changes within
European society as a whole: the consolidation of the modern national
state, the rise of capitalism, the Renaissance, the Reformation, the birth
of modern science, and the emergence of secular and rational trends in
European society.

Jewish history in this multifaceted era simultaneously demonstrated
signs of traditionalism and modernism, engagement with Western civilization and disengagement, and new economic and political opportunities
alongside persisting restrictions and discrimination. Portents of political,
social, and cultural changes for European Jews were visible by the end of
the period. Yet, despite radical migratory shifts, new intellectual and cultural liaisons between the Jews and Christians in the West, the ferment of
kabbalistic messianism and its anarchic tendencies, and the cultural and
spiritual reawakening of Eastern European Jewry, the political and social
foundations of traditional Jewish society still remained virtually intact.

SAMUEL USQUE'S CONSOLATION FOR ISRAEL'S TRIBULATIONS

The expulsion of the Jews from Spain in 1492 left many of the exiles in a state of shock. The finality of their exit forced them to reflect on the ultimate purpose of Jewish existence and Jewish belief. Why had their generation been singled out for suffering? Had their faith in divine providence been misguided? Where was God in their hour of need, and what future could they expect as wandering, unwanted castoffs? The plight of the *conversos* (those who converted to Christianity) in Spain and later in Portugal also weighed heavily on those who sought meaning in the troublesome events of their era.

Samuel Usque, a former Portuguese *converso*, addressed these same questions in a book he published in Ferrara, Italy, in 1553, written in Portuguese primarily to an audience of *conversos*. The work, *A Consolation for the Tribulations of Israel*, offered a plea to the disillusioned among the Jewish and *converso* communities to restore their faithful hope in the destiny of their people. Israel had suffered because of its sins but, at this juncture, its present misfortunes were about to end. Setting his narrative in the framework of a pastoral dialogue among three shepherds—Ycabo (Jacob, the personification of the Jewish people), Numeo (Nahum, "the comforter"), and Zicario (Zachariah, "the remembrancer")—Usque sought to review all of Jewish history from the biblical period to his own generation. By holding up the mirror of the past to the present, he hoped to convince his readers, especially those *conversos* living in Portugal and Spain, that divine redemption was imminent and that they should return to the Jewish fold.

The passage below is excerpted from Numeo's summary of eight compelling reasons why his generation should remain hopeful. Among these reasons he includes the argument that the Jewish dispersal among the nations precludes their complete annihilation; Spain may destroy its Jewish community but, at the same time, Ferrara and Turkey openly welcome the exiles. Moreover a beneficent and wealthy Jewess named Dona Gracia Nasi, a former *converso* herself, offers her coreligionists full material and emotional support.

READING 5-1

Let me return. Even when God inflicted corporeal punishment, which troubles you so greatly, His compassion made it possible in many ways for you to endure it patiently, and for many benefits to accrue to you because of it.

Firstly, He meted out your punishment gradually, so that your full punishment might not consume you and destroy you. Thus He said through the prophet's lips, "I shall punish you little by little, but consume you I shall not."

Secondly, He punished you immediately after each sin, so that your unrequited iniquities should not accumulate, and so that you should take measures to remedy your works after every lash. The Lord told you this in these words: "Your affliction shall teach you and your travails shall reprove you."

Thirdly, by scattering you among all peoples, He made it impossible for the world to destroy you, for if one kingdom rises against you in Europe to inflict death upon you, another in Asia allows you to live. And if the Spaniards burn you in Spain and banish you, the Lord wills for you to find someone in Italy who welcomes you and lets you live in freedom. And if the Lord had not dispersed you but instead, as your iniquities merit, had isolated you in one corner of the earth, like your brethren, the Ten Tribes, your life would be in jeopardy and the die for your destruction cast. You would long ago have perished from the wrath of only one of the peoples who had subjected you. . . .

The fifth road to consolation is the great benefit which has come of your misfortunes in Spain and Portugal, of which you so bitterly complain; for when a person's limbs are being devoured by herpes, it is best to cut them off with the knife or the fire, so as to prevent the spread of the disease and save the rest of the body. At such a time the cruel surgeon is the instrument of recovery. Therefore, since you had forgotten your ancient Law, and feigned Christianity with all your might solely to save your life and property, without realizing that you were jeopardizing your soul, it was proper that in such a perilous and mortal illness the Lord should not be apprehensive about applying the cautery to cure you. Truly, if you consider matters carefully, His mercy was great in being cruel to you, for the noxious wound penetrated your body so rapidly that in a few years it would have killed the memory of Judaism in your children. And no more merciful remedy would have sufficed to save your limbs, which are now out of danger. Therefore cut away your flesh which is wasting, if you desire life. Let the great benefit you are receiving soften the unyielding pain of your rigorous cure. And throw these waters of consolation upon the flames of the Inquisition, that the heat you suffer may be lessened. . . .

The eighth and most signal way by which you will rise to a higher degree of consolation is in the great nation of Turkey. This country is like a broad and expansive sea which our Lord has opened with the rod of His mercy, as Moses did for you in the Exodus from Egypt, so that the swells of your present misfortunes, which relentlessly pursue you in all kingdoms of Europe like the infinite multitude of Egyptians, might cease and be consumed in it. Here the gates of liberty are always wide open for you that you may fully practice your Judaism; they are never closed. Here you may restore your true character, transform your nature, change your ways, and banish false and erring opinions. Here you have begun to embrace your true ancient faith and to abandon the practices opposed to God's will, which you have adopted under the pressures of the nations in which you have wandered. This is a sublime mercy from the Lord, for He has granted you such abundant freedom in these realms that you may now take the first step toward your belated repentance. Consider this a great consolation, and you will find relief for your tribulations in a refuge so certain and sure. For here you may come to terms with your soul, and be unafraid that pressures will remove it from His Law, as has happened in other kingdoms.

SOLOMON IBN VERGA'S ANALYSIS OF
THE CAUSES OF JEWISH SUFFERING

Solomon ibn Verga composed his Hebrew work, *Shevet Yehudah* ("The Scepter of Judah"), in the 1520's after escaping Portugal where he had lived as a forced Christian convert. His book was published by his son only a year after Usque's. Like the *Consolation*, it consists of a series of imaginary dialogues interspersed in a comprehensive history of persecutions that serves as a backdrop for exploring contemporary tribulations. But, unlike Usque, ibn Verga used his dialogues first to probe the sociological and psychological causes of Christian persecution toward Jews before resorting to a more traditional theological response.

The selection below is part of an imaginary dialogue between a typical Hispanic king named Alphonso and his trusted royal adviser, Thomas. In the mouths of his imaginary characters, the author charges that arrogance, conspicuous consumption, social standoffishness, and usury were all factors in explaining Spanish hatred toward the Jews. Elsewhere in his work, however, ibn Verga again considered the causes of Jewish suffering, responding in his own name and in a more traditional manner. As Solomon Alami and earlier Spanish Jewish writers had argued before him, he attributed the tribulations of the Jews to their own moral inadequacies.

READING 5-2

The answer of Thomas: I have never seen an intelligent person who hates the Jews. They are hated only by the masses—and for good reason. First, the Jews are proud and are always seeking to domineer. They do not consider that they are exiles and serfs, driven from land to land. On the contrary, they try to present themselves as lords and nobles, and therefore the people envy them. The Sage [King Solomon, traditional author of the book of Proverbs] has said that the hatred which is caused by envy can never be overcome. My lord will find empirical confirmation in the fact that when the Jews came to his kingdom they came as serfs and exiles, wearing tattered clothes. For many years they neither put on an expensive garment nor evinced any haughtiness. In those days did my lord hear that any blood accusations were made against them? If such had been made, they would have been recorded in the chronicles of the kings of Spain, as is the good and proper custom, in order to learn from them for the future. There can thus be no question that as long as they gave no cause for envy, they were beloved. But now the Jew is ostentatious. If he has two hundred pieces of gold, he immediately dresses himself in silk and his children in embroidered clothing. This is something that not even nobles who possess an annual income of a thousand doubloons would do. Therefore accusations are leveled against them, which may perhaps lead to their expulsion from the kingdom. In the city of Toledo their pride brought them to such presumption that they struck

Christians, and their leaders were constrained to proclaim that whoever struck a Christian would be punished by their laws. In this regard we can apply Solomon's statement: "For three things the earth doth quake . . . for a servant when he reigneth . . ."

A second reason for the hatred is that when the Jews came to my lord's kingdom they were poor and the Christians were rich. Now it is the opposite, since the Jews are clever and achieve their purposes with cunning. Moreover, they became very rich by lending on interest. My lord will note that three-quarters of all the lands and estates of Spain are all in the hands of the Jews [a gross exaggeration]—and this on account of the heavy interest.

A HANDBOOK OF HEBREW RHETORIC IN THE SETTING OF RENAISSANCE ITALY

Simultaneously with the decline of Hispanic-Jewish life, Jewish communities began to flourish throughout northern Italy. These communities were composed of the Jews who had migrated from southern and central Italy, Germany, France, and, later, from Spain. Living in a relatively open social and economic environment and exposed to new currents of thought and cultural modes associated with the Renaissance, a limited but noticeable number of Italian Jews participated fully in the intellectual pursuits of Italian culture, while maintaining an intense awareness of their own specific identity.

Judah Messer Leon, a Jewish doctor and rabbinic scholar living in the second half of the fifteenth century, composed a Hebrew work entitled *Nofet Ẓufim* ("The Honeycomb's Flow") which was published before 1480. In his work Messer Leon introduced a new genre of rhetorical writing to his Italian Jewish readers which placed him in the center of Italian humanism, a new and dominant expression of Renaissance culture in the fifteenth century. The humanists reclaimed rhetoric as a significant and independent part of a new curriculum of studies that included grammar, poetry, history, and moral philosophy. All of which would shape, they believed, a new breed of educated civil leaders claiming both wisdom and eloquence.

Messer Leon's rhetorical compendium similarly projected the ideal of a good and righteous man who combined knowledge and noble character, and provided a new and effective leadership for the Jewish community. He claimed that the model of classical oratory was initially conceived not in Greece nor Rome but in Israel; the Hebrew Bible was the font and exemplar of the rhetorical art. By Judaizing the humanist ideal, he offered the Jews a satisfying reassurance regarding the intrinsic worth of their own cultural legacy in the context of Renaissance culture.

READING 5-3

Not only is this the case here, but every science, every rationally apprehended truth that any treatise may contain, is present in our holy Torah and in the books of those who speak by the Holy Spirit—present, that is, for those who thoroughly understand the subjects involved, and for whom the Lord has enlightened the eyes of understanding as perfectly as possible. This is what the Psalmist, upon whom be peace, means when he says: The law of the Lord is perfect, restoring the soul. In this verse he has included two ideas. The first is that the Torah is so complete—meaning that nothing is lacking therein, for such is completeness—that it is a Law entirely perfect, deficient in no single respect; from this it necessarily follows that the Torah must include the entirety of all truths, either implicitly or explicitly. The other idea is that the Torah is able to restore the soul to the place whence she was hewn for this the soul needs nothing else, since the Torah is in itself alone sufficient. For as the Torah includes all perfection, so it includes all that is necessary for the ultimate perfection, the survival of the soul and her cleaving to God. The latter and concluding portion of the verse is thus the necessary consequence of its beginning, for since the Torah is complete it must necessarily be equal to the task of restoring the soul to the citadel on high: if she returned unto her father's house as in her youth, the Lord alone shall lead her, and . . . no strange god with Him.

In the days of Prophecy, indeed, in the months of old, when out of Zion, the perfection of beauty, God shined forth, we used to learn and know from the holy Torah all the sciences and truths of reason, including all that were humanly attained, for everything is either latent therein or plainly stated. What other peoples possessed of these sciences and truths was, by comparison with us, very little, so that the nations which heard the fame of us were wont to say: "Surely this great nation is a wise and understanding people." But after the indwelling Presence of God departed from our midst because of our many iniquities, when Prophecy and insight ceased, and the science of our men of understanding was hid we were no longer able to derive understanding of all scientific developments and attainments from the Torah's words; this condition, however, persists due to our own falling short, our failure to know the Torah in full perfection. Thus the matter has come to be in reverse; for if, after we have come to know all the sciences, or some part of them, we study the words of the Torah, then the eyes of our understanding open to the fact that the sciences are included in the Torah's words, and we wonder how we could have failed to realize this from the Torah itself to begin with. Such has frequently been our own experience, especially in the science of Rhetoric. For when I studied the words of the Torah in the way now common amongst most people, I had no idea that the science of Rhetoric or any part of it was included therein. But once I had studied and investigated Rhetoric, searched for her as for hid treasures out of the treatises written by men of nations other than our own, and afterwards came back to see what is said of her in the Torah and the Holy Scriptures, then the eyes of my understanding were opened; and I saw that it is the Torah which was the giver. Between the Torah's pleasing words and stylistic elegancies—and, indeed, all the statutes and ordinances of Rhetoric which are included within the Holy Scriptures—and all of the like that all other nations possess, the difference is so striking that to compare them is like comparing the hyssop . . . in the wall with the cedar that is in Lebanon; and I marvel how previously the spirit of the Lord passed me by aforetime, so that I did not know her place, where it is. You could apply the same comparison to all other sciences.

A CHRISTIAN SCHOLAR LEARNS THE *KABBALAH*

The most significant interaction between Jewish and Italian Renaissance culture occurred in Florence at the end of the fifteenth century in the home of the illustrious philosopher Giovanni Pico della Mirandola (1463–94). In a relatively unprecedented manner a select but influential group of Christian Neoplatonic scholars, inspired by Pico's example, actively desired to understand the Jewish religion, its culture and texts in order to penetrate their own spiritual roots more deeply.

Pico and his colleagues were drawn to Jewish study, especially to the study of the *kabbalah* (Jewish mysticism), because of their belief in the concept of "ancient theology"—a single truth that pervaded all historical periods. By studying the ancient authors, Jewish and Christian, a unity and harmony of religious insight could be discovered. While "ancient theology" led Pico to Judaism, his concept of "poetic theology" facilitated his concentration on the *kabbalah*. For Pico the ancient pagan religions had concealed their secret truths through a kind of "hieroglyphic" imagery of myths and fables; so too Moses had addressed the Hebrews in a veiled manner called the *kabbalah*. The *kabbalah* therefore constituted that part of Judaism where the divine truths could be located; it was the key to laying bare the secrets of Judaism, to reconcile them with the mysteries of other religions and cultures, and thus to Christianize and universalize them.

The selection below constitutes part of the appendix to Pico's commentary on the first part of the Book of Genesis, called the *Heptaplus*. It represents Pico's exposition of the first word of the Bible, "bereshit" (in the beginning), illustrating how a Christian author familiar with kabbalistic techniques could use them for Christian theological purposes. Pico thus transformed Jewish *kabbalah* into a Christian *kabbalah*.

READING 5-4

Exposition of the First Expression, Namely, "In the Beginning"

Now has come the end of the work with the exposition of the whole text having been surveyed in its seven forms. However, I recognize that as yet there has been something left by me untouched and undiscussed which it seemed should have been explained even at the first, namely, what the first expression of the law means, that is, "In the beginning." . . .

I should like to explain the first expression of the work, which by the Hebrews is read "Bereshit" and by us "In the beginning," to see if I also, using the rules of the ancients, could draw out into the light thence something worthy to know. And beyond my hope, beyond my conjecture, I found what not even I, finding it, could believe, nor what others could easily believe—the whole arrangement of the creation of the world and of all things revealed and explained in that one expression.

I do say a marvelous, unheard of, and unbelievable thing. But if you will pay attention, you will believe it at once, and the very thing will prove me right. That expression by the Hebrews is written in this manner: . . . Berescith. From this if we unite the third letter to the first, it becomes . . . "AB." If to the first one doubled, we add the second one, it becomes . . . "BEBAR." If we read all of them except the first, it becomes . . . "RESIT." If we unite the fourth and the first and the last, it becomes . . . "SCIABAT." If we put the first three in the order in which they are, it becomes . . . "BARA." If with the first omitted, we put down the three following ones, it becomes . . . "ROSC." If leaving out the first and the second ones, we put the two following ones, we have . . . "ES." If we leave off the first three ones, we put together the fourth and the last one, we have . . . "SETH." Again if we unite the second to the first one, we have . . . "RAB;" if we put after the third, the fourth and then the fifth ones, we have . . . "HISC;" if we unite the first two with the last two, we have . . . "REBITH." If we unite the last to the first, we obtain the twelfth and the last word, . . . "THOB," turning the THAU into the letter THETH, which is a very common proceeding in Hebrew.

Let us see what these words mean in Latin, then what may be revealed about the mystery of the whole nature of those not ignorant of philosophy. AB means the father; BEBAR means in the son and through the son (in fact, the prefix BETH means both); RESIT indicates the beginning; SABATH the rest and the end; BARA, created; ROSC, head; ES fire; SETH, foundation; RAB, of the great; HISC, of the man; BERIT, with an agreement; THOB, with goodness.

If, following this order, we rebuild the expression, it will be like this: "The Father, in the Son and through the Son, the beginning and end, or rest, created the head, the fire, and the foundation of the great man with a good agreement." This entire discourse results from the taking apart and the putting together of that first expression. It cannot be clear to all how deep and full of all meaning this teaching is. But, if not all, at least some of the ideas are signified to us by these words that are clear to all. By all Christians it is known what is meant by the saying "the Father created in the Son and through the Son," and likewise what is meant by "the Son is the beginning and the end of all things." In fact, He is the Alpha and Omega, (as John writes), and He called Himself the Beginning, and we have shown that He is the End of all things in which they may be brought back to their beginning.

The rest is a little more obscure: namely, what do the head, the fire, and the foundation of the great man mean, and what is the "agreement," and why is it called "good"? In fact, not everyone can see present here every law of the four worlds of which I spoke, the whole plan, their relationship, and, likewise, their happiness, about which I explained at the end. First then, we must remember that the world was called by Moses, "great man." In fact, if man is a small world, necessarily the world is a great man. Hence with the opportunity seized, he pictures, very appropriately, the three worlds, the intellectual, the heavenly, and the corruptible ones, through the three parts of man, not only showing with this figure that in man are contained all the worlds, but also explaining briefly which part of man corresponds to each world.

Let us consider then the three parts of man: the higher is the head; then that which from the neck stretches to the navel; the third, that which extends from the navel to the feet. And these parts in the figure of man are also well defined and separated with a certain variety. But it is astonishing how beautifully and how perfectly they correspond by a very precise plan, by analogy, to the three parts of the world.

The brain, source of knowledge, is in the head; the heart, source of movement, life, and heat, is in the chest; the genital organs, the beginning of reproduction, are located in the lowest part. By the same token, in the world the highest part, which is the angelic or intellectual world, is the source of knowledge because such nature is made for the understanding; the middle part, that is the sky, is the beginning of life, of movement, heat, and is controlled by the sun as the heart in the chest. It is known to all that below the moon is the beginning of creation and corruption. See how appropriately all these parts of the world and of man correspond reciprocally. Indeed, he designated the first one with its appropriate name, the head; he called the second one fire, because of this name the heavens are valued by many, and because in us this part is the principle of heat. He called the third one foundation because by it (as is known by all) is founded and sustained the whole body of man. He added finally that God created them with a good agreement because between them, through the law of divine wisdom, an agreement of peace and friendship was decreed on the kinship and on the mutual agreement of their natures. This agreement is good because it is thus arranged and set in order toward God, Who is goodness itself, so that, just as the whole world is one in the totality of its parts, so also like this, at the end, it is one with its Maker.

Let us also imitate the holy agreement of the world, so that we may be one together in mutual love, and that simultaneously through the true love of God, we may all happily ascend as one with Him.

AN ITALIAN JEW COMPARES THE JEWISH GOD WITH THAT OF THE ANCIENT PAGANS

Pico's universal theology of Christianity not only influenced Christian thought of the Renaissance and Reformation but contemporary Jewish thought as well. One of Pico's major Jewish teachers, a prolific writer and physician named Yoḥanan Alemanno (ca. 1435–1505), even recast the *kabbalah* in a Neoplatonic and magical perspective, very much in the style of his Florentine student.

Another Italian Jewish doctor and student of the *kabbalah* named Abraham b. Ḥananiah Yagel (1553–after 1628) apparently was familiar with Alemanno's and Pico's writings and utilized them in his own compositions. In an encyclopedia of the natural and metaphysical world which he called *Bet Ya'ar ha-Levanon* ("The House of the Forest of Lebanon"), composed at the end of the sixteenth century, he devoted one section (printed below) to elucidating the Jewish view of God. In order to demonstrate the similarity of the Jewish conception with that of the ancient pagan philosophers, he unhesitatingly evoked the testimony of such ancient pagan philosophers and magicians as Orpheus, Zoroaster, Apuleius, and Plato. He even translated into Hebrew a prayer of the ancient "magus" Hermes, from his *Pimander*, following the Latin translation of Marsilio Ficino.

So blatant a utilization of pagan magical sources discloses his remarkable belief in the concept of "ancient theology" (articulated by the Florentine school) that every philosophy and every religion possesses a common nucleus of universal truth. By equating the Jewish God with that of Hermes and the other pagans, he appeared to undermine the unique character of Jewish belief. Yagel's use of ancient theology provides a striking illustration of the influence of Renaissance cultural ideals on Jewish thought.

READING 5-5

The important sages among the gentiles, who never saw the lights of the Torah nor of worship, prophecy, wonders and miracles [acknowledged the idea of one God]. . . . Listen to what these sages spoke about the creator:

Firstly, the following quotation ascribed to the ancient Orpheus is found in ancient books: "The angels and the heavenly forces attribute their origin, their existence and their beginning to the singular master and king and creator, whose ability is above all forces and whose power is infinite. From this unique being everything comes into being, according to his desire, one by one, according to their degrees: earth, air, water, fire, day and night. He created them out of his love and compassion and gave them power. With this love of his, He created everything which will remain forever etc." At this point he continued to relate the initial creation of the higher and lower beings and the love common to all of them. . . .

The ancient sage Zoroaster wrote: "Deus is an essence, located in every place, who experiences no deficient action nor deterioration. He is not born nor does He give birth; He is the first and the last. He is father and creator of all great and wonderous things. His acts are holy and just; He is the light of all living and the bestower of perfection to the nature of all creatures."

The ancient philosopher Apuleius wrote: "He is the king of the wondrous world of nature and its causality. There is nothing like Him nor does anything participate with Him. No place limits Him; no time can capture Him and no thought or concept can conceptualize Him. . . . He is light and force and life of everything. All creation desires to worship Him for He is the king of glory."

These are the words of the great Hermes and his prayer to God as he wrote it at the end of the first chapter of the *Pimander*, after he related the manner of creation and existence of the world. This [prayer] is close to what is found in the Torah of Moses, if one understands all the details of its statements precisely, without the intrusion of any false thoughts, doubt or suspicion. He said that with all the strength of his soul, upon seeing [God's] acts, he praises and extols God and says:

"God is holy, the father and creator of everything. God is holy whose will is more perfect than its essential powers. God is holy who reveals himself to those who love Him. You are holy for by your word you made everything. You are holy for your image is found in all natural beings. You are holy for you were never fashioned from any natural being. . . . Hear me and fortify me and appear in the splendor of your influence to people who are found with the vanities of the world. . . . For I am your servant who believes in you and testifies to your greatness with faithful testimony. By this I elevate myself with life and with light. . . ."

DAVID REUVENI'S TRAVELS IN ITALY

Messianic activity also marked the cultural ambiance of Italian Jewry of the Renaissance. In the aftermath of the expulsion from Spain, messianic speculation and activity were particularly widespread among Sephardic Jews and *conversos*. This enthusiasm for predicting the end was also shared by Christians. Astrological events, political and military upheavals, the Reformation and the Counter-Reformation, as well as the discovery of new lands and new peoples, were tabulated by Jewish and Christian messianic prognosticators alike.

In 1524 David Reuveni (d. 1538?), a dark-skinned Jew, arrived in Italy from Israel and claimed to be a representative of the ten lost tribes. He eventually was granted an audience with the pope to advance his plan to organize a joint Jewish-Christian force to overthrow the Turks and regain the Holy Land. Despite detractors, Reuveni was able to muster support from Christian and Jewish eschatological enthusiasts who considered him to be a messianic figure.

The major source for Reuveni's activity is an autobiographical diary which he is purported to have written. Whatever the actual origin of this mysterious figure and the actual author of the diary, its account of Reuveni's wanderings in Italy retains a surprisingly authentic air of reality and can be corroborated by other sources. The excerpts below describe some of Reuveni's Italian adventures, including his meeting with Cardinal Egidio (Giles) of Viterbo (a noted Christian Hebraist), Pope Clement VII, and notables of the Jewish community. Reuveni's conversation with the affluent Jewish banker Ishmael of Rieti is especially revealing. When asked whether he more desired Jerusalem or his native Siena, Ishmael answered, "I have no desire in Jerusalem but only in Siena."

READING 5-6

I, David, the son of King Solomon, of righteous memory, from the wilderness of Habor, entered the gate of the City of Rome on the 15th day of Adar, 1524, and a Gentile from Venice came to me and spoke with me in Arabic, and I was angry with him. I went to the Pope's palace, riding on horseback, and my servant before me, and the Jews also came with me, and I entered the presence of Cardinal Egidio; and all the Cardinals and Princes came to see me, and with the said Cardinal was R. Joseph Ashkenazi, who was his teacher, and the physician Rabbi, Joseph Sarphati; and I spoke to the Cardinal, and my interpreter was the learned man who came with me, and the Jews heard all that I spoke to the Cardinal, and I said to him that to the Pope I would complete my message. I stayed with the Cardinal all day till the eve of Sabbath, and he promised to bring the matter before the Pope tomorrow. I went away with R. Joseph Ashkenazi and with R. Raphael, the old man who lived in the same house, and we took our Sabbath meal and slept till the morning; and I went with them to the Synagogue in order to pronounce the blessing of deliverance from peril before the scroll of the Law. Men, women, and children came to meet us all the way until we entered the house of the said R. Raphael, and I fasted on that Sabbath day. All day long men and women, Jews and Gentiles came to visit me until evening. Cardinal Egidio sent for R. Joseph Ashkenazi to tell me that the Pope was very pleased, and wished to see me on Sunday before 11. And so in the morning, before prayers, they gave me a horse and I went to Borghetto Santo Gile to the house of an old man, the brother-in-law of R. Joseph Sarphati, before morning prayer; and I prayed there, and many Jews came to me, may God keep them and multiply them a thousand fold! At eight o'clock I went to the house of the Pope and entered Cardinal Egidio's room, and with me were about twelve old and honoured Jews. As soon as the Cardinal saw me, he rose from his chair and we went, I and he, to the apartment of the Pope, and I spoke with him, and he received me graciously and said, "The matter is from the Lord"; and I said to him, "King Joseph and his elders ordered me to speak to thee that thou shouldst make peace between the Emperor and the French King, by all means, for it will be well with thee and them if thou makest this peace, and write for me a letter to these two Kings, and they will help us and we will help them; and write also for me to King Prester John (i.e. the King of Abyssinia). The Pope answered me, "As to the two kings between whom thou askest me to make peace, I cannot do it, but if thou needest help the King of Portugal will assist thee, and I will write to him and he will do all, and his land is near to thy country and they are accustomed to travel on the great sea every year, more than those in the lands of those other Kings"; and I replied to the Pope, "Whatever thou wishest I will do, and I will not turn to the right or left from what thou biddest me, for I have come for God's service, and not for anything else, and I will pray for thy welfare and good all the days of my life." And the Pope asked the Cardinal, "Where does the Ambassador lodge?" and he answered, "The Jews asked him to go with them," and the honourable Jews who were with the Pope told him, "Let the Ambassador stay with us, for we will honour him for the sake of thy honour," and the Pope said to them, "If you will do honour to him I will pay all your expenses"; and I said to the Pope, "I wish to come before thee once every two days, for to see thee is as seeing the face of God"; and the Pope answered me that he ordered Cardinal Egidio to come with me every time I came to see him, and I took leave of the Pope and went from before him, and I went with the Jews and rejoiced and was glad of heart. . . .

When I left Viterbo, Jews on ten horses accompanied me and we stayed at Bolsena over sabbath in the house of the said R. Joseph, and remained there until Sunday, and they showed us great honour, more than proper. Thence we journeyed to Siena and came to the house of the honourable Ishmael of Rieti, who took us and made room in his house, and prepared for me a bed and separate room. He has a large dwelling and is very rich, and I said to him, "What desirest thou more, Jerusalem or thy own place?" and he answered, "I have no desire in Jerusalem but only in Siena"; and I was much surprised at him that he cannot do meritorious deeds with the wealth that God has given him. "He that loveth silver shall not be satisfied with silver." He promised to do kindness unto my servants, but repented and did not keep his promise and did not desire to earn a good name before all Israel.

We journeyed from Siena on the Monday and arrived at Pisa in the house of R. Jechiel, may he be remembered with a thousand times a thousand blessings, he and his mother Signora Laura and his grandmother Signora Sarah, may they be blessed among women. Amen! . . .

The household of R. Jechiel gave me all kinds of food and spices and flowers and apple water, and served me with all the delicacies of the world, and did all kindness and truth with me and sent me great presents and silk robes, and gave money to all my servants and, on the great fast, they came to me with honour to the house of R. Jechiel. His wife, called Diamante, the daughter of R. Asher Meshullam, of Venice, and the mother of R. Jechiel, Signora Laura, and her mother, Signora Sarah, and other young women used to dance in the room where I was and the wife of R. Jechiel played the harp and they said to me, "We are come here for your honour's sake, and in order that the sorrow may go from the fast and that you may rejoice"; and they asked me if I had any delight in the sound of the harp, and in dancing and I answered, "You are very kind," but God knows my thoughts that I did not wish to listen to the sound of the harp and the flute and rejoicings. The Gentiles of Pisa came to me to R. Jechiel's house and blew trumpets and made great sounds in order to get money, and the said R. Jechiel wrote a scroll of the law with his own hand, and I made the blessing over that scroll several Sabbaths. . . .

After a few days the King of Portugal sent to Rome as Ambassador Don Martin instead of Don Miguel, and as soon as Don Martin arrived in Rome he wrote to me to Pisa that "the King of Portugal has heard about thee that thou has come to serve him; he is glad and will do thee kindness, therefore prepare and go with this ship.". . .

A CONTEMPORARY PORTRAIT OF SOLOMON MOLKHO

When Reuveni arrived in Portugal, he found an anxious following of *conversos* who mistook his coming for the imminence of the messianic age. In Lisbon he attracted one young follower who took the name Solomon Molkho (ca. 1500–32), circumcised himself, and left Portugal with his newly discovered spiritual mentor. Molkho, in contrast to Reuveni, had few inhibitions about declaring himself the messiah. Arriving in Salonika, he attracted the attention of some of the most illustrious rabbis of the city, publishing a book of electrifying sermons he apparently had delivered there. He then visited Italy where he was noticed by Jews and Christians alike. While in Italy he and Reuveni enjoyed the complete protection of the papacy. When visiting the Holy Roman emperor, Charles V, in search of further support for their cause, however, both were captured. Molkho was tried by the Inquisition and burned at the stake; Reuveni was incarcerated for the remainder of his life. The Reuveni-Molkho episode dramatically discloses the deeply rooted and persistent messianic strains within the consciousness of sixteenth-century Jewry, some three decades after the Spanish expulsion.

The following excerpt is taken from the description of Molkho by the contemporary Jewish historian, Joseph ha-Cohen (1496–1578).

READING 5-7

Now there came out of Portugal a noble whose name was Solomon Molko. He was of those who had fled there in the days of the Inquisition. While he was still a youth, he served as one of the secretaries of the king (John III, 1521–1557). But when he saw David Reubeni, the Lord touched his heart and he returned to the Lord, the God of our ancestors, and he was circumcised.

At that time he knew nothing of the Law or the Scriptures. After he was circumcised, the Lord endowed him with wisdom. Soon he became the wisest of men, arousing much wonder. He went to Italy, and with great daring spoke of the Divine Law in the presence of kings. Thence he went to Turkey, and later returned to Rome. He spoke with Pope Clement (VII, 1523–1534) who, against the desire of his intimates, extended every kindness to him. The Pope gave him a letter of safe-conduct, signed with his own hand, permitting him to live as he pleased, and without delay Solomon lived openly as a Jew.

Now Solomon became learned in the wisdom of the Kabbalah. From his lips came words of grace, for the spirit of the Lord was upon him and His word was constantly on his tongue. He continually drew forth marvelous words from the deep fountain of the Kabbalah and he wrote them upon tablets. But I have not yet seen them. He preached to large audiences in Bologna and in other places. Many followed him both to hear his wisdom and to test him with riddles, but Solomon answered all their questions. Nothing was hidden from him. When they heard Solomon's words of wisdom they said, "What we heard about you was a true report. You have gained wisdom even exceeding your fame."

Many clothed themselves with envy, but they could inflict no harm upon him in Italy, for he was beloved by the nobles. He united himself with David Reubeni; in those days they were as one. . . .

Now Solomon was accustomed to discuss the beliefs and faith with the emperor (Charles V). When the emperor was in Ratisbon (in 1532), he went there and talked with him. But the emperor was unresponsive and, because of his ill temper, he would not listen to him. The emperor commanded that he be clapped into prison, he and his friend Prince David and their followers. And they remained there several days.

After the Turks were repulsed there was a period of respite and the emperor left Ratisbon. He returned to Italy, and took all the prisoners, bound in fetters, in wagons, setting a special guard over them. Then, in accordance with his imperial custom, the emperor discussed them with his advisers. . . . They found Solomon guilty and condemned him to death. And they said, "Bring him forth, and let him be burned." In order to prevent him from addressing the people, they put a bridle on his jawbones, and thus he came before them. The whole population surged about him, as he stood facing the crackling flames. And one of the emperor's nobles said, "Take the bridle from between his teeth, for I have a message to him from the King." When this was done, he said to Solomon, "The emperor sent me to you to say this: 'If you repent, your repentance will be accepted and you shall live.' He shall provide for you and you shall be one of his court; but if not—death is your fate." He did not move an eyelash. Even as a saint or an angel of God, he said, "Because I have lived your religion, my heart is bitter and grieved. Now do as you please. My soul, I know, will return to her Father's house where it will be better off than here."

And they were incensed, and cast him upon the burning woodpile. He was as a burnt offering to the Lord, and He smelled the sweet savour, and took to Him his pure soul. Then they brought his servants from the prison and they suffered the same fate. None escaped the destruction, except the noble David Reubeni, his friend; over him they set a guard. Whereupon the emperor went to Bologna, and they brought along Reubeni, bound in fetters, in a wagon, and took him to Spain. There he lived for a long time and died in the prison house.

During these days there were many in Italy who believed that Solomon Molko had, by his wisdom, delivered himself from his enemies, and that the fire did not touch his body. Some even took an oath before the community and the assembly that he was in his home eight days after the auto-da-fé, and that he left there and was never again seen. Almighty God alone knows the truth. Would to God I could write down with certainty whether his words were true or false.

THE BURNING OF THE *TALMUD* IN ITALY

The relatively tolerant climate that Renaissance Italy offered its small Jewish community was unfortunately short-lived. As a result of the oppressive policy of Pope Paul IV (1476–1559) and his successors, the Italian Jewish community experienced a radical deterioration of its legal status and physical welfare. The Italian Jews suddenly faced a major offensive against their community and religious heritage, which culminated in the public burning of the *Talmud* in 1553, and in restrictive legislation leading to increased impoverishment, ghettoization, and expulsion. The situation was further aggravated by severe pressures for conversion which included compulsory appearance at Christian preaching in synagogues and the establishment of houses for potential new converts. Whether motivated primarily by the need to fortify Catholic domination over all dissidence of Christian and non-Christian alike, or driven by a renewed missionary zeal for immediate and massive conversion, the papacy acted resolutely to undermine the previous status of this small Jewish community living in the heart of western Christendom.

Joseph ha-Cohen lived through the harrowing events of 1553 and vividly described them in the following excerpt. Note especially Joseph's emphasis on the role of recent Christian converts from Judaism in fomenting the anti-Jewish measures.

READING 5-8

In those days certain scoundrels went forth from our midst and did impute things that were not true against the Torah of the Lord our God and stiffened their neck and went astray from the Lord. They rejected the covenant which God had made with our fathers and followed after the Gentiles, concerning whom the Lord had commanded that they should not do like them. They provoked Him very much with their vanities and sinned heavily.

They brought up an evil report against the Talmud to the Pope Julius III [1550–1555], saying: "There is a certain Talmud widely spread among the Jews and its laws are diverse from those of all peoples. It calumniates your Messiah and it ill befits the Pope to suffer it." The impetuous Julius became very angry and his fury raged within him and he said: "Get hold of it and let it be burnt." No sooner had the command left his lips than the officers went forth, rushing out in haste, and entered the houses of the Jews and brought the books found there into the city-square and burnt them on the Sabbath day, on the festival of New Year in the year 5314, that is, 1553. And the children of Israel bewailed the burning which the enemies of God had kindled.

These are the names of those informers who were our troublers: Hananel da Foligno, Joseph Moro, Solomon Romano. O, Lord, do not blot out their sin. Deal with them in the time of thine anger.

Fleet messengers went forth to the tall and "tonsured" people [the clergy] throughout the Romagna so that in Bologna and Ravenna innumerable books were burnt on the Sabbath, and the children of Israel sighed and cried aloud but had no power to help themselves. In Ferrara and Mantua, too, the books were burnt by order of the Pope who commanded that they were to be destroyed. There was no one to save them in the day of the Lord's wrath.

In Venice, too, the Pope reached out and did not withdraw his hand from destroying. A certain adversary and enemy there, who had also deserted the divine Torah, Eleazar ben Raphael, the physician, gnashed at them with his teeth. There, too, innumerable books were burnt in the month of Elul, that is, the eighth month [October or November, 1553]. They sought to lay their hands even on the Holy Scriptures in the ark, but the congregational heads stood in the breach and saved them from their hands.

And in all the rest of the places to which the command of the Pope came there was great mourning among the Jews and fasting and weeping and wailing. The house of Israel humbled themselves and cried out to God saying: "The Lord, He is righteous," and when they humbled themselves the fierce wrath of God turned from them and He would not destroy them altogether. In the Duchies of Milan and Montferrat they did not even make a search, for the command of the Pope was odious to Don Ferrante [Gonzaga, d. 1557], the Viceroy. The Lord made the chiefs of the community to be pitied in his eyes and no one listened to the voice of the Pope. (The corrector [who added notes to Joseph ha-Cohen's account] says: The merit of the Talmudical academy which was in that cream of cities, Cremona, stood them in good stead. For verily the Lord raised up for them a redeemer, the great scholar, the honored Rabbi Joseph Ottolengo, who spread Torah in Israel. On them the wrath of the Lord did not fall, for their delight was in the law of the Lord; day and night they did not cease its study, and God saved them. It was not until the year 5319 [1559, when the Inquisition seized and burnt about 11,000 Hebrew volumes in Cremona] that the evil reached them, for then the academies came to an end and over them, too, passed the poisonous cup of reeling of the princes, and there was no longer peace for those who fight the battle of the Torah.) The Cardinal of Mantua [Ercole Gonzaga, d. 1563], the brother of Don Ferrante, also spoke to the Jews several times before he did anything at all in order that they might know what to do. Remember them, my God, for good.

The community leaders went to the Pope and he received them graciously in that he allowed them to keep the works of the later [Jewish] lawmakers, so as to leave them a remnant in the land, but he would not listen to them with respect to the books of the Talmud. And now, O Lord, consider and see for there is no might in us to stand before those who rise against us, neither know we what to do, but our eyes are upon you.

LEONE MODENA'S LIFE IN LOMBARDY

Leone Modena (1571–1648), although living in the era of Italian Jewry's decline, is still considered the most illustrious exemplar of Renaissance Jewish culture. A prolific writer in Hebrew and Italian, a gifted preacher, a formidable polemicist, a passionate lover of music, and an incessant gambler, he exemplified in his colorful personality and career many of the diversified trends of Italian Jewish culture. Despite his extraordinary intellectual interests and accomplishments, his life clearly reflects the growing anxiety and insecurity of Italian Jewry of the late sixteenth and early seventeenth centuries. His cultural pursuits also were constantly interrupted by problems of financial insecurity, a dilemma faced by many of his contemporaries.

Leone vividly described his early life in his *Ḥayyei Yehudah* ["Judah's (= Leone's) Life"], a Hebrew autobiography, from which the selection below is excerpted. Note especially the twenty-six occupations Leone admits he had attempted in the course of his life.

READING 5-9

Now there was a very great and powerful earthquake in the city of Ferrara, the like of which had not been known in any country, just as is written in the book *Light of the Eyes* by the sage Azariah dei Rossi [a sixteenth-century Italian-Jewish scholar]. And my father and his houshold fled for their very lives to Venice.

While they were there I, the bitter and hasty, was born on Monday between the eighteenth and nineteenth hour on the 23rd of April, 1571. Well-nigh like Job and Jeremiah may I curse that day, for wherefore did I come forth to see toil and wrath, distress and straits and evil alone all the while?

The birth was extremely hard for my mother, and when I came forth I was doubled over with my breech facing outwards, even then having to do with reverses. At the end of eight days I was circumcised with great joy by the renowned scholar and kabbalist, Rabbi Menahem Azariah of Fano, and my father and Mistress Sarah, daughter of my uncle Shemaiah, were my godparents; and my Hebrew name was called Judah Arieh. May the Lord have mercy on my soul and may the upsets of my life be an atonement for my sins and transgressions.

They dwelt in Venice for about eight months and then returned to Ferrara. While they were on the way to Francolino, near Ferrara, they left the ship and gave me to a gentile porter, who fled and bore me away in his bosom. As soon as they saw that I had vanished, his honor Master Samson Meshullam of blessed memory, who was my father's guide, pursued him about two miles and caught up with him and took me. Then he thrashed him thoroughly, and brought me back to my parents; and we came to Ferrara and dwelt there.

I began to learn the alphabet from a certain teacher known as Hazaneto, afterwards from Rabbi Isaac Supino, and afterwards from the Rabbi Azriel Basola. And though it is said, "Let a stranger praise thee but not thine own mouth," I may admit since I am now fully grown and it is no longer praise that in truth I did well with my studies from the very beginning. When I was two and a half years old, I said the Haphtarah in the synagogue, and when I was three I recognized my Creator and the value of study and knowledge, and I would explain the portion of the week and understand it.

And so I passed from class to class.

One day I was walking about in the garden and fell from a stone and twisted my hand and was sick for some time, to say nothing of the worms which troubled me. A certain woman gave me rock oil, and I fainted, and almost remained in that faint. A little later I became sick with smallpox; and these were all things that happened to me before I was four, yet are as clear in my mind and memory as if they happened yesterday; for I still know what my thoughts were then.

In 1575 we left Ferrara and went to live in Colonia, a small town belonging to Venice, to conduct a pawnshop. My father went to a great deal of trouble to prepare a ritual bath for the womenfolk in his house and to draw suitable water there. At the end of 1576 it was declared fitting, and at the time I was studying Mishna together with Rabbi Gershon Cohen, who is now the head of a Yeshibah in Poland, and was then a boy like me.

The teacher went somewhere, and both of us went down to the bath to play, as boys do; and I fell in to it when it was full to the brim, and the other boy ran away shouting, and the housefolk heard him and came dashing with my father and mother and looked for me here and there and did not know where I had fallen. And meanwhile an hour passed while I kept hold of a ledge round the bath until the housefolk came. Then a servant girl jumped into the water and took me out; and they carried me to bed as though I had been dead of dread and fear. . . .

I also learnt to play instruments, to sing, to dance, to do fine penmanship, and a little Latin. But on account of two servant women who hated me and embittered my life, I returned home when the year was over. So in the spring of 1581 my father of blessed memory sent me to Padua to the house of Rabbi Samuel Archivolti of blessed memory, to board with him and learn Torah from him. From him I learnt the craft of versifying and how to write prose, and he loved me very much until the day of his death; for he used to say that I was one of the pupils who was his very likeness and image in wisdom.

I was there for a whole year and then my father summoned me home. Now since my parents wanted to keep me there, the Lord provided us in the spring of 1582 with a young man from Italy who, however, came at the time from Safed. His name was Moses, son of Benjamin della Rocca, a grandson of the scholar Rabbi Moses Basola and a knowledgeable and understanding man. And this Moses became my teacher and from him I learnt much. During two years he was with me, after which he left for Cyprus where he married. While still a fine young man, he was summoned to the Upper Assembly. When I heard this sad news, I wrote laments for him and particularly the Hebrew and Italian *ottava rima* which is printed in my volume of sermons *Midbar Yehudah;* at the time I was thirteen years old. All the poets saw it and praised it, and up to the present it is a wonder for Christian and Jewish sages alike. Thereafter I ceased to study with any regular teacher, but only on my own, though I was not in a large city where comrades might have helped me to maintain my studies. Alas that I dwelt during the best period for study without a teacher and rabbi! . . .

In the month of Elul, 1589, my mother and I came to Venice to journey to Ancona in order to recover the property and goods which had been in the hands of my brother of blessed memory; for his wife had taken them and we did not see as much as a shoelace. Still, afterwards we decided not to go, and stayed in Venice. While we were there, my mother and her sister and the kinsfolk again took up the matter of the match; and we came to an agreement and gave our hands on it, and I took possession at the betrothal with great joy, and to my mother I pointed out the color of the clothes and ornaments which I had described to her more than a year earlier, when I had seen her in my dream. She was indeed a beautiful woman and wise, and I said that the words of Proverbs would apply about her and not the words of Ecclesiastes. (In Ecclesiastes, however, there is a verse, "A woman more bitter than death I have found.")

When the time of the wedding came, which was on the 13th day of Sivan, 1590, I wrote to my father, who was then in Bologna, and he came. And I summoned all my friends and relations and we went immediately after Shebuoth, all of us rejoicing and merry at heart, to Venice. When we got there, we found the bride in bed; but everybody said that there was nothing more serious than a little diarrhea, which would soon be cured. But from day to day the sickness grew worse, till she was on the verge of dying; but her heart was as the heart of a lion, and she was not frightened.

On the day of her death she called me and embraced and kissed me, saying, "I know that this is shamelessness. But God knows that during the whole year of our match we have not touched one another, even with the little finger. And now at the hour of death, the right of death is permitted me. I did not merit to be your wife. What shall I do if it is decreed from on high? Let the Lord do His Will."

Then she requested that a sage be called for her to confess; and he came and she said the death confession and requested the blessing of her parents and my mother. And on the eve of Sabbath, the 24th of Sivan, 1590, almost the anniversary of the time my brother died, my bride departed as the bride Sabbath came in, with a life of vanity to a life of eternity; and she passed away to her own place. There was much weeping in and out of the house among all who knew her; and she was laid to rest in all honor.

Immediately after she was buried all the kinsfolk came to my mother and me and said, "The sister who follows her is as good as she is. Why should we not maintain the kinship and give comfort to the father and mother of the girl?"

And they pressed me unceasingly to take her sister Rachel as my wife. So I wrote to my father, who replied to me as he always replied regarding this matter, as follows: "Do what you wish, for you have to make the choice. Today or tomorrow I shall be taken from you, but you and your children will stay with her. Therefore understand what lies before you and do as the hand of the Lord doth show you."

So in order to give satisfaction to my mother and the dead girl after the fashion she had hinted in her words, I agreed and took the aforesaid Mistress Rachel as my wife. And we immediately wrote the contract and made the wedding on Friday, the 5th of Tammuz, 1590, under a good star. . . .

Here I wish to write down for a memorial the number of ways I sought to earn my living; and I tried and did not succeed:

1. Jewish pupils. 2. Gentile pupils. 3. Teaching how to write. 4. Sermons. 5. Sermons written for others. 6. Acting as cantor. 7. Secretary of charitable and other societies. 8. Officiating as rabbi. 9. Decisions in ritual law. 10. Officiating as judge.

11. Daily lessons in the synagogue. 12. Conferring rabbinical diplomas. 13. Letters written in the names of others. 14. Music. 15. Verses for weddings and tombstones. 16. Italian sonnets. 17. Writing comedies. 18. Producing them. 19. Drawing up legal documents. 20. Translation. 21. Printing my own writings. 22. Proofreading. 23. Teaching the writings of charms and talismans. 24. Selling books of charms. 25. Commercial agent. 26. Matchmaker.

MARTIN LUTHER AND THE JEWS

Some Jews had high hopes that Martin Luther's challenge to the hegemony of the Catholic Church in 1517 and the beginning of the Reformation might signal a positive change for Jewish-Christian relations. Luther's initial statement about the Jews seemed to confirm such hopes. In a work written as early as 1523, *That Jesus Christ Was Born a Jew*, Luther evinced a sympathetic posture toward the Jews, hoping, however, that Jews would embrace his version of Christianity.

Jews did not flock to the Protestant camp as Luther had expected. He became increasingly bitter and disillusioned by Jewish indifference and, exactly twenty years after his first pronouncement, composed a revised statement entitled *Concerning the Jews and Their Lies*. His anti-Jewish remarks rivaled those of the most vociferous anti-Jewish antagonists within the Catholic camp both in tone and substance. They provided striking testimony that, with respect to their attitudes about the Jews, German Protestants and Catholics remained very much alike.

Ironically, Luther's distasteful pamphlet was read and quoted frequently by later anti-Semites. Excerpts from both of Luther's writings are found below.

READING 5-10A

That Jesus Christ Was Born a Jew

I will therefore show by means of the Bible the causes which induce me to believe that Christ was a Jew born of a virgin. Perhaps I will attract some of the Jews to the Christian faith. For our fools—the popes, bishops, sophists, and monks—the coarse blockheads! have until this time so treated the Jews that to be a good Christian one would have to become a Jew. And if I had been a Jew and had seen such idiots and blockheads ruling and teaching the Christian religion, I would rather have been a sow than a Christian.

For they have dealt with the Jews as if they were dogs and not human beings. They have done nothing for them but curse them and seize their wealth. Whenever they converted them, they did not teach them either Christian law or life but only subjected them to papistry and monkery. When these Jews saw that Judaism had such strong scriptural basis and that Christianity [Catholicism] was pure nonsense without Biblical support, how could they quiet their hearts and become real, good Christians? I have myself heard from pious converted Jews that if they had not heard the gospel in our time [from us Lutherans] they would always have remained Jews at heart in spite of their conversion. For they admit that they have never heard anything about Christ from the rulers who have converted them.

I hope that, if the Jews are treated friendly and are instructed kindly through the Bible, many of them will become real Christians and come back to the ancestral faith of the prophets and patriarchs. . . .

I would advise and beg everybody to deal kindly with the Jews and to instruct them in the Scriptures; in such a case we could expect them to come over to us. If, however, we use brute force and slander them, saying that they need the blood of Christians to get rid of their stench and I know not what other nonsense of that kind, and treat them like dogs, what good can we expect of them? Finally, how can we expect them to improve if we forbid them to work among us and to have social intercourse with us, and so force them into usury?

If we wish to make them better, we must deal with them not according to the law of the pope, but according to the law of Christian charity. We must receive them kindly and allow them to compete with us in earning a livelihood, so that they may have a good reason to be with us and among us and an opportunity to witness Christian life and doctrine; and if some remain obstinate, what of it? Not every one of us is a good Christian.

I shall stop here now until I see what the results will be. May God be gracious to us all. Amen.

READING 5-10B

Concerning the Jews and Their Lies

What then shall we Christians do with this damned, rejected race of Jews? Since they live among us and we know about their lying and blasphemy and cursing, we can not tolerate them if we do not wish to share in their lies, curses, and blasphemy. In this way we cannot quench the inextinguishable fire of divine rage (as the prophets say) nor convert the Jews. We must prayerfully and reverentially practice a merciful severity. Perhaps we may save a few from the fire and the flames [of hell]. We must not seek vengeance. They are surely being punished a thousand times more than we might wish them. Let me give you my honest advice.

First, their synagogues or churches should be set on fire, and whatever does not burn up should be covered or spread over with dirt so that no one may ever be able to see a cinder or stone of it. And this ought to be done for the honor of God and of Christianity in order that God may see that we are Christians, and that we have not wittingly tolerated or approved of such public lying, cursing, and blaspheming of His Son and His Christians. . . .

Secondly, their homes should likewise be broken down and destroyed. For they perpetrate the same things there that they do in their synagogues. For this reason they ought to be put under one roof or in a stable, like gypsies, in order that they may realize that they are not masters in our land, as they boast, but miserable captives, as they complain of us incessantly before God with bitter wailing.

Thirdly, they should be deprived of their prayer-books and Talmuds in which such idolatry, lies, cursing, and blasphemy are taught.

Fourthly, their rabbis must be forbidden under threat of death to teach any more. . . .

Fifthly, passport and traveling privileges should be absolutely forbidden to the Jews. For they have no business in the rural districts since they are not nobles, nor officials, nor merchants, nor the like. Let them stay at home. . . .

Sixthly, they ought to be stopped from usury. All their cash and valuables of silver and gold ought to be taken from them and put aside for safe keeping. For this reason, as said before, everything that they possess they stole and robbed from us through their usury, for they have no other means of support. This money should be used in the case (and in no other) where a Jew has honestly become a Christian, so that he may get for the time being one or two or three hundred florins, as the person may require. This, in order that he may start a business to support his poor wife and children and the old and feeble. Such evilly acquired money is cursed, unless, with God's blessing, it is put to some good and necessary use. . . .

Seventhly, let the young and strong Jews and Jewesses be given the flail, the ax, the hoe, the spade, the distaff, and spindle, and let them earn their bread by the sweat of their noses as is enjoined upon Adam's children. For it is not proper that they should want us cursed *Goyyim* [Gentiles] to work in the sweat of our brow and that they, pious crew, idle away their days at the fireside in laziness, feasting, and display. And in addition to this, they boast impiously that they have become masters of the Christians at our expense. We ought to drive the rascally lazy bones out of our system.

If, however, we are afraid that they might harm us personally, or our wives, children, servants, cattle, etc. when they serve us or work for us—since it is surely to be presumed that such noble lords of the world and poisonous bitter worms are not accustomed to any work and would very unwillingly humble themselves to such a degree among the cursed *Goyyim*—then let us apply the same cleverness [expulsion] as the other nations, such as France, Spain, Bohemia, etc., and settle with them for that which they have extorted usuriously from us, and after having divided it up fairly let us drive them out of the country for all time. For, as has been said, God's rage is so great against them that they only become worse and worse through mild mercy, and not much better through severe mercy. Therefore away with them. . . .

To sum up, dear princes and nobles who have Jews in your domains, if this advice of mine does not suit you, then find a better one so that you and we may all be free of this insufferable devilish burden—the Jews.

DAVID GANS ON WITNESSING THE ASTRONOMICAL OBSERVATORY OF TYCHO BRAHE NEAR PRAGUE

Despite the decline of Jewish life in Germany and Central Europe in the sixteenth century, islands of Jewish refuge remained. Jews still inhabited important communities in Worms, Vienna, and Frankfort, and in the adjacent Bohemian capital of Prague. From the end of the sixteenth through the early seventeenth century, particularly during the reign of Rudolph II and his successor, Matthias, Prague emerged as a Renaissance center, importing art and literature from Italy and Germany, attracting astronomers, alchemists, and magicians from all over Europe. In such an atmosphere Jewish society and culture flourished. The Jews distinguished themselves particularly in science, mathematics, history, and theology.

One of the most outstanding cultural luminaries of this era was David Gans (1541–1613). Gans wrote an important historical work called *Zemah David* ["Offspring of David"] in the tradition of Spanish Jewish writing of the earlier sixteenth century. His most original Hebrew composition, entitled *Neḥmad ve-Na'im* ["Delightful and Pleasant"], focused on the latest geographical and astronomical discoveries of his day. At the end of the work he even described, in inspired tones, his visit to the astronomical observatory of the Dutch scientist, Tycho Brahe, at the castle of Benatek outside Prague. Excerpts of this report appear below.

READING 5-11

Before completing this book of mine, I will relate the news that in the year 1600, His Majesty the Emperor Rudolph [the second] . . . because he was filled with wisdom, understanding and exceptional knowledge in the discipline of astronomy and because he loves scholars, honors and supports them, sent a message to the kingdom of Denmark and invited the exceptional investigator, the most learned astronomer of any who had come before him . . . called Tycho Brahe. He placed him in the castle of Benatek, five parasangs from his capital city of Prague. There he lived a solitary life with his students. He was provided with an income of 3000 thaler a year, bread, wine, and beer, as well as with many other gifts . . . . [He continues to describe Brahe's twelve colleagues who all received (along with Brahe) their own room and telescope].

And I, the writer, was also present three times, each time lasting for five consecutive days. I sat with them in the observational rooms and saw what was happening—the wonderful things—not only the planets but most of the fixed stars. They would call each star by name as it crossed the midnight skyline. They would measure them with three different kinds of instruments, each of which was manned by two scholars. Everything instantaneously was recorded in a book: the time of the appearance of each star at the midnight skyline—the hour and the [exact] minutes of the hour. . . .

Such great observations we have never seen nor heard in all our days; nor have our forefathers told us nor did we see it in any book either from the children of Israel or from the nations of the world. . . . Thus they changed many of the Ptolemaic principles of astronomy, all on the basis of reason and good taste, [discovering] new and wonderful matters, things which the ancients never had imagined. [He concludes with four specific innovative conclusions reached through Brahe's observations.]

NATHAN HANOVER'S EULOGY ON THE LIFE OF EASTERN EUROPEAN JEWRY

By the seventeenth century the Jewish community of Eastern Europe had reached unsurpassed heights demographically, politically, and economically. The Jewish population reached 150,000 souls; the Jews took full advantage of diversified economic opportunities, and Jewish self-government surpassed all previous Diaspora communities. In so receptive a political and social climate, Judaic learning flourished.

The community experienced a major setback, however, when, in 1648, the Cossacks of the Ukraine revolted against the Polish crown and nobility. The Jews were conspicuously associated with the Roman Catholic Poles through economic activities. When the Cossacks, together with the Crimean Tatars and Greek Orthodox Ukrainian peasants, went on a rampage from city to city, the Jews became prime targets for brutality; thousands were slaughtered, died from famine or plague, or expired as martyrs.

The major chronicle of the Cossack pogroms is *Yeven Meẓulah* ("The Abyss of Despair"), written by the contemporary author Nathan Hanover. The final chapter of his work, excerpted below, movingly describes the social and religious life of Eastern European Jewry. Following Nathan's elaborate depictions of Jewish suffering, it functions as a kind of eulogy to the victims of the massacre and to the values their community embodied.

READING 5-12

And now I will begin to describe the practices of the Jews in the Kingdom of Poland, which were founded on principles of righteousness and steadfastness.

It is said in Tractate Aboth: Simon the Just was one of the last survivors of the Great Synagogue. He used to say: "Upon three things the world is based: Upon the Torah, upon divine service, and upon the practice of charity." Rabban Simeon, the son of Gamaliel said: "By three things is the world preserved: by truth, by judgment and by peace." All the six pillars upon which the world rests were in existence in the Kingdom of Poland.

The Pillar of the Torah: Matters that are well known need no proof, for throughout the dispersions of Israel there was nowhere so much learning as in the Kingdom of Poland. Each community maintained academies, and the head of each academy was given an ample salary so that he could maintain his school without worry, and that the study of the Torah might be his sole occupation. The head of the academy did not leave his house the whole year except to go from the house of study to the synagogue. Thus he was engaged in the study of the Torah day and night. Each community maintained young men and provided for them a weekly allowance of money that they might study with the head of the academy. And for each young man they also maintained two boys to study under his guidance, so that he would orally discuss the Gemara (Talmud), the commentaries of Rashi, and the Tosafoth, which he had learned, and thus he would gain experience in the subtlety of Talmudic argumentation. The boys were provided with food from the community benevolent fund or from the public kitchen. If the community consisted of fifty householders it supported not less than thirty young men and boys. One young man and two boys would be assigned to one householder. And the young man ate at his table as one of his sons. Although the young man received a stipend from the community, the householder provided him with all the food and drink that he needed. Some of the more charitable householders also allowed the boys to eat at their table, thus three persons would be provided with food and drink by one householder the entire year.

There was scarcely a house in all the Kingdom of Poland where its members did not occupy themselves with the study of the Torah. . . .

The Pillar of Charity: There was no measure for the dispensation of charity in the Kingdom of Poland, especially as regards hospitality. If a scholar or preacher visited a community, even one which had a system of issuing communal tickets [meal tickets] to be offered hospitality by a householder, he did not have to humiliate himself to obtain a ticket, but went to some community leader and stayed wherever he pleased. The community beadle then came and took his credentials to collect funds to show it to the synagogue official or the community leader for the month, and they gave an appropriate gift which was delivered by the beadle in dignified manner. He was then the guest of the householder for as many days as he desired. Similarly all other transients who received tickets, would be the guests of a householder, whose turn it was by lot, for as many days as he wished. A ticket was good for at least three days. The guest was given food and drink, morning, noon and evening. If they wished to depart they would be given provisions for the road, and they would be conveyed by horse and carriage from one community to another. . . .

The Pillar of Justice was in the Kingdom of Poland as it was in Jerusalem before the destruction of the Temple, when courts were set up in every city, and if one refused to be judged by the court of his city he went to the nearest court, and if he refused to be judged by the nearest court, he went before the great court. For in every province there was a great court. Thus in the capital city of Ostrog there was the great court for Volhynia and the Ukraine, and in the capital city of Lwow there was the great court for [Little] Russia. There were thus many communities each of which had a great court for its own province. . . .

The Pillar of Truth: Every community appointed men in charge of weights and measures, and of other business dealings, so that everything would be conducted according to truth and trustworthiness.

The Pillar of Peace: For it is said: "The Lord will give strength unto His people; the Lord will bless His people with peace." There was in Poland so much interest in learning that no three people sat down to a meal without discussing the words of Torah, for throughout the repast everyone indulged in debating matters of the Law and puzzling passages in the Midrashim, in order to observe: "Thy law is in my inmost parts." And the Holy One blessed be He, recompensed them so that even when they were in the land of their enemies, He did not despise them and did not break his covenant with them. And wherever their feet trod the ground among our brothers of the House of Israel they were treated with great generosity, above all, our brethren of the House of Israel who were in distress and in captivity among the Tartars. For the Tartars led them to Constantinople, a city that was a mother in Israel, and to the famed city of Salonica, and to other communities in Turkey and Egypt, and in Barbary and other provinces of Jewish dispersion where they were ransomed for much money, as mentioned above. To this day they have not ceased to ransom prisoners that are brought to them each day. The Lord recompense them.

Those who escaped the sword of the enemy in every land where their feet trod, such as Moravia, Austria, Bohemia, Germany, Italy, were treated with kindness and were given food and drink and lodging and garments and many gifts, each according to his importance, and they also favored them with other things. Especially in Germany did they do more than they could. May their justice appear before God to shield them and all Israel wherever they are congregated, so that Israel may dwell in peace and tranquility in their habitations. May their merit be counted for us and for our children, that the Lord should hearken to our cries and gather our dispersed from the four corners of the earth, and send us our righteous Messiah, speedily in our day. Amen, Selah.

THE MESSIANIC MOOD OF SIXTEENTH-CENTURY SAFED

Of all the Jewish communities inhabited by Spanish emigrés throughout the Ottoman Empire in the sixteenth century, the modest town of Safed in the northern Galilee seemed the most unlikely to emerge as a major religious center. Yet, by the end of the sixteenth century the Jewish population there numbered 10,000, of whom many earned a living from the manufacture and trade of cloth. More importantly, Safed attracted some of the most distinguished rabbinic and kabbalistic scholars to its academies of learning, even eclipsing the venerable academies of Jerusalem. R. Joseph Caro (1488–1575), the most influential rabbinic scholar and codifier of the sixteenth century, settled in Safed in the 1530's; his student, R. Moses Cordovero (1522–70), the major expositor and systematizer of Spanish *kabbalah*, also flourished there. The spiritual revival of Safed was characterized especially by messianic agitation, precipitated in part by the memory of the Spanish expulsion. This mood was reinforced by assemblies of worship and spiritual meditation that helped produce a deeply felt sense of spiritual ecstasy and religious mission among the town's congregations.

The two selections below convey a sense of the ideological and psychological climate of Safed. The first is the poem *Lekha Dodi* ("Come, my Beloved") written by Solomon Alkabetz, a close friend of Joseph Caro. In this hymn, now a part of the Friday night liturgy, the poet personifies the Sabbath as Israel's divine bride and calls for Jerusalem to arise from its ruins with the imminent arrival of messianic redemption. The second selection represents portions of a personal account about Safed's Jewish community by Solomon Shloemel Meinstrl after his arrival there in 1602 from his native Moravia.

READING 5-13A

Come, my friend to meet the bride, the Sabbath let us welcome.

'Observe' and 'Remember' in a single commandment
God the Only One gave us to hear.
The Lord is one, and one His name,
For fame, for glory and for praise.
          Come, my friend, etc.

To greet the Sabbath let us go,
For it is ever a fount of blessing
Poured forth of old, at the very beginning,
Last act in creation, first in God's plan.
          Come, my friend, etc.

Thou shrine of the King, thou royal city,
Arise, come forth from amidst thy ruins.
Too long hast thou dwelt in the valley of weeping;
Now will God have compassion upon thee.
>   Come, my friend, etc.

Shake off thy dust now and arise,
Array thee in raiment of beauty, my people;
God has made with thee a covenant of peace;
So pray: Be Thou nigh to my soul; redeem it.
>   Come, my friend, etc.

Bestir thyself! Bestir thyself!
For thy light has come, arise and shine.
Awake! awake! and sing thy song,
For the glory of God in thee is revealed.
>   Come, my friend, etc.

Be not ashamed! Be not abashed!
Why be downcast? Why be sad?
My afflicted people in thee will take shelter,
In the city rebuilt on its ancient site.
>   Come, my friend, etc.

Despoiled be all that would despoil thee,
And banished all that would destroy thee;
Thy God will take delight in thee
As a bridegroom rejoicing in his bride.
>   Come, my friend, etc.

Thou wilt spread abroad to right and left,
And in gratitude adore thy God,
Delighting ever in His salvation;
Then will we rejoice and be glad.
>   Come, my friend, etc.

O come in peace, thy husband's crown,
Come in joy and exultation,
Amidst the faithful of God's treasured people,
Come, Sabbath bride! Come, Sabbath bride!
>   Come, my friend, etc.

READING 5-13B

I HAVE come to inform you that the God of blessing in his great lovingkindness has vouchsafed me the merit of making my dwelling in the Holy Land, here in Safed, may she be rebuilt speedily and in our days, in the Upper Galilee; and I have now been here for five years in the midst of the Land, thank God, with no business other than the study of the Torah and the service of his blessed Name. The day I became twenty-two my Maker moved me and awakened my heart and said unto me: How long, O sluggard, wilt thou sleep in the slumber of idleness? Rise now, gird up thy loins like a warrior and pursue the knowledge of the Torah and of the commandments, and become an understanding youth. . . .

So I arrived in the holy city of Safed in the mid-days of the Feast of Booths of 5363 [autumn, 1602], arriving in peace and finding a holy congregation. For this is a great city before God with close on to three hundred great rabbis, all of them pious and men of works. Eighteen talmudic academies I found here, as well as twenty-one synagogues and a large House of Study with close on to four hundred children in the charge of four teachers, who give them free instruction. For there are wealthy folk in Constantinople who pay the hire of the teachers, and likewise send them clothes every year. And in all the synagogues, after the Morning and Evening Prayer, the entire congregation gather together and sit before their rabbis, five or six groups in every synagogue, each group engaging in study before they forsake the synagogue.

Before they begin to pray, the great and pious rabbi, our master Rabbi Moses Galante [mystic and talmudist; successor to Joseph Caro in the rabbinate of Safed], may his Rock and Maker guard him, ascends the pulpit and utters mighty words and rouses Israel to fear of the Name and brings them to love the Creator, by means of his sweet tongue, great wisdom, and erudition and vast sanctity. Afterward there ascend two heads of academies, great and pious scholars and men of good deeds.

Then they begin to pray in awe and fear and great dread, their eyes weeping like two fountains of water. Who has ever seen the like of those great and bitter prayers and outcries of all Israel that weep and as one man let tears fall over the Exile and the Destruction because of our many sins; how they confess their iniquities!

Then every New Moon's eve they follow the practices of the eve of the Day of Atonement until midnight, proclaiming a stoppage of work until that hour. And all Israel gather together in one great synagogue or proceed to the grave of Hosea ben Beeri the prophet, over which there is a magnificent building formed like a dome, and they enter inside; or else they proceed to the cave of the divine teacher, Abba Saul, may he rest in peace; or else they assemble before the grave of Rabbi Judah bar Ilai [Palestinian rabbis of the first centuries, C.E.]; all of which saints are buried near the city. There they pray an awesome prayer until the noon, sometimes spending the entire day there praying and preaching.

Apart from this, I found that the entire Holy Land is filled with the blessing of the Lord, with great plenty and a great cheapness which is beyond all estimation and imagining and telling. Now when I perceived the great plenty to be found in the Holy Land, and saw that all this bounty is being consumed by the nations of the world while Israel are dispersed and have not the merit to eat of its fruits or be seated with its goodness, I wept greatly and I said: Would that our brethren the children of Israel knew but a tenth of all this plenty and goodness and great satiety which are now to be found in the Land of Israel! For then they would weep day and night over their exile and over this pleasant, good and spacious land which they have lost, which even in its ruins brings forth fruits and oil and wine and silk for a third of the world, from Venice and Spain, and France, and Portugal, and Constantinople, and load up with corn and olive oil, raisins, and cakes of figs, and honey, and silk, and good soap, all of which are as plentiful as the sand of the seashore. . . .

Now the Lord who is the true God and King of the universe knew my heart and saw my good intention, how with all my heart and all my soul I entreated the Lord to answer me in my time of trouble and to deliver me. So he gave me all I desired of him, may he be blessed, and he brought me in peace to the Land of Israel, on the Feast of Booths in the year 5364, where he had appointed for me as my helpmate a good and God-fearing woman, the daughter of a great and very exalted and pious scholar, whose vast holiness and tremendous piety are known to all Israel. He is the sage, our honored master, Rabbi Israel Sarug of blessed memory [disciple of Isaac Luria, leader of the circle of mystics in Safed].

The Holy One, blessed be he, has given me the merit of possessing all the writings prepared by that holy and godly man and teacher of all Israel, our master Rabbi Isaac Luria of blessed memory; more than are in the possession of any of the sages of the Land of Israel. I came to them through the wife I married in the Land of Israel, who inherited them from her honored father, our master Rabbi Israel Sarug of blessed memory, who tirelessly sought them out all his life long and expended more than two hundred thalers on them until he obtained them all.

I now have them praise God, and I delight in them every day; and the blessed Name has caused me to find favor and friendship among all the sages of Safed. My rabbi and teacher, before whom I sit and from whom I learn Torah, particularly the wisdom of the Kabbalah, is the perfect and very humble sage, our honored master Rabbi Masud, the Great Light of Fez, may the Merciful guard him and redeem him. He is famous in all Israel by reason of his great holiness and vast knowledge and erudition in the entire Torah, may the blessed Name guard and preserve him.

THE LIFE OF ISAAC LURIA

Isaac Luria (1534–72) was drawn to Safed in 1569 only three years before his death. Although he never reached the scholarly stature of Caro or Cordovero, he eventually became the cultural hero of his generation and the following generations. Much of Luria's mystical teachings had been anticipated by earlier kabbalists; what was novel about his approach was its dramatic focus on the end of creation rather than its beginning, and its emphasis on national redemption within the context of the entire universe. Lurianic *kabbalah* constituted a daring mythical imagery that responded directly to the spiritual needs of a community in turmoil. Through the diffusion and percolation of the arcane mysteries of Luria's teachings by his disciples, expecially Ḥayyim Vital Calebrese (1543–1620), Lurianic *kabbalah* gradually was transformed from esoteric to exoteric lore and became increasingly familiar to large numbers of sixteenth- and seventeenth-century Jews.

The following hagiographic account of Luria was written by the same Solomon Shloemel Meinstrl.

READING 5-14

During his youth he lived in Egypt although he was born in Jerusalem. At his birth Elijah, of blessed memory, appeared to his father—for he was very pious, as was his mother too—and said to him: "Take heed, now, on the day of the circumcision, not to circumcise this child until you see me standing beside you in the synagogue."

Now when the eighth day came and they took the child to the synagogue for the circumcision the father looked around on all sides for Elijah but did not see him there. By some sort of a pretext, the father delayed for about a half an hour or more and kept the congregation standing. They wondered why he held off so long and finally they all rebuked him. He, however, paid no attention to their complaint but waited till finally Elijah did come. He said to the father: "Sit down on the chair," and the father sat down with the infant in his arms. Then Elijah came, sat down on the father's lap, took the child from the parent, put him on his own lap and held him with his own two arms. The man who performed the circumcision went ahead with his work and saw nothing, of course, but the father. After the child had been circumcised Elijah returned him to the father, saying: "Here is your child. Take good care of him for a great light shall shine forth from him upon all the world."

Later when he was still a lad his father died. Because of poverty he went down to Egypt to the home of his uncle who was a very rich man. Luria developed into a brilliant student noted for his keenness, powers of argumentation, and sound reasoning, so that by the time he was fifteen years of age he was superior to all the sages of Egypt in his understanding of and his ability to debate in Talmudic law. His uncle then gave him his daughter to wife. After the marriage he studied alone with our honored teacher, Rabbi Bezalel Ashkenazi [important talmudist and chief rabbi of Cairo], for seven years, and after this he studied by himself for six years. In addition to this, for two years in succession, he kept himself in seclusion in a certain house built along the Nile river and sanctified himself by an unusual piety. He was altogether alone and spoke with no one. On the eve of the Sabbath, just before it grew dark, he would return to his home, but even here, too, he would talk to no one, not even his wife, except when it was absolutely necessary, and then only in Hebrew and very briefly.

It was there on the banks of the Nile that he merited for himself the descent of the Holy Spirit. At times Elijah the prophet revealed himself to him and taught him the secrets of the Torah, and he was found so worthy that throughout the night his soul would mount on high, and troops of ministering angels would come to guard him on the way till they had led him into the heavenly assembly, and there they would ask of him in which college he wished to study. . . .

After these two years of extreme asceticism in Egypt, Elijah appeared to him. Luria was at that time only thirty-six years of age; and he was thirty-eight years old when, from here in Safed—may it be rebuilt and reestablished speedily in our days—he was summoned to the Academy on High, because of our many sins. Elijah had said to him: "The time of your death is approaching. And now go up to Safed. There you will find a certain scholar whose name is Rabbi Hayyim Calabrese—may God guard and deliver him. Anoint him in your stead. Lay your hands upon him and teach him all your lore for he will take your place. The sole purpose of your coming into the world has been to "improve" the soul of Rabbi Hayyim, for it is a precious one. Through you he will merit wisdom, and a great light shall shine forth from him upon all Israel. I assure you that I will reveal myself to you whenever you need me; I will lay bare before you the secrets of the upper and the nether worlds, and God, too, will pour out upon you his Holy Spirit a thousand times more than you are able to acquire here in Egypt."

All these things did our Master Luria—of blessed memory—reveal to our teacher Rabbi Hayyim Calabrese, and he in turn revealed them intimately to a chosen few of his associates in Palestine. But our teacher Hayyim, however, wrote in the book which he composed that it appeared to him that Luria was the Messiah ben

Joseph but the Master would not admit it to him because of his exceeding humility. However his disciples could surmise it from what Luria had told them. . . .

Luria knew all the deeds of men and even their thoughts. He could read faces, look into the souls of men, and recognize souls that migrated from body to body. He could tell you about the souls of the wicked which had entered into trees and stones or animals and birds; he could tell you what commandments a man had fulfilled and what sins he had committed since youth; he knew wherein a sinful man had been punished by God and would prescribe "improvements" to remove a moral blemish, and knew just when such a moral defect had been corrected. He understood the chirping of birds, and through their flight he divined strange things, as is referred to in the verse: "For a bird of the air shall carry the voice, and that which hath wings shall tell the matter." All of this he acquired because of the piety, asceticism, purity, and holiness that he had exercised since his youth.

A CHRISTIAN EYE-WITNESS ACCOUNT OF SHABBETAI ZEVI

Some one hundred years after Isaac Luria died, Jewish communities experienced an explosion of millenarian fervor unparalleled in Jewish history since the first century C.E. The focus of this frenzied behavior was a self-proclaimed messiah named Shabbetai Zevi (1626–76), who attracted wide appeal even after he had seemingly proven himself a false pretender. Born in Izmir in Turkey, Shabbetai wandered through various cities in Greece, Egypt, and Israel before meeting his son-to-be chief prophet, Nathan of Gaza, in 1665. Nathan was early convinced of Shabbetai's messiahship and proclaimed his coming. Arousing the suspicion of the Turkish authorities, Shabbetai was arrested in 1666. They offered him conversion to Islam or death; he chose the former for which he was awarded an honorific title and a government pension.

The matter seemed to be over for most of his followers, but for his most ardent disciples the paradox of his apostasy could not be attributed to insincerity but had to be understood ideologically. Using the conceptual framework of Lurianic *kabbalah*, they discovered a new rationale for the conversion that also legitimated their own break from traditional Jewish norms. The final outcome of the movement of Shabbetai Zevi was a major spiritual crisis within the Jewish community, a revolution against Jewish rabbinical authority, and intense acrimony between the followers and opponents of the false messiah.

The following account of Shabbetai Zevi was written by Sir Paul Rycaut 1678–1700, a Christian diplomat from England who served many years in the Ottoman Empire and composed a history of the Turks. Note especially Rycaut's attempt to connect Shabbetai's appearance with the year (1666), a year of Christian millennial stirring throughout Europe.

READING 5-15

ANNO 1666

We shall begin this year with the strange rumor and disturbance of the Jews, concerning Shabbethai Zebi, their pretended Messiah which, for being most principally acted in Turkey, may properly belong to the history of this time and place. . . .

According to the predictions of several Christian writers, especially of such who comment upon the *Apocalypse* or *Revelations*, this year of 1666 was to prove a year of wonders, of strange revolutions in the world, and particularly, of blessing to the Jews. . . .

Strange reports flew from place to place of the march of multitudes of people from unknown parts into the remote deserts of Arabia, supposed to be the ten tribes and a half, lost for so many ages. That a ship was arrived in the northern parts of Scotland, with her sails and cordage of silk, navigated by mariners who spoke nothing but Hebrew, and with this motto on their sails, "The Twelve Tribes of Israel." . . .

In this manner millions of people were possessed when Shabbethai Zebi first appeared at Smyrna, and published himself to the Jews for their Messiah, relating the greatness of their approaching kingdom, the strong hand whereby God was about to deliver them from bondage, and gather them from all parts of the world. It was strange to see how this fancy took and how fast the report of Shabbethai and his doctrine flew through all parts where Jews inhabited, and so deeply possessed them with a belief of their new kingdom and riches, and many of them with promotion to offices of government, renown, and greatness; that in all places from Constantinople to Buda (which it was my fortune that year to travel) I perceived a strange transport in the Jews, none of them attending to any business, unless to wind up former negotiations, and to prepare themselves and families for a journey to Jerusalem. All their discourses, their dreams, and disposal of their affairs tended to no other design but a reestablishment in the Land of Promise, to greatness and glory, wisdom and doctrine of the Messiah [Shabbethai], whose origin(al), birth, and education is first to be recounted.

Shabbethai Zebi was son of Mordecai Zebi, an inhabitant and natural of Smyrna who gained his livelihood by being broker to an English merchant in that place; a person who before his death was very decrepit in his body, and full of the gout and other infirmities. But his son Shabbethai Zebi, addicting himself to study and learning, became a notable proficient in the Hebrew and Arabic languages. And especially in divinity and metaphysics he was so cunning a sophister that he vented [expressed] a new doctrine in their Law, and drew to the profession of it so many disciples as raised one day a tumult in the synagogue; for which afterwards he was, by censure of the Hakams (who are the expounders of the Law), banished out of the city.

During the time of his exile he traveled to Thessalonica, now called Salonica. . . . And being now free from the encumbrances of a family, his wandering head moved him to travel through the Morea [southern Greece], thence to Tripoli in Syria, Gaza, and Jerusalem . . . and meeting there with a certain Jew called Nathan, a proper instrument to promote his design, he communicated to him his condition, his course of life, and intentions to declare himself the Messiah of the world, so long expected and desired by the Jews.

This design took wonderfully with Nathan; and because it was thought necessary, according to Scripture and ancient prophecies, that Elijah was to precede the Messiah, as St. John Baptist was the forerunner of Christ, Nathan thought no man so proper to act the part of the prophet as himself. And so no sooner had Shabbethai declared himself the Messiah, but Nathan discovers himself to be his prophet, forbidding all the fasts of the Jews in Jerusalem, and declaring that the Bridegroom [the Messiah] being come, nothing but joy and triumph ought to dwell in their habitations; writing to all the assemblies of the Jews to persuade them to the same belief. And now the schism being begun, and many Jews really believing what they so much desired, Nathan took the courage and boldness to prophesy that [in 1666] one year from the 27th of Kislev . . . the Messiah was to appear before the Grand Signior [the Sultan of Turkey], and to take from him his crown, and lead him in chains like a captive. . . .

And now all the cities of Turkey, where the Jews inhabited, were full of the expectation of the Messiah; no trade or course of gain was followed. Every one imagined that daily provisions, riches, honors, and government were to descend upon him by some unknown and miraculous manner. An example of which is most observable in the Jews at Thessalonica, who now full of assurance that the restoration of their kingdom and the accomplishment of the times for the coming of the Messiah was at hand . . . applied themselves immediately to fastings; and some in that manner beyond the abilities of nature, that having for the space of seven days taken no sustenance, were famished.

Others buried themselves in their gardens, covering their naked bodies with earth, their heads only excepted, remained in those beds of dirt, until their bodies were stiffened with the cold and moisture. Others would endure to have melted wax dropt upon their shoulders; others to roll themselves in snow and throw their bodies in the coldest season of the winter into the sea, or frozen waters. But the most common manner of mortification was first to prick their backs and sides with thorns and then to give themselves thirty-nine lashes. All business was laid aside; none worked or opened shop, unless to clear his warehouse of merchandise at any price. Who[ever] had superfluity in household stuff sold it for what he could. . . .

The Grand Signior, having by this time received divers informations of the madness of the Jews and the pretenses of Shabbethai, grew big with desire and expectation to see him; so that he no sooner arrived at Adrianople, but the same hour he was brought before the Grand Signior. . . . The Grand Signior . . . declared that, having given public scandal to the professors of the Mahometan religion and done dishonor to his sovereign authority by pretending to withdraw from him so considerable a portion as the land of Palestine, his treason and crime could not be expiated without becoming a Mahometan convert: which if he refused to do, the stake was ready at the gate of the seraglio to impale him.

Shabbethai, being now reduced to his last game and extremity (not being in the least doubtful what to do, for to die for what he was assured was false was against nature and the death of a mad man), replied with much cheerfulness that he was contented to turn Turk and that it was not of force, but of choice; having been a long time desirous of so glorious a profession, he esteemed himself much honored that he had an opportunity to own it first in the presence of the Grand Signior [September, 1666]. . . .

The news of Shabbethai turning Turk and of the Messiah to a Mahometan quickly filled all parts of Turkey. The Jews were strangely surprised at it, and ashamed of their easiness of belief, of the arguments with which they had persuaded others, and of the proselytes they had made in their own families. Abroad they became the common derision of the towns where they inhabited. The boys hooted after them, coining a new word at Smyrna (*poustai!*) which every one seeing a Jew, with a finger pointed out, would pronounce with scorn and contempt; so that this deceived people for a long time after remained with confusion, silence, and dejection of spirit.

And yet most of them affirm that Shabbethai is not turned Turk, but his shadow only remains on earth, and walks with a white head, and in the habit of a Mahometan; but that his body and soul are taken into heaven, there to reside until the time appointed for accomplishment of these wonders. And this opinion began so commonly to take place, as if this people resolved never to be undeceived, using the forms and rules for devotion prescribed them by their Mahometan Messiah. Insomuch that the Hakams of Constantinople, fearing the danger of this error might creep up and equal the former, condemned the belief of Shabbethai being Messiah as damnable, and enjoined them to return to the ancient method and service of God, upon pain of excommunication. . . .

And thus the . . . Jews [returned] again to their wits, following their trade and profession of brokage as formerly, with more quiet and advantage than the means of regaining their possessions in the Land of Promise. And thus ended this mad frenzy amongst the Jews, which might have cost them dear, had not Shabbethai renounced his Messiahship at the feet of Mahomet [IV. Sultan, 1648–1687].

FROM JACOB FRANK'S "WORDS OF THE MASTER"

There was a more radical anarchist branch associated with Shabbetai's ideology. It preached the holiness of sin; it affirmed that Shabbetai Ẓevi's behavior was to be emulated by others. The two most extreme groups within this faction were the Donmeh in Turkey and the Frankists in Poland. The first group, prominent from the end of the seventeenth through the eighteenth century, converted to Islam as their redeemer had done. The Frankists, named after the diabolical figure of Jacob Frank (1726–71), saw themselves as the direct continuation of the Donmeh. Frank declared himself the reincarnation of Shabbetai, advocated the nullification of Jewish law, and dreamed of an army of disciples "to follow their leader step by step" in a territory of his own.

In 1759 Frank openly converted to Christianity with a thousand of his followers. He soon was caught by the Inquisition, which incarcerated him until his death. Some of his followers, forced to go underground for fear of governmental harassment, continued to cling to their delusional beliefs well into the next century. Whatever their actual number of adherents, the Donmeh and Frankist sects sent shock waves through the established Jewish communities of Turkey and Eastern Europe.

The following excerpts are taken from a book called *Slona Panskie* ("The Words of the Master," apparently first written in Hebrew), a collection of nearly 2300 sayings and stories attributed to Frank and compiled by his followers at the end of the eighteenth century.

READING 5-16

Honor your master. How? In this manner: by releasing oneself from all laws and beliefs, to follow after me step by step.

Speech is not the essential thing but action. For many years already our fathers and the fathers of our fathers spoke. Yet what good did their words do and what did they achieve? But here a silent burden! Here one must be silent and carry the crucial matter and this is the task. For this helpers are necessary for everyone will help. Some with a whole hand and some with only a finger, everyone according to his own ability.

I say to you: When the spilling of blood will begin, if, God forbid, one of you will have in your heart a blemish of Torah, even as much as a hairsbreadth, this man with all the members of his household and even with his neighbors will be totally destroyed. For this place toward which we are going cannot tolerate any law, for all of the latter comes from the Devil (literally "the side of death") and we are going to life.

I wanted to send you to all the Jews to inform them that they should be ready when the hour arrives for the time of war; for they should learn the art of warfare, even the women and children should not be weak. Not one man will be destroyed who listens to my voice.

Poland is the land that was promised to our fathers. If I was given all the lands filled with precious stones, I would never leave Poland for it is an inheritance of God and an inheritance of our fathers.

When the matter will be fulfilled and the Jews will enter the religion of Edom (Christianity), then all their children from the age of six on, will practice from their childhood with military weapons. My soul yearns for ten million soldiers chosen from Israel and at least another million from among the gentiles. Whether they will be needed by me or not, the matter will be fulfilled as it is written: and Israel makes war—the children of Israel will gather together to fight.

In every place that the first man passed, a city was established. But in every place that I will step, everything will be destroyed for I have only come to destroy everything. But afterwards, everything which I will build will stand forever.

When dogs fight, even if a man will try to separate them by hitting them with sticks, they will not pay him any attention nor will they stop biting each other. Thus the spilling of blood must take place in the world. And in this utter confusion we will find the destruction that we seek. For when water is dirty it is good to catch fish and when the world will be filled with bloodshed then we will be able to catch the matter that is important to us.

All the beliefs and all the mores and all the books that have been written up until this time and everyone who has read them direct their vision backward and look upon things which have already died. All this comes from the gate of death. But the eyes of a wise man are always ahead for he needs to look at the one who walks in front of him.

A man once had a precious unblemished stone. He had travelled from city to city searching for an artisan who could put a hole in his stone without damaging it, offering large payment for anyone who could do this. Yet no artisan would accept this type of work. This man was even ready to pay a thousand rubies to the most skillful of all the artisans but he too refused to accept this work. The man didn't know what to do with his stone so he went to the apprentice of one of the artisans during a time when the artisan was not at home. He ordered the apprentice to immediately put a hole in his stone, offering him hard cash for his work. Without fear, the apprentice inserted the hole. The man paid him his wages and went on his way full of joy. This is also the case in this matter of mine. Many wise men wanted to insert a hole but they were not able because of their fear. But I was chosen to make the great restitution and to diminish the *Kelipah* [evil] because I am a common man and I will make the hole and do everything that is needed.

Everything must be with self-sacrifice. The day will come when men will wish to make you distant from me and they will say to you: "Go farther away," but one who will turn away from me will be distant and will be banished forever while one who remains with me will be worthy to be with me for eternity.

Everything that has happened up until this day was done in order to perpetuate the seed of the Jews and that the name of Israel would never be forgotten. But now there is no need for commandments nor for prayer but only to listen and to do and to advance until we have arrived at the one hidden place.

THE *BA'AL SHEM TOV* AND EARLY HASIDISM

In the last decades of the eighteenth century, years of decline and economic impoverishment for Eastern European Jewry, a new pietist movement called Hasidism arose in Jewry's poorest regions of Podolia and Volhynia. It was founded by an itinerant wonder-worker named Israel ben Eliezer (1700–1760), the *Ba'al Shem Tov* (master of the good [divine] name). His followers were the poor and disfranchised of the neglected regions from which he came. He and his followers articulated an ideology of Judaism that heightened the human dignity and religious function of common Jews. They sought to purify Lurianic *kabbalah* of the heretical excesses of Frankist messianism and to reinforce traditional values. They also succeeded in introducing a new image of the religious leader within the Jewish community, called the *ẓaddik*, the righteous one, a mystic sage with social concern who succeeded in inspiring others by extolling their virtues and by providing an example to them through his own behavior.

The following short selections from the voluminous Hasidic literature of theological speculation and teaching parables illustrate some of the basic teachings of the movement. The first selection emphasizes the fact that the religious experience, real apprehension of God, is not the same as "book" learning. The second and third selections illustrate Hasidism's negative posture towards Shabbetai Ẓevi and his followers. The fourth selection portrays the Hasidic ideology of the *ẓaddik*. The *ẓaddik* is first described philosophically as the form that gives life to matter (the people). He is then described as the leader who willingly descends to the level of his constituency to raise them up to his level (a reinterpretation of the dangerous concept of the followers of Shabbetai Ẓevi: descending into the evil *kelipah* to extract the divine spark.)

READING 5-17A

How the Maggid Was Converted

I heard a certain Ḥasid tell what happened when Rabbi Dov Baer [the Maggid of Mezeritch, the major leader of Hasidism after the death of the *Ba'al Shem Tov*] of blessed memory heard of the fame of the holy Rabbi the Baal Shem Tov; how all the people flock to him and how he achieves awesome and tremendous things by the power of his prayers. Now Rabbi Dov Baer of blessed memory was a most acute scholar, thoroughly familiar with the whole of the Talmud and all the Codes and he possessed ten measures of knowledge in the science of the Kabbalah. Astonished at the reports he had heard concerning the high rank of the Baal Shem Tov he decided that he would journey to meet him in order to put him to the test. Since Rabbi Dov Baer was very industrious in his studies, it came about, after two or three days of his journey, during which time he was unable to concentrate on his studies with the same application as in his own home, that he was sorry for having decided to go. When eventually he came to the Baal Shem Tov of blessed memory, he thought that he would hear some words of Torah from him, but instead the Baal Shem Tov told him a tale of how he had undertaken a journey of many days during which he had no bread to give to his uncircumcised coach driver and how a poor Gentile came along with a sack of loaves so that he was able to buy some bread wherewith to feed his coach driver. He told him other tales of this sort. When he came the next day the Baal Shem Tov told him of how on that journey he had no fodder to give to his horses and it happened, etc. Now all these tales related by the Baal Shem Tov contained great and marvelous wisdom if one could only understand it, but since Rabbi Dov Baer of blessed memory failed to appreciate this he returned to his inn, saying to his servant: "I wish to return home right away, but since it is so dark we shall stay on here until the moon shines brightly and then we shall be on our way." At midnight, just as Rabbi Dov Baer was getting ready to depart, the Baal Shem Tov sent his servant to summon him and he heeded the summons. The Baal Shem Tov of blessed memory asked him: "Are you a scholar?" and he answered in the affirmative. "So have I heard, that you are a scholar," said the Baal Shem Tov. "And do you know the science of the Kabbalah?" "Yes, I do," replied Dov Baer. The Baal Shem Tov then instructed his servant to bring a copy of the book *Ètz Ḥayyim* (The Tree of Life) [a kabbalistic work written by Ḥayyim Vital (1543–1620), the major disciple of Isaac Luria] and the Baal Shem Tov showed Rabbi Dov Baer a passage in this book. Rabbi Dov Baer said that he would look at the passage and after doing so he expounded it to the Baal Shem Tov of blessed memory. But the Baal Shem Tov said: "You have not the slightest degree of understanding of this passage." So he looked at it again. He then said to the Baal Shem Tov: "The correct interpretation of this passage is as I have stated it, but if your honor knows of another meaning let him tell it to me and I shall judge which is more correct." Upon which the Baal Shem Tov said: "Arise!" and he rose to his feet. Now this particular text contained many names of angels and no sooner did the Baal Shem Tov of blessed memory begin to recite the text than the whole house was filled with light, and fire burned around it, and they actually saw the angels mentioned in the text. He said to Rabbi Dov Baer of blessed memory: "It is true that the meaning of the text was as you stated it to be, but your study of the text had no soul in it." On the spot Rabbi Dov Baer ordered his servant to journey home while he himself remained in the home of the Baal Shem Tov from whom he learned great and deep topics of wisdom. The Ḥasid heard all this from Rabbi Dov Baer's own holy mouth, his memory be for a blessing.

READING 5-17B

The Dream of Rabbi Jacob Joseph

Rabbi Joel told me that once the rabbi [Jacob Joseph of Polonnoye, the major "transcriber" of the *Ba'al Shem Tov*'s oral teachings] saw in his dream that one member of his minyan [a quorum of ten Jewish men for prayer] had been converted to Christianity. The rabbi awoke trembling with fear. He sent someone to wake up the others in the minyan, and he saw that all of them, thank God, were faithful. He asked them: "Perhaps one of you has secretly committed a crime, God forbid." And he told them of his dream.

One pious man, Rabbi Eliezer of Tomashpol, answered: "I don't know of anything I did wrong, but before I went to bed I looked through the book, Ḥemdat ha-Yamim [an anonymous work first printed in Turkey in 1731–32, associated with the heresy of Shabbetai Ẓevi].

READING 5-17C

The Besht (Ba'al Shem Tov) and Shabbetai Tsevi

Rabbi Joel told me, in addition, that Shabbetai Tsevi came to the Besht to ask for redemption. Rabbi Joel said in these words: "The *tikkun* [Lurianic concept of restitution of divine sparks; redemption] is done through the connection of soul with soul, spirit with spirit, and breath with breath." The Besht began to establish the connection moderately. He was afraid as Shabbetai Tsevi was a terribly wicked man. Once the Besht was asleep, and Shabbetai Tsevi, may his name be blotted out, came and attempted to tempt him again, God forbid. With a mighty thrust the Besht hurled him to the bottom of hell. The Besht peered down and saw that he landed on the same pallet with Jesus.

Rabbi Joel said that the Besht said that Shabbetai Tsevi had a spark of holiness in him, but that Satan caught him in his snare, God forbid. The Besht heard that his fall came through pride and anger. I was reluctant to write it down, but nevertheless I did so to show to what extent pride can be dangerous.

READING 5-17D

The Preacher Who Spoke Evil of the Jews

I heard from the rabbi of our community that he heard the following from the Ḥasid, our teacher Ze'ev of Olyka. Once the Besht observed the Sabbath in that holy community with a householder who was an elder of the community. On the Sabbath the householder went to the synagogue for Minhah [the afternoon service] to listen to a sermon of a visiting preacher, and the Besht waited to begin the third meal until he arrived from the synagogue. While waiting the Besht heard that the preacher was vilifying the Jews. The Besht became angry, and he told the gabbai to go and call the householder. The gabbai reported to a few people that the Besht was angry at the preacher. The preacher saw that the people dropped out one by one, and he stopped preaching.

The following day the preacher came to the Besht and greeted him. The Besht asked him who he was, and he replied: "I am the preacher. Why did you become angry with me?"

The Besht jumped up and tears poured from his eyes. He said: "You speak evil of the Jewish people. A Jew goes to the market every day, but toward evening, when it becomes dark, he becomes anxious. 'Oy, I'll skip Minhah.' He goes to a house and prays the Minhah. Even if he does not know what he is saying, the seraphim and the *ofannim* [various classes of angels] are stirred by it."

READING 5-17E

Man is created out of form and matter, which are two opposites, matter tending toward material domination [*kelipot*] and form yearning for spiritual things. The purpose of man's creation is that he should convert matter into form, creating a unity. As this is the purpose of the creation of the individual man, so is it with the nation as a whole. The masses are called "people of the earth," because their concern is with earthly, material things, and so they are "matter." The zaddikim, who engage in Torah and prayer, are "form." The purpose of all this is that matter should be transformed into form, as it is said, "The lips of the priest do keep knowledge, and they should seek Torah from his mouth; for he is the messenger of the Lord of Hosts. The law of truth was in his mouth, and unrighteousness was not found on his lips; he walked with Me in peace and uprightness, and did turn many away from iniquity."

The principal purpose of the creation of man, who was made out of form and matter, is that he should strive all his days to turn matter into form. After he has achieved this in himself, he should endeavor to transform others, for the zaddik is the form or soul of the whole world, while the wicked are the matter or body of the whole world. The zaddik must strive all his days to change matter into form, to bring the wicked under the wings of the *Shechinah* [the Divine Presence], which is the goal and purpose of everything."

READING 5-17F

I have heard a parable concerning a prince whose father banished him to a distant village so that he might yearn for the table of his father, the king, but the prince, because of his folly, mixed with the strangers in the village, learned their deeds and forgot the royal pleasures. So the king sent one of his nobles to bring the prince back but he failed, until finally one clever noble removed his royal clothing and dressed in peasant clothing like the villagers. He succeeded. . . .

By this deed he [the zaddik] is able to join with the people who are of lowly deed in order to speak to their hearts, to stir them into the realization that they are far from the table of the King of kings and that they should return to Him as in the tale above. Now, surely, the wise man acts for the love of the King and may indeed bring the son back to his father. Nonetheless *he enters into danger*. It is possible that, after speaking in an intimate manner with the prince once or twice, he may return him; it is also possible that the prince, though reared in royal fashion, has become so accustomed to the evil ways of the villagers as to have become one of them, forgetting all the pleasures of his youth.

ELVIRA DEL CAMPO BEFORE THE SPANISH INQUISITION

Twelve years before the expulsion of the Jews from Spain, Ferdinand and Isabella established the Spanish Inquisition, an ecclesiastical court to root out heresy. Although officially under the jurisdiction of the pope, it essentially was under the monarch's control. The Inquisition was concerned particularly with the alleged heresy of the *conversos* (recent converts from Judaism), their supposedly insincere conversions to Christianity, and their clandestine observance of Jewish customs. Besides Spain, the Inquisition was established throughout Europe, including Portugal and Italy, and in the New World, surviving for well over three centuries. During this prolonged period thousands of converts were tried by inquisitional tribunals. Many inquisitors used threats of torture to extract confessions; many victims were severely punished and some even were burned at the stake. Throughout the sixteenth and seventeenth centuries, thousands of *conversos* fled the Iberian peninsula for fear of inquisitional harassment and in search of havens from persecution.

The following account of Elvira del Campo is a typical example of the Inquisition at work. In 1567–69, she was tried by the Inquisition of Toledo on a charge of not eating pork and of putting on clean linen on Saturdays. She admitted being guilty of these practices but pleaded that she had no heretical intention. She eventually was tortured and sentenced to a relatively light sentence of prison for three years. Although released after six months, her property was confiscated and she was publicly disgraced.

READING 5-18

She was carried to the torture-chamber and told to tell the truth, when she said that she had nothing to say. She was ordered to be stripped and again admonished, but was silent. When stripped, she said "Señores, I have done all that is said of me and I bear false-witness against myself, for I do not want to see myself in such trouble; please God, I have done nothing." She was told not to bring false testimony against herself but to tell the truth. The tying of the arms was commenced; she said "I have told the truth; what have I to tell?" She was told to tell the truth and replied "I have told the truth and have nothing to tell." One cord was applied to the arms and twisted and she was admonished to tell the truth but said she had nothing to tell. Then she screamed and said "I have done all they say." Told to tell in detail what she had done she replied "I have already told the truth." Then she screamed and said "Tell me what you want for I don't know what to say." She was told to tell what she had done, for she was tortured because she had not done so, and another turn of the cord was ordered. She cried "Loosen me, Señores and tell me what I have to say: I do not know what I have done, O Lord have mercy on me, a sinner!" Another turn was given and she said "Loosen me a little that I may remember what I have to tell; I don't know what I have done; I did not eat pork for it made me sick; I have done everything; loosen me and I will tell the truth." Another turn of the cord was ordered, when she said "Loosen me and I will tell the truth; I don't know what I have to tell—loosen me for the sake of God—tell me what I have to say—I did it, I did it—they hurt me Señor—loosen me, loosen me and I will tell it." She was told to tell it and said "I don't know what I have to tell—Señor I did it—I have nothing to tell—Oh my arms! release me and I will tell it." She was asked to tell what she did and said "I don't know, I did not eat because I did not wish to." She was asked why she did not wish to and replied "Ay! loosen me, loosen me—take me from here and I will tell it when I am taken away—I say that I did not eat it. She was told to speak and said "I did not eat it, I don't know why." Another turn was ordered and she said "Señor I did not eat it because I did not wish to—release me and I will tell it." She was told to tell what she had done contrary to our holy Catholic faith. She said "Take me from here and tell me what I have to say—they hurt me—Oh my arms, my arms!" which she repeated many times and went on "I don't remember—tell me what I have to say—O wretched me!—I will tell all that is wanted, Señores—they are breaking my arms—loosen me a little—I did everything that is said of me." She was told to tell in detail truly what she did. She said "What am I wanted to tell? I did everything—loosen me for I don't remember what I have to tell—don't you see what a weak woman I am?—Oh! Oh! my arms are breaking." More turns were ordered and as they were given she cried "Oh! Oh! loosen me for I don't know what I have to say—Oh my arms!—I don't know what I have to say—if I did I would tell it." The cords were ordered to be tightened when she said "Señores have you no pity on a sinful woman?" She was told, yes, if she would tell the truth. She said "Señor tell me, tell me it." The cords were tightened again, and she said "I have already said that I did it." She was ordered to tell it in detail, to which she said "I don't know how to tell it señor, I don't know." Then the cords were separated and counted, and there were sixteen turns, and in giving the last turn the cord broke.

She was then ordered to be placed on the *potro* [a ladder with sharp rungs]. She said "Señores, why will you not tell me what I have to say? Señor, put me on the ground—have I not said that I did it all?" She was told to tell it. She said "I don't remember—take me away—I did what the witnesses say." She was told to tell in detail what the witnesses said. She said "Señor, as I have told you, I do not know for certain. I have said that I did all that the witnesses say. Señores release me, for I do not remember it." She was told to tell it. She said "I do not know it. Oh! Oh! they are tearing me to pieces—I have said that I did it—let me go." She was told to tell it. She said "Señores, it does not help me to say that I did it and I have admitted that what I have done has brought me to this suffering—Señor, you know the truth—Señores, for God's sake have mercy on me. Oh Señor, take these things from my arms—Señor release me, they are killing me." She was tied on the *potro* with the cords, she was admonished to tell the truth and the *garrotes* [twisting sticks] were ordered to be tightened. She said "Señor do you not see how these people are killing me? Señor, I did it—for God's sake let me go." She was told to tell it. She said "Señor, remind me of what I did not know—Señores have mercy upon me—let me go for God's sake—they have no pity on me—I did it—take me from here and I will remember what I cannot here." She was told to tell the truth, or the cords would be tightened. She said "Remind me of what I have to say for I don't know it—I said that I did not want to eat it—I know only that I did not want to eat it," and this she repeated many times. She was told to tell why she did not want to eat it. She said, "For the reason that the witnesses say—I don't know how to tell it—miserable that I am that I don't know how to tell it—I say I did it and my God how can I tell it?" Then she said that, as she did not do it, how could she tell it—"They will not listen to me—these people want to kill me—release me and I will tell the truth." She was again admonished to tell the truth. She said, "I did it, I don't know how I did it—I did it for what the witnesses say—let me go—I have lost my senses and I don't know how to tell it—loosen me and I will tell the truth." Then she said "Señor, I did it, I don't know how I have to tell it, but I tell it as the witnesses say—I wish to tell it—take me from here—Señor as the witnesses say, so I say and confess it." She was told to declare it. She said "I don't know how to say it—I have no memory—Lord, you are witness that if I knew how to say anything else I would say it." I know nothing more to say than that I did it and God knows it." She said many times, "Señores, Señores, nothing helps me. You, Lord, hear that I tell the truth and can say no more—they are tearing out my soul—order them to loosen me." Then she said, "I do not say that I did it—I said no more." Then she said, "Señor, I did it to observe that Law." She was asked what Law. She said, "The Law that the witnesses say—I declare it all Señor, and don't remember what Law it was—O, wretched was the mother that bore me." She was asked what was the Law she meant and what was the Law that she said the witnesses say. This was asked repeatedly, but she was silent and at last said that she did not know. She was told to tell the truth or the *garrotes* would be tightened but she did not answer. Another turn was ordered on the *garrotes* and she was admonished to say what Law it was. She said "If I knew what to say I would say it. Oh Señor, I don't know what I have to say—Oh! Oh! they are killing me—if they would tell me what—Oh, Señores! Oh, my heart!" Then she asked why they wished her to tell what she could not tell and cried repeatedly "O, miserable me!" Then she said "Lord bear witness that they are killing me without my being able to confess." She was told that if she wished to tell the truth before the water was poured she should do so and discharge her conscience. She said that she could not speak and that she was a sinner. Then the linen *toca* [funnel] was placed [in her throat] and she said "Take it away, I am strangling and am sick in the stomach." A jar of water was then poured down, after which she was told to tell the truth. She clamored for confession, saying that she was dying. She was told that the torture would be continued till she told the truth and was admonished to tell it, but though she was questioned repeatedly she remained silent. Then the inquisitor, seeing her exhausted by the torture, ordered it to be suspended.

THE LETTERS OF ELIA DA MONTALTO TO PEDRO RODRIGUES

Elia da Montalto was one of the *conversos* who fled Portugal at the end of the sixteenth century. Owing to his reputation as a distinguished doctor and scientist, he was invited to serve as a personal physician of

Marie de Medici, the wife of Henry IV, the king of France. He later was invited to teach medicine at the University of Pisa, spent some time in Venice, where he published a number of medical treatises, and eventually arrived in France and worked for the queen until his death in 1616.

In Venice he formally declared himself a Jew and assumed the role of defender and polemicist for Judaism against those *conversos* who had failed to renounce their Christian faith and reenter the Jewish fold. Pedro Rodrigues and his wife, Isabella de Fonseca, a sister of Montalto's wife, also had escaped Portugal as *conversos* and settled in Southern France, but failed to return to Judaism. In a series of letters, two of which are presented below, Montalto attempted to persuade Rodrigues to follow his example and affirm his Jewishness. The letters* are typical examples of the apologetic literature written in Western European languages, emerging from the *converso* communities in Europe of the seventeenth century. They consist of exchanges between believers and nonbelievers, between *conversos* who had rediscovered their ancestral religion and those who were opportunists or committed skeptics, unable to accept any traditional faith.

READING 5-19

Venice, 8 May 1612

Dearest Doctor,

Although you have caused me much grief I want to give you truthfully this title, for the more I feel affection for a person the more I care for his or her welfare. A sufficient time has passed, indeed, during which a man as intelligent as you could have thanked me for having enlightened him and freed him from the darkness in which he had lived up to now. And if you still have not the understanding to see the bright light of Divine truth, you have at least the obligation to show where you stand. But if you believe that you have something on which you can base your explanation, then do it in order that I may show you with the clearest evidence that there is no reason for it.

I believe that I would succeed in convincing you as I did some days ago with a Dominican friar, lector of theology in Padua, who came to see me and who raised objections against the Divine law, using a number of carefully prepared arguments. I listened to them up to the end in the Latin language which he spoke very well; and when he had finished I answered in the same language according to the order of his arguments without bringing up any new reasons but only confuting his own. I disposed of his arguments with so much success that, by the Lord who created heaven and earth and by the most Divine law that I profess, he, after having heard me, suddenly said that the same happened to him that had happened to the Queen of Sheba when she came to visit King Solomon and found him, as she said, filled with much more wisdom than had been reported about him. And he confessed that no-

---

*Reprinted from Franz Kobler, *Letters of Jews Through the Ages*, by permission of Hebrew Publishing Company.

body could convince any learned Jew. He went away confused and tied up, showing himself very much ashamed that his arguments had come to nought.

Those who defame us, know very well the weakness of their arguments and the strength of ours, and for this reason they never want to enter into a contest without making use of certain verses of the Divine Scripture falsely translated and without consideration of what precedes and what follows. They explain Scripture with one-sided interpretations and vain allegories. . . . I believe that with regard to your age and understanding, if not of the Divine Scripture at least of universal literature, you should be able to convince yourself of the truth.

There are so many arguments that prove the truth which the prophets of Israel profess that I have only to open Scripture anywhere. [Here follow extensive quotations and interpretations of biblical passages.] I wish I had time to demonstrate to you how every verse of Scripture has to be compared with others, but I am obliged to stop and to leave it for another time to continue to do so. If you will consider the truth you will find that it is so clear that nobody has an excuse for not being able to understand it. And I protest incessantly against your following a road which must lead you to the precipice and to the undoing of your soul. . . .

May our Lord have pity on your soul and take you away from that blind idolatry, and give you the good that you want. I wish this to you and to your wife, Isabella da Fonseca, and all of us send you the most affectionate greetings.

The friend of your Worship and friend of your soul,

Dr. Eliau da Luna Montalto

Venice, 6 September 1612

Señor Doctor,

. . . Open your eyes, for entirely blind must he be who does not see such a clear thing:

First consider that these punishments (viz. the curses contained in Deuteronomy XXVIII, referred to in the course of the preceding arguments) have come to us for not having obeyed the Law and observed the ceremonies which the Lord has given Moses on Sinai.

Secondly, you read here of the destruction made by the Romans because the one made by the Chaldeans would not apply here since they were neighbours of the Land of Israel, and they were not from far, from the end of the earth and their language was not unknown to the Jews. It applies to the Romans because they lived very far from the Land of Israel, and they carried Bretons, English and other occidental nations with them, as Josephus and the other historians record. . . .

Thirdly, you read here the description of the present captivity and the violent tyranny with which the kings of France, of Castile, of Portugal, of England and other kingdoms forced the Jews to adore their false gods and their idols of wood and stone, gods which neither the Jews nor their fathers have known. Of what other sect does Scripture speak if not of the erroneous one which you follow . . . and which you entered not from conviction nor by Divine inspiration but through the force of the kings Don Manuel and Don Juan permitted by the Lord as punishment in conformity with what is said elsewhere?. . . Thus you are not a Christian, simply because your father (of whom we know that he lived and died secretly as a Jew) for fear did not dare to reveal his will to you when you were a child, and in this way you have become used to these errors and inclined to these worldly things.

Fourthly, you read here also the description of the institution of the Inquisition. Note that Scripture says: it will be no use to serve the gods of Spain and Portugal (which are at the end of the earth of which the prophecy speaks) in order to have peace in that country, but by means of this punishment the Lord brings you to the country of Liberty in order that you may recognize the truth and free yourself from an abominable blindness and torpid idolatry in which you have lived up to now, in order that you may come to know and to follow the true God: Creator and not creature, living and not dead, infinite and not corporeal, most high and not subject to human miseries and weaknesses. . . .

My soul is extremely sorry about your misfortune and your losses. Everything I can do or that the Lord gives me shall always be yours because I love you like my soul. Don't get discouraged because the Lord will remedy everything. May He keep you, comfort you, make you prosper and may He enlighten your Worship together with signora Isabella da Fonseca, according to our wishes.

FROM URIEL DA COSTA'S AUTOBIOGRAPHY

By the seventeenth century Amsterdam was one of the few communities in Europe willing to receive *converso* refugees. Thousands of *conversos* fled to Amsterdam, where they played a leading role in the burgeoning capitalistic economy of the city. Highly educated, originally reared as Christians, literate in Latin and conversant in Spanish and Portuguese, they chose to return to Judaism as adults and to enter a traditional social and religious milieu totally alien to their previous identity and background. Their migration from Catholicism to Judaism involved both an intellectual as well as psychological passage from one world to another. Their reemergence within the Jewish community was not without painful emotional, religious, and educational stress for which their former Christian lives hardly had prepared them.

Such was the case of one *converso* named Uriel da Costa (1585–1640). Born in Oporto, Portugal, he fled to Amsterdam only to discover that his version of Judaism, fashioned from reading the Bible, was at variance with that of the community. He ultimately was incapable of reconciling what he had hoped Judaism might be with what it actually was. He criticized the "Pharisees of Amsterdam" as rigid and ritualistic and objected to the rabbinic oral law which supplemented and superseded the written one. He also argued that the doctrine of the immortality of the soul could not be derived from the Bible and was thus not part of Jewish belief. He left the Jewish community, only to return some time later after having been excommunicated and publicly humiliated. His autobiography, the *Exemplar Humanae Vitae*, from which a selection appears below, documents his anguished efforts to return to Judaism. He apparently committed suicide soon after writing this work.

READING 5-20

I was born in Portugal in a city of the same name but commonly called Oporto. My parents were of the nobility, originally descended from those Jews who were forced to embrace Christianity in that kingdom. My father was a true Christian and a man of unquestioned honor and integrity. I had a good education at home, servants always at my command, and I rode a Spanish jennet to perfect myself in horsemanship, an art in which my father was so skilled and in which I endeavored to follow his steps. At length, being grown up, and as well accomplished in the liberal arts as young gentlemen generally are, I applied myself to the study of law. As to my character and disposition, I was by nature very pious and compassionate. So much so that I could not hear the story of any person's misfortunes without melting into tears. I had so strong an innate sense of modesty that I dreaded nothing so much as to suffer disgrace. Not that I had the least degree of cowardice in my nature. When there was reasonable justification I was not free from resentment. It is for this reason that I always had an aversion to that haughty and insolent tribe of men who are inclined to despise and trample upon others, and I therefore took every opportunity to defend the oppressed and to make their cause my own.

Religion has brought incredible suffering into my life. According to the custom of the country, I was educated in Roman Catholicism. When I was but a youth the dread of eternal damnation made me anxious to observe all its doctrines punctiliously. I employed my leisure time in reading the Gospels, the Breviaries of the Confessors and other religious literature. But the more time I devoted to them, the more perplexed did I become. Little by little this caused me such difficulties, doubts and conflicts that I was overwhelmed with grief and melancholy.

Reflection led me to believe that the obtaining of a plenary absolution by the confession of sins and the fulfillment of all that the Church required was impossible. This consequently made me despair of salvation inasmuch as it was to be obtained only by such special rules. But as it was very difficult to shake off quickly a religion in which I had been educated from my infancy and which by a long unquestioning faith had taken deep root, I began, when I was about twenty years old, to question the teachings concerning the afterlife. I asked myself whether or not they were forgeries and whether belief in them was consistent with reason. My reason perpetually suggested to me conclusions that were just the contrary. Under the shadow of this doubt I continued for some time, and finally I was persuaded that salvation could not be obtained in the prescribed manner.

During this time I continued to apply myself to the study of law. When I was in my twenty-fifth year an opportunity presented itself whereby I obtained an ecclesiastical benefice as treasurer in the church. But I was unable to find the satisfaction I wanted in the Catholic church. I wanted, however, to attach myself to a religion and, aware of the great dispute between the Christians and the Jews, I made a study of the *Books of Moses* and of the *Prophets*. I found some things sharply contradictory to the doctrines of the New Testament. There seemed to be less difficulty in believing those things which were revealed by God Himself. Besides, the Old Testament was assented to by both Jews and Christians whereas the New Testament was believed only by Christians. Hence I decided to become a convert to the Law of Moses. As he declared himself to be only a deliverer of what was revealed by God Himself, being called to that mission or rather constrained to accept it, I thought it my duty to make the Law the rule of my life. Having made this decision and finding it unsafe to profess this religion in Portugal, I began to think of changing my residence and leaving my native home. In order to do this, I immediately resigned from my ecclesiastical benefice in favor of another, uninfluenced either by profit or honor, the two prevailing motives among the people of our country. I also left a beautiful house situated in the best part of the city, which my father had built. When I had concluded all the necessary arrangements, my mother, brothers and myself boarded a ship, not without danger for it is illegal for those who are descended from Jews to depart without a special permit from the King. I must tell the reader that out of natural affection, I had communicated to my family my sentiments of the falsity of our religion even though the discovery of it might have proved fatal to me—so dangerous is it in that country to speak freely on this subject, even to one's dearest friends. At the end of our voyage we arrived at Amsterdam where we found the Jews professing their religion with great freedom, as the Law directs them. We immediately fulfilled the precept concerning circumcision.

I had not been there very long before I observed that the customs and ordinances of the modern Jews were quite different from those commanded by Moses. Now if the Law was to be observed according to the letter, as it expressly declares, the Jewish interpreters are not justified in adding to it interpretations quite contrary to the original text. This provoked me to oppose them openly. Nay, I looked upon the open defense of the Law against such innovations as a service to God. The modern rabbis, like their ancestors, are an obstinate and stiffnecked race of men, vigorous advocates of the teachings and institutions of the Pharisees, not without a view to gain and, as is justly imputed to them, vainly fond of the conspicuous seats in the synagogue and greetings in the market place. Men of this character could not bear my differing with them in the slightest degree. They insisted that I follow unswervingly their prescribed regulations or else suffer exclusion from the synagogue and the full sentence of excommunication. But it would have been unworthy of him who had so recently left his native country and been content to forego many other temporal advantages for liberty of conscience to be overawed and to submit to men who had no right to such power. Besides, I thought it both sinful and beneath a man to be a slave in things pertaining to the conscience. Therefore I resolved to suffer the worst they could inflict rather than recant. Accordingly they excommunicated me from their congregation. Even my own brothers who before had looked upon me as their teacher, dared not take any notice of me as they passed me in the streets, for fear of the rabbis.

This state of affairs led me to write a tract in defense of myself and to prove plainly out of the Law of Moses the vanity and the invalidity of the traditions and ordinances of the Pharisees as well as their conflict with the Law. After I had begun this work (for I consider myself obliged to relate everything clearly and circumstantially), it so happened that I entirely agreed with the opinion of those who confine the rewards and punishments proposed in the Old Testament to this life only and are little concerned with the future life or the immortality of the soul. The following argument, among others, led to this viewpoint: The Law of Moses is completely silent as to the latter problems and proposes only temporal rewards and punishments to observers and transgressors thereof. The discovery that I entertained such opinions was no small triumph to my adversaries who felt that as a result they had the Christians as their allies, who by their faith in the Gospel which expressly mentions eternal rewards and punishments, do believe and preach the immortality of the soul. It was with the idea of rendering me odious to the Christians and of silencing me completely that, even before my tract went to press, they employed a certain scholar [Samuel da Silva] to publish a book entitled *Of the Immortality of the Soul*. In it the scholar inveighed bitterly against me as one who defended the philosophy of Epicurus and who by denying the immortality of the soul disputed the very existence of God. At that very time I had, in reality, an incorrect idea of Epicurus and, prejudiced by my unsavory relations with other persons without even hearing what he had to say for himself, I did not scruple to censure him freely. But now that I have heard from impartial lovers of the truth some estimate of this philosopher and his teaching, I have found reason to change my opinion and to be sorry for the injustice I did him then when I pronounced him a ridiculous madman even though, being an utter stranger to his writings, I was far from being competent to judge his opinions.

The next step they took was to set their children upon me in the streets. They insulted me en masse as I walked along, abusing and railing at me. They cried out, "There goes a heretic, there goes an imposter." At other times they assembled before my doors, flung stones at the windows and did everything they could to disturb and annoy me so that I could not live at peace in my own house. After the abovementioned book was published, I immediately set about my own defense. I wrote an answer in which I opposed with all the power at my command the doctrine of the immortality of the soul, incidentally dealing with the deviations of the Pharisees from Mosaic institutions. No sooner had this appeared in print than the elders and officials of the Jews agreed to make a complaint against me before the public magistrate. They asserted that I had published a book to disprove the immortality of the soul in order to subvert, not only the Jewish, but also the Christian religion. As a result, I was apprehended and sent to prison from which, after a confinement of eight or ten days, I was discharged upon giving security. For the magistrate fined me three hundred florins and confiscated my recently published books.

Let me here declare my mind freely. What should hinder a man from speaking the truth without reservation, who is just about to make his exit and to leave behind him a sad though true example of human misery? Sometime after this (as age and experience are apt to bring new discoveries to the mind of man and consequently to alter his judgment of things) I began to ask myself whether the law of Moses should be considered the law of God inasmuch as there were many arguments which seemed to persuade or rather determine the contrary. At length I came to the conclusion that it was nothing but a human invention, like many other religious and legal systems in the world, and that Moses was not really its author. I noted that it contained many things contrary to the laws of nature; and God, who was the author of those laws, could not contradict Himself, which He must have done had He given to mankind rules and regulations contrary to the laws of nature. . . .

BARUKH SPINOZA'S CRITIQUE OF JUDAISM

The polarized intellectual and religious climate of seventeenth-century Amsterdam helps to explain the genesis of the thinking of its most original and creative philosopher, Barukh Spinoza (1632–77). Born in Amsterdam of a family of former *conversos*, Spinoza gradually ceased his

Jewish observance, withdrew from the community, and devoted his life to a philosophical system ultimately antithetical to Jewish culture and faith. His devastating critique of Judaism, the *Tractatus theologico-politicus*, was published in 1670. In this work he polemicized especially with the rationalist philosophy of Moses Maimonides, objecting to what he considered the arbitrariness, artificiality, and downright cynicism of Maimonides' allegorical interpretation of the Bible, his identification of prophecy with philosophy, and his ideal of the state grounded in divine law.

For Spinoza scripture was to be studied and evaluated on its own terms. It was not synonymous with philosophy but inferior to it. Reason in Spinoza's view had come to judge biblical and Jewish faith on its own assumptions and had found them lacking. Spinoza's scathing formulation placed Jewish rabbinic authority in direct opposition to the views of Western philosophical thinking. In offering a religious experience based exclusively on personal autonomy, whose only guide was reason, Spinoza had presented a formidable challenge to every subsequent thinker hoping to legitimate and justify Jewish particularity, rabbinic law, and traditional Jewish faith in the modern era. The selection below is from the fifth chapter of the *Tractatus*, "Of the Ceremonial Law." Here Spinoza argues that Jewish ceremonial observance is not synonymous with the rational divine law; it "has nothing to do with blessedness and virtue." His argument mirrors the traditional Christian critique of Jewish law.

READING 5-21

In the foregoing chapter we have shown that the Divine law, which renders man truly blessed, and teaches them the true life, is universal to all men; nay, we have so intimately deduced it from human nature that it must be esteemed innate, and, as it were, ingrained in the human mind.

But with regard to the ceremonial observances which were ordained in the Old Testament for the Hebrews only, and were so adapted to their state that they could for the most part only be observed by the society as a whole and not by each individual, it is evident that they formed no part of the Divine law, and has nothing to do with blessedness and virtue, but had reference only to the election of the Hebrews, that is, (as I have shown in Chap. III), to their temporal bodily happiness and the tranquility of their kingdom, and that therefore they were only valid while that kingdom lasted. If in the Old Testament they were spoken of as the law of God, it is only because they were founded on revelation, or a basis of revelation. Still as reason, however sound, has little weight with ordinary theologians, I will adduce the authority of Scripture for what I here assert, and will further show, for the sake of greater clearness, why and how these ceremonials served to establish and preserve the Jewish kingdom. Isaiah teaches most plainly that the Divine law in its strict sense signifies that universal law which consists in a true manner of life, and does not signify ceremonial observances. In chapter 1., verse 10, the prophet calls on his countrymen to harken to the Divine law as he delivers it, and first excluding all kinds of sacrifices and all feasts, he at length sums up the law in these few words,

"Cease to do evil, learn to do well: seek judgment, relieve the oppressed." Not less striking testimony is given in Psalm xl. 7–9, where the Psalmist addresses God: "Sacrifice and offering Thou didst not desire; mine ears hast Thou opened; burnt offering and sin offering hast Thou not required; I delight to do Thy will, O my God; yea, Thy law is within my heart." Here the Psalmist reckons as the law of God only that which is inscribed in his heart, and excludes ceremonies therefrom, for the latter are good and inscribed on the heart only from the fact of their institution, and not because of their intrinsic value.

Other passages of Scripture testify to the same truth, but these two will suffice. We may also learn from the Bible that ceremonies are no aid to blessedness, but only have reference to the temporal prosperity of the kingdom; for the rewards promised for their observance are merely temporal advantages and delights, blessedness being reserved for the universal Divine Law. In all the five books commonly attributed to Moses, nothing is promised, as I have said, beyond temporal benefits, such as honors, fame, victories, riches, enjoyments, and health. Though many moral precepts besides ceremonies are contained in these five books, they appear not as moral doctrines universal to all men, but as commands especially adapted to the understanding and character of the Hebrew people, and as having reference only to the welfare of the kingdom. For instance, Moses does not teach the Jews as a prophet not to kill or to steal, but gives these commandments solely as a lawgiver and judge: he does not reason out the doctrine, but affixes for its non-observance a penalty which may and very properly does vary in different nations. So, too, the command not to commit adultery is given merely with reference to the welfare of the state; for if the moral doctrine had been intended with reference not only to the welfare of the state, but also to the tranquility and blessedness of the individual, Moses would have condemned not merely the outward act, but also the mental acquiescence, as is done by Christ, Who taught only universal moral precepts, and for this cause promises a spiritual instead of a temporal reward. Christ, as I have said, was sent into the world, not to preserve the state nor to lay down laws, but solely to teach the universal moral law, so we can easily understand that He wished in nowise to His sole care was to teach moral doctrines, and distinguish them from the laws of the state; for the Pharisees, in their ignorance, thought that the observance of the state law and the Mosaic law was the sum total of morality; whereas such laws merely had reference to the public welfare, and aimed not so much at instructing the Jews as at keeping them under constraint. But let us return to our subject, and cite other passages of Scripture which set forth temporal benefits as rewards for observing the ceremonial law, and blessedness as reward for the universal law.

THE OPENING OF GLÜCKEL OF HAMELN'S DIARY

Glückel of Hameln (1646–1724) was a memorable woman who lived in the Jewish communities of Hamburg, Hameln, and Metz in the seventeenth and early eighteenth centuries. In her memoirs written to "her dear beloved children" in Judaeo-German, she described her colorful childhood, her marriage of thirty years, her child rearing, her husband's death, and her unfortunate second marriage. Her life story is set against the backdrop of the political, economic, and cultural life of Central European

Jewry. She sees the world from the perspective of a middle-class woman and loving mother. She enjoys moralizing to her children and relishes the opportunity of reciting her favorite story to educate them in proper moral conduct. Her style recalls the popular ethical will of Jewish fathers, but throughout her narrative her own refreshing individuality clearly is perceptible. The following selection* is from the introductory passages of her book.

READING 5-22

In my great grief and for my heart's ease I begin this book in the year of Creation 5451—God soon rejoice us and send us His redeemer soon. Amen.

. . . . . .

With the help of God, I began writing this, my dear children, upon the death of your good father in the hope of distracting my soul from the burdens laid upon it, and the bitter thought that we have lost our faithful shepherd. In this way I have managed to live through many wakeful nights, and springing from my bed have shortened the sleepless hours.

I do not intend, my dear children, to compose and write for you a book of morals. Such I could not write, and our wise men have already written many. Moreover, we have our holy Torah in which we may find and learn all that we need for our journey through this world to the world to come. Of our beloved Torah we may seize hold. . . . We sinful men are in the world as if swimming in the sea and in danger of being drowned. But our great, merciful and kind God, in his great mercy, has thrown ropes into the sea that we may take hold of them and be saved. These are our holy Torah where is written what are the rewards and punishments for good and evil deeds. . . .

Dear children, I do not want to speak at length upon this, for if I would penetrate too deeply into this matter ten books were not sufficient. Read in the German 'Brandspiegel', in 'Leb Tob' [both are moralistic books], or, for those who can study, in [other] books of morals; there you will find everything.

I pray you this, my children: be patient, when the Lord, may He be praised, sends you a punishment, accept it with patience and do not cease to pray to Him; perhaps He will have mercy upon you. . . . Therefore, my dear children, whatever you lose, have patience, for nothing is our own, everything is only a loan. . . . We men have been created for nothing else but to serve God and to keep His commandments and to obey the Torah, for 'He is thy life, and the length of thy life.'

The kernel of the Torah is: 'Thou shalt love thy neighbour as thyself.' But in our days we seldom find it so, and few are they who love their fellow-men with all their heart. On the contrary, if a man can contrive to ruin his neighbour nothing pleases him more. . . .

The best thing for you, my children, is to serve God from your heart without falsehood or deception, not giving out to people that you are one thing while, God forbid, in your heart you are another. Say your prayers with awe and devotion.

---

*Reprinted from Franz Kobler, *Letters of Jews Through the Ages*, by permission of Hebrew Publishing Company.

During the time for prayers do not stand about and talk of other things. While prayers are being offered to the Creator of the world, hold it a great sin to engage another man in talk about an entirely different matter—shall God Almighty be kept waiting until you have finished your business?

Moreover, set aside a fixed time for the study of the Torah, as best you know how. Then diligently go about your business, for providing your wife and children with a decent livelihood is likewise a mitzwah—the command of God and the duty of man. We should, I say, put ourselves to great pains for our children, for on this the world is built, yet we must bear in mind that if children did as much for their parents, the children would quickly tire of it.

A bird once set out to cross a windy sea with its three fledglings. The sea was so wide and the wind so strong that tht father bird was forced to carry his young, one by one, in his claws. When he was half-way across with the first fledgling the wind turned to a gale, and he said: 'My child, look how I am struggling and risking my life in your behalf. When you are grown up, will you do as much for me and provide for my old age?' The fledgling replied: 'Only bring me to safety, and when you are old I shall do everything you ask of me.' Whereat the father bird dropped his child into the sea, and it drowned, and he said: 'So shall it be done to such a liar as you.' Then the father bird returned to the shore, set forth with his second fledgling, asked the same question, and receiving the same answer, drowned the second child with the cry 'You, too, are a liar!' Finally he set out with the third fledgling, and when he asked the same question, the third and last fledgling replied: 'My dear father, it is true you are struggling mightily and risking your life in my behalf, and I shall be wrong not to repay you when you are old, but I cannot bind myself. This though I can promise: when I am grown up and have children of my own, I shall do as much for them as you have done for me.' Whereupon the father bird said: 'Well spoken, my child, and wisely; your life I will spare and I will carry you to shore in safety.'

Above all, my children, be honest in money matters, with both Jews and Gentiles, lest the name of Heaven be profaned. If you have in hand money or goods belonging to other people, give more care to them than if they were your own, so that, please God, you do no one a wrong. The first question put to a man in the next world is, whether he was faithful in his business dealings. Let a man work ever so hard amassing great wealth dishonestly, let him during his lifetime provide his children fat dowries and upon his death a rich heritage—yet woe, I say, and woe again to the wicked man who for the sake of enriching his children has lost his share in the world to come! For the fleeting moment he has sold Eternity.

When God sends evil days upon us, we shall do well to remember the remedy contrived by the physician in the story told by Rabbi Abraham ben Sabbatai ha-Levi. A great king, he tells us, once imprisoned his physician, and had him bound hand and foot with chains, and fed on a small dole of barley-bread and water. After months of this treatment, the king dispatched relatives of the physician to visit the prison and learn what the unhappy man had to say. To their astonishment he looked as hale and hearty as on the day he entered his cell. He told his relatives he owed his strength and well-being to a brew of seven herbs he had taken the precaution to prepare before he went to prison, and of which he drank a few drops every day. 'What magic herbs are these?' they asked; and he answered: 'The first is trust in God, the second is hope, and the others are patience, recognition of my sins, joy that in suffering now I shall not suffer in the world to come, contentment that my punishment is not worse, as well it could be, and, lastly, knowledge that God who thrust me into prison can, if He will, at any moment set me free.'

However, I am not writing this book in order to preach to you, but, as I have already said, to drive away the melancholy that comes with the long nights. So far as my memory and the subject permit, I shall try to tell everything that has happened to me from my youth upward. Not that I wish to put on airs or pose as a good and pious woman. No, dear children, I am a sinner. Every day, every hour, and every moment of my life I have sinned, nearly all manner of sins. God grant that I may find the means and occasion for repentance. But, alas, the care of providing for my orphaned children, and the ways of the world, have kept me far from that state.

If God will that I may live to finish them, I shall leave you my Memoirs in seven little books. And so, as it seems best, I shall now begin with my birth.

FROM LESSING'S *NATHAN THE WISE*

By the beginning of the eighteenth century, although Jews still lacked equal political status with other citizens throughout Europe, portents of change were more visible than at any other previous time. Within an increasingly vocal sector of elite Western European society, ideas of religious tolerance, universal suffrage, and the separation of the powers of church and state were gaining widespread legitimacy and currency. John Locke and John Toland in England openly expressed enlightened views regarding the moral self-sufficiency of the state and the elimination of Christianity as a political factor in governmental policy.

In Germany, Gotthold Ephraim Lessing (1729–81), the celebrated dramatist and literary critic, published a play called *Nathan the Wise* that held out the promise of a new evaluation of the Jews in Christian society. Lessing had developed a close relationship with the Jewish philosopher Moses Mendelssohn (1729–86). For this German Christian, Mendelssohn the Jew embodied the Enlightenment ideal: that non-Christians were also capable of producing noble and rational individuals. In Nathan, modeled after Mendelssohn, Lessing created a character who spoke for all humanity despite his Jewish upbringing.

The selection from the play, below (Act 3, Scene 7), is based on the famous parable of the three rings, made famous by Giovanni Boccaccio's *Decameron* of the fourteenth century. All three major religions are portrayed by three sons of a generous father who gives each an identical ring, although each claims his alone is authentic. Such a tolerant view as that of Lessing still indicated only a possibility of restructuring the social and political status of European Jewry, but, nevertheless, it was one voiced with increasing regularity and moral cogency throughout the eighteenth century.

READING 5-23

NATHAN.

In days of yore, there dwelt in Eastern lands
A man, who from a valued hand received
A ring of priceless worth. An opal stone
Shot from within an ever-changing hue,
And held this virtue in its form concealed,
To render him of God and man beloved,
Who wore it in this fixed unchanging faith.
No wonder that its Eastern owner ne'er
Withdrew it from his finger, and resolved
That to his house the ring should be secured.
Therefore he thus bequeathed it: first to him
Who was the most beloved of his sons,
Ordaining then that he should leave the ring
To the most dear among his children; then,
That without heeding birth, the fav'rite son,
In virtue of the ring alone, should still
Be lord of all the house. You hear me, Sultan?

SALADIN.

I understand. Proceed.

NATHAN.

From son to son,
The ring at length descended to a sire
Who had three sons, alike obedient to him,
And whom he loved with just and equal love,
The first, the second, and the third, in turn,
According as they each apart received
The overflowings of his heart, appeared
Most worthy as his heir, to take the ring,
Which, with good-natured weakness, he in turn
Had promised privately to each; and thus
Things lasted for a while. But death approached,
The father now embarrassed, could not bear
To disappoint two sons, who trusted him.
What's to be done? In secret he commands
The jeweller to come, that from the form
Of the true ring, he may bespeak two more.
Nor cost nor pains are to be spared, to make
The rings alike—quite like the true one. This
The artist managed. When the rings were brought
The father's eye could not distinguish which
Had been the model. Overjoyed, he calls
His sons, takes leave of each apart—bestows
His blessing and his ring on each—and dies.
You hear me?

SALADIN (*who has turned away in perplexity*).
        Ay! I hear. Conclude the tale.
                NATHAN.
'Tis ended, Sultan! All that follows next
May well be guessed. Scarce is the father dead,
When with his ring, each separate son appears,
And claims to be the lord of all the house.
Question arises, tumult and debate—
But all in vain—the true ring could no more
Be then distinguished than—(*after a pause, in which he
    awaits the Sultan's reply*) the true faith now.
                SALADIN.
Is that your answer to my question?
                NATHAN.
                        No!
But it may serve as my apology.
I cannot venture to decide between
Rings which the father had expressly made,
To baffle those who would distinguish them.
                SALADIN.
Rings, Nathan! Come, a truce to this! The creeds
Which I have named have broad, distinctive marks,
Differing in raiment, food, and drink!
                NATHAN.
                    'Tis true!
But then they differ not in their foundation.
Are not all built on history alike,
Traditional or written? History
Must be received on trust. Is it not so?
In whom are we most likely to put trust?
In our own people? in those very men
Whose blood we are? who, from our earliest youth
Have proved their love for us, have ne'er deceived,
Except in cases where 'twere better so?
Why should I credit my forefathers less
Than you do yours? or can I ask of you
To charge your ancestors with falsehood, that
The praise of truth may be bestowed on mine?
And so of Christians.
                SALADIN.
                By our Prophet's faith,
The man is right. I have no more to say.
                NATHAN.
Now let us to our rings once more return.
We said the sons complained; each to the judge
Swore from his father's hand immediately
To have received the ring—as was the case—
In virtue of a promise, that he should

One day enjoy the ring's prerogative.
In this they spoke the truth. Then each maintained
It was not possible that to himself
His father had been false. Each could not think
His father guilty of an act so base.
Rather than that, reluctant as he was
To judge his brethren, he must yet declare
Some treach'rous act of falsehood had been done.

SALADIN.

Well! and the judge? I'm curious now to hear
What you will make him say. Go on, go on!

NATHAN.

The judge said: If the father is not brought
Before my seat, I cannot judge the case.
Am I to judge enigmas? Do you think
That the true ring will here unseal its lips?
But, hold! You tell me that the real ring
Enjoys the secret power to make the man
Who wears it, both by God and man, beloved.
Let that decide. Who of the three is loved
Best by his brethren? Is there no reply?
What! do these love-exciting rings alone
Act inwardly? Have they no outward charm?
Does each one love himself alone? You're all
Deceived deceivers. All your rings are false.
The real ring, perchance, has disappeared;
And so your father, to supply the loss,
Has caused three rings to fill the place of one.

SALADIN.

O, charming, charming!

NATHAN.

And,—the judge continued:—
My counsel, be it so. I recommend
That you consider how the matter stands.
Each from his father has received a ring:
Let each then think the real ring his own.
Your father, possibly, desired to free
His power from one ring's tyrannous control.
He loved you all with an impartial love,
And equally, and had no inward wish
To prove the measure of his love for one
By pressing heavily upon the rest.
Therefore, let each one imitate this love;
So, free from prejudice, let each one aim
To emulate his brethren in the strife
To prove the virtues of his several ring,
By offices of kindness and of love,
And trust in God. And if, in years to come,

The virtues of the ring shall reappear
Amongst your children's children, then, once more,
Come to this judgment-seat. A greater far
Than I shall sit upon it, and decide.
So spake the modest judge.

SALADIN.
Oh God, O God!

NATHAN.
And if now, Saladin, you think you're he—

SALADIN.
(*Approaches* NATHAN, *and takes his hand, which he retains
to the end of the scene.*)
This promised judge—I?—Dust! I?—Nought! oh God!

NATHAN.

NATHAN.
What is the matter, Sultan?

SALADIN.
Dearest Nathan!
That judge's thousand years are not yet past;
His judgment-seat is not for me. But go,
And still remain my friend.

6

Roads from the Ghetto
(1789 to 1914)

Michael Stanislawski

For the Jews the modern age was characterized by new challenges and opportunities that transformed internal Jewish history as well as the role of Jews in civilization as a whole. The two centuries since the French Revolution included both the most successful integration of Jews into non-Jewish society and the most extensive murder of Jews ever. Vibrant Jewish centers came into being in new parts of the world at the same time as old Jewish communities were destroyed. A searing crisis of belief and self-perception tore many Jews away from their ancestral faith; new ideologies and philosophies emerged to guide other Jews through the unprecedented maze of the modern world.

The complex, often paradoxical history of the Jews in the last two centuries has revolved around the relationship of the Jews to the three major revolutions that have defined modern life—what might be called the intellectual, the political, and the social revolutions. The sources that follow proceed roughly in chronological order, and geographically from Western to Eastern Europe in line with the major currents of modern Jewish history until World War I. The selections attempt to highlight—in a necessarily incomplete manner—the ways in which the Jews responded to the three revolutions of modernity: how they invented new forms and patterns of Jewish life while participating wholeheartedly in the creation of the modern world.

MOSES MENDELSSOHN ON JUDAISM AND ENLIGHTENMENT

Moses Mendelssohn (1729–86) was a major philosopher of the German Enlightenment and the primary exponent of a synthesis between Judaism and the Enlightenment. Many historians have regarded Mendelssohn as the first modern Jew. In this selection from his work *Jerusalem*,

Mendelssohn addresses the problem of the relationship between Jewish law and Jewish participation in society at large.

READING 6-1

And even today, no better advice than this can be given to the House of Jacob: Adopt the mores and constitution of the country in which you find yourself, but be steadfast in upholding the religion of your fathers, too. Bear both burdens as well as you can. True, on the one hand, people make it difficult for you to bear the burden of civil life because of the religion to which you remain faithful; and, on the other hand, the climate of our time makes the observance of your religious laws in some respects more burdensome than it need be. Persevere nevertheless; stand fast in the place which Providence has assigned to you; and submit to everything which may happen, as you were told to do by your Lawgiver long ago.

Indeed, I cannot see how those who were born into the household of Jacob can in good conscience exempt themselves from the observance of the law. We are permitted to reflect on the law, to search for its meaning, and occasionally, where the Lawgiver himself provides no reason [for a particular law], to surmise that it must perhaps be understood in terms of a particular time, place, and set of circumstances. Therefore, the law can perhaps also be changed according to the requirements of a particular time, place, and set of circumstances, but only if and when it pleases the supreme Lawgiver to let us recognize His will—to make it known to us just as openly, publicly, and beyond any possibility of doubt and uncertainty, as He did when He gave us the law itself. As long as this has not happened, as long as we can show no such authentic dispensation from the law, no sophistry of ours can free us from the strict obedience we owe to it. Reverence for God must draw a line between speculation and observance, beyond which no conscientious person may go. . . .

Here it seems obvious that "what God has joined together, man may not tear asunder." I cannot understand how any one of us, even if he were to convert to the Christian religion, could believe that he would thereby have appeased his conscience and freed himself from the yoke of the law. Jesus of Nazareth was never heard to declare that he had come to release the House of Jacob from the law. Indeed, he explicitly and emphatically said the opposite and, what is more, did the opposite himself. Jesus of Nazareth himself observed not only the law of Moses but also the ordinances of the rabbis; and whatever in his recorded speeches and actions seems to contradict this fact, actually only appears to do so at first glance. . . .

And you, my brothers and fellowmen, who are followers of the teachings of Jesus, how can you blame us for doing what the founder of your religion himself has done and sanctioned by his authority? Can you seriously believe that you cannot reciprocate our love as citizens and associate yourselves with us for civic purposes as long as we are outwardly distinguished from you by our ceremonial law, do not eat with you, or do not marry you? As far as we can see, the founder of your religion himself would not have done these things or have permitted us to do them either.

If this should be and remain your true conviction—which one can hardly believe of truly Christian people—if we can be united with you as citizens only on the condition that we deviate from the law which we still consider binding, then we sincerely regret the necessity of declaring that we shall renounce our claim to civil [equality and] union with you. . . .

It is beyond our power to yield in this matter; but it is nevertheless also within our power, if we have integrity, to love you as our brothers and to implore you as brothers to make our burdens as tolerable as you possibly can. Regard us, if not as brothers and fellow citizens, at least as fellowmen and coinhabitants of this country. Show us ways and provide us with means of becoming better fellow residents, and let us enjoy, together with you, the rights of humanity, as far as time and circumstances will permit. We cannot forsake the law in good conscience—and without a conscience of what use would fellow citizens be to you?. . .

At least prepare the way for your more fortunate descendants to [reach] that height of culture, that universal tolerance for which reason is still sighing in vain. Reward and punish no doctrine; hold out no allurement or bribe to anyone for the adoption of a particular faith. Let every man who does not disturb the public welfare, who obeys the law, acts righteously toward you and his fellowmen be allowed to speak as he thinks, to pray to God after his own fashion or after the fashion of his fathers, and to seek eternal salvation where he thinks he may find it. Permit no one in your country to search someone else's heart or to judge someone else's thoughts. Let no one usurp a right which the Omniscient has reserved to Himself. If we render unto Caesar what is Caesar's, then let us also render unto God what is God's. Love truth! Love peace!

THE DEBATE OVER EMANCIPATING THE JEWS OF FRANCE

The French Revolution of 1789 was based on the principle laid out in the Declaration of the Rights of Man, enacted by the National Assembly on August 26, 1789: "All men are born, and remain, free and equal in rights. . . . No person shall be molested for his opinions, even such as are religious. . . ." Soon the question arose: did this equality include the Jews? Should the Jews be emancipated as citizens of the new French state? The following selection is a part of the most famous speech in favor of the emancipation of the Jews made by a deputy to the Assembly, Count Clermont-Tonnerre.

READING 6-2

I will deal now with religion. You have already addressed this point in stating in the Declaration of Rights that no one shall be persecuted for his religious beliefs. Is it not profound persecution of the citizen to want to deprive him of his dearest right because of his opinions? The law cannot affect the religion of a man. It can take no hold over his soul; it can affect only his actions, and it must protect those actions when they do no harm to society. God wanted us to reach agreement among ourselves on issues of morality, and he has permitted us to make moral laws, but he has given to no one but himself the right to legislate dogmas and to rule over [religious] conscience. So leave man's conscience free, that sentiments or thoughts guided in one manner or another toward the heavens will not be crimes that society punishes by the loss of social rights. Or else create a national religion, arm yourself with a sword, and tear up your Declaration of Rights. [But] there is justice, there is reason. . . .

Every religion must prove but one thing—that it is moral. If there is a religion that commands theft and arson, it is necessary not only to refuse eligibility to those who profess it, but further to outlaw them. This consideration cannot be applied to the Jews. The reproaches that one makes of them are many. The gravest are unjust, the others are merely wrong. Usury, one says, is permitted them. This assertion is founded on nothing but a false interpretation of a principle of charity and brotherhood which forbids them to lend at interest among themselves. . . . Men who possess nothing but money cannot live but by making that money valuable, and you have always prevented them from possessing anything else. . . . This people is insatiable, one says. This insatiability is [however] not certain.

The Jews should be denied everything as a nation, but granted everything as individuals. They must be citizens. It is claimed that they do not want to be citizens, that they say this and that they are [thus] excluded; there cannot be one nation within another nation. . . . It is intolerable that the Jews should become a separate political formation or class in the country. Every one of them must individually become a citizen; if they do not want this, they must inform us and we shall then be compelled to expel them. The existence of a nation within a nation is unacceptable to our country. . . .

THE EMANCIPATION OF THE SEPHARDIM

The debate over emancipating the Jews dragged on with neither side convincing the other. By the beginning of 1790 a compromise was reached between the supporters and opponents of emancipation: the small Sephardic community, already integrated into French culture and society, would be granted equal rights before any decision would be made on the larger Ashkenazic community of northern France. On January 28, 1790, the three thousand Sephardim of France were emancipated by the following decree.

READING 6-3

All the Jews, known in France, under the name of Portuguese, Spanish, and Avignonese Jews, shall continue to enjoy the same rights they have hitherto enjoyed, and which have been granted to them by letters patent.

In consequence thereof, they shall enjoy the rights of active citizens, if they possess the other requisite qualifications, as enumerated in the decrees of the national assembly.

THE FRENCH CONSTITUTION

The debate over the emancipation of the Ashkenazim was interrupted by the promulgation of the Constitution of the new French state. The following provision of that constitution rendered Jewish emancipation inevitable.

READING 6-4

TITLE I.

FUNDAMENTAL REGULATIONS GUARANTEED BY THE CONSTITUTION.

The Constitution guarantees, as natural and civil rights,

1. That all the citizens are admissible to places and employments, without any other distinction than that of *virtue* and *talents*.
2. That all taxes shall be equally divided amongst all the citizens, in proportion to their abilities.
3. That the same crimes shall be subject to the same punishments, without any distinction of persons.

The Constitution in like manner guarantees, as natural and civil rights, liberty to every man to go, stay, or depart, without being arrested, or detained, except according to the forms determined by the Constitution.

Liberty to every man to speak, write, print and publish his thoughts, without the writings being subjected to censure or inspection before their publication, and to exercise the religious worship to which he is attached.

THE EMANCIPATION OF THE ASHKENAZIM

When the National Assembly again deliberated on the fate of the Jews, one deputy pointed out that any further argument was in violation of the spirit of the Constitution, and hence out of order. Thus, without resolving the debate over whether the Jews could become equal citizens of France, the following decree was enacted on September 27, 1791.

READING 6-5

The National Assembly, considering that the conditions requisite to be a French citizen, and to become an active citizen, are fixed by the constitution, and that every man who, being duly qualified, takes the civic oath, and engaged to fulfill all the duties prescribed by the constitution, has a right to all the advantages it insures;—Annuls all adjournments, restrictions, and exceptions, contained in the preceding decrees, affecting individuals of the Jewish persuasion, who shall take the civic oath, which shall be considered as a renunciation of all privileges granted in their favour.

RESPONSE OF THE FRENCH JEWS

Most of the French Jews viewed their emancipation as a blessing. Indicative of their response is the following selection from a letter written by a prominent Jewish businessman and politician, Berr Isaac Berr, the day after the emancipation. Berr praised the National Assembly for its act, and explicitly described the contract the Jews had entered into upon their emancipation.

READING 6-6

Gentlemen and dear brethren,

At length the day is arrived when the veil, by which, parted from our fellow-citizens, we were kept in a state of humiliation, is rent; at length we recover those rights which have been taken from us more than *eighteen centuries* ago. How much are we at this moment indebted to the clemency of the God of our forefathers!

We are now, thanks to the Supreme Being, and to the sovereignty of the nation, not only Men and Citizens, but we are Frenchmen!—What a happy change thou hast worked in us, merciful God! So late as the 27th of September last, we were the only inhabitants of this vast empire who seemed doomed to remain for ever in bondage and abasement; and on the following day, on the 28th, a day for ever sacred among us, thou inspirest the immortal legislators of France. They pronounce, and more than sixty thousand unfortunate beings, mourning over their sad fate, are awakened to a sense of their happiness by the liveliest emotions of the purest joy. . . .

What orator could presume to express to the nation and to its king, all the extent of our gratitude, and of our unalterable submission? But neither the king nor the representatives of the nation seek for praises or acknowledgments; their only wish is to behold people happy. In that they expect and they will find their reward. Let us then, dear brethren, let us conform to their wishes; let us examine with attention what remains to be done, on our part, to become truly happy, and how we may be able to shew, in some measure, our grateful sense for all the favours heaped upon us. On this subject, gentlemen and dear brethren, give me leave to submit to your judgment the result of some reflections, which our change of condition has suggested to me.

The name of active citizen, which we have just obtained, is, without a doubt, the most precious title a man can possess in a free empire; but this title alone is not sufficient; we should possess also the necessary qualifications to fulfil the duties annexed to it: we know ourselves how very deficient we are in that respect; we have been in a manner compelled to abandon the pursuit of all moral and physical sciences, of all sciences, in short, which tend to the improvement of the mind, in order to give ourselves up entirely to commerce, to be enabled to gather as much money as would insure protection, and satisfy the rapacity of our persecutors. . . .

We must then, dear brethren, strongly bear this truth in our minds, that till such a time as we work a change in our manners, in our habits, in short, in our whole education, we cannot expect to be placed by the esteem of our fellow citizens in any of those situations in which we can give signal proofs of that glowing patriotism so long cherished in our bosoms. God forbid that I should mean any thing derogatory to our professed religion, or to our established form of worship. . . .

But I cannot too often repeat to you how absolutely necessary it is for us to divest ourselves entirely of that narrow spirit, of *Corporation* and *Congregation*, in all civil and political matters, not immediately connected with our spiritual laws; in these things we must absolutely appear simply as individuals, as Frenchmen, guided only by a true patriotism and by the general good of the nation: to know how to risk our lives and fortunes for the defence of the country, to make ourselves useful to our fellow citizens, to deserve their esteem and their friendship, to join our efforts to theirs in maintaining public tranquility, on which that of individuals depends; such ought to be the principal aim of our daily employment; and as we are not yet able to fulfil those noble functions ourselves, we must turn our minds to the means necessary to be acquired, and, above all, in our attention on our children, and procure for them all the necessary instructions.

EXTENSION OF EMANCIPATION

As the ideals of the Revolution were spread through Western Europe by the French Army, so too was Jewish emancipation brought to neighboring countries by the French forces. In many places this meant the physical abolition of ghetto walls. Here is the decree ordering the destruction of the ghetto in Padua.

READING 6-7

Liberty   Equality

In the Name
Of the French Republic
One and Indivisible

The Central Government of the Delta Districts of Rovigo and Adria,

Having heard the report of Department III for Legislation and Chief Police about the proposed levelling with the ground of the Gates, Arches and simple precinct Walls of the former Ghetto, and

Whereas it is necessary to remove all vestiges of a separation which is contrary to the rights of free Men, and whereas the said levelling is consistent with the new title of Via Libera given to that residential section, and as following the Government Decree of Fruttidor 11,

Decrees:

First.—The municipal police committee shall carry out the solemn levelling with the ground of the Gates, Arches and simple precinct Walls of the ex-*Ghetto* in such a manner that no vestige shall remain of the ancient separation from other neighboring streets.

Secondly.—This performance shall take place in all the communities of the department where Ghettos should exist.

Padua, Fruttidor 29, year V of the French Republic and year I of Italian Liberty, September 15, 1797.

EMANCIPATION IN PRUSSIA

Even in countries not occupied by France the spirit of reform resulted in new laws extending the rights of the Jews. In Prussia the Jews were emancipated in 1812 according to the following decree, though it was not enforced for many years.

READING 6-8

We, Friedrich Wilhelm, by the Grace of God, King of Prussia, etc., have resolved to grant the adherents of the Jewish faith in Our monarchy a new constitution suitable to the general welfare, and declare all laws and regulations concerning Jews [issued] hitherto, which are not confirmed by the present Edict as abolished, and decree as follows:

1

Jews and their families domiciled at present in Our States, provided with general privileges, patent letters of naturalization, letters of protection and concessions, are to be considered as natives [*Einländer*] and as Prussian state citizens.

2

The continuance of this qualification as natives and state citizens conferred upon them shall however be permitted only under the following obligation:
that they bear strictly fixed family names, and that they shall use the German or another living language not only in keeping their commercial books but also upon drawing their contracts and declaratory acts, and that they should use no other than German or Latin characters for their signatures. . . .

4

After having declared and determined his family name, everyone shall receive a certificate from the Provincial Government of his domicile that he is a native and a citizen of the state, which certificate shall be used in the future for himself and his descendants in place of the letter of protection. . . .

7

Jews considered as natives . . . shall enjoy equal civil rights and liberties with Christians, in so far as this Order does not contain anything to the contrary.

8

They may therefore administer academic school teaching and municipal offices for which they qualified themselves.

9

As far as the admission of Jews to other public services and government offices is concerned, We leave to Ourselves its regulation by law in course of time.

10

They are at liberty to settle in the towns as well as in the open country.

11

They may acquire real estate of any kind same as the Christian inhabitants and they may carry on any permitted trade, with the provision that they observe the general legal regulations.

12

Freedom of trade ensuing from the right of state citizenship also includes commerce. . . .

14

Native Jews as such must not be burdened with special taxes. . . .

JEWISH RIGHTS IN ENGLAND

In England the Jews were never formally emancipated, because the nature of English law and custom precluded the necessity of a specific act proclaiming the Jews to be citizens. Once in Britain, the only limitation on the Jews and other nonconformist religious groups was access to public positions that required an oath to be sworn in conformity with the rites of the Church of England. From the late 1820's on, these restrictions began to fall as a result of a movement for social and political reform. In the following document, the Jewish Disabilities Removal Act of July 31, 1845, restrictions on Jews elected to municipal offices were rescinded. Thirteen years later, the Jews won the right to sit in Parliament.

READING 6-9

An Act for the Relief of Persons of the Jewish Religion Elected to Municipal Offices.

Whereas the Declaration prescribed by an Act of the Ninth Year of the Reign of King George the Fourth, intituled An Act for repealing so much of several Acts as imposes the Necessity of receiving the Sacrament of the Lord's Supper as a Qualification for Certain Offices and Employments, upon Admission into Office in Municipal Corporations, cannot conscientiously be made and subscribed by Persons of the Jewish Religion: Be it therefore enacted by the Queen's most Excellent Majesty, by and with the Advice and Consent of the Lords Spiritual and Temporal, and Commons, in this present Parliament assembled, and by the Authority of the same, that, instead of the Declaration required to be made and subscribed by the said recited Act, every Person of the Jewish Religion be permitted to make and subscribe the following Declaration within One Calendar Month next before or upon his Admission into the office of Mayor, Alderman, Recorder, Bailiff, Common Councilman, Councillor, Chamberlain, Treasurer, Town Clerk, or any other Municipal Office in any City, Town Corporate, Borough, or Cinque Port, within England and Wales or the Town of Berwick-upon-Tweed:

"I, A. B., being a Person professing the Jewish Religion, having conscientious Scruples against subscribing the Declaration contained in an Act passed in the Ninth year of the Reign of King George the Fourth, intituled An Act for repealing so much of several Acts as imposes the Necessity of receiving the Sacrament of the Lord's Supper as a Qualification for certain Offices and Employments, do solemnly, sincerely, and truly declare, That I will not exercise any Power or Authority or Influence which I may possess by virtue of the Office of _____ to injure or weaken the Protestant Church as it is by Law established in England, nor to disturb the said

Church, or the Bishops and Clergy of the said Church, in the Possession of any Right or Privileges to which such Church or the said Bishops and Clergy may be by Law entitled."

II. And be it enacted, That such Declaration shall, with respect to any such office, be of the same Force and Effect as if the Person making it had made and subscribed the Declaration aforesaid contained in the said Act of the Ninth year of the Reign of King George the Fourth.

THE REFORM OF JUDAISM

In response to the attractions of the outside world, many Jews were no longer satisfied with the Judaism of their parents or with the Enlightenment philosophy of Moses Mendelssohn and the other adherents of the Jewish Enlightenment. In Germany Jews invented a variety of new ideologies and movements dedicated to a synthesis between Judaism and modernity. The first such attempt was the Reform movement, which arose in the first half of the nineteenth century.

The following selections from the deliberations at a conference of Reform rabbis at Frankfurt in 1845 reflect the fundamental commitment of the new movement to the notion that true Judaism has no national boundaries. Thus the Jews in Germany were simply "Germans of the Mosaic persuasion" parallel to "Germans of the Christian persuasion." In line with this view the messianic hope was transformed from a belief in a personal messiah who would lead the Jews back to Palestine to a belief in universal brotherhood and freedom.

READING 6-10

The concept of the Messiah is closely linked to the entire ceremonial law. The believer in the Talmud finds his salvation only in the reconstruction of the state, the return of the people, the resumption of sacrifices, etc. Here lies the cause for all our lamentations over the destruction of the Temple, and our yearnings for the ruins of the altar. Ardent belief and unshakable courage were expressed in these hopes, uttered forth from the dark caves of our miserable streets.

But now our concepts have changed. There is no need any more for an extended ceremonial law. The earlier approach restricted divine guidance to the land [of Israel] and the people; the deity, it was believed, enjoyed bloody sacrifices, and priests were needed for penance. With increasing zeal, the prophets spoke up against this restricted view. Everybody knows the passage: "It hath been told thee, O man, what is good, and what the Lord doth require of thee; only to do justly, and to love mercy, and to walk humbly with thy God." The decline of Israel's political independence was at one time deplored, but in reality it was not a misfortune, but a mark of progress; not a degradation, but an elevation of our religion, through which Israel has come closer to fulfilling its vocation. The place of the sacrifices has been taken by sacred devotion. From Israel, the word of God had to be carried to the four corners of the earth, and new religions have helped in carrying out the task. Only the Talmud moves in circles; we, however, favor progress. . . .

The wish to return to Palestine in order to create there a political empire for those who are still oppressed because of their religion is superfluous. The wish should rather be for a termination of the oppression, which would improve their lot as it has improved ours. The wish, moreover, is inadmissible. It turns the messianic hope from a religious into a secular one, which is gladly given up as soon as the political situation changes for the better. But messianic hope, truly understood, is religious. It expresses either a hope for redemption and liberation from spiritual deprivation and the realization of a Kingdom of God on earth, or for a political restoration of the Mosaic theocracy where Jews could live according to the Law of Moses. This latter religious hope can be renounced only be those who have a more sublime conception of Judaism, and who believe that the fulfillment of Judaism's mission is not dependent on the establishment of a Jewish state, but rather by a merging of Jewry into the political constellations of the fatherland. Only an enlightened conception of religion can displace a dulled one.

In all contemporary additions to the prayerbook our modern conception of the Messiah may clearly be stated, including the confession that our newly gained status as citizens constitutes a partial fulfillment of our messianic hopes. . . .

Resolution adopted by the majority: The messianic idea should receive prominent mention in the prayers, but all petitions for our return to the land of our fathers and for the restoration of a Jewish state should be eliminated from the liturgy. . . .

POSITIVE-HISTORICAL JUDAISM

A prominent group of German rabbis and scholars at first allied themselves with the Reform movement but soon felt that the Reformers had gone too far in abandonment of Jewish traditions and belief. In favor of emancipation, but equally dedicated to preserving the hope of the return to the Land of Israel, this group began to advocate what it called "Positive-Historical Judaism"—a moderate approach to the reform of Judaism based on historical research and the idea that Judaism was a continuously evolving tradition. The following selection is from the writings of Rabbi Zecharias Frankel, the leader of this group.

READING 6-11

For centuries Judaism has engaged in a successful struggle with the world. Through the ages Judaism has shed its light abroad and illumined the way of many nations who even today, whether consciously or unconsciously, make use of its enlightenment. Not in vain did Judaism oppose paganism, materialism, sensuality, and the striving after earthly things. Through many generations Judaism sustained and guarded the sparks of divine spirit, and in helping them to develop, developed itself. Shall we assume that its power is now exhausted and consumed, that its living high spirit has lost its force? Does the spirit of the age really rise against it with might and strength?. . .

Judaism ties its teachings to divine revelation, which is an expression of the highest will of God. The eternal truths regarding the Godhead and morality flow from this source, and around these there are grouped other laws which are saturated with the same spirit, and in which the high ideas of the nobility of man and his closeness to God find expression. These revealed laws are the guardians of Judaism, the never-slumbering watchman of the holiest elements within it. They are designed to protect the highest truths and they have faithfully carried out this mission to the present day. These laws have one of two purposes. Some have the purpose within themselves, though it may not always be clearly evident in each particular law. Thus the dietary laws aim at cultivating restraint of appetite; the sexual laws at inculcating chastity and purity of morals. Other laws which mirror the power of God as the creator have another function—to remind man of God. . . .

We have, then, reached a decisive point in regard to moderate changes, namely, that they must come from the people and that the will of the entire community must decide. Still, this rule alone may accomplish little. The whole community is a heavy unharmonious body and its will is difficult to recognize. It comes to expression only after many years. We must find a way to carry on such changes in the proper manner, and this can be done by the help of the scholars. Judaism has no priests as representatives of faith nor does it require special spiritual sanctimoniousness in its spokesmen. The power to represent it is not the share of any one family, nor does it pass from father to son. Knowledge and mastery of the law supply the sanctity, and these can be attained by everybody. In Jewish life, spiritual and intellectual ability ultimately took the place of the former priesthood which, even in early times, was limited in its function primarily to the sacrificial cult. Even in early days, Judaism recognized the will of the people as a great force and because of this recognition a great religious activity came into being. But this activity, in turn, was translated into a living force by the teachers of the people through the use of original ordinances and through interpretation of the Scriptures. At times these actions of the sages lightened the amount of observance; at times they increased it. That the results of the studies and research of the teachers found acceptance among the people proves, on the one hand, that the teachers knew the character of their time, and, on the other hand, that the people had confidence in them and that they considered them true representatives of their faith.

Should Jewish theologians and scholars of our time succeed in acquiring such a confidence, then they will attain influence with the introduction of whatever changes may be necessary. The will of the community of Israel will then find its representatives and knowledge will be its proper exercise.

ORTHODOX JUDAISM

The third new movement in German-Jewish life was the Orthodox movement, which insisted on the eternal truth of all aspects of Talmudic Judaism while at the same time advocating Jewish emancipation. Led by Rabbi Samson Raphael Hirsch from whose works the following selection is taken, German Orthodoxy attempted to present the teachings of the *Torah* in a vocabulary acceptable to university-trained Jews, and was prepared to accept a limited number of external modifications of Jewish liturgy.

READING 6-12

Emancipation

You ask me for my opinion on the question which at present so greatly agitates the minds of men; namely emancipation. You wish to know whether I consider it feasible and desirable according to the spirit of Judaism. The new conception of Judaism which you have acquired, dear Benjamin, has rendered you so uncertain as to whether such ideas could be reconciled with the eternal ideals of our faith. You have begun to doubt whether the acceptance of these new relations is in harmony with the spirit of Judaism, inasmuch as it approximates to a close union with that which is different and alien, and a severance of the ties which bind us all to Israel's lot. You doubt its desirability, because, through too much intimacy with the non-Jew, Israel's own special characteristics might easily be obliterated. I respect your scruples, and will communicate to you my own opinion. Let us first examine whether it is in harmony with the spirit of Judaism.

When Israel began its great wandering through the ages and among the nations, Jeremiah proclaimed it as Israel's duty to:

"Build houses and dwell therein; plant gardens and eat the fruit thereof; take wives unto yourselves, and beget sons and daughters, and take wives for your sons and give your daughters in marriage that they bear sons and daughters, and that you multiply *there*, and diminish not. *And seek the peace of the city whither I have exiled you, and pray for it to the Lord, for in its peace there will be unto you peace.*"

To be pushed back and limited upon the path of life is, therefore, not an essential condition of the *Galuth*, Israel's exile among the nations. On the contrary, it is our duty to join ourselves as closely as possible to the state which receives us into its midst, to promote its welfare and not to consider our own well-being as in any way separate from that of the state to which we belong.

This close connection with states everywhere is not at all in contradiction to the spirit of Judaism, for the independent national life of Israel was never the essence or purpose of our existence as a nation, but only a means of fulfilling our spiritual mission.

Land and soil were never Israel's bond of union. That function was always fulfilled solely by the common task set by the Torah. Therefore the people of Israel still forms a united body, though it is separated from a national soil. Nor does this unity lose any of its reality though Israel accept everywhere the citizenship of the nations among which it is dispersed. This spiritual unity (which may be designated by the Hebrew terms *am* and *goy*, but not by the term "nation," unless we are able to separate from that word the inherent concept of common territory and political power) is the only communal bond we possess, or ever expect to possess, until that great day shall arrive when the Almighty shall see fit in His inscrutable wisdom to unite again His scattered servants in one land, and the Torah shall be the guiding principle of a state, a model of the meaning of Divine Revelation and the mission of humanity. . . .

I bless emancipation when I notice that no spiritual principle, not even one of foolish fanaticism, stands in its way, but that it is opposed only by those passions which are degrading to humanity, namely, greed for gain and narrow selfishness. I rejoice when I perceive that in this concession of emancipation, regard for the natural rights of men to live as equals among equals is freely extended without force or compulsion, but purely through the power of their own inner truth. I welcome the sacrifice of the base passions wherever it is offered, as the dawn of reviving humanity in mankind, and as a preliminary step to the universal recognition of God as the sole Lord and Father, and of all human beings as the children of the All-One.

But for Israel I only bless it if, at the same time, there will awaken in Israel the true spirit which strives to fulfill the mission of Israel regardless of whether or not there is to be emancipation, to elevate and ennoble ourselves, to implant the spirit of Judaism in our souls, in order that it may generate a life in which that spirit shall be reflected and realized. I bless it, if Israel will regard emancipation not as the goal of its vocation, but only as a new condition of its mission, and as a new test, much severer than the trial of oppression. But I should grieve if Israel understood itself so little, and had so little comprehension of its own spirit that it would welcome emancipation as the end of the *Galuth*, and as the highest goal of its historic mission. If Israel should regard this glorious concession merely as a means of securing a greater degree of comfort in life, and greater opportunities for the acquisition of wealth and enjoyment, it would show that Israel had not comprehended the spirit of its own Law, nor learned anything from exile. And sorrowfully indeed would I mourn if Israel were so far to forget itself as to deem emancipation not too dearly purchased through capricious curtailment of the Torah, capricious abandonment of the chief element of our very being. We must become Jews, Jews in the true sense of the word, imbued with the spirit of the Law, accepting it as the fountain of spiritual and ethical life. Then Judaism will gladly welcome emancipation as affording a greater opportunity for the fulfillment of its task, the realization of a noble and ideal life.

THE CULMINATION OF EMANCIPATION IN GERMANY

Only in France and England did the Jews' civil rights survive in the period of reaction of the mid-nineteenth century. The revolutions of 1848 briefly led to a new emancipation of the Jews which, however, fell by the wayside with the collapse of the revolutionary regimes.

In the 1860's and early 1870's, with the drive for national unification in Germany and Italy and with the restructuring of the Austro-Hungarian empire, pragmatic political calculations resulted in a thorough emancipation of the Jews of Central Europe. The following document was issued in Germany on July 3, 1869.

READING 6-13

Law Concerning the Equality of All Confessions in Respect to Civil and Political Rights.

We, Wilhelm, by the Grace of God, King of Prussia, etc., with the approval of the *Bundesrath* and of the *Reichstag* decree in the name of the North German Confederation as follows:

All still existent restrictions on civil and political rights derived from the difference in religious confession are hereby repealed. In particular, the qualification for participation in communal and provincial representative bodies and for holding the public offices shall be independent of religious confession.

Authentically under Our Most High Signature and with the Seal of the Confederation affixed,

Done at the Castle of Babelsberg, July 3, 1869

Wilhelm
Count of Bismarck—Schoenhausen.

FINAL EMANCIPATION IN ITALY

Following Germany, the Italian principalities, uniting in one state, rescinded all restrictions that still obtained in regard to the Jews.

READING 6-14

ROYAL DECREE BY VIRTUE OF WHICH IN ROME AND IN THE RO-MAN PROVINCES ALL INEQUALITIES SHALL CEASE AMONGST CITIZENS REGARDLESS OF THE RELIGION WHICH THEY PROFESS, CONCERNING THE ENJOYMENT AND EXERCISE OF CIVIL AND POLITICAL RIGHTS AND COMPETENCE TO HOLD PUBLIC OFFICES.

Vittorio Emanuele II

By the Grace of God and the Will of the Nation King of Italy

Having considered Article 24 of the Statute, and having heard the Council of Ministers, and on the proposal by the Keeper of Our Seals, Minister Secretary of State for the Affairs of Charity and Justice of Religions,

We have decreed and hereby decree:

Art. 1. In Rome and in the Roman provinces all inequality between citizens whatever religion they may profess shall cease with regard to the enjoyment and the exercise of civil and political rights and to the competence for public offices.

Art. 2. Every law and disposition contrary to the present Decree which becomes effectual immediately upon its publication, is abrogated.

We order that the present Decree, provided with the Seal of the State, shall be inserted in the Official Digest of the Laws and Decrees of the Kingdom of Italy, instructing all concerned to observe same and to enforce the observation thereof.

Done at Firenze, on the day of October 13, 1870

Vittorio Emanuele

JEWISH SOCIETY IN EASTERN EUROPE: THE TRIUMPH OF HASIDISM

Emancipation was far off for the largest Jewish community in the world—that of the Russian empire. Since the Polish partitions at the end of the eighteenth century, more than a million Jews lived in a part of the world politically and socially similar to Western Europe in the sixteenth or seventeenth centuries. These Jews were, therefore, in a situation analogous to that of the Jews of the West before the rise of the modern state, the Enlightenment, and the Industrial Revolution.

Most of the Jews in Russia and Poland, and even in Galicia, the eastern province of the Austrian Empire, were by this time devout adherents of the Hasidic movement. The following selection describes a famous, if uncharacteristic, Hasidic master, Rabbi Menahem Mendel of Kotsk, who lived and attracted followers in the first half of the nineteenth century.

READING 6-15

I Am Not a God: A Hasidic Tale

It was a bitter frosty winter. One night, Menahem Mendel, the old rebbe of Kotsk, sat all alone by his stove, deep in study of the Gemara. The windows were covered with frost. He was reciting aloud at the top of his voice. He did not see or hear a sleigh pulling up before his house and a man asking to see him.

In the vestibule, the rebbe's attendant dozed by the stove. When the man, dressed in a fur coat and covered with frost, entered, the attendant awoke and asked what he wanted.

The man put down the driver's whip near the door, shook off some of the ice, rubbed his hands. "I must see the rebbe, I have come from a village many miles away, on behalf of my only daughter who has been three days in labor. It is a matter of life and death. Let me see the rebbe."

So absorbed was the rebbe in his study, reciting so loudly, the attendant was afraid to enter. The man pleaded with him, even promising him vodka. But the attendant stood tiptoe at the door, listening. The man became impatient, as if he were on hot coals. He cajoled and he threatened, but it was no use. It was no small matter interrupting the rebbe at his studies! The man, seeing the attendant was afraid to enter, said: "I will go in myself." The attendant tried to stop him, they struggled; the man pushed the attendant aside, and threw open the door. He began to weep: "Sainted rebbe, a daughter of Israel is in danger. She has been three days in labor. There is no doctor in the village and the weather is too frosty to bring her into town. Rebbe, have pity, pray for her!"

The rebbe looked at him, then he went to the door and shouted: "I am not a god. What do you want of me? Why are you pleading with me? Plead with God!"

He told the man to leave and returned to his studies. The man was so upset that the attendant tried to comfort him: "God will help. With God's help, your daughter will be all right. Don't worry, the rebbe knows what he's doing."

But the man would not be comforted. With renewed courage, once again he burst open the door to the rebbe's study and fell at the rebbe's feet, imploring him. The rebbe's wife and children came running to see what was the matter. The women, too, began weeping, and the rebbe's wife entreated: "Mendel, say something to him. It is a matter of life and death."

The rebbe did not reply, his head still bent over the Gemara. The man still lay on the floor, bleating like a calf. The neighbors, too, had come running. Then, pacing up and down his study, the rebbe shouted, "What do these village Jews think? Do they think I am a priest that they kiss my shoes? I am not a god. Go home, pray to God, and your daughter will be well."

But the man kept wailing. "Rebbe, help me; only you, sainted rebbe; I will stay here until you promise me that the birth will go well."

The study was full now. The neighbors were crying, some women even said the man was right to insist on the rebbe's blessing. The rebbe himself stood at a window, his head pressed against a frozen pane. The room was heavy with anguish. Then the rebbe cried out: "Fools, dolts, why have you come here? Do you think I am a god? That I can bring the dead back to life? You think that I, Mendel Kotsker, have influence in Heaven? That if I choose I can turn the frost into a heat wave? Fools, asses. Out! Out! Out!"

The attendant drove all the people out of the study, but the man would not leave. He remained on the floor, like a madman. The rebbe returned to the Gemara, his voice rising ever higher as if he wanted to blot out the incident. The man lay on the floor, perhaps an hour, sighing from time to time. When the rebbe finished, he put his kerchief on the Gemara, and turned to the man. They looked at each other. Then the rebbe said, "Your horse must be frozen. Why are you waiting?" The man began to weep anew: "I cannot go home, rebbe, unless you help me!"

"How can I help you?" asked the rebbe calmly. "I am not a doctor and certainly not a god. Go home. God will probably help you."

His words took effect. The man arose and said goodbye. He took his whip, got into his sleigh, and quickly drove away.

The next day the man returned, cheerful. The attendant asked, "Are congratulations in order?"

"Double congratulations. My daughter had two boys."

The rebbe received him with a smile; "Did you need my blessing?"

"Rebbe," replied the man, "Your last words yesterday helped. At the very moment you were telling me to go home my daughter gave birth."

THE PALE OF SETTLEMENT

Before inheriting the huge number of Jews from the Polish state it destroyed, the Russian empire had never allowed Jews in its midst. In order to deal with the Jews it now controlled, the Russian government ruled that the Jews could remain in the areas seized from Poland but not move to most other parts of the empire. The area permitted to Jewish residence became known as the Pale of Settlement. It was established in the late eighteenth century, but its borders were not formally fixed until 1835 in the following decree by Tsar Nicholas I.

READING 6-16

. . . 3. A permanent residence is permitted to the Jews: (a) In the provinces: Grodno, Vilna, Volhynia, Podolia, Minsk, Ekaterinoslav. (b) In the districts: Bessarabia, Bialystok.

4. In addition to the provinces and districts listed in the preceding section, a permanent residence is permitted to the Jews, with the following restrictions: (a) in Kiev province, with the exception of the provincial capital, Kiev; (b) in Kherson province, with the exception of the city of Nikolaev; (c) in Tavaria province, with the exception of the city of Sebastopol; (d) in Mogilev and Vitebsk provinces, ex-

cept in the villages; (e) in Chernigov and Poltava provinces, but not within the government and Cossack villages, where the expulsion of the Jews has already been completed; (f) in Courland province permanent residence is permitted only to those Jews who have been registered until the present date with their families in census lists. Entry for the purpose of settlement is forbidden to the Jews from other provinces; (g) in Lithland province, in the city of Riga and the suburb Shlok, with the same restrictions as those applying in Courland province. . . .

11. Jews who have gone abroad without a legal exit-permit are deprived of Russian citizenship and not permitted to return to Russia.

12. Within the general area of settlement and in every place where the Jews are permitted permanent residence, they are allowed not only to move from place to place and to settle in accordance with the general regulations, but also to acquire real estate of all kinds with the exception of inhabited estates, the ownership of which is strictly forbidden to Jews. . . .

23. Every Jew must be registered according to the law in one of the legal estates of the realm. Any Jew not complying with this regulation will be treated as a vagrant.

MAX LILIENTHAL IN RUSSIA

Under Nicholas I the Russian government began to intervene in unprecedented ways into the internal workings of Jewish society. Beginning in 1827 it conscripted the Jews into the army in a manner designed specifically to erode Jewish unity; in 1844 it abolished the Jewish communal boards; in the late 1840's and 1850's it joined hands with Russian Jewish enlighteners to create new secular schools for Jewish children.

To supervise this educational reform, the government hired Dr. Max Lilienthal, a German Reform rabbi. After several years Lilienthal abandoned his Russian mission and emigrated to America where he became an important rabbi. The following selection from Lilienthal's memoirs recounts the opposition to his educational project on the part of the Jews of Minsk in 1842.

READING 6-17

On the following Sabbath I visited the synagogues, but met with the same cold and reserved treatment. Meetings were held all over the city at which the firm resolution was voiced by all present to defeat my scheme at once. It was said: "If Vilna gave ear to these dangerous reforms of the educational system it is not to be wondered at, since for many a year all misfortunes have been caused by the intrigues and irreligion of the Berliners; the better ones in the Jewish metropolis have been intimidated by the threats of godless informers, and hence the unmanly and ungodly submissiveness on the part of the Jewish authorities of Vilna. But Minsk, thank God," they continued, "is not afraid of the consequences that decided opposition will bring; we are ready for martyrdom, and by setting a glorious example to all our sister cities, we will deserve well of our religion like the heroes of old.". . .

I pitied not myself, but my friends, against whom all kinds of fanatical threats were uttered, and with an uneasy heart I went into the large rooms of the vestry at 6 o'clock in the evening.

They were crowded to the utmost. The presiding officers of the congregation were not present as yet, and the utmost disorder prevailed. The greatest indignation against the proposed reform of the schools was unanimously manifested. The leading members of the *Beth Hamidrash* [House of Study] threatened with banishment and excommunication anyone who would dare support such a frivolous scheme. The *Melamdim* [Talmud teachers] unfaltering and united like a phalanx described in gloomy colors the future punishment awaiting those who would lead the innocent children to apostacy. . . .

I could not recognize any more the usual quiet and calm of the Russian Jew; roused by fanaticism, they were like infuriated lions. I perceived the uselessness of advocating in this meeting the cause to which I had devoted my best energies. Some of my best friends, afraid of the result of this meeting and the treatment I was risking, advised me to leave the assembly, saying that they would inform me of its result at the close of the debate. . . .

The public joy over the defeat was as intense the next morning as had been the efforts to accomplish this defeat the day before. I was shunned everywhere in the streets. No one greeted me, everyone being afraid of coming in contact with him who was considered almost an outlaw; and when three days afterwards I left the city none of my friends were with me to bid me farewell. The scorn and derision of wanton children were the last sounds that accompanied me out of the city of Minsk.

"AWAKE, MY PEOPLE!"

Despite the intense opposition to modern education exhibited by the majority of East European Jewry, the Jewish Enlightenment movement did find fertile soil in Russia. Here, the striving for a modern Jewish consciousness expressed itself not in philosophy, scholarship, or movements for religious reform, as in the West, but in literature. In the mid-nineteenth century there was a remarkable explosion of Jewish creativity among Russian Jewry.

The chief exponent of the Jewish Enlightenment movement in Russia was the Hebrew poet Judah Leib Gordon (1830–92), whose poem, "Awake, My People!" was the most influential and famous expression of the belief in the possibilities of progress for the Jews in Russia.

READING 6-18

Awake, my people! How long will you slumber?
The night has passed, the sun shines bright.

Awake, lift up your eyes, look around you—
Acknowledge, I pray you, your time and your place. . . .

The land in which now we live and are born—
Is it not thought to be part of Europe?
Europe—the smallest of Earth's regions,
Yet the greatest of all in wisdom and reason.

This land of Eden [Russia] now opens its gates to you,
Her sons now call you "brother"!

How long will you dwell among them as a guest,
And why do you now affront them?

Already they have removed the weight of suffering from your shoulder,
They have lifted off the yoke from your neck,
They have erased from their hearts gratuitous hatred and folly,
They give you their hand, they greet you with peace.

Raise your head high, straighten your back,
And gaze with loving eyes upon them.
Open your heart to wisdom and knowledge,
Become an enlightened people, and speak their language.

Every man of understanding should try to gain knowledge;
Let others learn all manner of arts and crafts;
Those who are brave should serve in the army;
The farmers should buy ploughs and fields.

To the treasury of the state bring your strength,
Take your share of its possessions, its bounty.
Be a man abroad and a Jew in your tent,
A brother to your countrymen and a servant to your king. . . .

THE MAY LAWS

The Russian Jewish enlighteners' belief in liberalism and eventual emancipation was dealt a severe blow in the last two decades of the nineteenth century. In the spring of 1881, Tsar Alexander II was assassinated in the streets of St. Petersburg, and many people accused the Jews of being responsible for this terrorist act. At Easter time a series of vicious attacks against the Jews broke out; the Russian word for such an attack—pogrom—became well-known abroad. Instead of working to ameliorate the lot of the Jews the Russian government blamed them for their own misfortunes and enacted a series of laws that further restricted the Jews' mobility and economic activity. The first of these decrees was issued on May 3, 1882 as a temporary measure, but it remained in effect until the tsarist regime collapsed in 1917.

READING 6-19

The Council of Ministers, having heard the presentation made by the Minister of Internal Affairs, regarding the execution of the Temporary Regulations regarding the Jews has concluded as follows:

1. As a temporary measure, and until a general re-examination of the laws pertaining to the Jews takes place by set order, it is henceforth forbidden for Jews to settle outside the cities and townships. Existing Jewish settlements which are engaged in agricultural work are exempted [from this ban].

2. The registration of property and mortgages in the name of Jews is to be halted temporarily; the approval of the leasing by Jews of real estate beyond the

precincts of the cities and townships is also to be halted temporarily. Jews are also prohibited from administering such properties.

3. It is forbidden for Jews to engage in commerce on Sundays and Christian holidays. . . .

4. The regulations contained in paragraphs one through three apply to those provinces in which the Jews permanently reside.

"J'ACCUSE"

At the same time that violence erupted against Jews in Russia, a new form of hatred of the Jews emerged in Western Europe. Combining a secularized version of traditional Christian hostility to the Jews with the pseudo-science of racism, a new movement was born called anti-Semitism. The most notorious manifestation of anti-Semitism occurred in France, the birthplace of emancipation. Captain Alfred Dreyfus was falsely accused of spying for Germany and was sent to Devil's Island. Even after evidence appeared proving Dreyfus' innocence, the fact that he was Jewish was sufficient to keep him in prison. By the end of the century, the "Dreyfus Affair" was the most controversial issue in French politics, splitting the nation into two camps. The famous writer Emile Zola stood at the head of the growing pro-Dreyfus forces after publishing a sharp attack on the government's handling of the case. The following is from Zola's letter to the French president.

READING 6-20

LETTER TO M. FÉLIX FAURE, PRESIDENT OF THE REPUBLIC

MONSIEUR LE PRÉSIDENT:

. . . I accuse Lieutenant-Colonel du Paty de Clam of having been the diabolical workman of judicial error—unconsciously, I am willing to believe—and of having then defended his calamitous work, for three years, by the most guilty machinations.

I accuse General Mercier of having made himself an accomplice, at least through weakness of mind, in one of the greatest iniquities of the century.

I accuse General Billot of having had in his hands certain proofs of the innocence of Dreyfus, and of having stifled them; of having rendered himself guilty of his crime of *lèse-humanité* and *lèse-justice* for a political purpose, and to save the compromised staff.

I accuse General de Boisdeffre and General Gonse of having made themselves accomplices in the same crime, one undoubtedly through clerical passion, the other perhaps through the *espirit de corps* which makes the war offices the Holy Ark, unassailable.

I accuse General de Pellieux and Major Ravary of having conducted a rascally inquiry—I mean by that a monstrously partial inquiry, of which we have, in the report of the latter, an imperishable monument of naïve audacity.

I accuse the three experts in handwriting, Belhomme, Varinard, and Couard, of having made lying and fraudulent reports, unless a medical examination should declare them afflicted with diseases of the eye and of the mind.

I accuse the war offices of having carried on in the press, particularly in *L'Éclair* and in *L'Écho de Paris*, an abominable campaign, to mislead opinion and cover up their faults.

I accuse, finally, the first council of war of having violated the law by condemning an accused person on the strength of a secret document, and I accuse the second council of war of having covered this illegality, in obedience to orders, in committing in its turn the judicial crime of knowingly acquitting a guilty man.

In preferring these charges, I am not unaware that I lay myself liable under Articles 30 and 31 of the press law of July 29, 1881, which punishes defamation. And it is willfully that I expose myself thereto.

As for the people whom I accuse, I do not know them, I have never seen them, I entertain against them no feeling of revenge or hatred. They are to me simple entities, spirits of social ill-doing. And the act that I perform here is nothing but a revolutionary measure to hasten the explosion of truth and justice.

I have but one passion, the passion for the light, in the name of humanity which has suffered so much, and which is entitled to happiness. My fiery protest is simply the cry of my soul. Let them dare, then, to bring me into the Assize Court, and let the investigation take place in the open day.

I await it.

Accept, *Monsieur le Président*, the assurance of my profound respect.

ÉMILE ZOLA

THE BIRTH OF ZIONISM

As a result of the "Dreyfus Affair," grave doubts began to gnaw at the self-confidence of the Jews of Western Europe: how could anti-Semitism explode with such fury in France of all places? These doubts combined with the search for a new kind of Jewish identity that had emerged in Russia even before the pogroms. Young Jews inspired by modern European nationalism despaired of the optimistic liberalism of their parents. They began to argue for the self-emancipation of the Jews.

After the pogroms, these ideas coalesced into a movement that argued that the only solution to anti-Semitism was the return of the Jews to the Land of Israel. This movement lacked coherence and effective leadership until Theodor Herzl, a Western European Jewish journalist covering the Dreyfus trial, came to similar conclusions independently. Herzl began to organize the Jews in the West and East who agreed with him and created the Zionist movement. The following selections are from *The Jewish State*, his blueprint for a Jewish homeland that was published in 1896.

READING 6-21

The idea which I develop in this pamphlet is an age-old one: the establishment of a Jewish State.

The world resounds with outcries against the Jews, and this is what awakens the dormant idea.

I am inventing nothing: let the reader bear this in mind particularly and at every point of my exposition. I am inventing neither the situation of the Jews, which has become a matter of history, nor the means to remedy it. The material components of the edifice I am sketching are in existence and within easy reach; any one can convince himself of that. If, therefore, anyone should wish to designate this attempt at a solution of the Jewish Question with a single word, it should not be called a "fantasy" but, conceivably, a "scheme." . . .

The Jewish Question exists. It would be foolish to deny it. It is an atavistic bit of medievalism which the civilized nations have not been able to shake off to this day, try as they might. They did show a magnanimous desire to do so when they emancipated us. The Jewish Question exists wherever Jews live in appreciable numbers. Where it does not exist, it is brought in together with Jewish immigrants. Naturally we move where we are not persecuted; our appearance then gives rise to persecution. This is a fact and is bound to remain a fact everywhere, even in highly developed countries—France is a case in point—as long as the Jewish Question is not solved politically. The unfortunate Jews are now importing anti-Semitism into England; they have already introduced it into America.

I believe I understand anti-Semitism, a highly complex movement. I view it from the standpoint of a Jew, but without hatred or fear. I think I can discern in it the elements of vulgar sport, of common economic rivalry, of inherited prejudice, of religious intolerance—but also of a supposed need for self-defense. To my mind, the Jewish Question is neither a social nor a religious one, even though it may assume these and other guises. It is a national question, and to solve it we must first of all establish it as an international political problem which will have to be settled by the civilized nations of the world in council.

We are a people, *one* people.

Everywhere we have sincerely endeavored to merge with the national communities surrounding us and to preserve only the faith of our fathers. We are not permitted to do so. . . .

Persecutions are no longer as vicious as they were in the Middle Ages? True, but our sensitivity has increased, so that we feel no diminution in our suffering. Prolonged persecution has overstrained our nerves.

And will some people say that the venture is hopeless, because even if we obtain the land and the sovereignty only the poor people will go along? They are the very ones we need first! Only desperate men make good conquerors.

Will anybody say, Oh yes, if it were possible it would have been done by now?

It was not possible before. It is possible now. As recently as a hundred, even fifty years ago it would have been a dream. Today it is all real. The rich, who have an epicurean acquaintance with all technical advances, know very well what can be done with money. And this is how it will be: Precisely the poor and plain people, who have no idea of the power that man already exercises over the forces of Nature, will have the greatest faith in the new message. For they have never lost their hope of the Promised Land.

Here it is, Jews! No fairy tale, no deception! Everyone may convince himself of it, for every man will carry over with him a little piece of the Promised Land: one in his brain, another in his brawn, a third in the possessions he has acquired.

Now, all this may seem to be a long-drawn-out affair. Even in the most favorable circumstances it might be many years before the founding of the State is under way. In the meantime, Jews will be ridiculed, offended, abused, whipped, plundered, and slain in a thousand different localities. But no; just as soon as we begin to implement the plan, anti-Semitism will immediately grind to a halt everywhere. . . .

CULTURAL ZIONISM

The Zionist movement soon split into many divergent groups: some espoused socialism, others capitalism; most were secularist but a few attempted to merge Zionism with religious orthodoxy; some stressed diplomatic activity and emigration, others cultural and educational work. The leader of the "cultural Zionists" was Ahad Ha'am, a brilliant Hebrew essayist who argued that the creation of a new Hebrew culture was more important for Zionism than mass immigration or diplomatic negotiations. The following selection is a citation from one of Ahad Ha'am's sharp attacks on the Western notion of emancipation, called "Slavery in Freedom."

READING 6-22

But the truth is that if Western Jews were not slaves to their emancipation, it would never have entered their heads to consecrate their people to spiritual missions or aims before it had fulfilled that physical, natural "mission" which belongs to every organism—before it had created for itself conditions suitable to its character, in which it could develop its latent powers and aptitudes, its own particular form of life, in a normal manner, and in obedience to the demands of its nature. Then, and only then, after all this had been achieved—then and only then, we may well believe, its development might lead it in course of time to some field of work in which it would be specially fitted to act as teacher, and thus contribute once again to the general good of humanity, in a way suited to the spirit of the modern world. And if *then* philosophers tell us that in this field of work lies the "mission" of our people, for which it was created, I shall not, indeed, be able to subscribe to their view; but I shall not quarrel with them on a mere question of terminology.

But alas! I shall doubtless be dead and buried before then. To-day, while I am still alive, I try mayhap to give my weary eyes a rest from the scene of ignorance, of degradation, of unutterable poverty that confronts me here in Russia, and find comfort by looking yonder across the border, where there are Jewish professors, Jewish members of Academies, Jewish officers in the army, Jewish civil servants; and when I see there, behind the glory and the grandeur of it all, a twofold spiritual slavery—moral slavery and intellectual slavery—and ask myself: Do I envy these fellow-Jews of mine their emancipation?—I answer, in all truth and sincerity: No! a thousand times No! The privileges are not worth the price! I may not be emancipated; but at least I have not sold my soul for emancipation. I at least can proclaim from the housetops that my kith and kin are dear to me wherever they are, without being constrained to find forced and unsatisfactory excuses. I at least can remember Jerusalem at other times than those of "divine service": I can mourn for its loss, in public or in private, without being asked what Zion is to me, or I to Zion. I at least have no need to exalt my people to Heaven, to trumpet its superiority above all other nations, in order to find a justification for its existence. I at least know "why I remain a Jew"—or, rather, I can find no meaning in such a question, any more than if I were asked why I remain my father's son. I at least can speak my mind concerning the beliefs and the opinions which I have inherited from my ancestors, without fearing to snap the bond that unites me to my people. I can even adopt that "scientific heresy which bears the name of Darwin," without any danger to my Judaism.

In a word, I am my own, and my opinions and feelings are my own. I have no reason for concealing or denying them, for deceiving others or myself. And this spiritual freedom—scoff who will!—I would not exchange or barter for all the emancipation in the world.

DIASPORA NATIONALISM

Other modern Jewish nationalists argued that the Zionist dream was hopelessly impractical. Instead, the Jews should strive to achieve cultural and national autonomy in the countries of Europe. This "Diaspora Nationalism" was shared by a group of liberals led by the important Jewish historian Simon Dubnov and by a growing number of Jewish socialists in Russia, who argued that national autonomy for the Jews and freedom for all oppressed peoples could only come about by means of a socialist revolution. These Jewish socialists founded the Jewish Workers' Bund which became an important political party.

Dubnov and his followers created a liberal "Autonomist" party based on the premise that nationalism had progressed to the point at which territory was superfluous. Dubnov argued this position in his "Letters on Old and New Judaism," a selection from which follows:

READING 6-23

All that has been presented in this Letter leads us to the following general theses:

(1) A nationality, in its over-all development, is a cultural-historical collectivity whose members are united originally by common descent, language, territory, and state, but who after some time reach a spiritual unity based upon a common cultural heritage, historical traditions, common spiritual and social ideals and other typical characteristics of development.

(2) A nationality which went through all these stages of development in the past, which disposes of a store of common ideas, sentiments and needs in the present, and which gives expression to aspirations of independent development in the future must have autonomy in one form or another (political or social or cultural), in keeping with its position in the family of nations.

(3) The consciousness of the nationality itself is the main criterion of its existence. "I think of myself as a nationality—therefore I am" is the formula of the national-cultural group. This consciousness manifests itself concretely in the strengthening of the national will to protect and defend its autonomy in its various social forms. A nationality which lacks the defensive protection of state or territory develops, instead, forces of inner defense and employs its national energy to strengthen the social and spiritual factors for unity which serve it as weapons in the struggle for national survival.

(4) The Jewish nationality which fulfills all these conditions is the highest type of cultural-historical or spiritual nation. Its long and unique historical development toughened the nation and energized its vital strength even though it had neither a unified state nor a territory. It will continue to exist as a nationality and strengthen

its national will as it has done in the past, although the forms will be different and more in keeping with modern cultural conditions.

(5) In point of fact, the Jewish people exists as a cultural nationality in the consciousness of the majority of its members who still think of themselves as a "religious nation" since national culture was identified with religion, and since religion dominated the life of the people for many generations. The inevitable secularization of the national idea will in due time change the traditional religious consciousness into the historical evolutionary consciousness. The rejection of Jewish nationality in favor of the concept of a "religious group" ("the Jews are a religious group among every nation of the world") is rooted in assimilation and represents merely an attempt of certain parts of Diaspora Jewry to fuse with the ruling people. . . .

(6) The teachings of Judaism, the creation of a national culture, approximate the culture of humanity through the principle of evolutionary development and not of tradition. The rejection of Judaism in this form by means of a change of religion means in fact exodus from the national community, separation from the congregation of Israel.

(7) Morally, Jewish nationalism must be understood as a manifestation of national individualism which has no connection whatever with national egotism.

These theses, presented thus far only in theoretical formulation, will be clarified in detail in the following Letters on the basis of data drawn from life in the past as well as the present.

(1897–1906).

MODERN JEWISH CULTURE

The founding of new Jewish parties and movements was paralleled by the increased prominence of Jews in European politics, just as the creation of a modern Jewish culture in Hebrew and Yiddish was matched by the centrality of Jews in modern European culture.

The following selection is a portion of one of the most powerful poems in modern Hebrew, "The City of Slaughter," written by the great Hebrew poet Hayyim Nahman Bialik, in response to the Kishinev pogrom of 1903.

READING 6-24

Arise and go now to the city of slaughter;
Into its courtyard wind thy way;
There with thine own hand touch, and with the eyes of thine head,
Behold on tree, on stone, on fence, on mural clay,
The spattered blood and dried brains of the dead.
Proceed thence to the ruins, the split walls reach,
Where wider grows the hollow, and greater grows the breach;
Pass over the shattered hearth, attain the broken wall
Whose burnt and barren brick, whose charred stones reveal
The open mouths of such wounds, that no mending
Shall ever mend, nor healing ever heal.

There will thy feet in feathers sink, and stumble
On wreckage doubly wrecked, scroll heaped on manuscript,
Fragments again fragmented—
Pause not upon this havoc; go thy way.
The perfumes will be wafted from the acacia bud
And half its blossoms will be feathers,
Whose smell is the smell of blood! . . .

Then wilt thou flee to a yard, observe its mound.
Upon the mound lie two, and both are headless—
A Jew and his hound.
The self-same axe struck both, and both were flung
Unto the self-same heap where swine seek dung;
Tomorrow the rain will wash their mingled blood
Into the runnels, and it will be lost
In rubbish heap, in stagnant pool, in mud.
Its cry will not be heard.
It will descend into the deep, or water the cockle-burr.
And all things will be as they ever were.

Descend then, to the cellars of the town,
There where the virginal daughters of thy folk were fouled,
Where seven heathen flung a woman down,
The daughter in the presence of her mother,
The mother in the presence of her daughter,
Before slaughter, during slaughter, and after slaughter!
Touch with thy hand the cushion stained; touch
The pillow incarnadined:
This is the place the wild ones of the wood, the beasts of the field
With bloody axes in their paws compelled thy daughters yield:
Beasted and swined!

Note also do not fail to note,
In that dark corner, and behind that cask
Crouched husbands, bridegrooms, brothers, peering from the cracks,
Watching the sacred bodies struggling underneath
The bestial breath,
Stifled in filth, and swallowing their blood!
Watching from the darkness and its mesh
The lecherous rabble portioning for booty
Their kindred and their flesh!

Crushed in their shame, they saw it all;
They did not stir nor move;
They did not pluck their eyes out; they
Beat not their brains against the wall!
Perhaps, perhaps, each watcher had it in his heart to pray:
A miracle, O Lord,—and spare my skin this day!
Those who survived this foulness, who from their blood awoke,
Beheld their life polluted, the light of their world gone out—

How did their menfolk bear it, how did they bear this yoke?
They crawled forth from their holes, they fled to the house of the Lord,
They offered thanks to Him, the sweet benedictory word.
The *Cohanim* [priests] sallied forth, to the Rabbi's house they flitted:
Tell me, O Rabbi, tell, is my own wife permitted?
The matter ends; and nothing more.
And all is as it was before.

Come, now, and I will bring thee to their lairs
The privies, jakes and pigpens where the heirs
Of Hasmoneans lay, with trembling knees,
Concealed and cowering,—the sons of the Maccabees!
The seed of saints, the scions of the lions!
Who, crammed by scores in all the sanctuaries of their shame,
So sanctified My name!
It was the flight of mice they fled,
The scurrying of roaches was their flight;
They died like dogs, and they were dead!
And on the next morn, after the terrible night
The son who was not murdered found
The spurned cadaver of his father on the ground.
Now wherefore dost thou weep, O son of man? . . .

7

The Golden Land
(1654 to 1932)

Michael Stanislawski

The millions of Jews who flocked to America in the years from 1881 to World War I found in their new home a vibrant Jewish community that dated back over two hundred years. After a rather inauspicious beginning, American Jewry slowly grew as successive waves of immigrants from Western, Central, and Eastern Europe were attracted to the promise of economic opportunity and political liberty.

The sources in this chapter chronicle the various stages by which America became a society uniquely receptive to Jews and American Jews became at once vital partners in the creation of America and members of the largest and freest Jewish community in the world.

RECEPTION OF THE FIRST JEWS IN AMERICA

In September 1654 twenty-three Jews from Recife in Brazil arrived in New Amsterdam—the first known Jewish settlers in America. The Dutch governor of New Amsterdam, Peter Stuyvesant, petitioned his superiors in the Dutch West Indies Company for permission to deport these Jews, but permission was denied. Stuyvesant's employers were indebted to Jewish investors in Amsterdam and recognized that the Jews from Brazil had suffered enough and would serve the North American colony well. The Jews were allowed to remain but not to practice their faith in public.

READING 7-1

Extract from a Certain Letter from Director Peter Stuyvesant to the Amsterdam Chamber, Dated Manhattan, September 22, 1654.

The Jews who have arrived would nearly all like to remain here, but learning that they (with their customary usury and deceitful trading with the Christians) were very repugnant to the inferior magistrates, as also to the people having the most affection for you; the Deaconry also fearing that owing to their present indigence they might become a charge in the coming winter, we have, for the benefit of this weak and newly developing place and the land in general, deemed it useful to require them in a friendly way to depart; praying also most seriously in this connection, for ourselves as also for the general community of your worships, that the deceitful race,—such hateful enemies and blasphemers of the name of Christ,—be not allowed further to infect and trouble this new colony, to the detraction of your worships and the dissatisfaction of your worships' most affectionate subjects.

THE AMERICAN CONSTITUTION

Within a century a secure and stable Jewish community had arisen in America. The religious egalitarianism of the Colonies and their acceptance of the twin beliefs in the equality of all men and the separation of church and state produced a society uniquely receptive to the Jews. After independence, the United States Constitution, adopted on September 17, 1787, and its First Amendment, enacted on November 3, 1791, certified the equality of the Jews in America without even having to mention them specifically.

READING 7-2

ARTICLE VI

. . . The Senators and Representatives before mentioned, and the Members of the several State Legislatures, and all executive and judicial Officers, both of the United States and of the several States, shall be bound by Oath or Affirmation, to support this Constitution; but no religious Test shall ever be required as a Qualification to any Office or public Trust under the United States.

Amendments *November 3, 1791*

ARTICLE I

Congress shall make no law respecting an establishment of religion, or prohibiting the free exercise thereof; or abridging the freedom of speech, or of the press; or the right of the people peaceably to assemble, and to petition the government for a redress of grievances.

BENJAMIN RUSH AT A JEWISH WEDDING

From the start American Jewry was not only legally free but also well integrated into American society. The following passage is from a letter by Benjamin Rush, a prominent physician and politician, in which he described a Jewish wedding he attended in Philadelphia in 1787. Rush's comments testify to the cordial relations between the Jews and non-Jews in America.

READING 7-3

My dear Julia,   Philadelphia, June 27, 1787

Being called a few days ago to attend in the family of Jonas Phillips, I was honored this morning with an invitation to attend the marriage of his daughter to a young man of the name of LEVY from Virginia. I accepted the invitation with great pleasure, for you know I love to be in the way of adding to my stock of ideas upon all subjects.

At 1 o'clock the company, consisting of 30 or 40 men, assembled in Mr. Phillips' common parlor, which was accommodated with benches for the purpose. The ceremony began with prayers in the Hebrew language, which were chaunted by an old rabbi and in which he was followed by the whole company. As I did not understand a word except now and then an Amen or Hallelujah, my attention was directed to the haste with which they covered their heads with their hats as soon as the prayers began, and to the freedom with which some of them conversed with each other during the whole time of this part of their worship. As soon as these prayers were ended, which took up about 20 minutes, a small piece of parchment was produced, written in Hebrew, which contained a deed of settlement and which the groom subscribed in the presence of four witnesses. In this deed he conveyed a part of his fortune to his bride, by which she was provided for after his death in case she survived him. This ceremony was followed by the erection of a beautiful canopy composed of white and red silk in the middle of the floor. It was supported by four young men (by means of four poles), who put on white gloves for the purpose. As soon as this canopy was fixed, the bride, accompanied with her mother, sister, and a long train of female relations, came downstairs. Her face was covered with a veil which reached halfways down her body. She was handsome at all times, but the occasion and her dress rendered her in a peculiar manner a most lovely and affecting object. I gazed with delight upon her. Innocence, modesty, fear, respect, and devotion appeared all at once in her countenance. She was led by her two bridesmaids under the canopy. Two young men led the bridegroom after her and placed him, not by her side, but directly opposite to her. The priest now began again to chaunt an Hebrew prayer, in which he was followed by part of the company. After this he gave to the groom and bride a glass full of wine, from which they each sipped about a teaspoonful. Another prayer followed this act, after which he took a ring and directed the groom to place it upon the finger of his bride in the same manner as is practised in the marriage service of the Church of England. This ceremony was followed by handing the wine to the father of the bride and then a second time to the bride and groom. The groom after sipping the wine took the glass in his hand and threw it upon a large pewter dish which was suddenly placed at his feet. Upon its breaking into a number of small pieces, there was a general shout of joy and a declaration that the ceremony was over. The groom now saluted his bride, and kisses and congratulations became general through the room. I asked the meaning, after the ceremony was over, of the canopy and of the drinking of the wine and breaking of the glass. I was told by one of the company that in Europe they generally marry in the open air, and that the canopy was introduced to defend the bride and groom from the action of the sun and from rain. Their mutually partaking of the same glass of wine was intended to denote the mutuality of their goods, and the breaking of the glass at the conclusion of the business was designed to teach them the brittleness and uncertainty of human life and the certainty of death, and thereby to temper and moderate their present joys.

Mr. Phillips pressed me to stay and dine with the company, but business and Dr. Hall's departure, which was to take place in the afternoon, forbade it. I stayed, however, to eat some wedding cake and to drink a glass of wine with the guests. Upon going into one of the rooms upstairs to ask how Mrs. Phillips did, who had fainted downstairs under the pressure of the heat (for she was weak from a previous indisposition), I discovered the bride and groom supping a bowl of broth together. Mrs. Phillips apologized for them by telling me they had eaten nothing (agreeably to the custom prescribed by their religion) since the night before.

Upon my taking leave of the company, Mrs. Phillips put a large piece of cake into my pocket for you, which she begged I would present to you with her best compliments. She says you are an old New York acquaintance of hers.

During the whole of this new and curious scene my mind was not idle. I was carried back to the ancient world and was led to contemplate the passovers, the sacrifices, the jubilees, and other ceremonies of the Jewish Church. After this, I was led forward into futurity and anticipated the time foretold by the prophets when this once-beloved race of men shall again be restored to the divine favor and when they shall unite with Christians with one heart and one voice in celebrating the praises of a common and universal Saviour.

LETTER OF NEWPORT SYNAGOGUE TO GEORGE WASHINGTON

As a symbol of their unique status in world Jewry, the Jews of Newport, Rhode Island, greeted George Washington, the first President, to their congregation. The following is the address made to Washington on August 17, 1790.

READING 7-4

Sir:—Permit the children of the stock of Abraham to approach you with the most cordial affection and esteem for your person and merit, and to join with our fellow-citizens in welcoming you to Newport.

With pleasure we reflect on those days of difficulty and danger when the God of Israel, who delivered David from the peril of the sword, shielded your head in the day of battle; and we rejoice to think that the same spirit which rested in the bosom of the greatly beloved Daniel, enabling him to preside over the provinces of the Babylonian Empire, rests and ever will rest upon you, enabling you to discharge the arduous duties of the Chief Magistrate of these States.

Deprived as we hitherto have been of the invaluable rights of free citizens, we now—with a deep sense of gratitude to the Almighty Disposer of all events—behold a government erected by the majesty of the people—a government which to bigotry gives no sanction, to persecution no assistance, but generously affording to all liberty of conscience and immunities of citizenship, deeming every one of whatever nation, tongue or language, equal parts of the great governmental machine.

This so ample and extensive Federal Union, whose base is philanthropy, mutual confidence and public virtue, we cannot but acknowledge to be the work of the great God who rules in the armies of the heavens and among the inhabitants of the earth, doing whatever seemeth to Him good.

For all the blessings of civil and religious liberty which we enjoy under an equal and benign administration, we desire to send up our thanks to the Ancient of days, the great Preserver of men, beseeching Him that the angels who conducted our forefathers through the wilderness into the promised land may graciously conduct you through all the difficulties and dangers of this mortal life; and when, like Joshua, full of days and full of honors, you are gathered to your fathers, may you be admitted into the heavenly paradise to partake of the water of life and the tree of immortality.

Done and signed by order of the Hebrew Congregation in Newport, Rhode Island.   MOSES SEIXAS, *Warden*
NEWPORT, *August* 17, 1790.

GEORGE WASHINGTON'S REPLY

The President responded with an eloquent reaffirmation of the principles of religious and political liberty.

READING 7-5

Gentlemen:—While I received with much satisfaction your address replete with expressions of esteem, I rejoice in the opportunity of assuring you that I shall always retain grateful remembrance of the cordial welcome I experienced on my visit to Newport from all classes of citizens.

The reflection on the days of difficulty and danger which are past is rendered the more sweet from a consciousness that they are succeeded by days of uncommon prosperity and security.

If we have wisdom to make the best use of the advantages with which we are now favored, we cannot fail, under the just administration of a good government, to become a great and happy people.

The citizens of the United States of America have a right to applaud themselves for having given to mankind examples of an enlarged and liberal policy—a policy worthy of imitation. All possess alike liberty of conscience and immunities of citizenship.

It is now no more that toleration is spoken of as if it were the indulgence of one class of people that another enjoyed the exercise of their inherent natural rights, for, happily, the Government of the United States, which gives to bigotry no factions [sanctions], to persecution no assistance, requires only that they who live under its protection should demean themselves as good citizens in giving it on all occasions their effectual support.

It would be inconsistent with the frankness of my character not to avow that I am pleased with your favorable opinion of my administration and fervent wishes for my felicity.

May the children of the stock of Abraham who dwell in this land continue to merit and enjoy the good will of the other inhabitants—while every one shall sit in safety under his own vine and fig tree and there shall be none to make him afraid.

May the father of all mercies scatter light, and not darkness, upon our paths, and make us all in our several vocations useful here, and in His own due time and way everlastingly happy.

                                                            G. WASHINGTON

COMMENCEMENT ADDRESS OF A COLUMBIA COLLEGE GRADUATE, 1800

The social integration of American Jewry was based on the essential religious pluralism of the new country. This tolerance was fortified by the Puritans' cultivation of the Hebrew language and biblical religion. Both these phenomena are evidenced in the following address given in Hebrew by Sampson Simson at the Commencement of Columbia College in 1800.

READING 7-6

Translation of Hebrew Address by Sampson Simson at the Commencement of Columbia College in the Year 1800

One of the professors of Columbia College has requested me to write something for Master Sampson to speak in public in the holy tongue on Commencement day, should you not object to his request.

Although not accustomed to speak in public, I rise with perfect confidence that you will kindly consent to listen to me and I earnestly crave your indulgence for any error I may commit in the course of my address. And if I have found grace in your eyes I shall essay to speak concerning my brethren residing in this land. It is now more than 150 years, since Israelites first came to this country, at the time when this province was under the dominion of Holland, but until now no one of them or their children has on a similar occasion been permitted thus to address a word in public, and I am a descendant of one of those who were among the first settlers here. It is known to you, that at the time when this province, then called New Amsterdam, was exchanged for the colony of Surinam, all the inhabitants remaining here came under the dominion of England. Among them were the Jews who until then could only congregate for worship in private rooms in their own dwellings until the year 5490 [1730] (according as we reckon in this city of New York). It was then that our regular Synagogue was built, where we have been serving Almighty God unmolested for upwards of seventy years. During this long period the Jews have not been as numerous as the other sects, for only few in number they came hither; but now, behold the Lord has enlarged and increased in this and in all the other provinces of these United States the descendants of those few families that came from Holland in the year 5420 [1660], one hundred and forty years ago. Among these was one man with his wife, one son and four daughters. The father and son died soon after they had reached this place, leaving the wife with her four daughters and behold they have exalted themselves in this city, and from them sprang forth many of the Congregation now known as "Shearith Israel". Afterwards, in the year 1696, there came from France some families by the way of England, who brought with them letters of denization from the king, constituting them freemen throughout all the provinces under his dominion. And in the year 1776 at the time when the people of this country stood up like one man in the cause of liberty and independence every Israelite that was among them rose up likewise and united in their efforts to promote the Country's peace & prosperity. And even now we endeavor to sustain the government of these provinces, free of any allegiance to any other whatsoever, monarchial or republican, and we exclaim in the language of King David, "Rid us, (O Lord!) from the hand of the children of the stranger, whose mouth speaketh vanity and whose right hand is the right hand of falsehood."

THE MARYLAND "JEW BILL"

Despite the legal equality assured by the federal Constitution, various states restricted the Jews from certain public offices. Most often these restrictions remained on the books but were not enforced. Soon they were formally rescinded. The following is the first form of the Maryland bill abolishing the restrictions; the final version was adopted in 1826.

READING 7-7

The First Form of the "Jew Bill," 1819

To extend to the sect of people professing the Jewish Religion the same rights and privileges that are enjoyed by Christians.

WHEREAS, It is the acknowledged right of all men to worship God according to the dictates of their own consciences. And whereas, it is declared by the thirty-sixth section of the bill of rights of this state, "That the manner of administering an oath to any person ought to be such as those of the religious persuasion, profession, or denomination of which such person is one, generally esteem the most effectual confirmation by the attestation of the divine Being. And whereas, religious tests for civil employment, though intended as a barrier against the depraved, frequently operate as a restraint upon the conscientious; and as the constitution of the United States requires no religious qualification for civil office, Therefore,

Sec. 1. *Be it enacted, By the General Assembly of Maryland,* That no religious test, declaration or subscription of opinion as to religion, shall be required from any person of the sect called Jews, as a qualification to hold or exercise any office or employment of profit or trust in this state.

Sec. 2. *And be it enacted,* That every oath to be administered to any person of the sect of people called Jews, shall be administered on the five books of Moses, agreeably to the religious education of that people, and not otherwise.

Sec. 3. *And be it enacted,* That if this act shall be confirmed by the General Assembly, after the next election of delegates, in the first session after such new election, as the constitution and form of government direct; that in such case, this act and the alterations and amendments of the constitution and form of government therein contained, shall be taken and considered, and shall constitute and be valid as part of the said constitution and form of government, to all intents and purposes, any thing in the declaration of rights, constitution and form of government contained, to the contrary notwithstanding.

Sec. 4. *And be it enacted,* That the several clauses and sections of the declaration of rights, constitution and form of government, and every part of any law of this state, contrary to the provisions of this act, so far as respects the sect of people aforesaid, shall be, and the same is hereby declared to be repealed and annulled on the confirmation hereof.

A JEWISH PEDDLER IN NEW ENGLAND

Between 1820 and 1870, 150,000 Jews from Germany came to the United States to escape narrowing economic opportunities and disappointing political conditions. These new immigrants eagerly spread out across the continent, peddling dry goods. Very quickly the peddlers were successful and became prominent merchants in large and small towns throughout the length and breadth of the United States. The following, written in 1842, is a selection from the diary of a typical German-Jewish peddler.

READING 7-8

Peddling in New England

Last week in the vicinity of Plymouth I met two peddlers, Lehman and Marx. Marx knew me from Fürth, and that night we stayed together at a farmer's house. After supper we started singing, and I sat at the fireplace, thinking of all my past and of my family. . . .

Today, Sunday, October 16th, we are here in North Bridgewater, and I am not so downcast as I was two weeks ago. The devil has settled 20,000 shoemakers here, who do not have a cent of money. Suppose, after all, I were a soldier in Bavaria; that would have been a bad lot. I will accept three years in America instead. But I could not stand it any longer.

As far as the language is concerned, I am getting along pretty well. But I don't like to be alone. The Americans are funny people. Although they sit together by the dozen in taverns, they turn their backs to each other, and no one talks to anybody else. Is this supposed to be the custom of a republic? I don't like it. Is this supposed to be the fashion of the nineteenth century? I don't like it either. "Wait a little! There will be more things you won't like." Thus I can hear my brother talking.

The week from the 16th to the 22nd of October found me feeling pretty cheerful, for I expected to meet my brother. Ah, it is wonderful to have a brother in this land of hypocrisy, guile, and fraud! How glad I was to meet my two brothers in Boston on Saturday, the 22nd! Now I was not alone in this strange country.

How much more could I write about this queer land! It likes comfort extremely. The German, by comparison, hardly knows the meaning of the word. The wife of an American farmer can consider herself more important than the wife of a Bavarian judge. For hours she can sit in her rocking chair shaking back and forth as she thinks of nothing but beautiful clothes and fine hairdo. The farmer, himself, unlike the German farmer who works every minute, is able to sit down for a few hours every day, reading his paper and smoking his cigar. . . .

This week I went, together with my brother Juda, from Boston to Worcester. We were both delighted, for the trip was a welcome change from our daily heavy work. Together we sat in the grass for hours, recalling the wonderful years of our youth. And in bed, too, we spent many hours in talking.

Today, the 30th of October, we are here in Northborough, and I feel happier than I have for a fortnight. Moses is in New York, and we will meet him, God willing, at Worcester on Tuesday. The sky is clear and cloudless, and nature is so lovely and romantic, the air so fresh and wholesome, that I praise God, who has created this beautiful country.

Yet, at the same time, I regret that the people here are so cold and that their watchword seems to be "Help yourself: that's the best help." I cannot believe that a man who adapts himself to the language, customs, and character of America can ever quite forget his home in the European countries. Having been here so short a time, I should be very arrogant if I were to set down at this time my judgments on America. The whole country, however, with its extensive domestic and foreign trade, its railroads, canals and factories, looks to me like an adolescent youth. He is a part of society, talking like a man and pretending to be a man. Yet he is truly only a boy. That is America! Although she appears to know everything, her knowledge of religion, history, and human nature is, in truth, very elementary. . . . American history is composed of Independence and Washington: that is all! On Sunday the

American dresses up and goes to church, but he thinks of God no more than does the horse that carries him there.

It seems impossible that this nation can remain a republic for many years. Millions and millions of dollars go each year to Europe, but only for the purchase of luxuries. Athens and Rome fell at the very moment of their flowering, for though commerce, art, and science had reached their highest level, luxury—vases of gold and silver, garments of purple and silk—caused their downfall. The merchant who seeks to expand too rapidly in his first years, whose expenses are not balanced by his income, is bound to become a bankrupt. America consumes too much, produces too little. Her inhabitants are lazy and too much accustomed to providing for their own comforts to create a land which will provide for their real and their spiritual needs. . . .

On Monday the 12th to Lyndeborough; Tuesday to Wilton; Wednesday to Mason Village; Thursday, New Ipswich; Friday, Ashburnham. On Saturday we came to Westminster, where we stayed over Sunday, the 18th of December. It was extremely cold this week, and there was more snow than we had ever seen in our lives. At some places the snow was three to four feet deep, and we could hardly get through with the sleigh. How often we thanked God that we did not have to carry our wares on our backs in this cold. To tramp with a heavy pack from house to house in this weather would be terrible.

O youth of Bavaria, if you long for freedom, if you dream of life here, beware, for you shall rue the hour you embarked for a country and a life far different from what you dream of. This land—and particularly this calling—offers harsh, cold air, great masses of snow, and people who are credulous, filled with silly pride, cold toward foreigners and toward all who do not speak the language perfectly. And, though "money is beauty, scarce everywhere," yet there is still plenty of it in the country. The Whig government, the new bankruptcy law, the high tariff bill—all combine to create a scarcity of ready cash the like of which I have never seen nor the oldest inhabitants of the land ever experienced.

A JEWISH SOLDIER IN THE CONFEDERATE ARMY

The German Jews rapidly adapted to America and even took on the regional coloration of the areas in which they lived. There were self-identified northern Jews and southern Jews, mid-westerners, and Californians, New Yorkers, and Bostonians. Indeed, when the Confederacy seceded in 1861, Jews were identified with both causes in the struggle, fought under both flags, and died on both sides. The following is a selection from the memoirs of Albert Moses Luria, who was born in Charleston, South Carolina, in 1843, was a second lieutenant in the Confederate Army, and died from a head wound at the Battle of Seven Pines (Fair Oaks) in May, 1862.

READING 7-9

One Saturday morning, the twentieth of April, 1861, I was sitting with the rest of the family around the breakfast table [at the Esquiline plantation, Columbus, Ga.]. We had finished, but were then only talking of one little matter and another, some standing, some sitting, when suddenly old Simmons, Cousin Edwin's boy [slave], appeared with a note from E. W. M. [Edwin Warren Moïse, a Columbus, Ga., lawyer] saying that our company was to leave for Norfolk, Va., that afternoon at four o'clock. It was then near eight in the morning, and the note stated that our company would have a call meeting at 10:00 A.M. So I had to hurry up and pack my trunk and say good-bye and get to town, five miles, in about two hours. I was very glad that my departure from home occurred under such circumstances, for I have always dreaded parting scenes.

I went into Columbus that morning and on my way stopped at Cousin Edwin's to bid adieu to his household. I saw them all and bade them an affectionate fare-well, having seen them as I thought then for the last time. But after getting in town, I made all my preparations and joined my company, [the] City Light Guards, [under] Captain Colquitt . . . at the armory, from which we marched to the depot, where we were met by an immense concourse of citizens, assembled to bid us God-speed. Among them were all the girls from home and Cousin Edwin's, except Alice [the sister of his sweetheart Eliza], come to bid me adieu.

I did not anticipate seeing them, for as it was Saturday I knew they could not ride and hardly expected that they would pay me the compliment of *walking in*. [Orthodox Jews do not ride on the Sabbath.] As I bade adieu to Azile her whole soul pressure of my hand was all that I could bear. I kissed her, and whispering a "God bless you," turned off, leaving home and friends with a happy heart, for I felt then and feel now that time cannot abate the warmth of her affection, and I felt fully that her feelings would undergo no change. No apprehension on that score has ever crossed my mind. However, I got on the trail and was soon hurrying off to Virginia, where I was to figure among mounted men and dashing youths. . . .

January, 1862.   Another year has passed away, another one of the semi-divisions have been swalled [swallowed] up in the grand *infinitessimos*. Time. The year of 1861 has gone! Time has gone around once more, and the click of the cog reminds us that one more part of the revolution of that great wheel has taken place. But though, hundreds of times, the cogs of the great wheel have been passed over, yet the one which represents the year 1861 will live forever, inperishable in the minds of men, long to be remembered as the year in which the great American republic found its downfall, as the period when the lovers of the great and glorious Union found that the pillars which supported the gigantic stature, the mighty fabric, had for years past been gnawed by political worms, and as the year when these pillars gave way, and the mighty republic of America fell, shattered in a thousand frag-ments.

As [John M.] Daniel, the editor of the Richmond *Examiner*, has it: "As the time when the government of the United States was crushed, not by the force of an assail-ing enemy, but by the rottenness of its own institutions." That country which was once "the land of the free and the home of the brave" is now the dominion of a military despot. That drivelling, baubling fool, Abraham Lincoln, unable to man-age the helm of the great ship of state, is governed by the whims and frivolities of a dissatisfied constituency. And the year which has but now passed away will live forever in the minds of men as the epoch at which the Southern states, having de-clared their resolution to have their rights "in the Union if they *could*, out of it if they must," were forced to accept the latter alternative, and struck the signal blow for their independence. During this year, a war has been waged which has not for circumstancial details a parallel in the pages of history, ancient or modern. Long life and prosperity to the Southern Confederacy, and the same for our first President, Jefferson Davis!!!

MASS IMMIGRATION FROM EASTERN EUROPE

The character of American Jewish life was permanently transformed by the immigration of over two million Eastern European Jews in the years 1881–1924. The following are the best statistics available about that mass migration.

READING 7-10

Jewish Immigration into the United States from 1881[1] to 1924

Year	Number	Year	Number
1881	8,193[2]	1903	76,203
1882	31,807	1904	106,236
1883	6,907	1905	129,910
1884	15,122	1906	153,748
1885	36,214	1907	149,182[4]
1886	46,967	1908	103,387
1887	56,412	1909	57,551
1888	62,619	1910	84,260
1889	55,851	1911	91,223
1890	67,450	1912	80,595
1891	111,284	1913	101,330
1892	136,742	1914	138,051
1893	68,569	1915	26,497
1894	58,833	1916	15,108
1895	65,309	1917	17,342
1896	73,255	1918	3,672
1897	43,434	1919	3,055
1898	54,630	1920	14,292
1899	37,415[3]	1921	119,036
1900	60,764	1922	53,524
1901	58,098	1923	49,989
1902	57,688	1924	10,292

[1]We have no, even approximately exact, figures of the Jewish immigration prior to 1881. Some 50,000 German Jews arrived up to 1848. No statistics are available about arrivals from central Europe after 1848. From 1869, when greater numbers of Jewish emigrants began to arrive from Russia, till 1880, an estimated total of 30,000 landed in the United States. Of smaller contingents of Jews from Austro-Hungary and Rumania who immigrated up to 1880 we have likewise no statistics.

[2]For 1881 to 1898 statistics are available only for the number of Jews admitted at the ports of New York, Philadelphia and Baltimore.

[3]For 1899 to 1907 figures are available for Jewish immigrants at all ports of the United States.

[4]Since 1908, statistics of departure as well as of arrivals have been kept on record.

THE BIRTH OF THE JEWISH UNIONS

Almost all of the new immigrants made their living in the garment trade. One of the most important features of East European immigrant life was the growth of labor unions in its midst. These organizations improved the lot of their members enormously, and were a major factor in the consolidation of the American labor movement. The following selection from the memoirs of a prominent union activist, Morris Hillquit, describes the beginnings of the Jewish unions.

READING 7-11

Aside from the roofs on Cherry Street our favorite gathering places were the East Side tea shops. There, particularly in the long winter nights, we would pass many hours talking and occasionally sipping weak tea served in tumblers, Russian style. A glass of tea and a "coffee twist" of ample proportions were, as a rule, the limit of a guest's consumption. The price of each was five cents.

I often wondered how the owners of the establishments could keep going on such meager income, and I suppose the owners were kept wondering harder than I. But they somehow managed. In some cases they were of the same kind and type as their guests, and they took it for granted that the tea shop was there not so much for drinking or eating as for discussions.

Of discussion there was plenty, but the purely vocal exercise did not long satisfy the enthusiastic young Socialists' yearning for action. They cast about for a promising field of practical work and inevitably discovered it among their own countrymen. . . . We resolved to undertake the task of bettering the lives of our laboring countrymen, of educating them to a realization of their human rights, of organizing them for resistance to their exploiters, and of securing for them tolerable conditions of labor and life.

It was a task beset with baffling difficulties. Several attempts to organize the Jewish workers of New York had been made before and had failed. A few spontaneous strikes had been quickly quelled. A few nuclei of labor unions had been stillborn. The Jewish workers seemed to be unorganizable. They had not been trained in any form of collective action in the countries of their birth. They were dull, apathetic, and unintelligent. And worst of all we did not speak their language, both figuratively and literally. Our language was Russian. The workers spoke Yiddish, a corrupted German dialect with several provincial variations. Few of us knew Yiddish well enough to embark on a campaign of propaganda. The only one among us who could speak Yiddish and did it fluently, lovingly, and artistically was Abraham Cahan, who subsequently made equally enviable places for himself in the English and Yiddish worlds of letters. Cahan was somewhat older than the rest of us. He was nearly thirty at that time, and we looked up to him with envy and respect, not only on account of his venerable age but also because of his incomparable knowledge of the language of the people.

We all began perfecting our Yiddish. Those of us who happened to know German had a somewhat easier task than those who spoke only Russian and had to labor at it word by word and idiom by idiom.

The next problem was to make contacts with the workers. This also proved a highly elusive undertaking. There were so many of them, and they were hopelessly scattered.

It would have taken decades to build a Jewish labor movement from the bottom up, educating individual workers, forming them into organized trade groups and finally uniting them into one coöperating body. We were forced to reverse the logical process and to attempt to build from the top down.

Taking the bull by the horns, we founded the "United Hebrew Trades" in October, 1888. It was a central labor body without affiliated labor unions, a mere shell within which we hoped in time to develop a solid kernel. . . .

I remember most vividly the origin and early history of the Knee Pants Makers' Union, and shall rapidly sketch them because they were typical of all tailoring trades.

In 1890 there were about one thousand knee pants makers employed in New York, all "green" and most of them illiterate. It was a sweat-shop industry *par excellence*. The work was done entirely on the contracting system. A contractor employed about ten workers on the average and usually operated his shop in his living-rooms. His sole function consisted of procuring bundles of cut garments from the manufacturer and having them made up by the workers. He did not even furnish the sewing machines. The operator provided his own machine as well as the needles and thread. The work day was endless, and the average earnings of experienced operators ran from six to seven dollars per week. Often the contractor would abscond with a week's pay; often the worker would be discharged because he was not fast enough to quit the contractor, and often he would be compelled to quit his job because of maltreatment or intolerable working conditions. Every time a knee pants maker changed contractors, he was compelled to put his sewing machine on his back and carry it through the streets to his new place of employment. It was at this point that their patience finally gave out. In the early part of 1890 they struck. The movement was spontaneous, without program, leadership, or organization. It was a blind outbreak of revolt and was destined to collapse if left to itself, sharing the fate of many similar outbursts in the past.

In this case the United Hebrew Trades stepped in during the very first hours of the strike. Through a committee of five, of whom I was one, it took complete charge of the situation.

Our first step was to hire a meeting hall large enough to accommodate all the strikers. There were about nine hundred, and we gathered them in from all shops and street corners. In the hall we held them in practically continuous session, day and night, allowing them only the necessary time to go home to sleep. We feared to let them go, lest they be tempted to return to work, and we entertained them all the time with speeches and such other forms of instruction and amusement as we could devise.

While the continuous performance was going on in the main hall, we tried to bring order and system into the strike and to organize the strikers into a solid and permanent union.

In consultation with the most intelligent men and women from the ranks of the strikers we worked out a list of demands centering upon the employer's obligation to furnish sewing machines and other work tools at his own expense. Then we chose pickets, relief committees, and settlement committees, all operating under our direct supervision and guidance.

The men did not know how to conduct meetings or transact business of any kind. They had never acted in concert. Our discourses on the principles of trade unionism and the philosophy of Socialism were interspersed with elementary lessons in parliamentary procedure and practical methods of organization. We tried to pick out the most promising among them and train them for leadership of their fellows. The strike was a course of intensive training and education, but it was of short duration. After one week without a break in the ranks of the workers, the contractors weakened; one Saturday night they became panicky and stormed the meeting hall of the strikers in a body, demanding an immediate and collective settlement on the workers' terms.

The United Hebrew Trades had scored a great victory and was encouraged to new efforts in other fields.

YOM KIPPUR BALLS

The internal controversies of East European Jewry crossed the ocean to America where they were able to develop in an atmosphere of political freedom. One of the most extreme, if colorful, ideologies was anarchism, represented in the following selection which describes an event that shocked even the least pious immigrant Jews in America.

READING 7-12

It happened in the year 1889. The Pioneers had rented the Clarendon Hall on Thirteenth Street for *Yom Kippur* eve, the night of *Kol Nidre* [the well-known prayer chanted on the eve of the Day of Atonement]. The Pioneers gave out thousands of leaflets . . . in shops and factories on the East Side. Some bolder Jewish *shkotzim* [ruffians] gave them out even near the synagogues. The leaflets called the Jewish workers to come and enjoy a pleasant evening at a ball instead of going to the synagogues to ask forgiveness for sins and transgressions which not they but their "bosses" had committed.

The announcement of the *Yom Kippur* ball fell like a bombshell in the Jewish quarter. The Orthodox element[s] were terribly upset. The very attempt at such a deed angered them deeply. This could not be possible! It just couldn't be true! It couldn't happen. They called meetings; they called on their German brethren to aid them; they turned to the Jewish politicians . . . to help prevent such sacrilege. Finally they found a "savior," one Levy, coroner of the state of New York. He made contact with powerful politicians who persuaded the police to influence the owner of the hall (a saloon keeper who depended upon police favors) to break his contract with the Pioneers and prevent the ball from taking place. The police . . . exerted pressure upon the proprietor, promised him the moon and the stars, and pledged their word that in return for this "favor" he would be rewarded. They also took it upon themselves to cover damage costs which the owner might incur.

It is almost impossible for me to describe the scene that took place around Clarendon Hall that *Yom Kippur* eve.

Thousands upon thousands of people crowded the streets . . .; many workers came with their wives and children, not knowing that the ball was canceled. Many curious people left their synagogues and came to see what would happen. In addition . . . many religious hoodlums came to fight the Lord's battle with sticks in their hands.

The owner refused to open the hall . . . A cry of protest arose which echoed in the streets. Our opponents were not silent either. They caused such a tumult that the police . . . began to scatter the crowds giving the usual excuse that they must clear the streets.

I was not a member of the Pioneers then, yet I succeeded in entering the hall. A crowd of reporters . . . encircled me and showered me with questions. I could not give them precise answers. . . .

. . . Nevertheless, the entire press came out the next morning with whole pages filled with fictitious reports in the minutest details about the extraordinary event, thereby rendering the Pioneers and their antireligious propaganda publicity which they did not think possible.

The anarchist crowd and the sympathizers gathered that night in the "locale" of the Pioneers which was situated (irony of ironies!) in a city-owned building and composed strong, moving protests. Through the night they printed these flyers and early the next morning, when the worshippers went to *shul* [synagogue], distributed them in the thousands. I, and Hilkowitch . . . who is now a lawyer, sweated over . . . this statement. The headline of the leaflet bore in large letters: "The finger of God—a policeman's club!" The text expressed the idea: "If there is a God let Him fight His own battles." It ridiculed the Orthodox who like dumb oxen were frightened to death of a red flag. Instead of appealing to God and waiting for His help, these religious fanatics appealed to the police who came to their immediate assistance.

Financially the Pioneers became rich from the canceled ball. The owner of the hall, fearing reprisal from labor organizations . . . appeased the Pioneers with . . . five hundred dollars—an oustandingly large sum for those times—and . . . because of the disrupted ball the Pioneers had gained more . . . than if it had taken place.

The complete episode, the audacity and courage of the Pioneers, formed a very strong impression on those radicals who until this point kept their distance. . . . Now, many of them came closer to the Jewish anarchist group in which they enrolled as members. I was one of them.

AMERICAN PATRIOTISM

The politics and culture of the East European immigrants were far removed from those of the German-Jewish elite. The ideology of the American Jewish establishment was based on a type of Reform Judaism that was more radical than the Reform movement in Germany. One of the leaders of American Reform, Rabbi Kaufman Kohler, explained his vision of American Jewry in the following words:

READING 7-13

For what is American Judaism, and for what does it stand? The very name has been challenged by those who assert that there is, and there should be, but *one* Judaism, Catholic Judaism, as they choose to call it, pointing to the traditional law, the Halakah, as the impregnable fortress and foundation of united Israel. As if this very law, with its diverse codes, as if this very Judaism of the centuries, was not the product of various lands and civilizations. Whether Palestinian or Babylonian, Alexandrian or Persian, Polish or Portuguese, medieval or modern, Judaism at all times received its peculiar traits, views and forms from its environments, which either broadened it or rendered it narrow and clannish. In the bright sunshine of Persian, Hellenic and Arabic culture it expanded in scope and vision to become a cosmopolitan power, giving rise to new systems of thought and higher conceptions and ideals of life. In the dreary Russian or medieval Ghetto its growth became stunted, and it deteriorated into a system of hairsplitting casuistry and superstition. True, there was wondrous sweetness and brightness behind those Ghetto walls. As the tossing billows of the ocean, built out of the very slime, cast forth by the oyster the thick shell that protects its tiny life, so did the floods of persecution and oppression render Talmudic legalism an armor or protection around Judaism to keep it intact. But how about the life when the shell opens? The wall had to give way before the trumpet blast of liberty, in order that Judaism might again thrive and rise to its full stature.

There is no room for Ghetto Judaism in America. Look at any of the creeds and churches in our free land! They are all more tolerant, more liberal, more humane and sympathetic in their mutual relations than those in Europe. Our free institutions, our common school education, our enlightening press and pulpit, with their appeal to common sense, enlarge the mental and social horizon and render progress the guiding maxim. Least of all could Judaism retain its medieval garb, its alien form, its seclusiveness, in a country that rolled off the shame and the taunt of the centuries from the shoulders of the wandering Jew, to place him, the former Pariah of the nations, alongside of the highest and the best, according to his worth and merit as *man*, and among a people that adopted the very principles of justice and human dignity proclaimed by Israel's lawgivers and prophets, and made them the foundation stones of their commonwealth. No, American Judaism must step forth, the equal of any church in broadness of view and largeness of scope, as a living truth, as an inspiring message to the new humanity that is now in the making, not as a mere memory of the past and a piece of Orientalism in the midst of vigorous, forward-pressing Occidental civilization.

American Judaism! What a power of inspiration lies in these two words! They spell the triumph of the world's two greatest principles and ideals, the consummation of mankind's choicest possessions, the one offered by the oldest, the other by the youngest of the great nations of history, the highest moral and spirtual and the highest political and social aim of humanity; the God of righteousness and holiness to unite and uplift all men and nations, and the Magna Charta of liberty and human equality to endow each individual with God-like sovereignty. . . .

IMMIGRATION BILLS, 1921 AND 1924

The split between the German and East European Jews in America was slowly healed in the wake of external problems that emerged in Europe and the United States. The Kishinev pogrom of 1903 led to concerted action by both communities, reinforced by the appearance of an American version of anti-Semitism: nativism. Most Americans rejected the racist ideology behind this movement, but nevertheless succumbed to the growing demand for the closing of the doors of the United States to further immigration from Eastern and Southern Europe. After vituperative debate, in 1921 and 1924 Congress passed the legislation reproduced in part below. The mass emigration of Jews from Russia and Poland was over just when political conditions were rapidly deteriorating there.

READING 7-14

SIXTY-SEVENTH CONGRESS. Sess. I. Ch. 8. 1921

Be it enacted by the Senate and House of Representatives of the United States of America in Congress assembled. . . .

. . . Sec. 2. (a) That the number of aliens of any nationality who may be admitted under the immigration laws to the United States in any fiscal year shall be limited to 3 per centum of the number of foreign-born persons of such nationality resident in the United States as determined by the United States census of 1910. . . .

. . . (d) When the maximum number of aliens of any nationality who may be admitted in any fiscal year under this Act shall have been admitted all other aliens of such nationality, except as otherwise provided in this Act, who may apply for admission during the same fiscal year shall be excluded. . . .

SIXTY-EIGHTH CONGRESS. Sess. I. Ch. 190. 1924.

Be it enacted by the Senate and House of Representatives of the United States of America in Congress assembled, That this Act may be cited as the "Immigration Act of 1924."

. . . Sec. 11. (a) The annual quota of any nationality shall be 2 per centum of the number of foreign-born individuals of such nationality resident in continental United States as determined by the United States census of 1890, but the minimum quota of any nationality shall be 100.

(b) The annual quota of any nationality for the fiscal year beginning July 1, 1927, and for each fiscal year thereafter, shall be a number which bears the same ratio to 150,000 as the number of inhabitants in continental United States in 1920 having that national origin (ascertained as hereinafter provided in this section) bears to the number of inhabitants in continental United States in 1920, but the minimum quota of any nationality shall be 100.

(c) For the purpose of subdivision (b) national origin shall be ascertained by determining as nearly as may be, in respect of each geographical area which under section 12 is to be treated as a separate country (except the geographical areas specified in subdivision (c) of section 4) the number of inhabitants in continental United States in 1920 whose origin by birth or ancestry is attributable to such geographical area. Such determination shall not be made by tracing the ancestors or descendants of particular individuals, but shall be based upon statistics of immigration and emigration, together with rates of increase of population as shown by successive decennial United States censuses, and such other data as may be found to be reliable.

8

Out of the Ashes
(1914 to 1945)

Michael Stanislawski

In many ways, the nineteenth century ended in 1914. The life and culture, even the national borders that millions of people knew and cherished were to be no more. The First World War and its aftermath shook European society's belief in unending progress and taught the world that the twentieth century could be the most violent yet.

The Jews of Europe, fully participating in all its dreams, squabbles, and illusions, experienced the period from 1914 to 1933 both as nationals of individual states and, uniquely, as Jews. Emancipation was triumphant throughout Europe, reaching even Russia and Poland. In many countries the integration of the Jews proceeded in ways previously unimaginable, while internal Jewish creativity thrived. Jews rose to positions of power and prominence in several European states and hope was strong that a Jewish commonwealth would be established in Palestine under British auspices.

By the late 1920's, however, signs of unprecedented danger were visible. The Nazi Party gained support and respectability in Germany; anti-Semitism became more rampant in East Central Europe; the revolutionary changes in Soviet society threatened Jewish national life in its midst; and the British became increasingly reluctant to live up to their promise of a Jewish homeland in Palestine.

From Hitler's accession to power in 1933 until the outbreak of World War II in September 1939, the Jewish world was traumatized by the eruption of anti-Semitic violence and madness in the heart of Western civilization. Emancipation was rescinded and integration abolished. But the most incredible was yet to happen: the murder of six million Jews in the course of World War II.

The selections that follow attempt to capture some of the major trends and events of this most confusing and destructive period.

THE BALFOUR DECLARATION

On November 9, 1917, *The Times* of London carried headlines proclaiming two pieces of recent news: "Palestine for the Jews" and "Lenin Seizes Power in Russia." On November 2, 1917 the British Government, in what came to be known as the "Balfour Declaration," announced its sympathy with the Zionist movement and called for the establishment of a Jewish homeland in Palestine. Five days later, the Bolsheviks seized power in Russia, overturning the Provisional Government that had ruled since March. Both these events would dramatically alter the life of Jews around the world.

Reproduced here is the Balfour Declaration, named after James Balfour, the British foreign secretary.

READING 8-1

His Majesty's Government view with favour the establishment in Palestine of a national home for the Jewish people, and will use their best endeavors to facilitate the achievement of this object, it being clearly understood that nothing shall be done which may prejudice the civil and religious rights of existing non-Jewish communities in Palestine, or the rights and political status enjoyed by Jews in any other country.

FRANZ ROSENZWEIG'S RETURN TO JUDAISM

In Weimar Germany extensive Jewish integration was matched by a significant return to Jewish culture and religiosity on the part of a small number of influential Jews. One of the most prominent of these men was Franz Rosenzweig, who became a major philosopher of modern Judaism. Selected here is a section of Rosenzweig's masterpiece, *The Star of Redemption*, dealing with "The Nations and Their States."

READING 8-2

And so the eternal people must forget the world's growth, must cease to think thereon. It must look upon the world, its own world, as complete, though the soul may yet be on the way: the soul can indeed overtake the final goal in one single leap. And if not, it must needs wait and wander on—to quote the wise Spanish proverb, "Patience, and a new shuffle of the cards." Waiting and wandering is the business of the soul, growth that of the world. It is this very growth that the eternal people denies itself. As nationality, it has reached the point to which the nations of the world still aspire. Its world has reached the goal. The Jew finds in his people the perfect fusion with a world of his own, and to achieve this fusion himself, he need not sacrifice a jot of his peculiar existence. The nations have been in a state of inner conflict ever since Christianity with its supernatural power came upon them. Ever since then, and everywhere, a Siegfried is at strife with that stranger, the man of the cross, in his very appearance so antagonizing a character. A Siegfried who, depending on the nation he comes from, may be blond and blue-eyed, or dark and small-boned, or brown and dark-eyed, wrestles again and again with this stranger who resists the continued attempts to assimilate him to that nation's own longing and vision. The Jew alone suffers no conflict between the supreme vision which is placed before his soul and the people among whom his life has placed him. He alone possesses the unity of myth which the nations lost through the influx of Christianity, which they were bound to lose, for their own myth was pagan, and, by leading them into this myth, led them away from God and their neighbor. The Jew's myth, leading him into his people, brings him face to face with God who is also the God of all nations. The Jewish people feels no conflict between what is its very own and what is supreme; the love it has for itself inevitably becomes love for its neighbor.

Because the Jewish people is beyond the contradiction that constitutes the vital drive in the life of the nations—the contradiction between national characteristics and world history, home and faith, earth and heaven—it knows nothing of war. For the peoples of antiquity, war was after all only one among other natural expressions of life: it held no fundamental contradiction. To the nations war means staking life in order to live. A nation that fares forth to war accepts the possibility of dying. This is not significant so long as nations regard themselves as mortal. While this conviction lasts, it is of no importance that of the two legitimate reasons for waging war as given by the great Roman orator—that of *salus* and that of *fides*, self-preservation and the keeping of the pledged word—the second may sometimes be in contradiction to the first. There is, after all, no good reason why Saguntum and its people shall not perish from the earth. But what it means becomes clear when Augustine, who is responsible for the clever refutation of Cicero, declares: the church cannot fall into such conflict between its own welfare and the faith pledged to a higher being; for the church, *salus* and *fides* are one and the same thing. What Augustine here says of the church holds in a narrower sense also for worldly communities, for nations and states which have begun to regard their own existence from the highest point of view. . . .

As against the life of the nations of the world, constantly involved in a war of faith, the Jewish people has left its war of faith far behind in its mythical antiquity. Hence, whatever wars it experiences are purely political wars. But since the concept of a war of faith is ingrained in it, it cannot take these wars as seriously as the peoples of antiquity to whom such a concept was alien. In the whole Christian world, the Jew is practically the only human being who cannot take war seriously, and this makes him the only genuine pacifist. For that reason, and because he experiences perfect community in his spiritual year, he remains remote from the chronology of the rest of the world, even though this has long ceased to be a chronology peculiar to individual peoples and, as Christian chronology, is accepted as a principle common to the world at large. He does not have to wait for world history to unroll its long course to let him gain what he feels he already possesses in the circuit of every year: the experience of the immediacy of each single individual to God, realized in the perfect community of all with God.

The Jewish people has already reached the goal toward which the nations are still moving. It has that inner unity of faith and life which, while Augustine may ascribe it to the church in the form of the unity between *fides* and *salus*, is still no more than a dream to the nations within the church. But just because it has that unity, the Jewish people is bound to be outside the world that does not yet have it. Through living in a state of eternal peace it is outside of time agitated by wars. Insofar as it has reached the goal which it anticipates in hope, it cannot belong to the procession of those who approach this goal through the work of centuries. Its soul, replete with the vistas afforded by hope, grows numb to the concerns, the doing and the struggling of the world. The consecration poured over it as over a priestly people renders its life "unproductive." Its holiness hinders it from devoting its soul to a still unhallowed world, no matter how much the body may be bound up with it. This people must deny itself active and full participation in the life of this world with its daily, apparently conclusive, solving of all contradictions. It is not permitted to recognize this daily solving of contradictions, for that would render it disloyal to the hope of a final solution. In order to keep unharmed the vision of the ultimate community it must deny itself the satisfaction the peoples of the world constantly enjoy in the functioning of their state. For the state is the ever changing guise under which time moves step by step toward eternity. So far as God's people is concerned, eternity has already come—even in the midst of time! For the nations of the world there is only the current era. But the state symbolizes the attempt to give nations eternity within the confines of time, an attempt which must of necessity be repeated again and again. The very fact that the state does try it, and *must* try it, makes it the imitator and rival of the people which is in itself eternal, a people which would cease to have a claim to its own eternity if the state were able to attain what it is striving for.

THE LAST WILL OF AN ASSIMILATED JEW

Despite the rejuvenation of Judaism many young Jews still desired nothing more than complete assimilation into European nations. An eloquent testimony of that wish is the last will of Marc Bloch (1886–1944), one of the greatest historians of the medieval world and of France. Bloch fought in the French Resistance during World War II and was killed by a Nazi firing squad.

READING 8-3

When death comes to me, whether in France or abroad, I leave it to my dear wife or, failing her, to my children, to arrange for such burial as may seem best to them. I wish the ceremony to be a civil one only. The members of my family know that I could accept no other kind. But when the moment comes I should like some friend to take upon himself the task of reading the following words, either in the mortuary or at the graveside.

I have not asked to have read above my body those Jewish prayers to the cadence of which so many of my ancestors, including my father, were laid to rest. All my life I have striven to achieve complete sincerity in word and thought. I hold that any compromise with untruth, no matter what the pretext, is the mark of a human soul's ultimate corruption. Following in this a far greater man than I could ever hope to be, I could wish for no better epitaph than these simple words:—DILEXIT VERITATEM. That is why I find it impossible, at this moment of my last farewell, when, if ever, a man should be true to himself, to authorize any use of those formulae of an orthodoxy to the beliefs of which I have ever refused to subscribe.

But I should hate to think that anyone might read into this statement of personal integrity even the remotest approximation to a coward's denial. I am prepared, therefore, if necessary, to affirm here, in the face of death, that I was born a Jew: that I have never denied it, nor ever been

tempted to do so. In a world assailed by the most appalling barbarism, is
not that generous tradition of the Hebrew Prophets, which Christianity at
its highest and noblest took over and expanded, one of the best justifica-
tions we can have for living, believing, and fighting? A stranger to all cre-
dal dogmas, as to all pretended community of life and spirit based on race,
I have, through life, felt that I was above all, and quite simply, a Frenchman. A family tradition, already of long date, has bound me firmly to my
country. I have found nourishment in her spiritual heritage and in her history. I can, indeed, think of no other land whose air I could have breathed
with such a sense of ease and freedom. I have loved her greatly, and served
her with all my strength. I have never found that the fact of being a Jew
has at all hindered these sentiments. Though I have fought in two wars, it
has not fallen to my lot to die for France. But I can, at least, in all sincerity,
declare that I die now, as I have lived, a good Frenchman.

When these words have been spoken, the same friend shall, if the text can be
obtained, read the citations which I received for service in the field.

REVISIONIST ZIONISM

In the course of the 1920's, and especially as the political status of the
Jews in East Central Europe declined, the appeal of Zionism grew
stronger every year. In the Zionist movement, a sharp difference of opinion developed between those who favored a moderate course of action in
regard to emigration and negotiations with Britain and those who demanded a more vociferous and activist approach. The latter, led by Vla-
dimir Jabotinsky, a brilliant Russian-Jewish journalist, called themselves
Revisionists and split off from the main Zionist movement.

The following selection is from Jabotinsky's platform.

READING 8-4

The first aim of Zionism is the creation of a Jewish majority on both sides of the
Jordan River. This is not the ultimate goal of the Zionist movement, which aspires
to more far-reaching ideals, such as the solution of the question of Jewish suffering
[*Judennotfrage*] throughout the entire world and the creation of a new Jewish culture. The precondition for the attainment of these noble aims, however, is a country
in which the Jews constitute a majority. It is only after this majority is attained that
Palestine can undergo a normal political development on the basis of democratic,
parliamentary principles without thereby endangering the Jewish national character of the country. . . .

Our attitude toward the Palestinian Arabs is determined by the full recognition
of an objective fact: even after the formation of a Jewish majority a considerable
Arab population will always remain in Palestine. If things fare badly for this group
of inhabitants then things will fare badly for the entire country. The political, economic and cultural welfare of the Arabs will thus always remain one of the main
conditions for the well-being of the land of Israel. In the future Jewish state absolute

equality will reign between residents of both peoples [*Volksstaemme*], both languages and all religions. All measures must be taken to develop the national autonomy of each of the peoples represented in the country with regard to communal affairs, education, cultural activities and political representation. We believe that in this way the Jewish people in Palestine will in the future be able to convince the Arabs inside and outside the country to reconcile themselves to [a Jewish majority in] the land of Israel.

It is a dangerous falsehood, however, to present such a reconciliation as an already existing fact. Arab public opinion in Palestine is against the creation of a Jewish majority there. The Arabs will continue to fight for a long time—sometimes energetically and sometimes apathetically, sometimes with political means and sometimes with other means—against all that which leads to the creation of this majority until the moment that the overwhelming might of the Jews in the country, i.e., the Jewish majority, becomes a fact. Only then will true reconciliation commence. To close our eyes to this state of affairs is unwise and irresponsible. We Revisionists are keeping our eyes open and want to be prepared for every eventuality. With all the sincere goodwill [we feel] toward the Arab people, we nevertheless firmly believe that the transformation of Palestine into a Jewish state is a postulate of the highest justice and that all opposition to it is unjust. One may neither come to terms with injustice or make any concessions to it. In this case especially, namely, the question of the formation of a majority, there is from our side no possibility to concede anything. One can only struggle against injustice, with peaceful means as long as it is not expressed in acts of violence, and with other means when it assumes the form of violence. . . .

Zionism appeals to the entire Jewish people for help in the reconstruction of the land of Israel. We call upon every Jew not only to give but to come and share the responsibility with us. But—and this must remain absolutely clear for all times—*the extent of responsibility depends on what is given.* From the Diaspora Zionism demands not only money, but belief—belief in the Zionist ideal. . . .

SOVIET JEWISH CULTURE

Diametrically opposed to the Zionists were those Jews both within and outside the Soviet Union who believed that communism would solve the Jewish problem. Jews were prominent in the Soviet Communist Party and government, and in communist and revolutionary movements throughout Europe.

Reproduced here is an example of the attempt, supported by the Soviet regime, at creating a "proletarian Yiddish culture"—the poem "Parade," by the Soviet Yiddish poet David Hofstein.

READING 8-5

Parade

We move with you, in your advancing ranks,
marching mankind,

the proud and the courageous, the seething and the chill—
step by step!
Held high on poles of shame, swaying, swaying there—
the old God.
Its tatters patched with air, there flutters still and flutters—
the old red banner—
no step back!
And sleepless drumsticks pour their pellets on stiff hides,
and cymbals clash—their sharpness hones the pliant air—
and flinging high its cry,
the gleaming trumpet . . .
Today I, too, am a piece of clanging brass—
I leap across
quiet velvet places,
I wake the weary,
I cover the sigh of the exhausted
with raucous laughter—
no step back!

MEIN KAMPF

The greatest problem facing European Jewry in the late 1920's and early 1930's was the rise of the National Socialist Party in Germany. The Nazis, led by Adolf Hitler, were dismissed by most Germans of any faith as an insignificant band of boorish thugs, but they gained increasing support among the disaffected and angry in German society.

In 1924 during a prison term Hitler wrote his manifesto, *Mein Kampf* (My Struggle), which exploded in a frenzy of anti-Semitic invective, typified by the following selection.

READING 8-6

The mightiest counterpart to the Aryan is represented by the Jew. In hardly any people in the world is the instinct of self-preservation developed more strongly than in the so-called 'chosen.' Of this, the mere fact of the survival of this race may be considered the best proof. . . .

If the Jews were alone in this world, they would stifle in filth and offal; they would try to get ahead of one another in hate-filled struggle and exterminate one another, in so far as the absolute absence of all sense of self-sacrifice, expressing itself in their cowardice, did not turn battle into comedy here too.

So it is absolutely wrong to infer any ideal sense of sacrifice in the Jews from the fact that they stand together in struggle, or, better expressed, in the plundering of their fellow men. . . .

Hence the Jewish people, despite all apparent intellectual qualities, is without any true culture, and especially without any culture of its own. For what sham culture the Jew today possesses is the property of other peoples, and for the most part it is ruined in his hands.

In judging the Jewish people's attitude on the question of human culture, the most essential characteristic we must always bear in mind is that there has never been a Jewish art and accordingly there is none today either; that above all the two queens of all the arts, architecture and music, owe nothing original to the Jews. What they do accomplish in the field of art is either patchwork or intellectual theft. Thus, the Jew lacks those qualities which distinguish the races that are creative and hence culturally blessed. . . .

The Jew has always been a people with definite racial characteristics and never a religion; only in order to get ahead he early sought for a means which could distract unpleasant attention from his person. And what would have been more expedient and at the same time more innocent than the 'embezzled' concept of a religious community? For here, too, everything is borrowed or rather stolen. . . .

Probably the Aryan was also first a nomad, settling in the course of time, but for that very reason he was never a Jew! No, the Jew is no nomad; for the nomad had also a definite attitude toward the concept of work which could serve as a basis for his later development in so far as the necessary intellectual premises were present. In him the basic idealistic view is present, even if in infinite dilution, hence in his whole being he may seem strange to the Aryan peoples, but not unattractive. In the Jew, however, this attitude is not at all present; for that reason he was never a nomad, but only and always a *parasite* in the body of other peoples. . . . He is and remains the typical parasite, a sponger who like a noxious bacillus keeps spreading as soon as a favorable medium invites him. And the effect of his existence is also like that of spongers: wherever he appears, the host people dies out after a shorter or longer period. . . .

THE NUREMBURG LAWS

After a series of electoral successes, Hitler became Chancellor of Germany on January 30, 1933. He immediately set about inciting far-reaching attacks on the Jews, a central part of his new program for Germany. Violence and economic boycotts were soon followed by laws that excluded the Jews from more and more areas of German life. In September 1935, the Nuremburg Laws (so called since they were drafted in that city) were enacted and soon became known as the most infamous anti-Semitic decrees ever.

READING 8-7

Law for the Protection of the German Blood and the German Honor

Imbued with the conviction that the purity of the German blood is prerequisite for the future existence of the German people, and animated with the unbending will to ensure the existence of the German nation for all the future, the Reichstag has unanimously adopted the following law, which is hereby proclaimed:

§ 1. (1) Marriages between Jews and state members (*Staatsangehörige*) of German or cognate blood are forbidden. Marriages concluded despite this law are invalid, even if they are concluded abroad in order to circumvent this law .

(2) Only the State Attorney may initiate the annulment suit.

§ 2. Extra-marital relations between Jews and state members of German or cognate blood are prohibited.

§ 3. Jews must not engage female domestic help in their households among state members of German or cognate blood, who are under 45 years.

§ 4. (1) The display of the Reich and national flag and the showing of the national colors by Jews is prohibited.

(2) However, the display of the Jewish colors is permitted to them. The exercise of this right is placed under the protection of the state.

§ 5. (1) Whosoever acts in violation of the prohibition of § 1, will be punished with penal servitude.

(2) Whosoever acts in violation of § 2, will be punished with either imprisonment or penal servitude.

(3) Whosoever acts in violation of § 3 or § 4, will be punished by imprisonment up to one year, with a fine or with either of these penalties. . . .

§ 7. This law goes into effect on the day following promulgation, except for § 3 which shall go into force on January 1, 1936.

September 15, 1935

COUNTER-EMANCIPATION

The Nuremburg Laws led to the "Reich Citizenship Laws" which formally rescinded the emancipation of the Jews of Germany.

READING 8-8

7. The Reich Citizenship Law

. . . § 2. (1) A Reich citizen (*Reichsbürger*) is only the state member (*Staatsangehöriger*) who is of German or cognate blood, and who shows through his conduct that he is both desirous and fit to serve in faith the German people and Reich.

(3) The Reich citizen is the only holder of full political rights in accordance with the provisions of the laws.

Nuremburg, September 15, 1935, on the Reich Party Day of Freedom.

8. First Decree to the Reich Citizenship Law
November 14, 1935

. . . § 4. (1) A Jew cannot be a citizen of the Reich. He cannot exercise the right to vote on political matters; he cannot hold public office.

(2) Jewish officials are to be retired on December 31, 1935. In case these officials served either Germany or her allies at the front in the World War, they shall receive as a pension, until they reach their age limit, the full salary last received;

they are not, however, to be promoted according to seniority. After they reach the age limit, their pension is to be calculated anew according to the salary last received, on the basis of which their pension was to be computed.

(3) Affairs of religious organizations are not affected therewith.

(4) The conditions of service of teachers in public Jewish schools remain unchanged until the forthcoming regulation of the Jewish school system.

§ 5. (1) A Jew is anyone who is descended from at least three full Jewish grandparents. § 2, clause 2, sentence 2 is to be applied.

(2) A Jewish state member of mixed descent (*Staatsangehöriger jüdischer Mischling*) who is descended from two full Jewish grandparents is also considered a Jew, if

a. He belonged to the Jewish religious community at the time this law was issued or joined the community later,

b. He was married to a Jew at the time when the law was issued, or if he married a Jew subsequently,

c. He is the offspring of a marriage with a Jew within the meaning of clause 1, which was contracted after the Law for the Protection of German Blood and Honor of September 15, 1935 (*RGBL*, i, p. 1146) went into effect,

d. He is the offspring of extra-marital intercourse with a Jew, within the meaning of clause 1, and will be born out of wedlock after July 31, 1936.

EXCLUSION FROM SCHOOLS

Soon the Jews were excluded from all aspects of German life. The following decree, passed in November 1938, dismissed all Jewish children from German schools.

READING 8-9

1. Jews are forbidden to attend German schools. They are permitted to attend Jewish schools only. Insofar as it has not yet happened all Jewish school boys and girls still attending German schools are to be dismissed immediately.

2. § 5 of the First Decree to the Reich Citizenship Law (*RGBL*, i, p. 1333) of November 14, 1935, specifies who is Jewish.

3. This regulation extends to all schools under the supervision of the Reich Minister of Education, including continuation schools.

THE FINAL SOLUTION

On September 1, 1939 Nazi Germany attacked Poland and began World War II. From the first the Jews were one of the principal targets of the Nazis. Brutal anti-Semitic violence was followed by legal restrictions, ghettoization, and mass murder.

It is impossible to know for certain exactly when Hitler and his advisers decided on what they called the "final solution of the Jewish

Problem"—the extermination of every Jewish man, woman, and child in Europe. The mechanisms for the extermination began to be available at the end of 1941: death camps. From evidence submitted at the Nuremburg Trials after the war, it is clear that on January 20, 1942 Nazi leaders gathered at a villa in a suburb of Berlin called Wannsee and laid out in detail the plans for the Final Solution. Selections from the minutes of that meeting follow.

READING 8-10

At the beginning of the discussion SS Obergruppenfuehrer HEYDRICH gave information that the Reich Marshal had appointed him delegate for the preparations for the final solution of the Jewish problem in Europe and pointed out that this discussion had been called for the purpose of clarifying fundamental questions. The wish of the Reich Marshal to have a draft sent to him concerning organisatory, factual and material interests in relation to the final solution of the Jewish problem in Europe, makes necessary an initial common action of all Central Offices immediately concerned with these questions in order to bring their general activities into line. . . .

Another possible solution of the problem has now taken the place of emigration, i.e. the evacuation of the Jews to the East, provided the Fuehrer agrees to this plan.

Such activities are, however, to be considered as provisional actions, but practical experience is already being collected which is of greatest importance in relation to the future final solution of the Jewish problem.

Approx. 11,000,000 Jews will be involved in this final solution of the European problem. . . .

Under proper guidance the Jews are now to be allocated for labor to the East in the course of the final solution. Able-bodied Jews will be taken in large labor columns to these districts for work on roads, separated according to sexes, in the course of which action a great part will undoubtedly be eliminated by natural causes.

The possible final remnant will, as it must undoubtedly consist of the toughest, have to be treated accordingly, as it is the product of natural selection, and would, if liberated, act as a bud cell of a Jewish reconstruction (see historical experience).

In the course of the practical execution of this final settlement of the problem, Europe will be cleaned up from the West to the East. Germany proper, including the protectorate Bohemia and Moravia, will have to be handled first because of reasons of housing and other social-political necessities.

The evacuated Jews will first be sent, group by group, into so-called transit-ghettos from which they will be taken to the East.

LIFE IN A GHETTO

The following is a stirring testimony of life in a ghetto as described by a survivor in a letter to friends immediately after the war.

READING 8-11

I remember it as if it was happening now—those first few days of surrender. On that Sunday, September 17, 1941, from the moment that first German appeared in the streets of the *shtetl* [small town], he showed us what he was planning and what he's known for throughout the world. An incredible barrage of firepower was kept up all day—not a soul dared show their face outside.

Our house overflowed with refugees. They were scattered all over and crowded together on the floor, trembling in fear. Suddenly, we heard the bloodcurdling scream of a Jewish boy we knew. I opened the door in terror and what I saw was a corpse lying on the threshold. This was the first time I really experienced the German's cruelty. I'm not mentioning this only because it's shocking, but because it ingrained itself in my mind as the first barbarous act of a supposedly civilized people. I endured a lot worse, and the more often it happened, the less it shocked me— this was the way it had to be.

My husband went through much hardship before he finally reached home. He was captured and held as a hostage many times. Both of us worked ourselves to the bone. We witnessed the most gruesome incidents. All my belongings were confiscated. White bands with the *mugen duvid* [Star of David] were wrapped around our arms. We were tortured at every turn. Every moment was pierced by the screams of Jews. We were constantly being beaten, tortured, or shot. Every morning, before they marched us off to work, we took leave of each other as if for the last time. Who knew if we'd still be alive by tomorrow?

The Yom Kippur of 1941 in Sarne will stay before my eyes forever. On Friday evening, this order was given: By morning, all Jews, without exception, must line up on the square wearing a new badge—one round, yellow, ten-centimeter-wide patch halfway down our backs, and another one on our right lapel. Anyone disobeying will be shot. That tragic night passed like a torture. We got ready to face the end. In the morning, the streets of our Jewish *shtetl* were swarming with yellow-spotted ghosts. We huddled together and waited—for what? A deep silence fell over the square. Machine guns were positioned on every side. Every now and then, a small child cried or screamed out for its mother. A light plane circled above to prevent our escape. An auto pulled up with the ranking officers and they ordered the *selektsye* [selection] of the artisans to begin. I can't describe our suffering to you. The *Schutzpolizei* [police] ran among us like dogs, beating and punishing whomever they got hold of. Several people were shot in the back through their patch as a sport. . . . It was only after many long hours that we were allowed to go home. I went through these punishment drills—*Appele* they called them—five times. To survive in Sarne was now beyond my strength. People said a ghetto was being planned. I was in my last month. The first reports about the mass murder of Jews were reaching us . . . more and more. My parents decided to bring us over to them, no matter the danger, and to have us share a common fate. Travel by train was forbidden us . . . and it meant certain death to go by coach. My father was the only one who would risk his life and come and get us. The conditions hadn't completely deteriorated in Rokitno. We still had our house, a large garden, and an orchard. I recuperated for a time, but not for long. A ghetto was imposed. Several streets were sealed off for Jews only.

My dear ones! I can't describe to you the horrors of the ghetto! People died from hunger, from epidemics. Most of us were swollen from malnutrition. The overcrowding stifled us. And this was the time I bore my child. Doctors weren't allowed to treat Jews. And it was forbidden to bring a Jew into the world. While I lay in bed, sick and terror-stricken, horrendous things were going on all around me. A German drunk accused my father of trying to poison him and he beat him terribly—he tried to kill him then and there. In the morning, my brother was attacked and beaten unconscious for not saluting properly. We were all confined to our beds. But my mother was heroic. She took care of us and comforted us—she saw to all our needs. My mother, who'd been sick herself, somehow now recovered her health. Each day, rumors spread and we suffered every moment. My husband was driven to exhaustion at slave labor. My younger brother, a very talented boy of eighteen, was the only one able to support us and he kept us alive. He worked as an electrician, a metalsmith, he fixed ovens and all kinds of things, he was a watchmaker, a painter, and many times they used him as an interpreter. And besides all this, he also had to work all day long at slave labor. This is how we were able to stay alive until August 26, 1942. My daughter was now a growing pretty, eight-month-old child.

Then, suddenly, an order was passed through the ghetto: everyone must assemble in the morning. . . . They accused us of having helped many Jews escape to the Russian partisan units. This was the time the first partisan units were forming. They wanted to investigate us and ordered a head count taken. The whole ghetto was overcome with despair. You could see terror on every face. Our sorrow knew no bounds now when we learned that [the assembly] in the neighboring *shtetl* of Selishtsh that same day ended with the murder of every last man, woman, and child. God! I can't just mention this in passing! My heart still cries out!

I broke into hysterical weeping. The men sat by mum, but my mother kept her head, she started comforting me and calmed me down. There was no way out. We were afraid to go to bed all night. How could we escape in the darkness? To whom? And with a baby! I begged the men not to think of us and to escape. But they didn't—we still wouldn't believe they were going to murder us!

The morning was especially beautiful and clear. My mother started to knead some dough, thinking she'd have time to bake it. My little girl sat up in her crib, looking just like a little angel. She had just woken up from her sweet, childish dreams. My brother left to go out into the street. The Jewish police started carrying out the order of chasing the people from their homes toward the square. My brother ran back into the house, pale as a ghost. I dressed my child quickly and we got ready to leave. My husband broke down in tears—it was a terrible thing to see. After him, we all did. Our home was filled with sobbing. A neighbor came to get us and then we walked out to the square. Big and small, everyone was lined up. Life had become so cheap to us, we were so apathetic, that at first it didn't seem there was anything out of the ordinary. There was only the chief of gendarmes to count how many we were. I can still see my mother when she came over to me with an expression of relief on her face and tried to comfort me: "See . . . there's no one here. Soon, they'll let us go home just like always." The count was taken quietly and quickly. We were only worried that they wouldn't let us go home soon. And suddenly, we heard an order: "Men to one side, women to the other, line up in rows of six!" We clung to each other. Everyone started panicking. We lost control of ourselves. I started trembling like I had a fever. My father, my husband, and my brother were separated from us. My mother held me by the hand, and it was very hard for me to keep a grip. She wanted to lighten my burden and took the child from my arms.

A moment later, a cry that pierced the heart rose from the 15,000 people and filled the skies: "Run, they're killing us!" The Germans and the police converged on the square. Shots rang out from behind the windows. I don't know how I reacted. I only remember this enormous weight suddenly falling on me. I started twisting and squirming and finally crawled free from under the dozens of bodies on top of me. I couldn't see where my mother and child lay. The bullets whistled past me. My dress was drenched with blood. I felt I was hit! No—someone had fallen on me. Whether they were dead or wounded I'll never know. The square was completely covered with bodies—some dead, others were wounded, and many were in shock and paralyzed with fear. Wild screams pierced the air. I couldn't get up anymore, there were people falling all over me. Slowly, I regained my senses. Death was staring me in the face. God!

. . . I found the truth of what happened. My mother and child managed to get back to the house. She put the child to sleep. A German broke in and beat them brutally, pushing them out toward the train with all the others. They were taken to Sarne, to the staging ground. My husband and brother had gotten away. They were caught the next day and forced to drag together all the corpses. . . .

Then, a day after, they were also brought to Sarne. They joined the others there—my mother and child.

They endured for three days. My husband carried water for my hungry child in his shoe.

A short time passed, a few days. The front was a few kilometers from our *shtetl*. We were bombarded from all sides. I became sick with typhus. Then my father got sick. His weakened heart couldn't stand the inhuman suffering. He died. I lost the most precious part of my life. I was left all alone.

My dears! My past is the past of the whole Jewish people. Be well.

UPRISING

In the ghettos of Warsaw, Vilna, Bialystok, Minsk, and Kovno, as well as several death camps, Jewish resistance groups rose up and bravely fought the Nazi murderers, knowing full well that there was no chance of victory. The uprisings were quelled, but nonetheless succeeded in symbolizing to the Jews and to the rest of the world the noble spirit of the Jewish victims of Nazism.

The following is from an eyewitness account of the uprising in the death camp of Treblinka recorded in 1945.

READING 8-12

. . . The small village of Treblinka lies near the little train depot on the Shedlets-Malkin line, six kilometers from Malkin. It's buried deep in the dense Polish forests. In the winter of 1942, it still functioned as a penal camp for "saboteurs"—like peasants who hadn't turned in their wheat quotas on time, or workers who'd reported to labor sites late. In the summer of 1942, this camp was made into a giant death factory. Millions of Jews were exterminated here—among them almost the whole of Warsaw Jewry, the Jews of Chenstokhov, Radom, Bialystok, and Shedlets. Jews from Germany, Czechoslovakia, Belgium, Holland, Greece, and other countries were also brought here. In July 1942, the gas chambers were installed and the people were poisoned by the different gases or asphyxiated when the chamber was turned into a vacuum and all the air was sucked out.

Huge transports are shipped in steadily and the Hitlerite murderers can no longer "dispose of" them quickly enough. During this time, a special structure is built containing twelve gas chambers, where from 6,000 to 7,000 people could be forced in at one time. The number of Jews exterminated in Treblinka before the uprising and the destruction of the death camp is over 3 million. Himmler, who was a steady "guest" at Treblinka, personally supervised his henchmen. On his advice, the bodies were carried out and burned on pyres to extinguish every last trace of them. The ash was collected to fertilize the neighboring fields.

We were divided into two labor battalions. The first numbered 700 men and worked at unloading people from the trains, sorting out the clothes and valuables. The second group of 300 people were the ones who carried the dead out of the gas chambers and burned them on the pyres. We were interned in two separate barracks, cut off one from the other by barbed wire.

During this whole time, there were very many individual acts of revenge by Jews who refused to take any more: the time the young Jew from Warsaw, after seeing his wife and child pushed into the gas chamber, attacked the SS man Max Bilo with a knife and stabbed him to death. From that day on, these SS units were named after that Hitlerite murderer. The plaque calling for revenge, which hung over their barracks, and the general slaughter the SS then started in retaliation, didn't intimidate us in the least—just the opposite: it aroused us and incited us to battle, to avenge ourselves and our people. The death of the young man from Warsaw became our rallying cry. The will to revenge, which lived in us, grew stronger all the time and took concrete shape. Especially when the Warsaw surgeon, Dr. Chorążycki, joined us. He worked at the camp dispensary where the Germans played their last evil hoax on the miserable victims before sending them into the gas chambers. He seemed like a very remote, formal person, making his rounds in a white coat and a Red Cross band just like he had once in his clinic, acting like he didn't care at all. But a warm Jewish heart beat under that uniform, and the burning desire for revenge. . . .

There were two ways of getting weapons: from the outside or on the inside—stealing them from the German and Ukrainian SS men. Attempts were made to take down the exact plan of the camp arsenal which was located at the very center of the SS barracks—they were all sitting right on this powder keg.

Only Germans were allowed in the area and there could be no thought of getting inside directly. Many plans were drawn up to dig a tunnel underground. But this might expose us to terrible danger and it was almost impossible to accomplish under those severe circumstances. It was decided to make a passkey, though, at any cost. This was an almost impossible obstacle because no one could get near the arsenal, let alone check its iron doors. But there was no other choice than waiting for the right moment. But to our surprise, in a very short time, the right opportunity presented itself. A defect was discovered in the arsenal lock. The Germans had to call on Jewish locksmiths. But they took such precautions that they forced all the work to be done in the locksmith workshops under their continuous watch. But a locksmith succeeded in pressing a mold of the key in shoe wax when the German guard looked the other way for a moment. A few days later, the leaders of the planned revolt got the finished key. It was guarded like a holy object. We awaited the right moment anxiously. . . .

During this month, the transports with the last Jews of the Warsaw Ghetto Uprising arrived. They were tortured mercilessly. Most of the train cars are full of dead ghetto fighters who were trapped, beaten, then jammed into the wagons. The few survivors told us of the Warsaw Ghetto Uprising. These new people weren't like the inert, broken inmates who'd arrived till now. They didn't carry tears in their eyes, but pocketfuls of explosives. We got many weapons from them.

The leadership was waiting for the best moment to start the revolt. . . . Those driven into the gas chambers demand that we avenge them.

Finally, our dream is realized. Engineer Galewski, the inmate "commandant," gives the signal for the uprising to begin. The date set was August 2, 1943, 5:15 P.M.

The plan at the outset was eluding the main "dogcatchers," then executing them; disarming the guards; cutting telephone lines; burning down and destroying all the apparatus of the "death factory"; and bringing the killing to a halt forever. We were also to liberate the "Polish" camp two kilometers away where many Jews were imprisoned, and join with them to form a huge partisan force.

Monday morning, everyone in camp is tense beyond endurance. The leaders assign special units to see to it that the daily work is carried out routinely, to avoid any suspicion. The combat group is divided up into platoons. When the signal is given, every unit must man its position. We report to the afternoon *Appel* as if nothing is going on. Then, Commandant Galewski announces that work will let off an hour earlier because *Schaarführer* Kitner is departing for Malkin to bathe in the Bug. He winks: another kind of "bath" is being gotten ready for him! At around two in the afternoon, the guns are handed out.

Almost immediately afterwards—the murderers are attacked! The telephone lines are cut. The guard towers set ablaze, the barracks, too—all with benzine. The benzine pumps in front of the garage are lit by Rudek and explode. Captain Zela hacks up two guards with an axe and breaks into our camp where he assumes overall command again. The garages are defended by a German armored assault vehicle which Rudek has commandeered and is using as a tank barricade. . . .

We, groundskeepers, storm the arsenal. The arms are passed around among the group. There are now around 200 of us who are fully armed, the others attack with axes, picks, and spades.

Commander Zela issued quick, new instructions. We're overcome with the rage of vengeance. No one thinks of his own life. We free still more guns. The heavy machine gun we've gotten is unstoppable. Rudolf Masaryk mans it and turns it on the "dove tower." He's spitting fire at the Ukrainian barracks and at the Germans. His cries are heard: "This is for my wife! And for my child, who never saw the world!! And this, scum, for humiliated and grieving humanity!!!"

The mock train depot with its macabre signs, "Bialystok-Wolkowysk," "Ticket Office," "Rest Lounge," and so on, is burned to the ground. The barracks named for the murderer Max Bilo go up in flames. The perimeter fences are cut through and the posts uprooted with cries of "Hurrah!"—the gas chambers are burned down, and then the "bath"!

German reinforcements are called in from all directions as the shooting rocks the entire region and the flames rise higher and higher. SS, MP's, and field gendarmes pour in from Malkin, *Luftwaffe* personnel are rushed in from the nearby airstrip at Kosów, and even elite SS commando forces from Warsaw are sent to take up positions in the camp. A major battle develops. Captain Zela leads the assault and rallies all our forces forward, until he's cut down by a Hitlerite bullet in the thick of the fighting.

Night is falling. Our ranks are thinning out. Ammunition's in short supply. The Germans are reinforced with wave after wave of men and matériel. But our revolt has succeeded 100 percent. The entire camp is in flames and completely destroyed. The hangmen are no more. They all got their punishment. We got rid of about 200 Germans and Ukrainian Fascists. The order is now given to break out of the siege any way possible and regroup in the surrounding forests. The majority of our combatants are cut down in this attempt. Only individuals break through, and most are then later murdered by the Polish assassins.

A PROTEST WITHOUT A RESPONSE

On May 12, 1943, Shmuel Zygelboim, the Jewish Workers' Bund representative to the Polish Government-in-Exile in London, committed suicide as a protest against the passivity of the world upon hearing of the murder of the millions of Jews by the Nazis. The following is the note he left behind.

READING 8-13

I take the liberty of addressing to you my last words and through you the Polish government and people of the Allied States and the conscience of the world.

From the latest information received from Poland, it is evident that without doubt the Germans with ruthless cruelty are now murdering the few remaining Jews in Poland. Behind the walls of the ghettos the last act of a tragedy unprecedented in history is being performed.

The responsibility for the crime of murdering all the Jewish population in Poland falls in the first instance on the perpetrators, but indirectly also it weighs on the whole of humanity, the peoples and governments of the Allied States which so far have made no effort toward a concrete action for the purpose of curtailing the crime. By passive observation of this murder of defenseless millions and the maltreatment of children and women, the men of those countries have become accomplices of criminals.

I have also to state that although the Polish government [in exile] has in a high degree contributed to stirring the opinion of the world yet it did so insufficiently for it did nothing extraordinary enough to correspond to the magnitude of the drama now being enacted in Poland.

Out of nearly 350,000 Polish Jews and about 700,000 Jews deported to Poland from other countries, there still lived in April of this year, according to the official information of the head of the underground Bund organization sent to the United States through a delegate of the government, about 300,000. And the murders are still going on incessantly.

I cannot be silent and I cannot live while the remnants of the Jewish people of Poland, of whom I am representative, are perishing.

My comrades in the Warsaw Ghetto perished with weapons in their hands in their last heroic impulse.

It was not my destiny to perish as they did together with them but I belong to them and their mass graves.

By my death, I wish to express my strongest protest against the inactivity with which the world is looking on and permitting the extermination of Jewish people. I know how little human life is worth, especially today. But as I was unable to do anything during my life, perhaps by my death I shall contribute to destroying the indifference of those who are able and should act in order to save now, maybe at the last moment, this handful of Polish Jews who are still alive from certain annihilation.

My life belongs to the Jewish people in Poland and therefore I give it to them. I wish that this handful that remains of the several million Polish Jews could live to see with the Polish masses the day of liberation—that it could breathe in Poland and in a world of freedom and in the justice of socialism in return for all its tortures and inhuman sufferings. And I believe that such a Poland will arise and that such a world will come.

I trust that the President and the Prime Minister will direct my words to all those for whom they are destined and that the Polish government will immediately begin appropriate action in the diplomatic and propaganda fields in order to save from extermination the Polish Jews who are still alive.

I bid farewell to all and everything dear to me and loved by me.

LIBERATION

By the time the Allies landed at Normandy on June 6, 1944, most of the Jews of Europe had been killed. In the last months of the war the Nazis diverted critical railroad cars from the front to transport Hungarian and other Jews to their death. On January 17, 1945 the Red Army liberated Warsaw and was on its way to Berlin; at the beginning of March, the United States First Army crossed the Rhine. On April 25, 1945 the American and Soviet armies met at the Elbe River; on May 1, it was announced that Hitler had died during the Battle of Berlin. Six days later, German army leaders surrendered to the Allies.

The following is a description by a Dachau concentration camp inmate of the liberation of the concentration camp by the American army.

READING 8-14

I was born in Poland in the city of Lódź. I'm fifteen years old now. At the age of nine, I was locked up inside the ghetto together with my family. We suffered hunger and misery. People swelled up and died. In 1943, the Germans took away all the children to the age of ten. I had a younger brother who was seven. We hid together with him, lying in an attic without food or drink. In a week, there was a new *aktsye* and the German SS charged into all the buildings looking for weak and emaciated people. I lay hidden along with my family and counted the shots. My father, like all the other men, had to go down into the courtyard for the *selektsye* and try to save the women and children this way. Can you imagine our heartbreak as our own *tahte* [father] stands out in the courtyard about to be shot or deported any second? We were ecstatic when we saw our father and husband again, though he came back with the news the Germans had sent away children and shot their mothers. In the end, we survived even these days filled with terror and were saved for a short while. But there was one thing which kept us alive and gave us courage, and this is that we were all together. I couldn't value as a young child what it means to have a family of a father and mother. I only really appreciate it now that it's too late, when I'm left all alone, with no one.

In the middle of 1944, we were transported to Auschwitz. How painful was this day in my life—as we were getting off the trains, the Germans tore the wives away from their husbands and the mothers from their children. These heart-piercing cries and not being able to say goodbye! The people just went limp. I was torn between my parents. My mother sent me across to my father and my father sent me back to my mother. My mother had my little brother by her side and she said through her red, tear-filled eyes, "Go. Be with your father."

This was her intuition—that the worst would happen to me if I didn't go with him. I was almost left all alone among this vast group of crying people. In a second, a Jew who worked at unloading the bundles from the train ran over to me and said I'd be better off going with my father, with the grown-up men. After looking all over, I finally found my father again as he stood with his head bowed, crying like all the others. I took a place in line next to my father, in front of the German officer who was selecting the healthy men out from among the weak ones. He sent away all the other people and all the children to be burned. I was very flushed from crying and packed around with a lot of clothes, so the officer thought I looked fit, and I went up to him and declared boldly that I was seventeen. He looked me over and sent me off behind my father. Two days after coming to Auschwitz, I was given thin clothes and sent away with my father to the labor camp at Kaufbeuren.

We were 600 men. On the first morning, we were sent out to the sites. My father worked in the forest for two days and caught pneumonia. I tried to muster all my strength for this work and was beaten hard all the time. After eight days, my father got better but he was still too weak for the labor gangs. They put him in the infirmary—which was very bad. He died in two days. I was left all alone, without anyone or any hope for tomorrow. The number of dead grew from day to day. Of 600 Jews, only 320 were left. The camp went on operating for another week, and by then, the last exhausted remnant of 125 people were transferred to Dachau. I looked like a corpse, with no strength left at all. We were put into the infirmary, but forty other people had died in the train on the way there—they couldn't have held out for another moment. Since I was the youngest here, the others gave me more food and I only started coming back to life after two long weeks. The doctor, who was French, felt sorry for me and didn't discharge me from the infirmary right away. He gave me light work to do inside the clinic. On April 25, all the Jews were packed into a transport that was headed for the Tyrol. This doctor tried to save me and write out a false diagnosis which confined me to bed, though I was already better. Both of us risked our lives doing this. But luckily, they crossed me off the transport list and I stayed behind in the infirmary.

On April 28, the Americans walked in. Thousands of people "rose from the dead" to come out on the grounds and stare at the liberators. The SS were marched past us with their hands stuck high in the air. I reacted coldly to all these signs of liberation—I had no reason to be glad. I fell into complete apathy. I watched the people sing and dance with joy and they seemed to me as if they'd lost their minds. I looked at myself and couldn't recognize who I was. I lost all sense of what had happened to me. After a long time, I began to understand. I was left all alone, without help and protection, without a living soul I could call my own. There were times I regretted having been left alive among these last survivors and handful of Jews. This was how the two months at Dachau passed. Many people died and many recovered. From Dachau, I was sent to a Jewish camp—Feldafing. I felt more at home here among my own brothers. The Jewish "Joint" did all it could to help. In a short while, I was sent to Heidelberg where, with the aid of the "Joint," I was put into the school for Jewish children. I only live today for the words my father said to me on his deathbed: "I'm already forty-three—I won't be able to survive this hell. But you—you're young, see to it our name isn't torn out from the pages of the world."

This keeps alive my spirit and I live with the hope for a better tomorrow.

THE SIX MILLION

The following is the best estimate of the number of Jews murdered by the Nazis as presented to the Nuremburg Trials in 1945.

READING 8-15

COUNTRY	ESTIMATED PRE-FINAL SOLUTION POPULATION	ESTIMATED JEWISH POPULATION ANNIHILATED
Poland	3,300,000	3,000,000
Baltic countries	253,000	228,000
Germany/Austria	240,000	210,000
Protectorate	90,000	80,000
Slovakia	90,000	75,000
Greece	70,000	54,000
The Netherlands	140,000	105,000
Hungary	650,000	450,000
SSR White Russia	375,000	245,000
SSR Ukraine*	1,500,000	900,000
Belgium	65,000	40,000
Yugoslavia	43,000	26,000
Rumania	600,000	300,000
Norway	1,800	900
France	350,000	90,000
Bulgaria	64,000	14,000
Italy	40,000	8,000
Luxembourg	5,000	1,000
Russia (RSFSR)*	975,000	107,000
Denmark	8,000	—
Finland	2,000	—
Total	8,861,800	5,933,900

*The Germans did not occupy all the territory of this republic.

9

Into the Future
(1945 to 1967)

_____ Michael Stanislawski _____

The documents in this chapter attempt to chart the transformation in the life of the Jews in the years from the end of World War II to the Six Day War of June 1967. The sources focus on the three main centers of Jewish life during this period, the State of Israel, the United States, and the Soviet Union, and demonstrate the continuing vitality and complexity of Jewish participation in the modern world.

Special emphasis is placed on the changes that occurred in these decades in the self-perception of the Jews around the world in the wake of the destruction of European Jewry and the creation of the Jewish state.

RECONSTRUCTION

The most important task facing the Jews after the destruction was finding a home for the survivors of the Nazi horror. International Jewish agencies banded together to help the Jews stranded in displaced persons camps find a safe haven. Many of the refugees wanted to go to Palestine, but the British authorities strictly limited the number of Jews permitted to move there. Many Jews left for the United States, Canada, Latin America, and Australia, where they attempted to rebuild their lives.

The following poignant selection is from the memoir of the painter Marika Frank Abrams, who was born in Hungary, was deported to Auschwitz and Bergen-Belsen, came to America in 1948, and settled in Seattle, Washington.

READING 9-1

We came on a small army transport boat in very bad weather. My cousin and I were determined to fight the seasickness. We would get up at five-thirty in the morning and run up and down the deck breathing fresh air. We were sleeping in large areas with people seasick all around, so it was a hard fight. And then we came out in New York, and it was depressing to feel so anxious in this glowing city.

We stopped in Chicago on the way to Seattle to visit the Foreign Student Service of the Hillel Foundation. Then we went west on a beautiful train, the Olympian Hiawatha. We had done a lot of research to inform ourselves about America—

we had never heard of Seattle until we got the scholarships. And we had a whole delegation meeting us, and I knew right away that it was a wonderful thing that was happening to me.

My experiences with the Americans at the consulate had been very humiliating. We were treated with such suspicion and animosity that it was one more experience with cruelty. Here we were, two little girls out of this inferno, and they were accusing us of lying. They wanted a paper for everything we said. They wanted me to chase up my concentration camp certificate. I came to Auschwitz in the summer of 1944, when they were killing so many people they didn't bother to tattoo us. And when a representative of the Joint Distribution Committee came to intercede for us it was made even more obvious that we were unwelcome and unwanted in the United States. So I had reason to be afraid. Actually I never believed I would be able to come.

Being here seemed such a dream, so unreal, so unbelievable. And the Hillel scholarship offered us everything. It paid for transportation, living costs, tuition at the University of Washington, transportation back to Europe—everything. The United States government wouldn't have granted us a visa unless somebody here promised that we would not be a public charge at any time.

The Jewish sorority paid for our room and board.

The sorority girls never became my friends. They were nice girls but we had nothing to talk about to each other. They were not at all aware of what the war meant to the Jewish people. They were really not aware of anything except their tiny, tiny little lives, their clothes, their boys and things like that. . . .

In 1948, shortly after I came, the new Displaced Persons Act was passed and I was able to apply for permanent residence. My status changed and by that time I was also married. My husband, Sid Abrams, was one of three Seattle boys who went to Europe to help bring immigrants to Palestine, and were involved in Aliyah Bet activities in Bulgaria, Italy and France. He came back to Seattle just after I arrived. We were introduced, fell in love and were married in two months. It was a very foolhardy thing to do because we were both so young and inexperienced, and we naturally had a very hard time. We're married twenty-eight years so I guess we worked out our problems, but it was really hard. . . .

I can look back on moments of great pleasure. In 1953, just after my son Eddie was born, I became an American citizen. I can remember that I had just learned to drive and I drove around with the baby in the car, being an American citizen. I felt like the queen of the world!

A kind of sadness, however, is always with me. I didn't know that others could see it until my son, only five or six years old, asked me once, "Mommy, why is your smile so sad?" And I realized that he divined my real feelings. I was always sad.

I used to go through periods of "violent witnessing." I would push my witnessing on people and be repulsed and very unhappy. And then I would give up and not say a word for a long time. You see, people say, "Oh, we don't want to ask you about your experiences because it must hurt to talk about it." But of course this is not true at all. They don't want to hear because *they* don't want to be hurt. I'm always hurt; I think about it all the time. . . .

I learned from my friends that social consciousness in this big loving country of ours doesn't include the Jewish experience. People get excited about going to the Peace Corps to work in Nigeria or Guatemala. They want to build a new Cuba and get very upset about the blacks and the Puerto Ricans. But the Jews, never—after all, who are the Jews? There are two hundred and ten million people living in this country and only six million Jews. It is hard to meet Jews; there are millions of gentiles who have never met a Jew. And they grow up feeling very ambivalent and have very confused ideas about what Jews are.

Finally after all these years a course in Jewish history is being given at the University of Washington. The Jewish community fought for this very hard, and even paid for it for a while. There is even a course on the Holocaust and, amazingly, over seventy students are enrolled. I was invited to speak to them; it was the first time that anybody wanted to hear what I have to say. All the societies in the Western world lived with Jews, legislated for Jews, against Jews, used Jews, killed Jews. The history of the Jews throughout the world is a touchstone. But nobody ever says a word about it. It is traditional to ignore Jews.

The Holocaust couldn't have happened if this wasn't so. The Germans did it, but they couldn't have done it without the backup of all Western civilization. And in spite of all this, thousands of us are leaving to be part of the gentile world. . . .

I guess I'm always searching for ways of understanding society and values. I lost the people who created me and the world I was created for, and America took my life over. The influences of my parents remained with me, however. My mother was a very positive sort of person, a very modern, very sophisticated woman: beautifully dressed, very chic, a good dancer. But she had a simple faith in God and gave us a lot of love. She had a sense of continuity and a feeling for justice which she gave to me especially. I remember on Sundays my father and mother would hire a horse and coach and go to the cemetery to visit the graves. She would put little stones on the graves of her beloved father and mother and aunts. Later I found out it had to do with a *Chasidic* legend that the souls come out at night and when they find a little stone they know their loved ones were there visiting them.

When I lived in Hungary I came from a small group of people with a certain vision of themselves as Jews and Hungarians. Now I have an entirely different concept of what it is to be a Jew. I feel guilty when I realize that I became what I really ought to have been thanks to the tragedy that befell all of us. If nothing had happened and the world of my childhood hadn't been destroyed I would never have become an artist. So here I am, flowering on the devastation.

PARTITION OF PALESTINE

After World War II relations between the Zionist movement and the British rulers of Palestine took a sharp turn for the worse, as the British vehemently opposed the creation of a Jewish state. The resistance forces of Jewish Palestine organized large-scale illegal immigration operations, as well as attacks against British forces. After much violence on both sides, the British government turned over the future of Palestine to the United Nations. On November 2, 1947 at the end of a long debate, the General Assembly voted more than two to one in favor of partitioning Palestine into two states: one Jewish, one Arab.

The following is the resolution adopted by the United Nations.

READING 9-2

The General Assembly. . . recommends to the United Kingdom, as the mandatory power for Palestine, and to all other members of the United Nations the adoption and implementation, with regard to future government of Palestine, of the Plan of Partition with Economic Union set out below:

. . . The mandatory Power shall use its best endeavors to ensure that an area situated in the territory of the Jewish State, including a seaport and hinterland adequate to provide facilities for a substantial immigration, shall be evacuated at the earliest possible date and in any event not later than February 1, 1948.

Independent Arab and Jewish States and the Special International Regime for the City of Jerusalem . . . shall come into existence in Palestine two months after the evacuation of the armed forces. . . .

DECLARATION OF INDEPENDENCE

Only part of the United Nations resolution was implemented: on May 14, 1948 the State of Israel was created. The Arabs refused to consider the very notion of a Jewish state in Palestine. Indeed, on the night of May 14 five Arab armies attacked the tiny country, and a bitter war was waged for over a year.

The following is the Declaration of Independence of the State of Israel.

READING 9-3

Declaration of the Establishment of the State of Israel

Eretz Israel was the birthplace of the Jewish people. Here their spiritual, religious and political identity was shaped. Here they first attained to statehood, created cultural values of national and universal significance and gave to the world the eternal Book of Books.

After being forcibly exiled from their land, the people kept faith with it throughout their Dispersion and never ceased to pray and hope for their return to it and for the restoration in it of their political freedom.

Impelled by this historic and traditional attachment, Jews strove in every successive generation to re-establish themselves in their ancient homeland. In recent decades they returned in their masses. Pioneers, ma'pilim and defenders, they made deserts bloom, revived the Hebrew language, built villages and towns, and created a thriving community, controlling its own economy and culture, loving peace but knowing how to defend itself, bringing the blessings of progress to all the country's inhabitants, and aspiring towards independent nationhood.

In the year 5657 (1897), at the summons of the spiritual father of the Jewish State, Theodor Herzl, the First Zionist Congress convened and proclaimed the right of the Jewish people to national rebirth in its own country.

This right was recognized in the Balfour Declaration of the 2nd November, 1917, and re-affirmed in the Mandate of the League of Nations which, in particular, gave international sanction to the historic connection between the Jewish people and Eretz-Israel and to the right of the Jewish people to rebuild its National Home.

The catastrophe which recently befell the Jewish people—the massacre of millions of Jews in Europe—was another clear demonstration of the urgency of solving the problem of its homelessness by re-establishing in Eretz-Israel the Jewish State, which would open the gates of the homeland wide to every Jew and confer upon the Jewish people the status of a fully-privileged member of the comity of nations.

Survivors of the Nazi holocaust in Europe, as well as Jews from other parts of the world, continued to migrate to Eretz-Israel, undaunted by difficulties, restrictions and dangers, and never ceased to assert their right to a life of dignity, freedom and honest toil in their national homeland.

In the Second World War, the Jewish community of this country contributed its full share to the struggle of the freedom- and peace-loving nations against the forces of Nazi wickedness and, by the blood of its soldiers and its war effort, gained the right to be reckoned among the peoples who founded the United Nations.

On the 29th November, 1947, the United Nations General Assembly passed a resolution calling for the establishment of a Jewish State in Eretz-Israel; the General Assembly required the inhabitants of Eretz-Israel to take such steps as were necessary on their part for the implementation of that resolution. This recognition by the United Nations of the right of the Jewish people to establish their State is irrevocable.

This right is the natural right of the Jewish people to be masters of their own fate, like all other nations, in their own sovereign State.

ACCORDINGLY WE, MEMBERS OF THE PEOPLE'S COUNCIL, REPRESENTATIVES OF THE JEWISH COMMUNITY OF ERETZ-ISRAEL AND OF THE ZIONIST MOVEMENT, ARE HERE ASSEMBLED ON THE DAY OF THE TERMINATION OF THE BRITISH MANDATE OVER ERETZ-ISRAEL AND, BY VIRTUE OF OUR NATURAL AND HISTORIC RIGHT AND ON THE STRENGTH OF THE RESOLUTION OF THE UNITED NATIONS GENERAL ASSEMBLY, HEREBY DECLARE THE ESTABLISHMENT OF A JEWISH STATE IN ERETZ-ISRAEL, TO BE KNOWN AS THE STATE OF ISRAEL.

WE DECLARE that, with effect from the moment of the termination of the Mandate, being tonight, the eve of Sabbath, the 6th Iyar, 5708 (15th May, 1948), until the establishment of the elected, regular authorities of the State in accordance with the Constitution which shall be adopted by the Elected Constituent Assembly not later than the 1st October, 1948, the People's Council shall act as a Provisional Council of State, and its executive organ, the People's Administration, shall be the Provisional Government of the Jewish State, to be called "Israel."

THE STATE OF ISRAEL will be open for Jewish immigration and for the Ingathering of the Exiles; it will foster the development of the country for the benefit of all inhabitants; it will be based on freedom, justice and peace as envisaged by the prophets of Israel; it will ensure complete equality of social and political rights to all its inhabitants irrespective of religion, race or sex; it will guarantee freedom of religion, conscience, language, education and culture; it will safeguard the Holy Places of all religions; and it will be faithful to the principles of the Charter of the United Nations.

THE STATE OF ISRAEL is prepared to cooperate with the agencies and representatives of the United Nations in implementing the resolution of the General Assembly of the 29th November, 1947, and will take steps to bring about the economic union of the whole of Eretz-Israel.

WE APPEAL to the United Nations to assist the Jewish people in the building-up of its State and to receive the State of Israel into the comity of nations.

WE APPEAL—in the very midst of the onslaught launched against us now for months—to the Arab inhabitants of the State of Israel to preserve peace and participate in the upbuilding of the State on the basis of full and equal citizenship and due representation in all its provisional and permanent institutions.

WE EXTEND our hand to all neighbouring states and their peoples in an offer of peace and good neighbourliness, and appeal to them to establish bonds of cooperation and mutual help with the sovereign Jewish people settled in its own land. The State of Israel is prepared to do its share in common effort for the advancement of the entire Middle East.

WE APPEAL to the Jewish people throughout the diaspora to rally round the Jews of Eretz-Israel in the tasks of immigration and upbuilding and to stand by them in the great struggle for the realization of the age-old dream—the redemption of Israel.

PLACING OUR TRUST IN THE ALMIGHTY, WE AFFIX OUR SIGNATURES TO THIS PROCLAMATION AT THIS SESSION OF THE PROVISIONAL COUNCIL OF STATE ON THE SOIL OF THE HOMELAND, IN THE CITY OF TEL-AVIV, ON THIS SABBATH EVE, THE 5th DAY OF IYAR, 5708 (14th MAY, 1948).

SOVIET JEWS GREET GOLDA MEIR

The dominant Jewish community in Europe remained that of the Soviet Union. Buoyed by the Soviet government's anti-Nazi stance and its support of the establishment of the state of Israel, the Soviet Jews retained their pride in their Jewishness while integrating into society around them.

This Jewish identity was dramatically manifested during the visit to Moscow in the fall of 1948 by Israel's first Minister to the Soviet Union, Golda Meyerson—later Meir. Here is Mrs. Meir's description of that famous encounter.

READING 9-4

As we had planned, we went to the synagogue on Rosh Hashanah. All of us—the men, women and children of the legation—dressed in our best clothes, as befitted Jews on a Jewish holiday. But the street in front of the synagogue had changed. Now it was filled with people, packed together like sardines, hundreds and hundreds of them, of all ages, including Red Army officers, soldiers, teenagers and babies carried in their parents' arms. Instead of the 2,000-odd Jews who usually came to the synagogue on the holidays, a crowd of close to 50,000 people was waiting for us. For a minute I couldn't grasp what had happened—or even who they were. And then it dawned on me. They had come—those good, brave Jews—in order to be with us, to demonstrate their sense of kinship and to celebrate the establishment of the State of Israel. Within seconds they had surrounded me, almost lifting me bodily, almost crushing me, saying my name over and over again. Eventually, they parted ranks and let me enter the synagogue, but there, too, the demonstration went on. Every now and then, in the women's gallery, someone would come to me, touch my hand, stroke or even kiss my dress. Without speeches or parades, without any words at all really, the Jews of Moscow were proving their profound desire— and their need—to participate in the miracle of the establishment of the Jewish state, and I was the symbol of the state for them.

I couldn't talk, or smile, or wave my hand. I sat in that gallery like a stone, without moving, with those thousands of eyes fixed on me. No such entity as the Jewish people, Ehrenburg had written. The State of Israel meant nothing to the Jews of the USSR! But his warning had fallen on deaf ears. For thirty years we and they had been separated. Now we were together again, and as I watched them, I knew that no threat, however awful, could possibly have stopped the ecstatic people I saw in the synagogue that day from telling us, in their own way, what Israel meant to them. The service ended, and I got up to leave; but I could hardly walk. I felt as though I had been caught up in a torrent of love so strong that it had literally taken my breath away and slowed down my heart. I was on the verge of fainting, I think. But the crowd still surged around me, stretching out its hands and saying *Nasha Golda* (our Golda) and *Shalom, shalom*, and crying.

Out of that ocean of people, I can still see two figures clearly: a little man who kept popping up in front of me and saying, "*Goldele, leben zolst du. Shana Tova!*" (Goldele, a long life to you and a Happy New Year), and a woman who just kept repeating, "Goldele! Goldele!" and smiling and blowing kisses at me.

It was impossible for me to walk back to the hotel, so although there is an injunction against riding on the Sabbath or on Jewish holidays, someone pushed me into a cab. But the cab couldn't move either because the crowd of cheering, laughing, weeping Jews had engulfed it. I wanted to say something, anything, to those people, to let them know that I begged their forgiveness for not having wanted to come to Moscow and for not having known the strength of their ties to us. For having wondered, in fact, whether there was still a link between them and us. But I couldn't find the words. All I could say, clumsily, and in a voice that didn't even sound like my own, was one sentence in Yiddish. I stuck my head out of the window of the cab and said, "*A dank eich vos ihr seit geblieben Yidden*" (Thank you for having remained Jews), and I heard that miserable, inadequate sentence being passed on through the enormous crowd as though it were some wonderful prophetic saying.

MURDER OF SOVIET-JEWISH WRITERS

After this demonstration, the Soviet government began a campaign against Jewish nationalism that was orchestrated by Stalin's newly emerging anti-Semitic obsessions. Jewish intellectuals, writers, and artists were arrested, accused of being agents of International Zionism and

American imperialism. On August 12, 1952 the elite of Soviet Jewish culture was executed in one fell swoop.

The following is an account of that massacre written in 1956 after the revelation of Stalin's crimes.

READING 9-5

Toward the end of last year, the General Prosecutor of Moscow called together the relatives of some twenty-six Yiddish writers arrested in 1948 and informed them, one by one, that they could never hope to witness the return of their father, husband, son or brother: the twenty-six had been shot on August 12, 1952. The magistrate added that it was a case of great injustice and that the victims would probably be rehabilitated if their families took the appropriate steps in Russian courts. Forty other Yiddish writers, victims of the same action, would not return because they had died of "natural causes" in the concentration camps of Vorkuta, Karaganda and Kolyma. Those who had been sent from Moscow to be executed without delay were the best poets, novelists, dramatists and essayists—part of an elite which determined the character of a literature and, dominating it, assured its future. Their non-Communist or opposition counterparts had been liquidated long before in the great purges. The majority of the twenty-six, however, had submitted, as had their Russian colleagues, to all of the imperatives of the regime. They had praised "the greatest man of all times and of all nations" and had cried "To death!" when it was required. Just like the others, they had betrayed their friends and their brothers on every occasion that loyalty to the party demanded them to do so; yet they had to die because they were incapable of betraying their language and their literature.

In the extermination of nearly six million European Jews, Hitler and his accomplices caused the demise of the greater part of the readership of Yiddish literature; in liquidating its writers, Stalin completed this work of destruction. This assassination is without precedent in the history of world literature and without example even in Jewish martyrology.

How could you not be indifferent to the fate of this assassinated literature? You are unaware of its works, their beauty and their power, and of everything they promised, which is now annihilated. And besides, untimely death is common in our times. The hibernation of that famous universal conscience is so deep that the cries of pain do not trouble it, even if those who are in power fail to stifle them in time.

One of the twenty-six who were shot was Peretz Markish, the best Yiddish poet of our generation. I met him in Vienna after the revolution, and I saw him again in Moscow in 1931. He resembled exactly the elating image an adolescent has of a poet; it was to become acquainted with his works that I learned to read Yiddish.

They say that, having gone mad, Markish sang and laughed unceasingly, even at the moment when the gun touched the nape of his neck. At his side died the great novelist David Bergelson. Speechless, with eyes that were three thousand years old, he studied his assassins. This "cosmopolitan without any heritage" had chosen as the title of his last book a saying of his ancestor, the psalmist: "Murdered, I will live on." He took his last words from the same psalmist: "Earth, oh earth, do not hide my blood."

COMMUNIST ANTI-SEMITISM IN EASTERN EUROPE

Stalin's anti-Semitism had an important effect on the status of the Jews in Soviet-controlled Eastern Europe. In Czechoslovakia, for example, a group of prominent Communist Party and government officials was charged with forming a Zionist conspiracy against the interests of the state and Party. Five of the accused were executed; three others were sentenced to life imprisonment.

The following selection from the memoirs of one of the latter, Artur London, details the anti-Semitic basis of the trumped-up accusations.

READING 9-6

Soon after my arrest, when I was confronted by a virulent, Nazi-type of anti-semitism, I thought it was limited to a few individuals. The Security Services couldn't be expected to recruit saints for such a dirty job. But I now realized that even if this mentality only appeared sporadically during the interrogations, it was nevertheless a systematic line.

As soon as a new name cropped up the interrogators insisted on knowing whether or not it was Jewish. The clever ones put the question like this: 'What was his name before? Didn't he change his name in 1945?' If the person really was of Jewish origin the interrogators managed to fit him into a report on some excuse or another which often had nothing to do with the matters in question. And this name was inevitably accompanied by the ritual adjective 'Zionist'.

They were trying to collect the maximum number of Jews in their reports. When I mentioned two or three names, if there was one which 'sounded Jewish', this was the only one they noted. However primitive this system of repetition, it succeeded in giving the impression that the defendant was in contact solely with Jews, or at least with a considerable number of Jews.

And yet the word 'Jew' was never actually used. When, for example, I was questioned about Hajdu, the interrogator crudely asked me to say whether each of the names mentioned was that of a Jew. But when he wrote out his report he replaced 'Jew' by 'Zionist'. 'We are in the Security Services of a people's democracy. The word Jew is an insult. That's why we write "Zionist".'

I pointed out that Zionist had political implications, but he replied that this was not true and that he was following orders. 'Besides,' he added, 'the word Jew is also forbidden in the USSR. They say Hebrew.'

I said there was a difference between Hebrew and Zionist, but it was no good. He explained that Hebrew sounded bad in Czech and he had orders to write 'Zionist'. That was that.

Until the end, the term Zionist was applied to men and women who had nothing to do with Zionism. And when they drew up the reports for the court, the interrogators refused to make any changes. This subsequently turned into a witch hunt. The discriminatory measures against the Jews increased on the pretext that they were foreigners in Czechoslovakia, cosmopolitans and Zionists, more or less involved in espionage.

To begin with, the interrogators vied with each other in their antisemitism. One day I told one of them that I didn't see how it could be applied to the group of former volunteers which, apart from Vales and me, contained no Jews. He answered perfectly seriously: 'You forget their wives. They're all Jewish and that comes to the same thing.' . . .

When my report was drawn up for the court and when they wrote 'Jewish nationality' (as they did for ten out of fourteen defendants) I asked an interrogator how they had reached this definition, particularly since my father and I were atheists. He replied by learnedly quoting Stalin on the problem of nationality, and concluded by saying that Stalin's five conditions of nationality corresponded to the definition of 'Jewish nationality'. Later the formulation became 'of Jewish origin'— I can't think why—and remained so in the records of the proceedings. . . .

THE POLISH EXODUS

Before Stalin's death, communist anti-Semitism charged the Jews with disloyalty to Stalin and the states he controlled. After Stalin's death, the Jews in Soviet-bloc lands were accused of being Stalinists and were punished for that.

In Poland the eruption of this new form of anti-Semitism convinced many Jews to leave the country. The Polish government opposed any anti-Semitic measures and issued the following decree, which had little effect.

READING 9-7

Discerning in occurrences of chauvinism, anti-Semitism, and racism a serious danger threatening the vital interests of our country and our party, the Central Committee appeals to the entire party, and calls for a determined struggle against such occurrences. We emphasize once more with the utmost determination the internationalist character of our party. There is and can be no place in it for people propagating nationalistic, chauvinistic, and racist views. . . . Particularly stringent demands in this respect must be put to comrades holding responsible party or state positions. . . .

We grant to all national minorities equality of national rights—the right of all minorities to schools in their native language and to full respect for and development of their national culture, the right to establish cultural associations, to publish newspapers in their native language, etc. We reaffirm the principle that every citizen has the right to national self-determination. . . .

The Party regards the tendency of the Jewish population to emigrate from Poland as the result of insufficient counteraction by the Party to anti-Semitism. We consider it to be one of the most urgent tasks of the party to wage war against it. At the same time we must persuade the Jewish population to stay in our country. This duty devolves in particular upon party committees in those localities where there is a considerable concentration of the Jewish population. Jewish party members in particular should be more active in their work in Jewish communities, and should take a determined stand against verbal and written propaganda and against an unjustified atmosphere of panic, fanned by Jewish nationalistic elements.

To this end the Central Committee considers it necessary to convene a national conference of activists of the Social and Cultural Association of Jews in Poland, to be attended by representatives of those . . . committees where there are Jewish communities. All party committees should discuss the Central Committee's letter at their meetings and draw appropriate conclusions for their activity in the fight against the nationalistic atmosphere.

JEWS AND AMERICAN CULTURE

In sharp contrast to the fate of the Jews in the Soviet bloc, the Jewish communities of the Western world flourished in the postwar years. Especially in the United States, barriers to the complete integration of the Jews disappeared, and Jews became an essential part of the fabric of American life and culture.

Particularly famous was a group of writers in New York City who transformed their experience as Jews into some of the most important works of American literature. Selected here is a representative sample of one of these writers, Alfred Kazin.

READING 9-8

When I was a child I thought we lived at the end of the world. It was the eternity of the subway ride into the city that first gave me this idea. It took a long time getting to "New York"; it seemed longer getting back. Even the I.R.T. [a subway line] got tired by the time it came to us, and ran up into the open for a breath of air before it got locked into its terminus at New Lots. As the train left the tunnel to rattle along the elevated tracks, I felt I was being jostled on a camel past the last way stations in the desert. Oh that ride from New York! Light came only at Sutter Avenue. First across the many stations of the Gentiles to the East River. Then clear across Brooklyn, almost to the brink of the ocean all our fathers crossed. All those first stations in Brooklyn—Clark, Borough Hall, Hoyt, Nevins, the junction of the East and West Side express lines—told me only that I was on the last leg home, though there was always a stirring of my heart at Hoyt, where the grimy subway platform was suddenly enlivened by Abraham and Straus's windows of ladies' wear. Atlantic Avenue was vaguely exciting, a crossroads, the Long Island railroad; I never saw a soul get in or out at Bergen Street; the Grand Army Plaza, with its great empty caverns smoky with dust and chewing-gum wrappers, meant Prospect Park and that stone path beside a meadow where as a child I ran off from my father one summer twilight just in time to see the lamplighter go up the path lighting from the end of his pole each gas mantle suddenly flaring within its corolla of pleated paper—then, that summer I first strayed off the block for myself, the steps leading up from the boathouse, the long stalks of grass wound between the steps thick with the dust and smell of summer—then, that great summer at sixteen, my discovery in the Brooklyn Museum of Albert Pinkham Ryder's cracked oily fishing boats drifting under the moon. . . .

We were of the city, but somehow not in it. Whenever I went off on my favorite walk to Highland Park in the "American" district to the north, on the border of

Queens, and climbed the hill to the old reservoir from which I could look straight across to the skyscrapers of Manhattan, I saw New York as a foreign city. There, brilliant and unreal, the city had its life, as Brownsville was ours. That the two were joined in me I never knew then—not even on those glorious summer nights of my last weeks in high school when, with what an ache, I would come back into Browns-ville along Liberty Avenue, and, as soon as I could see blocks ahead of me the Labor Lyceum, the malted milk and Fatima signs over the candy stores, the old women in their housedresses sitting in front of the tenements like priestesses of an ancient cult, knew I was home.

We were the end of the line. We were the children of the immigrants who had camped at the city's back door, in New York's rawest, remotest, cheapest ghetto, enclosed on one side by the Canarsie flats and on the other by the hallowed middle-class districts that showed the way to New York. "New York" was what we put last on our address, but first in thinking of the others around us. *They* were New York, the Gentiles, America; we were Brownsville—*Brunzvil*, as the old folks said—the dust of the earth to all Jews with money, and notoriously a place that measured all success by our skill in getting away from it. So that when poor Jews left, *even* Ne-groes, as we said, found it easy to settle on the margins of Brownsville, and with the coming of spring, bands of Gypsies, who would rent empty stores, hang their rugs around them like a desert tent, and bring a dusty and faintly sinister air of carnival into our neighborhood.

THE RISE IN JEWISH SOLIDARITY

At the same time as Western Jews became more successful in all realms of life and more essential to their society, they continued to be vi-tally concerned with Jewish culture and creativity. Profoundly affected by the murder of European Jewry and the establishment of the State of Is-rael, Jews everywhere acknowledged that solidarity with the Jewish peo-ple was compatible with integration in a pluralistic society.

The following is one example of post-Holocaust Jewish creativity in the West: the American Yiddish poet Jacob Glatstein's reflection on the theological implications of the destruction.

READING 9-9

Without Jews

Without Jews there is no Jewish God.
If we leave this world
The light will go out in your tent.
Since Abraham knew you in a cloud,
You have burned in every Jewish face,
You have glowed in every Jewish eye,
And we made you in our image.
In each city, each land,
The Jewish God

Was also a stranger.
A broken Jewish head
Is a fragment of divinity.
We, your radiant vessel,
A palpable sign of your miracle.

Now the lifeless skulls
Add up into millions.
The stars are going out around you.
The memory of you is dimming,
Your kingdom will soon be over.
Jewish seed and flower
Are embers.
The dew cries in the dead grass!

The Jewish dream and reality are ravished,
They die together.
Your witnesses are sleeping:
Infants, women,
Young men, old.
Even the Thirty-six,
Your saints, Pillars of your World,
Have fallen into a dead, an everlasting sleep.

Who will remember you?
Who deny you?
Who yearn for you?
Who, on a lonely bridge,
Will leave you—in order to return?

The night is endless when a race is dead.
Earth and heaven are wiped bare.
The light is fading in your shabby tent.
The Jewish hour is guttering.
Jewish God!
You are almost gone.

MASS MIGRATIONS TO ISRAEL

The new State of Israel opened its doors to all Jews and hundreds of thousands responded. In the first three years after the establishment of the Jewish state, 684,201 Jews from 42 different countries immigrated to Israel. While most of these Jews came as individuals, there were some important communal migrations as well: virtually the entire Jewish communities of Yemen, Iraq, Libya, and Bulgaria came to Israel. With these migrations, the population of Israel became increasingly Oriental in origin.

Following are selections from accounts of the flight of Yemenite Jews to the state of Israel.

READING 9-10

They did not proceed from these places all at the same time, nor in the same fashion. From some—cities like San'a, Haulan, Sharab, Sa'da, Ibb, Dhamar—went on the road in fairly compact and continuous groups of forty or fifty or a hundred persons. Of the smaller localities, many were emptied of their Jews at one stroke, overnight. From dozens of villages they proceeded in small detachments, individual families, a man and his wife and his children. . . .

They descended mostly from the densely populated central and southern highlands, but they also came from the far north, whence they had to traverse the mountain line from the Saudi Arabian border and for three hundred miles across the whole length of the Yemen. They came from the humid lowlands and the hot, sandy desert stretches along the Red Sea in the West. . . . They came from places where the existence of Jews had never been suspected. Some made the journey in ten or twelve days. These were the lucky ones. For most of them it took four or six weeks; for some a harrowing three months.

We were instructed by the Rabbi of our village to transfer all we had to the Arabs and whatever they agreed to pay we should accept, for the Miracle of the Redemption was at hand. We did as we were instructed and made ready for the journey. The orders were that no one in the village travel alone, but the whole village together. The money must be divided equally among rich and poor so that all might reach the Land together. Afterward they would return the money given to them as a loan. This we did before we made our way to the city of San'a. The flour and the bread we transported on the camels and the asses together with the oil and the coffee.

I don't really know how to describe the mass of humanity pouring in. . . . They were hungry and sick, and most of them had terrible sores. Soon there were so many they covered every inch of the ground. You had to pick your way not to step on them. . . . Then came a time when there were nearly fourteen thousand people here, and you can imagine what it meant to wash, feed and clothe them. . . . There would be a day-long queue only for food, and more faintings and pushing and shouting and restlessness. There were still too few tents, only more sun and more sandstorms, and more people to lie about in the open, with little water to go round, no shade, no sanitary facilities; those toilets were not enough; they would urinate and excrete in the sand all about them; there was a smell I would not like to describe, it was felt for a mile round the camp; and they ate and slept in the sand, and women gave birth in the open, on the sand; and others died there.

ISRAELI IDENTITY

In the Jewish state the reception and absorption of masses of immigrants were coupled with the attempt at forging a new kind of Jewish culture and personality. Among the first questions facing Israel were its relationship to world Jewry and to the centuries-old question of "Who is a Jew?"

One of the most graphic manifestations of this problem was the case of Brother Daniel. A Polish Jew born in 1922, Brother Daniel was active in the Zionist movement and the Jewish Underground in World War II. Caught by the Nazis, he escaped and found refuge in a convent, where he was converted to Christianity. At the end of the war he became a member of the Carmelite Order and moved to Israel. There he applied for citizenship, claiming that he was a Jew by nationality and a Christian by religion. The government decided that anyone who regards himself as a member of another religion cannot be considered a Jew and denied Brother Daniel's petition. He appealed to the Israeli Supreme Court, whose majority upheld the government's view. Both the majority and the dissenting opinions of the Court are summarized here.

READING 9-11

Judge Silberg:

"Whether he is religious, non-religious or anti-religious, the Jew living in Israel is bound, willingly or unwillingly, by an umbilical cord to historical Judaism from which he draws his language and its idiom, whose festivals are his own to celebrate and whose great thinkers and spiritual heroes . . . nourish his national pride. Would a Jew who has become a Christian find his place in all this? What can all this national sentiment mean to him? Certainly, Brother Daniel will love Israel. . . . But such love will be from without—the love of a distant brother. He will not be a true inherent part of this Jewish world."

Judge Cohn:

"The tests provided by religious law cannot apply to the Law of Return. . . . In the absence of an objective test provided by the Law itself, there is no alternative . . . but to assume that the Legislature intended to content itself with the subjective test, that is to say, that the right to return to Israel belongs to any person who declares that he is a Jew returning to his homeland and wishes to settle there. . . . The further provision . . . that the right belongs only to those who profess no other than the Jewish religion exceeds . . . the powers of the Government, whose duty it is merely to carry out the Law."

THE JEWS OF SILENCE

In the mid-1960's the fate of Soviet Jewry became an issue of grave concern to the Jews in the West. This concern was intensified in the aftermath of the Six Day War of June 1967 when Jews around the world, including the Soviet Union, displayed new pride in their Jewish roots and Jewish culture.

One of the first works to focus the attention of American Jews on the situation of Soviet Jewry was Elie Wiesel's *The Jews of Silence*. The following is the beginning and the end of that work.

READING 9-12

Their eyes—I must tell you about their eyes. I must begin with that, for their eyes precede all else, and everything is comprehended within them. The rest can wait. It will only confirm what you already know. But their eyes—their eyes flame with a kind of irreducible truth, which burns and is not consumed. Shamed into silence before them, you can only bow your head and accept the judgment. Your only wish now is to see the world as they do. A grown man, a man of wisdom and experience, you are suddenly impotent and terribly impoverished. Those eyes remind you of your childhood, your orphan state, cause you to lose all faith in the power of language. Those eyes negate the value of words; they dispose of the need for speech.

Since my return I have often been asked what I saw in the Soviet Union, what it was I found there. My answer is always the same: eyes. Only eyes, nothing else. . . .

That is enough. I visited many cities, was shown what a tourist is shown, and have forgotten it all. But still the eyes which I cannot forget pursue me; there is no escaping them. Everything I have I would give them, as ransom for my soul.

I saw thousands, tens of thousands of eyes: in streets and hotels, subways, concert halls, in synagogues—especially in synagogues. Wherever I went they were waiting for me. At times it seemed as though the entire country was filled with nothing but eyes, as if somehow they had assembled there from every corner of the Diaspora, and out of ancient scrolls of agony.

All kinds of eyes, all shades and ages. Wide and narrow, lambent and piercing, somber, harassed. Jewish eyes, reflecting a strange unmediated reality, beyond the bounds of time and farther than the farthest distance. Past or future, nothing eludes them; their gaze seems to apprehend the end of every living generation. God himself must surely possess eyes like these. Like them, He too awaits redemption.

If they could only speak . . . but they do speak. They cry out in a language of their own that compels understanding. What did I learn in Russia? A new language. That is all, and that is enough. It is a language easily learned in a day, at a single meeting, a single visit to a place where Jews assemble, a synagogue. The same eyes accost you in Moscow and Kiev, in Leningrad, Vilna and Minsk, and in Tbilisi, the capital of the Georgian Republic. They all speak the same language, and the story they tell echoes in your mind like a horrible folk tale from days gone by. . . .

For the second time in a single generation, we are committing the error of silence.

One may question whether we have any way of knowing that the Jews of Russia really want us to do anything for them. How do we know that our shouts and protests will not bring them harm? These are very serious questions, and I put them to the Russian Jews themselves. Their answer was always the same: "Cry out, cry out until you have no more strength to cry. You must enlist public opinion, you must turn to those with influence, you must involve your governments—the hour is late."

In Kiev a Jew said to me, "I hope you will not have cause to regret that you have abandoned us." And in Moscow a religious Jew said, "The preservation of human life takes precedence over all six hundred thirteen commandments. Don't you know that? Don't our cries reach you? Or do they reach you but not move you?

If that is so, then we are truly lost, because you live in a world wholly guilty, and your hearts have become foul." In every city I heard dozens of cries like these, almost without variation. I was not to forget, I was to tell it all, I was to warn the Jewish communities of the world that their continued indifference would be accounted a horrible crime in the years to come. I promised I would do it, but I wept before them as I promised. I wept because I knew that nothing would help. Our Jews have other problems on their minds. When you tell them what is expected of them in Russia, they shrug their shoulders. It is exaggerated; or, we can do nothing about it; or, we must not do too much lest we be accused of interfering in the cold war. The Jewish brain has killed the Jewish heart. That is why I wept.

I believe with all my soul that despite the suffering, despite the hardship and the fear, the Jews of Russia will withstand the pressure and emerge victorious. But whether or not we shall ever be worthy of their trust, whether or not we shall overcome the pressures we have ourselves created, I cannot say. I returned from the Soviet Union disheartened and depressed. But what torments me most is not the Jews of silence I met in Russia, but the silence of the Jews I live among today.

RESPONSE TO THE SIX DAY WAR

The astounding victory of the Israeli forces in June 1967 changed the political map of the Middle East and led to new controversies that are still at the center of world politics. Inside Israel the conquest of the West Bank of the Jordan River with its large Arab population has led to continuing self-scrutiny and debate with enormous cultural and political ramifications. The following poem by the important contemporary Israeli poet Yehuda Amichai is one expression of that self-examination.

READING 9-13

[On the Day of Atonement]

On the Day of Atonement in 1967, I
put on my dark holiday suit and went
to the Old City in Jerusalem. I stood,
for some time, before the alcove of an
Arab's shop, not far from Damascus
Gate, a shop of buttons and zippers
and spools of thread in all colours, and
snaps and buckles. A glorious light and
a great many colours like a Holy Ark
with its doors ajar.

I told him in my heart that my father,
too, had such a shop of threads and
buttons. I explained to him in my
heart all about the tens of years and the

reasons and the circumstances because of which I am now here and my father's shop is in ashes there, and he is buried here.

By the time I had finished, it was the hour of 'the locking of the Gates'. He too pulled down the shutter and locked the gate, and I went back home with all the worshippers.

Acknowledgments and Citations
of Source Readings

The authors and publisher gratefully acknowledge permission to reprint material from the following sources.

Selections from the Hebrew Bible in chapters 1 and 2 are from *The Torah*, *The Prophets*, and *The Writings: A New Translation of the Holy Scriptures*, Philadelphia: The Jewish Publication Society of America, 1962, 1978, 1982. Copyright by The Jewish Publication Society of America and reprinted by permission of the JPSA. Bibliographical citations of all other source readings follow.

CHAPTER 1

1-1A. Adapted from "The Sumerian Flood Story," trans. M. Civil. © Oxford University Press 1969. Reprinted from *Atra-Hasis: The Babylonian Story of the Flood*, by W.G. Lambert and A.R. Millard, 1969, pp. 143, 145, by permission of Oxford University Press.

1-2A. Jacob J. Finkelstein, "An Old Babylonian Herding Contract and Genesis 31:38f.," *Journal of the American Oriental Society*, 88 (1968), p. 31. Reprinted by permission of the American Oriental Society.

1-2B. The Laws of Hammurapi, Paragraph 267, trans. W.W. Hallo.

1-3A. Adapted from M. Held, "Philological Notes on the Mari Covenant Rituals," *Bulletin of the American Schools of Oriental Research*, vol. 200, 1970, p. 33. By permission of the American Schools of Oriental Research, 4243 Spruce Street, Philadelphia, PA, 19104.

1-3B. Adapted from O.R. Gurney, *The Hittites*, Pelican Books 1952, p. 151. © O.R. Gurney, 1952, 1954. Reprinted by permission of Penguin Books Ltd.

1-4A. W.K. Simpson, *The Literature of Ancient Egypt*, New Haven: Yale University Press, 1972, pp. 92–96. Copyright © 1972 by Yale University Press. Reprinted by permission.

1-5A. The Report of a Frontier Official, trans. John A. Wilson in James B. Pritchard, *Ancient Near Eastern Texts: Relating to the Old Testament*, 3rd ed. with Supplement, p. 259. Copyright © 1969 by Princeton University Press. Adapted by permission of Princeton University Press.

1-5B, C. Ricardo A. Caminos, *Late Egyptian Miscellanies*, Brown Egyptological Studies, I, 1954, pp. 106 and 491. Reprinted by permission of Oxford University Press.

1-6A. Adapted from Brian Lewis, *The Sargon Legend* (ASOR Dissertation Series), Philadelphia, 1980, pp. 24–25. By permission of the American Schools of Oriental Research, 4243 Spruce Street, Philadelphia, PA, 19104.

1-7A. Barbara Bell, "The Dark Ages in Ancient History: I. The First Dark Age in Egypt," in *American Journal of Archaeology* vol. 75, 1971, pp. 12–13. Reprinted by permission.

1-8A–E.   Excerpts from Hittite and Akkadian suzerainty treaties, trans. W.W. Hallo.

1-9A.   The Laws of Eshnunna, Paragraphs 53–55, trans. W.W. Hallo.

1-9B.   The Laws of Hammurapi, Paragraphs 250–252, trans. W.W. Hallo.

1-10A.   The Story of Sinuhe, trans. John A. Wilson in James B. Pritchard, *Ancient Near Eastern Texts: Relating to the Old Testament*, 3rd ed. with Supplement, pp. 19–20. Copyright © 1969 by Princeton University Press. Reprinted by permission of Princeton University Press.

1-11A.   Baruch A. Levine, "The Deir 'Alla Plaster Inscriptions," *Journal of the American Oriental Society,* 101 (1981), pp. 195–205. Reprinted by permission of the American Oriental Society.

1-12A.   The Israel Stela, in D. Winton Thomas, *Documents from Old Testament Times*, London, 1958, p. 139. Reprinted by permission of Professor D. Winton Thomas and Thomas Nelson and Sons, Ltd., Publishers.

1-13A.   A Syrian Interregnum, trans. John A. Wilson in James B. Pritchard, *Ancient Near Eastern Texts: Relating to the Old Testament*, 3rd ed. with Supplement, p. 260. Copyright © 1969 by Princeton University Press. Reprinted by permission of Princeton University Press.

1-17A.   D.B. Redford, "Studies in Relations between Palestine and Egypt during the First Millenium B.C.," in J.W. Wevers and D.B. Redford, editors, *Studies on the Ancient Palestinian World*, Toronto: The University of Toronto Press, 1972, pp. 153–154. © University of Toronto Press 1972. Reprinted by permission.

1-17B.   William W. Hallo, "A Sumerian Amphictyony," *Journal of Cuneiform Studies*, vol. 14, October 1960, p. 92. By permission of the American Schools of Oriental Research, 4243 Spruce Street, Philadelphia, PA, 19104.

1-18A.   Jerrold S. Cooper, "Gilgamesh and Agga: A Review Article" *Journal of Cuneiform Studies*, vol. 33, July-October 1981, pp. 235–236. By permission of the American Schools of Oriental Research, 4243 Spruce Street, Philadelphia, PA, 19104.

1-19.   Shalmaneser III: The Fight Against the Aramean Coalition, trans. A. Leo Oppenheim in James B. Pritchard, *Ancient Near Eastern Texts: Relating to the Old Testament*, 3rd ed. with Supplement, pp. 278–279. Copyright © 1969 by Princeton University Press. Reprinted by permission of Princeton University Press.

1-20A.   Shalmaneser III: The Fight Against the Aramean Coalition, trans. A. Leo Oppenheim in James B. Pritchard, *Ancient Near Eastern Texts: Relating to the Old Testament*, 3rd ed. with Supplement, p. 281. Copyright © 1969 by Princeton University Press. Reprinted by permission of Princeton University Press.

1-20B.   Louis D. Levine, "Two Neo-Assyrian Stelae from Iran," Occasional Paper 23, Art and Archaeology Department, Royal Ontario Museum, Toronto, 1972, p. 19. Reprinted by permission.

1-20C.   Stephanie Page, "Joash and Samaria in a New Stela Excavated at Tell al Rimah, Iraq," *Vetus Testamentum*, vol. 19, 1969, pp. 483–484. Reprinted by permission of E.J. Brill, Leiden.

1-22A.   A.K. Grayson, *Assyrian and Babylonian Chronicles*, Locust Valley, New York: J.J. Augustin Publisher, 1975, pp. 72–73. Reprinted by permission.

1-23A.   N. Na'aman, "Sennacherib's Campaign to Judah and the Date of the *LMLK* Stamps," *Vetus Testamentum*, vol. 29, 1979, pp. 61–62. Reprinted by permission of E.J. Brill, Leiden.

1-23B.   William W. Hallo, "The Royal Correspondence of Larsa: I. A Sumerian Prototype for the Prayer of Hezekiah?" pp. 215–221 in *Kramer Anniversary Volume*. Edited by Barry L. Eichler. Alter Orient und Altes Testament, Band 25. Verlag Butzon & Bercker, Kevelaer und Neukirchner Verlag des Erziehungsvereins GmbH, Neukirchen-Vluyn, 1976.

1-24A.   The Vassal Treaties of Esarhaddon, trans. Erica Reiner in James B. Pritchard, *Ancient Near Eastern Texts: Relating to the Old Testament*, 3rd ed. with Supplement, pp. 538–539. Copyright © 1969 by Princeton University Press. Reprinted by permission of Princeton University Press.

1-25A.   William W. Hallo, "Nebukadnezar Comes to Jerusalem," in *Through the Sound of Many Voices: Writings Contributed on the Occasion of the 70th Birthday of Gunther Plaut*, ed. Jonathan V. Plaut, Toronto: Lester & Orpen Denys, 1982, pp. 48–49.

Chapter 2

2-2A.   Babylonian Historical Documents, trans. A. Leo Oppenheim, in James B. Pritchard, *Ancient Near Eastern Texts: Relating to the Old Testament*, 3rd ed. with Supplement, p. 308. Copyright © 1969 by Princeton University Press. Reprinted by permission of Princeton University Press.

2-3A.   Nabonidus and the Clergy of Babylon, trans. A. Leo Oppenheim, in James B. Pritchard, *Ancient Near Eastern Texts: Relating to the Old Testament*, 3rd ed. with Supplement, p. 313. Copyright © 1969 by Princeton University Press. Reprinted by permission of Princeton University Press.

2-3B.   Prayer of Nabonidus, trans. W.W. Hallo.

2-4.   Morton Smith, "II Isaiah and the Persians," *Journal of the American Oriental Society*, 83 (1963), pp. 415–421. Reprinted by permission of the American Oriental Society.

2-5.   Edict of Cyrus, trans. A. Leo Oppenheim in James B. Pritchard, *Ancient Near Eastern Texts: Relating to the Old Testament*, 3rd ed. with Supplement, p. 316. Copyright © 1969 by Princeton University Press. Reprinted by permission of Princeton University Press.

2-6.   Petition for Authorization to rebuild the Temple of Yaho, trans. H.L. Ginsberg in James B. Pritchard, *Ancient Near Eastern Texts: Relating to the Old Testament*, 3rd ed. with Supplement, p. 492. Copyright © 1969 by Princeton University Press. Reprinted by permission of Princeton University Press.

2-7.   H.V. Hilprecht and A.T. Clay, *Business Documents of Murashû Sons of Nippur*, The Babylonian Expedition of the University of Pennsylvania, Series A: Cuneiform Texts, The University Museum, University of Pennsylvania, 1898, vol. 9, pp. 32–33. Reprinted by permission.

2-8.   William W. Hallo, "The First Purim," *Biblical Archaeologist*, vol. 46, 1983, p. 20. Reprinted by permission.

2-11.   "Papyri of the Fourth Century B.C. from Daliyeh," trans. by Frank Moore Cross, from *New Directions in Biblical Archaeology*, by David Noel Freedman and Jonas C. Greenfield, Garden City, 1969, pp. 42–43. Copyright © 1969 by Committee on Biblical Research. Reprinted by permission of Doubleday & Company, Inc.

2-12.   *Catalogue général des antiquités égyptiennes du Musée du Caire*, no. 59075. Trans. by Naphtali Lewis.

2-13A.   A.K. Grayson, *Babylonian Historical-Literary Texts*, Toronto: University of Toronto Press, 1975, pp. 33–35. © University of Toronto Press, 1975. Reprinted by permission.

2-14A.   I Maccabees 4:36–59. From the Revised Standard Version Apocrypha, copyrighted © 1957 by the Division of Christian Education of the National Council of the Churches of Christ in the USA, and used by permission.

2-14B.   Babylonian Talmud, Soncino edition, Shabbath 21b, pp. 92–93. Reprinted by permission of the Soncino Press Ltd., London and New York.

2-15.   I Maccabees 15:26–36. From the Revised Standard Version Apocrypha, copyrighted © 1957 by the Division of Christian Education of the National Council of the Churches of Christ in the USA, and used by permission.

2-16.   Judah Goldin, trans., *The Fathers According to Rabbi Nathan*, New Haven: The Yale University Press, 1955, pp. 35–37. Copyrighted 1955 by Yale University Press. Reprinted by permission.

2-17.   Josephus, *Jewish Antiquities*, trans. Louis H. Feldman, Loeb Classical Library, Cambridge, Mass.: Harvard University Press, 1965, vol. 9, pp. 9–23. Reprinted by permission of the publishers and The Loeb Classical Library.

2-18.   Josephus, *Jewish Antiquities*, trans. Louis H. Feldman, Loeb Classical Library, Cambridge, Mass.: Harvard University Press, 1965, vol. 9, pp. 49–51. Reprinted by permission of the publishers and The Loeb Classical Library.

2-19.   Acts 2:5–11. From the Revised Standard Version of the Bible, copyrighted 1946, 1952 ©, 1971, 1973, and used by permission of the Division of Christian Education of the National Council of the Churches of Christ in the USA.

CHAPTER 3

3-1.   Josephus, *The Jewish War*, trans. H. St. J. Thackeray, Loeb Classical Library, Cambridge, Mass.: Harvard University Press, 1961, vol. 3, pp. 611–615. Reprinted by permission of the publishers and The Loeb Classical Library.

3-2.   Judah Goldin, trans., *The Fathers According to Rabbi Nathan*, New Haven: The Yale University Press, 1955, p. 34. Copyright 1955 by Yale University Press. Reprinted by permission.

3-3.   Josephus, *Against Apion*, trans. H. St. J. Thackeray, Loeb Classical Library, Cambridge, Mass.: Harvard University Press, 1976, pp. 351, 367–369, 405–407, 409–411. Reprinted by permission of the publishers and The Loeb Classical Library.

3-4A.   H. Danby, trans., *The Mishnah*, Aboth 1, Oxford: Oxford University Press, 1933, pp. 446–447. Reprinted by permission.

3-4B.   H. Danby, trans., *The Mishnah*, Pesaḥim 10, Oxford: Oxford University Press, 1933, pp. 150–151. Reprinted by permission.

3-4C.   Judah Goldin, *The Song at the Sea*, New Haven: Yale University Press, 1971, pp. 189–197. Copyright © 1971 by Yale University Press. Reprinted by permission.

3-4D.   Babylonian Talmud, Soncino edition, Yoma 82a–82b, pp. 403–405. Reprinted by permission of the Soncino Press Ltd., London and New York.

3-5.   Mark 12:1–12 and John 8:21–47. From the Revised Standard Version of the Bible, copyrighted 1946, 1952 ©, 1971, 1973 and used by permission of the Division of Christian Education of the National Council of the Churches of Christ in the USA.

3-6. Wayne A. Meeks and Robert L. Wilken, *Jews and Christians in Antioch in the First Four Centuries of the Common Era*, Chico, CA: Scholars Press, 1978, pp. 87–90. © 1978 by the Society of Biblical Literature. Reprinted by permission of Scholars Press on behalf of SBL.

3-7. St. Augustine, *The Writings Against the Manichaeans*, in *A Select Library of the Nicene and Post Nicene Fathers of the Christian Church*, Grand Rapids, Michigan: Wm. B. Eerdmans Publishing Company, vol. 4, pp. 186–188. Reprinted by permission.

3-8. Jacob R. Marcus, *The Jew in the Medieval World*, New York, 1969, pp. 4–6. Copyright © 1938 by the Union of American Hebrew Congregations. Reprinted by permission.

3-9. Jacob R. Marcus, *The Jew in the Medieval World*, New York, 1969, pp. 111–113. Copyright © 1938 by the Union of American Hebrew Congregations. Reprinted by permission.

3-10. *The Koran*, trans. N.J. Dawood, Penguin Classics, 3rd revised edition, reprinted 1971, pp. 333, 336–338. Copyright © N.J. Dawood 1956, 1959, 1966, 1968. Reprinted by permission of Penguin Books.

3-11. Norman Stillman, *The Jews of Arab Lands*, Philadelphia, Jewish Publication Society of America, 1979, pp. 157–158. Copyright by the Jewish Publication Society of America and reprinted by permission of the JPSA.

3-12. Norman Stillman, *The Jews of Arab Lands*, Philadelphia, Jewish Publication Society of America, 1979, pp. 163–164. Copyright by the Jewish Publication Society of America and reprinted by permission of the JPSA.

3-13. Norman Stillman, *The Jews of Arab Lands*, Philadelphia, Jewish Publication Society of America, 1979, pp. 171, 172–173, 174–175. Copyright by the Jewish Publication Society of America and reprinted by permission of the JPSA.

3-14. Alexander Altmann, trans., The Book of Beliefs and Opinions, in *Three Jewish Philosophers*, New York, 1973, pp. 44–46. Reprinted by permission of the Publishers, Hebrew Publishing Company, Copyright ©. All rights reserved. Reprinted by permission.

3-15. Leon Nemoy, *Karaite Anthology*, New Haven: Yale University Press, 1952, pp. 75–78. Copyright 1952 Yale University Press. Reprinted by permission.

3-16. Kenneth Stow, "Agobard of Lyons and the Medieval Concept of the Jew," *Conservative Judaism*, vol. 29, 1974, p. 65. Copyright 1975 by The Rabbinical Assembly and reprinted by permission of The Rabbinical Assembly.

CHAPTER 4

4-1. Norman Stillman, *The Jews of Arab Lands*, Philadelphia: The Jewish Publication Society of America, 1979, p. 210. Copyright by The Jewish Publication Society of America and reprinted by permission of the JPSA.

4-2. *Miscellany of Hebrew Literature*, trans. A.I.K.D., London, 1872, vol. 1, pp. 92–93, 101–103.

4-3. Leon J. Weinberger, trans., *Jewish Prince in Moslem Spain: Selected Poems of Samuel Ibn Nagrela*, University, Alabama: The University of Alabama Press, 1973, pp. 34–35, 39–41. Copyright © 1973 The University of Alabama Press. Reprinted by permission.

4-4. Bernard Lewis, "An Anti-Jewish Ode: The Qasida of Abu Ishaq against Joseph ibn Nagrella," in *Salo Wittmayer Baron Jubilee Volume*, Jerusalem: American

Academy for Jewish Research, 1974, vol. 2, pp. 659–663. Reprinted by permission of Professor Bernard Lewis and the American Academy for Jewish Research.

4-5.   Jacob R. Marcus, *The Jew in the Medieval World*, New York: 1969, pp. 374–377. Copyright © 1938 by the Union of American Hebrew Congregations. Reprinted by permission.

4-6A.   *Selected Poems of Moses ibn Ezra*, trans. Solomon Solis Cohen, Philadelphia: The Jewish Publication Society of America, 1945, pp. 40–41, 47, 120–121.

4-6B.1.   Judah Halevi, "Wedding Song," trans. Nina Davis, in *Jewish Quarterly Review*, Old Series, vol. 11, 1899, pp. 300–301. Reprinted by permission of Dropsie College.

4-6B.2.   Judah Halevi, "Where Shall I Find Thee," trans. Nina Davis, in *Jewish Quarterly Review*, Old Series, vol. 10, 1898, pp. 117–118. Reprinted by permission of Dropsie College.

4-6B.3,4.   *Selected Poems of Jehudah ha-Levi*, trans. Nina Salaman, Philadelphia: The Jewish Publication Society of America, 1924, pp. 2, 20. Copyright by The Jewish Publication Society of America and reprinted by permission of the JPSA.

4-7.   I. Heinemann, trans., The Kuzari in *Three Jewish Philosophers*, New York, 1973, pp. 72–75. Reprinted by permission of the Publishers, Hebrew Publishing Company, Copyright ©. All rights reserved. Reprinted by permission.

4-8A.   Moses Maimonides, *The Book of Knowledge*, trans. Moses Hyamson, New York: Feldheim Publishers, 1974, pp. 34a–35b. Reprinted by permission of Philipp Feldheim, Inc., 200 Airport Executive Dr., Spring Valley, NY, 10977.

4-8B, C.   Moses Maimonides, *The Guide of the Perplexed*, trans. Shlomo Pines, Chicago: The University of Chicago Press, 1963, pp. 523–524 and 618–620. © 1963 by the University of Chicago. All rights reserved. Published 1963. Reprinted by permission.

4-9A, B, C.   Franz Kobler, *Letters of Jews Through the Ages*, London: 1953, vol. 1, pp. 194–196, 197–198, 211–212. Reprinted by permission of the Publishers, Hebrew Publishing Company. Copyright © 1952. All rights reserved. Reprinted by permission.

4-10.   Robert Chazan, *Church, State, and Jew in the Middle Ages*, New York: Behrman House, 1980, pp. 58–59. Reprinted by permission of Behrman House Publishers Inc., 1261 Broadway, New York, NY, 10001 and Professor Robert Chazan.

4-11.   Jacob R. Marcus, *The Jew in the Medieval World*, New York, 1969, pp. 115–118. Copyright © 1938 by the Union of American Hebrew Congregations. Reprinted by permission.

4-12.   *St. Bernard of Clairvaux as Seen Through his Selected Letters*, trans. Bruno Scott James, 1953, pp. 265–269. Reprinted by permission of Burnes and Oates, London.

4-13.   Francis James Child, ed., *English and Scottish Ballads*, vol. 8, Boston: 1859, pp. 47–54, 78–83.

4-14.   Jacob R. Marcus, *The Jew in the Medieval World*, New York, 1969, pp. 127–130. Copyright © 1938 by the Union of American Hebrew Congregations. Reprinted by permission.

4-15.   Robert Chazan, *Church, State, and Jew in the Middle Ages*, New York: Behrman House, 1980, pp. 266–269. Reprinted by permission of Behrman House

Publishers Inc., 1261 Broadway, New York, NY, 10001 and Professor Robert Chazan.

4-16A, B. Israel Abrahams, ed., *Hebrew Ethical Wills*, Philadelphia: The Jewish Publication Society of America, 1976, pp. 56–59, 61–62, 69–70, 80–81, 208–211, 214–216, 217–218. Copyright 1926, 1954 by the Jewish Publication Society of America and reprinted by permission of the JPSA.

4-17A, B, C, D. Irving Agus, *Rabbi Meir of Rothenberg*, 2nd ed., New York: Ktav Publishing House, Inc., 1970, pp. 215–216, 244–245, 485–486, 500. Reprinted by permission.

4-18A. Benzion Halper, *Post Biblical Hebrew Literature*, Philadelphia: The Jewish Publication Society of America, 1921, pp. 178–181. Copyright by the Jewish Publication Society of America and reprinted by permission of the JPSA.

4-18B. Nahum Glatzer, *The Judaic Tradition*, New York: Behrman House, pp. 427–428. Copyright © 1969 by Nahum Glatzer. Reprinted by permission of Nahum Glatzer and Behrman House Inc., 1261 Broadway, New York, NY, 10001.

4-19. Nahum Glatzer, *The Judaic Tradition*, New York: Behrman House, pp. 397–400, 402–403. Copyright © 1969 by Nahum Glatzer. Reprinted by permission of Nahum Glatzer and Behrman House Inc., 1261 Broadway, New York, NY, 10001.

4-20. Franz Kobler, *Letters of Jews Through the Ages*, London, 1953, vol. 1, pp. 277–282. Reprinted by permission of the Publishers, Hebrew Publishing Company. Copyright © 1952. All rights reserved. Reprinted by permission.

4-21. Leo W. Schwarz, *Memoirs of My People*, New York: Rinehart & Company, 1943, pp. 46–47. Reprinted by permission of Mrs. Leo W. Schwarz.

CHAPTER 5

5-1. Samuel Usque, *Consolation for the Tribulations of Israel*, trans. Martin Cohen, Philadelphia: The Jewish Publication Society of America, 1965, pp. 227, 229, and 231. Copyright by The Jewish Publication Society of America and reprinted by permission of the JPSA.

5-2. Michael A. Meyer, *Ideas of Jewish History*, New York: Behrman House, 1974, pp. 112–113. Reprinted by permission of Behrman House Publishers, Inc., 1261 Broadway, New York, NY, 10001 and Professor Michael A. Meyer.

5-3. Judah Messer Leon, *The Book of the Honeycomb's Flow*, edited and translated by Isaac Rabinowitz, Ithaca: Cornell University Press, 1983, pp. 143 and 145. Copyright © 1983 by Cornell University Press. Used by permission of the publisher.

5-4. Pico della Mirandola, *Heptaplus*, trans. Jessie Brewer, New York: Philosophical Library, 1977, pp. 110, 112–114. Reprinted by kind permission of the Philosophical Library.

5-5. Abraham ben Hananiah Yagel, *Beit Ya'ar ha-Levanon* ("The House of the Forest of Lebanon"), Book 2, Chap. 3. English translation by David Ruderman, MS Reggio 9, fol. 47v–48r. Bodleian Library, Oxford. By courtesy of the Curators.

5-6. Elkan N. Adler, *Jewish Travellers*, 2nd ed., New York: Sepher-Hermon Press, 1966, pp. 270–272, 280–282. Reprinted by permission of Sepher-Hermon Press, Inc., New York.

5-7. Leo W. Schwarz, *Memoirs of My People*, New York: Rinehart & Company, 1943, pp. 62–63, 66–67. Reprinted by permission of Mrs. Leo W. Schwarz.

5-8. Jacob R. Marcus, *The Jew in the Medieval World*, New York, 1969, pp.

170–172. Copyright © 1938 by the Union of American Hebrew Congregations. Reprinted by permission.

5-9.   Leo W. Schwarz, *Memoirs of My People*, New York: Rinehart & Company, 1943, pp. 75–79. Reprinted by permission of Mrs. Leo W. Schwarz.

5-10A, B.   Jacob R. Marcus, *The Jew in the Medieval World*, New York, 1969, pp. 166–169. Copyright © 1938 by the Union of American Hebrew Congregations. Reprinted by permission.

5-11.   David Gans, *Neḥmad ve-Na'im*, (Jesnitz, 1743), p. 82b, trans. D. Ruderman.

5-12.   Nathan Hanover, *The Abyss of Despair*, trans. Abraham Mesch, New York: 1950, pp. 110–111, 117–119. Copyright © 1983 by Transaction Inc. Reprinted by permission.

5-13A.   *Lekha Dodi* in *Sabbath Prayer Book*, trans. Eugene Kohn, New York: Jewish Reconstructionist Foundation, 1975, pp. 21–25. Reprinted by permission.

5-13B.   Kurt Wilhelm, *Roads to Zion*, trans. I.M. Lask, New York: Schocken Books, 1948, pp. 57–64. Copyright © 1948, copyright renewed 1976, by Schocken Books. Reprinted by permission of Schocken Books Inc.

5-14.   Jacob R. Marcus, *The Jew in the Medieval World*, New York, 1969, pp. 257–259. Copyright © 1938 by the Union of American Hebrew Congregations. Reprinted by permission.

5-15.   Jacob R. Marcus, *The Jew in the Medieval World*, New York, 1969, pp. 262–264, 266–267. Copyright © 1938 by the Union of American Hebrew Congregations. Reprinted by permission.

5-16.   Jacob Frank, *Words of the Master*, trans. D. Ruderman from Hebrew translation in Isaiah Shaḥar, *A Change of Values in Jewish Society in the Second Half of the Eighteenth Century*, Akadamon (Jerusalem, 1969), pp. 1–3.

5-17A.   Louis Jacobs, *Hasidic Thought*, New York: Behrman House, 1976, pp. 3–4. Reprinted by permission of Behrman House Publishers, Inc., 1261 Broadway, New York, NY, 10001 and Professor Louis Jacobs.

5-17B–E.   Dan Ben-Amos and Jerome Minz, editors and translators, *In Praise of the Baal Shem Tov (Shivhei ha-Besht): The Earliest Collection of Legends of the Founder of Hasidism*, Bloomington: The University of Indiana Press, 1970, pp. 86–87, 182–183. Reprinted by permission of the University of Indiana Press.

5-17F.   Samuel H. Dresner, *The Zadik*, New York: Schocken Books, 1974, pp. 136–137, 212–213. Copyright © 1960 by Samuel H. Dresner. Reprinted by permission of Schocken Books Inc.

5-18.   H.C. Lea, *A History of the Inquisition of Spain*, New York: Macmillan Publishing Company, 1907, vol. 3, pp. 24–26. Reprinted by permission of Macmillan Publishing Company.

5-19.   Franz Kobler, *Letters of Jews Through the Ages*, London: 1953, vol. 2, pp. 432–435. Reprinted by permission of the Publishers, Hebrew Publishing Company. Copyright © 1952. All rights reserved. Reprinted by permission.

5-20.   Leo W. Schwarz, *Memoirs of My People*, New York: Rinehart & Company, 1943, pp. 84–88. Reprinted by permission of Mrs. Leo W. Schwarz.

5-21.   Benedict de Spinoza, *A Theologico-Political Treatise*, trans. R.H.M. Elwes, New York: Dover Publications, 1951, pp. 69–71. Copyright © 1951 by Dover Publications Inc., N.Y. Reprinted by permission.

5-22.   Franz Kobler, *Letters of Jews Through the Ages*, London, 1953, vol. 2, pp.

565–568. Reprinted by permission of the Publishers, Hebrew Publishing Company. Copyright © 1952. All rights reserved. Reprinted by permission.
5-23.   *The Dramatic Works of G.E. Lessing*, ed. Ernest Bell, London, 1878, pp. 305–309.

CHAPTER 6

6-1.   Moses Mendelssohn, *Jerusalem and Other Jewish Writings*, trans. Alfred Jospe, New York: Schocken Books, 1969, pp. 104–107, 110. Copyright © 1969 by Schocken Books Inc. Reprinted by permission of Schocken Books Inc.

6-2.   *The Jew in the Modern World: A Documentary History*, by Paul R. Mendes Flohr and Jehuda Reinharz, New York: Oxford University Press, 1980, pp. 103–104. Copyright © 1980 by Oxford University Press, Inc. Reprinted by permission.

6-3.   M. Diogene Tama, trans., *Transactions of the Parisian Sanhedrin*, London, 1807, pp. 3–4.

6-4.   Benjamin Flower, *The French Constitution*, London, 1792, p. 23.

6-5.   M. Diogene Tama, trans., *Transactions of the Parisian Sanhedrin*, London, 1807, pp. 6–7.

6-6.   M. Diogene Tama, trans., *Transactions of the Parisian Sanhedrin*, London, 1807, pp. 11, 13–16.

6-7.   Raphael Mahler, ed., *Jewish Emancipation: A Selection of Documents*, New York: Research Institute on Peace and Post-War Problems, The American Jewish Committee, 1941, p. 28. Reprinted by permission.

6-8.   Raphael Mahler, ed., *Jewish Emancipation: A Selection of Documents*, New York: Research Institute on Peace and Post-War Problems, The American Jewish Committee, 1941, pp. 32–33. Reprinted by permission.

6-9.   Raphael Mahler, ed., *Jewish Emancipation: A Selection of Documents*, New York: Research Institute on Peace and Post-War Problems, The American Jewish Committee, 1941, pp. 42–43. Reprinted by permission.

6-10.   *The Jew in the Modern World: A Documentary History*, by Paul R. Mendes-Flohr and Jehuda Reinharz, New York: Oxford University Press, 1980, pp. 163–165. Copyright © 1980 by Oxford University Press, Inc. Reprinted by permission.

6-11.   Mordechai Waxman, ed., *Tradition and Change: The Development of Conservative Judaism*, New York: Burning Bush Press, 1958, pp. 43–50. Copyright 1958 by the Rabbinical Assembly of America, reprinted by permission of the Rabbinical Assembly.

6-12.   Samson Raphael Hirsch, *The Nineteen Letters on Judaism*, ed. Jacob Breuer, Jerusalem and New York: Feldheim Publishers, 1969, pp. 106–107, 109–111. Reprinted by permission of Philipp Feldheim, Inc., 200 Airport Executive Dr., Spring Valley, NY, 10977.

6-13.   Raphael Mahler, ed., *Jewish Emancipation: A Selection of Documents*, New York: Research Institute on Peace and Post-War Problems, The American Jewish Committee, 1941, pp. 57–59. Reprinted by permission.

6-14.   Raphael Mahler, ed., *Jewish Emancipation: A Selection of Documents*, New York: Research Institute on Peace and Post-War Problems, The American Jewish Committee, 1941, p. 59. Reprinted by permission.

6-15.   Lucy S. Dawidowicz, *The Golden Tradition*, New York: Holt, Rinehart and Winston, 1967, pp. 101–102. Copyright © 1967 by Lucy S. Dawidowicz. Reprinted by permission of Holt, Rinehart, and Winston, Publishers.

6-16.   *The Jew in the Modern World: A Documentary History*, by Paul R. Mendes Flohr and Jehuda Reinharz, New York: Oxford University Press, 1980, p. 307. Copyright © 1980 by Oxford University Press, Inc. Reprinted by permission.

6-17.   David Philipson, *Max Lilienthal, American Rabbi*, New York: Bloch Publishing Co., 1915, pp. 308–310, 312. Reprinted by permission.

6-18.   *The Jew in the Modern World: A Documentary History*, by Paul R. Mendes Flohr and Jehuda Reinharz, New York: Oxford University Press, 1980, pp. 312–313. Copyright © 1980 by Oxford University Press, Inc. Reprinted by permission.

6-19.   *The Jew in the Modern World: A Documentary History*, by Paul R. Mendes Flohr and Jehuda Reinharz, New York: Oxford University Press, 1980, p. 309. Copyright © 1980 by Oxford University Press, Inc. Reprinted by permission.

6-20.   Robert Chazan and Marc Lee Raphael, eds., *Modern Jewish History: A Source Reader*, New York: Schocken Books, 1974, pp. 103, 112–113. Copyright © 1974 by Schocken Books Inc. Reprinted by permission of Schocken Books Inc.

6-21.   Theodor Herzl, *The Jewish State*, New York: The Herzl Press, 1970, pp. 27, 33, 109. Reprinted by permission of The Herzl Press.

6-22.   *Selected Essays of Ahad Ha-am*, trans. Leon Simon, New York: 1981, pp. 192–194. Copyright by The Jewish Publication Society of America and reprinted by permission of the JPSA.

6-23.   Simon Dubnow, *Nationalism and History*, ed. Koppel Pinson, New York: 1958, pp. 98–99. Copyright by The Jewish Publication Society of America and reprinted by permission of the JPSA.

6-24.   Hayyim Nahman Bialik, "The City of Slaughter," trans. A.M. Klein, in *Complete Poetic Works of Hayyim Nahman Bialik*, New York: Histadruth Ivrit, 1948, pp. 129–135. Reprinted by permission of Bloch Publishing Inc./Histadruth Ivrit.

CHAPTER 7

7-1.   *Publications of the American Jewish Historical Society*, vol. 18, 1909, pp. 4–5. Reprinted by permission of the American Jewish Historical Society.

7-2.   Raphael Mahler, ed., *Jewish Emancipation: A Selection of Documents*, New York: Research Institute on Peace and Post-War Problems, The American Jewish Committee, 1941, p. 24. Reprinted by permission.

7-3.   L.H. Butterfield, ed., *The Letters of Benjamin Rush*, vol. 1, 1761–1792, Princeton: The American Philosophical Society, 1951, pp. 429–430. Reprinted by permission of The American Philosophical Society.

7-4.   Lewis Abraham, "Correspondence between Washington and Jewish Citizens," *Publications of the American Jewish Historical Society*, vol. 3, 1895, pp. 90–91. Reprinted by permission of the American Jewish Historical Society.

7-5.   Lewis Abraham, "Correspondence between Washington and Jewish Citizens," *Publications of the American Jewish Historical Society*, vol. 3, 1895, pp. 91–92. Reprinted by permission of the American Jewish Historical Society.

7-6.   *Publications of the American Jewish Historical Society*, vol. 27, 1920, pp. 373–374. Reprinted by permission of the American Jewish Historical Society.

7-7.　Joseph L. Blau and Salo W. Baron, *The Jews of the United States, 1790–1840: A Documentary History,* New York: Columbia University Press, 1963, vol. 1, pp. 39–40. 1963, Columbia University Press. Reprinted by permission.

7-8.　"A Jewish Peddler's Diary, 1842–1843," by Abram Vossen Goodman, *American Jewish Archives,* vol. 3, June 1951, pp. 100–101. Reprinted by permission.

7-9.　"Albert Moses Luria, Gallant Young Confederate," *American Jewish Archives,* vol. 7, January 1955, pp. 92 and 103. Reprinted by permission.

7-10.　Mark Wischnitzer, *To Dwell in Safety: The Story of Jewish Migration Since 1800,* Philadelphia: The Jewish Publication Society of America, 1948, p. 289. Copyright by The Jewish Publication Society of America and reprinted by permission of the JPSA.

7-11.　Morris Hilquit, *Loose Leaves from a Busy Life,* 1934, reprint ed. New York: Da Capo Press, 1971, pp. 15, 17–18, 22–24.

7-12.　Azriel Eisenberg, ed., *Eyewitnesses to American Jewish History,* Part 3, New York: Union of American Hebrew Congregations, 1979, pp. 49–51. Reprinted by permission of the author.

7-13.　Kaufman Kohler, *Hebrew Union College and Other Addresses,* Cincinnati: Ark Publishing, 1916, pp. 198–200.

7-14.　Congressional Record, 1921 (67th Congress) and 1924 (68th Congress).

CHAPTER 8

8-1.　"Palestine for the Jews," *The Times* of London, November 9, 1917, p. 7. Reprinted by permission.

8-2.　Nahum N. Glatzer, *Franz Rosenzweig: His Life and Thought,* New York: Schocken Books, 1953, pp. 336–339. Copyright © 1953 by Schocken Books Inc.; Copyright © 1961 by Schocken Books Inc. Reprinted by permission of Schocken Books Inc.

8-3.　Marc Bloch, *Strange Defeat,* trans. Gerard Hopkins, 1949, New York: W.W. Norton, 1968, pp. 177–178. Reprinted by permission of Oxford University Press.

8-4.　*The Jew in the Modern World: A Documentary History,* by Paul R. Mendes Flohr and Jehuda Reinharz, New York: Oxford University Press, 1980, pp. 462–465. Copyright © 1980 by Oxford University Press, Inc. Reprinted by permission.

8-5.　"Parade" by David Hofstein, trans. by Allen Mandelbaum, in Irving Howe and Eliezer Greenberg, eds., *A Treasury of Yiddish Poetry,* New York: Holt, Rinehart and Winston, 1969, p. 175. Copyright © 1969 by Irving Howe and Eliezer Greenberg. Reprinted by permission of Holt, Rinehart and Winston, Publishers.

8-6.　Adolf Hitler, *Mein Kampf,* trans. Ralph Manheim, Boston: Houghton Mifflin Company, 1943, pp. 300, 302–305. Copyright 1943 and © renewed 1971 by Houghton Mifflin Company. Reprinted by permission of Houghton Mifflin Company. Also reprinted by permission of Hutchinson Publishing Group Ltd.

8-7.　B.D. Weinryb, *Jewish Emancipation Under Attack,* New York: Research Institute on Peace and Post-War Problems, The American Jewish Committee, 1942, p. 45. Reprinted by permission.

8-8.　B.D. Weinryb, *Jewish Emancipation Under Attack,* New York: Research Institute on Peace and Post-War Problems, The American Jewish Committee, 1942, p. 46. Reprinted by permission.

8-9.   B.D. Weinryb, *Jewish Emancipation Under Attack*, New York: Research Institute on Peace and Post-War Problems, The American Jewish Committee, 1942, p. 55. Reprinted by permission.

8-10.   John Mendelsohn, editor, *The Holocaust*, New York: Garland Press, 1982, vol. 11, pp. 2, 5, 7–8. Reprinted by permission.

8-11.   Isaiah Trunk, *Jewish Responses to Nazi Persecution*, New York: Stein and Day, 1979, pp. 154–160. Copyright © 1978 by Isaiah Trunk. Reprinted with permission of Stein and Day Publishers.

8-12.   Isaiah Trunk, *Jewish Responses to Nazi Persecution*, New York: Stein and Day, 1979, pp. 263–268. Copyright © 1978 by Isaiah Trunk. Reprinted with permission of Stein and Day Publishers.

8-13.   *The New York Times*, June 4, 1943. Copyright © 1943 by The New York Times Company. Reprinted by permission.

8-14.   Isaiah Trunk, *Jewish Responses to Nazi Persecution*, New York: Stein and Day, 1979, pp. 326–328. Copyright © 1978 by Isaiah Trunk. Reprinted with permission of Stein and Day Publishers.

CHAPTER 9

9-1.   Sylvia Rothschild, ed., *Voices from the Holocaust*, New York: New American Library, 1981, pp. 314–321. Copyright © 1981 by the William E. Wiener Oral History Library of the American Jewish Committee. Reprinted by arrangement with New American Library, N.Y., N.Y. Also reprinted by permission of the author and the William E. Wiener Oral History Library of the American Jewish Committee.

9-2.   *The New York Times*, November 30, 1947. Copyright © 1947 by The New York Times Company. Reprinted by permission.

9-3.   *Encyclopaedia Judaica*, Jerusalem: Keter Publishing House, 1972, vol. 5, p. 1453. Reprinted by permission of Keter Publishing House, Jerusalem, Ltd.

9-4.   Golda Meir, *My Life*, New York: G.P. Putnam's Sons, 1975, pp. 250–251. Copyright © 1975 by Golda Meir. Reprinted by permission of G.P. Putnam's Sons.

9-5.   Gerard Israel, *The Jews in Russia*, trans. Sanford L. Chernoff, New York: St. Martin's Press, 1975, pp. 201–202. Copyright © 1975 by Gerard Israel. Reprinted by permission of St. Martin's Press.

9-6.   Artur London, *The Confession*, trans. Alastair Hamilton, New York: William Morrow and Company, 1970, pp. 200–202. French edition (by Artur and Lise London) published by Editions Galimard, Paris, under the title *L'Aveu*, © Editions Galimard 1968. Translation Copyright © 1970 by Macdonald and Company Publishers Ltd. Reprinted by permission of William Morrow & Company, Editions Galimard, and Macdonald and Company, Publishers.

9-7.   Josef Banas, *The Scapegoats: The Exodus of the Remnants of Polish Jewry*, London: Weidenfeld and Nicholson, 1979, pp. 29–30. Reprinted by permission of Dr. Josef Banas.

9-8.   Alfred Kazin, *A Walker in the City*, New York: Harcourt, Brace, and World, 1951, pp. 8–12. Copyright 1951, 1979 by Alfred Kazin. Reprinted by permission of Harcourt Brace Jovanovich, Inc.

9-9.   "Without Jews," by Jacob Glatstein, trans. by Nathan Halper, in Irving Howe and Eliezer Greenberg, eds., *A Treasury of Yiddish Poetry*, New York: Holt,

Rinehart and Winston, 1969, pp. 331–332. Copyright © 1969 by Irving Howe and Eliezer Greenberg. Reprinted by permission of Holt, Rinehart and Winston, Publishers.

9-10.   Joseph B. Schechtman, *On the Wings of Eagles*, New York: 1961, pp. 61, 66. Reprinted by permission of Mrs. Rachael Schechtman.

9-11.   Asher F. Landau, *Selected Judgments of the Supreme Court of Israel*, Jerusalem: Ministry of Justice, 1971, pp. 1–2.

9-12.   Elie Wiesel, *The Jews of Silence*, trans. Neal Kozodoy, New York: Holt, Rinehart, and Winston, 1966, pp. 3–5, 102–103. Copyright © 1966 by Holt, Rinehart, and Winston. Reprinted by permission of Holt, Rinehart, and Winston, Publishers.

9-13.   Yehuda Amichai, "On the Day of Atonement," in T. Carmi, ed. and trans., *The Penguin Book of Hebrew Verse*, London: Allan Lane, 1981, p. 571. Copyright © 1981 by T. Carmi. Reprinted by permission of Penguin Books, Ltd.

Index of Source Readings

Project Funders

Funding for this publication and other college materials created for *Heritage: Civilization and the Jews* was provided by the Charles H. Revson Foundation and the National Endowment for the Humanities. Additional educational funding was provided by The Brookdale Foundation, The Endowment Fund of the Greater Hartford Jewish Foundation, and The Jaffe Foundation.

Funding for the production of *Heritage: Civilization and the Jews* and for related activities was provided by the following generous contributors:

The Charles H. Revson Foundation, Milton Petrie, and the National Endowment for the Humanities.

The Frances and John L. Loeb Foundation, the Bank Leumi le-Israel Group and Israel Discount Bank of New York, the Nate B. and Frances Spingold Foundation, Inc., the Crown Family, and Joseph Meyerhoff.

The Columbia Foundation, the Corporation for Public Broadcasting, The Green Fund, Inc., and the Norman and Rosita Winston Foundation. The Ann L. Bronfman Foundation, Mr. and Mrs. Ludwig Jesselson, Carl Marks and Company, Inc., Public Television Stations, the Billy Rose Foundation, Inc., The Samuel and David Rose Foundation, John M. Schiff, and the Miriam and Ira D. Wallach Foundation. Irwin S. Chanin, Max M. Fisher, William S. and Selma Ellis Fishman, the Morris and Rose Goldman Foundation, Leonard E. Greenberg, The Isermann Family, The Ethel and Phillip M. Klutznick Charitable Trusts, The Louis B. Mayer Foundation, the Samuel I. Newhouse Foundation, Arthur Rubloff, The Swig Foundation, Laurence A. Tisch, and The Weiler-Arnow Family.

Nathan S. Ancell, The Goldstein Family Philanthropic Fund, Integrated Resources, Inc., the Morris L. and Barbara Levinson Philanthropic Fund, the Henry and Lucy Moses Fund, Inc., Louis Rogow,

Morris A. Schapiro, the Louis and Martha Silver Foundation, Inc., the Herbert and Nell Singer Philanthropic Fund of the Jewish Communal Fund, the George D. Smith Fund, the Tauber Foundation, Inc., and Florrie and Herbert Tenzer.

The Sidney Stern Memorial Trust, Adele and Leonard Block, Marvin H. Davidson, Mr. and Mrs. Jerome L. Greene, Mr. and Mrs. Harry L. Marks, The Richard and Dorothy Rodgers Foundation, Melvin Simon, Uzi Zucker, Arthur Ross, The Ritter Foundation, Inc., Jane B. Hart, and Carl A. Morse. The Eugene and Estelle Ferkauf Foundation, Jewelcor Incorporated, Mr. and Mrs. Fred Kayne, William Petschek Philanthropic Fund, The Sarah and Matthew Rosenhaus Peace Foundation, and the Michael Tuch Foundation, Inc.

Robert P. Balgley, Peter Bienstock, Samuel J. and Ethel LeFrak Foundation, The Joe and Emily Lowe Foundation, Inc., Sunny and Abe Rosenberg, Philip and Helen Sills Foundation, Inc., and the Slade Foundation, Inc., The Henry and Elaine Kaufman Foundation, Inc., Mr. and Mrs. Robert N. Armour, Irving M. Geszel, Shumer S. Lonoff, the Leon Lowenstein Foundation, Inc., Frederick R. Adler, The Duray Foundation, Inc., Mr. and Mrs. Ronald L. Gallatin, the Giesser Family Fund at Brandeis University, the Reuben A. and Lizzie Grossman Foundation, Phyllis and Murray Horowitz, M. David Hyman, the Morris J. and Betty Kaplun Foundation, Kenneth Lipper, Bernice Manocherian, Martin E. Segal, Mr. and Mrs. J. Jacques Stone, William Ungar, Eli Wachtel, and the Erving Wolf Foundation, Neil R. Austrian, the Forbes Foundation, Raymond M. Galante, Rodger Hess, the Alex Hillman Family Foundation, Inc., Mrs. M. S. Lowenstein, Doris and Walter Marks, Harry and Adele Oppenheimer, Mr. and Mrs. Sam S. Schahet, Ellen and Stephen Schwarzman.

About the Editors

William W. Hallo, the editor of the chapters on the ancient period, is an eminent scholar in the field of ancient Near East history. His area of specialization is Assyriology and he is the curator of the Babylonian Collection at the Sterling Library at Yale University. He graduated from Harvard College with a B.A. and received an M.A. and Ph.D. from the University of Chicago in Near Eastern Languages and Literature. Professor Hallo has written many articles and is the author of a widely used introductory text, *The Ancient Near East: A History.* He has received numerous honours including a Fulbright Fellowship, a Guggenheim Fellowship, and a National Endowment for the Humanities grant.

David B. Ruderman, the editor of the chapters on the medieval period, is Professor of the History of Judaism, Department of Religious Studies, Yale University. His area of specialization is Italian Jewish history. He received his B.A. from the City College of New York, his M.A. from Columbia, his rabbinic degree from The Hebrew Union College—Jewish Institute of Religion, and his Ph.D. from Hebrew University. Professor Ruderman is the author of *The World of a Renaissance Jew: The Life and Thought of Abraham b. Mordechai Farissol,* for which he received the National Jewish Book Award in History in 1982. He is also the author of many articles and reviews on medieval and early modern Jewish history.

Michael Stanislawski, the editor of the chapters on the modern period, is Assistant Professor of Jewish History on the Miller Foundation at Columbia University. His area of specialization is East European Jewish history. He received his A.B., A.M., and Ph.D. degrees from Harvard University. Professor Stanislawski is the author of *Tsar Nicholas I and the Jews: The Transformation of Jewish Society in Russia, 1825–1855,* for which he received the National Jewish Book Award in History in 1984. He is also the author of numerous articles on Jewish and Russian history.

319

Benjamin R. Gampel, editorial coordinator, is a visiting Assistant Professor of Jewish history at the University of Maryland. He has also taught at the Jewish Theological Seminary of America and Rockland Community College. A specialist in medieval Spanish Jewry, he received his doctorate from Columbia University, where he wrote his dissertation entitled *Medieval Jewry on the Eve of Dissolution: The Last Years of Jewish Life in the Kingdom of Navarre.*

Russell H. Herman, editorial coordinator, is a specialist in early modern Jewish and European history. He is completing his doctorate in Italian-Jewish history at Columbia University. Mr. Herman holds an M.A. from the Jewish Theological Seminary of America and an M.Phil. from Columbia University.